POLITICS
OF
LETTERS

POLITICS
OF
LETTERS

Richard Ohmann

 WESLEYAN UNIVERSITY PRESS
MIDDLETOWN, CONNECTICUT

Excerpt from *Rabbit Redux* by John Updike copyright © 1971 by Alfred A. Knopf. Used by permission of Alfred A. Knopf.

The following chapters appeared originally in: (Chapter 1) *ADE Bulletin*, 82 (Winter 1985); (Chapter 3) *Only Connect* (March 1986); (Chapter 7) *New Literary History*, 11:2 (Winter 1980); (Chapter 8) *Critical Theory and the Teaching of Literature*, Proceedings of the Northeastern University Center for Literary Studies, 3, 1985; (Chapter 9) *Berkshire Review*, 1981; (Chapter 10) *University of Hartford Studies in Literature*, 16:2:3, 1984; (Chapter 13) *The CEA Forum*, 6:1, 1975; (Chapter 14) *The Radical Teacher*, #13 (Summer 1979); (Chapter 15) *College English*, 47:7 (November 1985); (Chapter 16) *The Chronicle of Higher Education*, 1976; (Chapter 17) *The Radical Teacher*, #31 (Fall 1986); (Chapter 18) *College English*, 41:4 (December 1979); (Chapter 20) *College English*, 44:1 (January 1982).

Chapter 2, copyright © 1978 by Indiana University Press. Reprinted from *What Is Criticism?* by Paul Hernadi, ed., by permission of Indiana University Press. Chapter 4, copyright © 1976 by The University of Chicago. All rights reserved. Reprinted from *Critical Inquiry*, vol. 3, 1976 by permission of The University of Chicago Press and Carol B. Ohmann. Chapter 5, copyright © 1978 by Indiana University Press. Reprinted from *What Is Criticism?* by Paul Hernadi, ed., by permission of Indiana University Press, 1978. It was published in full in *Critical Inquiry*, vol. 10, 1983. Used by permission of Indiana University Press and The University of Chicago Press.

LIBRARY OF CONGRESS CATALOGING-IN-PUBLICATION DATA

Ohmann, Richard M. (Richard Malin), 1931–
  Politics of letters.
  Bibliography: p.
  Includes index.
    1. American literature—20th century—History and criticism.   2. Politics and literature—United States.   3. American literature—Study and teaching—United States.   4. Social classes in literature.   5. Marxist criticism—United States. 6. Canon (Literature).   7. United States—Intellectual life—20th century. 8. United States—Popular culture—20th century.   I. Title.
PS228.P6O36   1987   810'.9'358   87-2152

ISBN 0-8195-5175-9

All inquiries and permissions requests should be addressed to the Publisher, Wesleyan University Press, 110 Mt. Vernon Street, Middletown, Connecticut 06457

Manufactured in the United States of America

FIRST EDITION, 1987
Wesleyan Paperback, 1988

To Jon Bailey, Danny Cantor, Sibel Goksel, John Houston, Jay Kilbourn, Alex Kotlowitz, Joel Lefkowitz, Dan Perlstein, Sarah Plotkin, Andy Polsky, Helen Schwartz, Josh Sparrow, Dan Zegart

Contents

Illustrations

Preface

The morning paper announces on page 1 that the president is intensifying his campaign against state-sponsored terrorism; a one-paragraph story on page 23 reports a Nicaraguan village burned by Contra forces, with eleven peasants killed. The reader takes in the news with only a muted sense of surprise, rushes off to her nine o'clock class, and there teaches a unit on usage to students who are mainly native speakers, but who, having failed to get it right in twelve years of required English, are now required by the college to take a thirteenth. Over a bag lunch in her office, the instructor skims a magazine article on teenage pregnancy and the culture of poverty, barely noting the ads that flank it, one for personal computers, one for Virginia Slims. In the late afternoon she manages an hour and a half in the library, researching an article on pastoral elegy which perhaps three hundred people will read, but the readers who count are the five who will review her work for tenure. In the evening she sits down before a stack of papers on "Leda and the Swan," slogs through the first one, notes that it digresses into personal opinions about rape, writes "C+" at the end of it, and adds a brief comment suggesting closer attention to syntax and metaphor.

A day in the life. Ordinary transactions of reading and writing, exchanges of value, exercises of authority. Mundanity. True, one sometimes gags on the commonplace: "state-sponsored terrorism"? Didn't our government fund that slaughter of villagers? Or, in a pensive moment, one may draw back critically from professional routines: "that student was telling me that rape frightens her too much to allow concentration on Yeats's syntax and his scheme of history—what kind of a human response is 'C+'?" Often, too, the routine gives routine discomfort; usage is a drag, and writing scholarship with an eye toward the tenure review is demeaning. Other verbal exchanges, like the bundle of messages that juxtaposes poverty and personal computers, pregnant adolescents and "You've come a long way, baby," strike one as bizarre, yet inevitable. That's how things are, that's how they will be.

Our experience naturalizes the odd and the appalling, offers them as common sense, in Gramsci's way of putting it. Domination filters through a thousand capillaries of transmission, a million habitual meanings. Most of the time it doesn't feel like domination, but like getting on with business. Raymond Williams points out that hegemony, as acted out in daily routines, is not in the first instance coercion or control,

or "manipulation" or "indoctrination." It is a whole body of practices and expectations, over the whole of living: our senses and assignments of energy, our shaping perceptions of ourselves and our world. It is a lived system of meanings and values . . . which as they are experienced as practices appear as reciprocally confirming. It thus constitutes a sense of reality for most people in the society.[1] (*Marxism and Literature*, Oxford, 1977, p. 11).

This book is about the process of hegemony in our society, mainly in the domain of verbal culture. (The chapter about television news and the extended discussion of visual advertising seemed insufficient warrant for using the broader word *Culture* in my title, in place of *Letters*.) Its topics include literacy, English composition, criticism, literature, teaching, academic and cultural institutions, advertising, mass media. Sometimes I take as starting point a practice or network of practices that seem natural and uncontested, such as the publishing, reception, criticism, and teaching of recent fiction. Sometimes I enter into an area already vexed with controversy, such as the debate over literacy and "basics." Either way, I try to see lines of conflict deeper than the immediate question of value or meaning.

"Deeper" in two ways: first, I scan the domain of letters for alignments of interest and power that are fundamental to the social process. Class is a central one; in particular I am concerned with the class to which I and the hypothetical English instructor of this preface belong, the class that includes teachers, ad men and women, journalists, editors, educational bureaucrats, writers, readers of the *New York Times*, and, as that last item suggests, many professionals and technicians and managers not so directly concerned with the production of verbal culture. I hold that this class has a special role in the hegemonic process, and in mediating relations of the other two main classes: the big bourgeoisie and the proletariat. If the oppositions and antagonisms that surround questions of letters are usually subdued into "common sense," one may often locate that normalizing in some project or custom of what I call the professional-managerial class.

The second way I try to look "deeper" at questions of letters is historically. The sense of reality that pervades our experience usually lacks a historical dimension. The newspaper, the idea of literacy, advertising, academic criticism, the English department, and so on feel like immutable features of a cultural landscape; yet they express and carry foward a particular history, just as they manifest class relations. The institutions and practices of letters with which I deal are, in fact, of recent origin. They either took shape or were transformed beyond recognition in the epoch of monopoly capital, a system of organizing our lives that figures centrally in many of these essays. It is hard to believe that my own life spans more than half of that epoch, and I say that not to proclaim my advanced years but to remark how new are the social arrangements that now seem so fixed. To grasp their history is to see them as contingent, less fixed, more open to change. I find that liberating.

Not that you and I could uproot the verbal culture of monopoly capitalism and remake it to our utopian wishes—not without uprooting a good deal more. But it is helpful to remember that—to quote Raymond Williams again—"A lived hegemony is always a process." And, as he goes on, "it does not just passively exist as a form of dominance. It has continually to be renewed, recreated, defended, and modified. It is also continually resisted, limited, altered, challenged by pressures not at all its own" (p. 112).[1] Culture is one arena of such conflict, yet not best seen as a *separate* arena, as I argue in many of the chapters to follow. Smokey Bear, the Virginia Slims ladies, the *New York Review of Books*, composition textbooks, General Electric, women's studies, and the Contras all participate in the same, what? Game? Struggle? I like to think of it as a struggle, though only at heightened historical moments does it feel more like that than like a game. Be that as it may, I enter it myself in a spirit of resistance. For of course a book like this does not stand over and apart from what it analyzes. Whatever claims some would make for the objectivity of intellectuals or of academic writing, there is no place to stand except in or against the hegemonic process. I hope that by making clear my allegiances in the *whole* process, I can add some clarity to the often mystifying politics of letters.

I wrote the essays in this volume over an eleven-year period, for various occasions and out of various exigencies. They come closer to carrying a single argument than I would have remembered had not Jeannette Hopkins of the Wesleyan University Press suggested collecting them, and initiated this agreeable labor of words. I have revised some of the essays extensively, and provided bridges between them here and there. But mainly I have let stand what I wrote, and I trust the reader to recognize that it, too, is historically contingent.

I gratefully acknowledge Wesleyan University's support of my research, a major assist from the Rockefeller Foundation, and a smaller one from the Indiana University Institute for Advanced Studies.

I wish I could acknowledge all the editors, conference organizers, colleagues, and friends, beyond those mentioned in the text, whose encouragement and ideas and criticism have helped shape this book, indeed made it happen. The list would be long: one does not write in a social vacuum. I do wish to mention, though not by individual name, my colleagues/comrades on *The Radical Teacher.* Their companionship in our project has meant much to me through precisely these eleven years. (Subscribe to the magazine—you can read their names on the masthead!) And I *have* mentioned, by name, in my dedication, another group of influentials. Their work with me as TAs and much more in 1976–77 gave heart, brain, and purpose to this enterprise. Let them stand for many other students, co-learners, friends.

I THE PROFESSION OF HUMANIST

1 The Function of English at the Present Time

I adapt my title from Matthew Arnold's, in part because this chapter includes a vest-pocket account of how humanistic criticism and the subject, English, fit into the broad movement of North American history, an account that responds to Arnold's questions, though not with his high hopes for literary culture. Also, the title leads into one of two anecdotes with which I want to begin.

Several years ago there was a conference on the humanities at the college where I teach. I agreed to respond to a lecture by one of the most respected critics of our time. She chose to use Arnold's title without change: "The Function of Criticism at the Present Time." She spoke of criticism's inherent value and of its value to the general society. It was a high-minded talk, and, as is customary with high-minded talks by practitioners, it made no mention of the circumstances within which practitioners actually work, or of functions their practice might have *for them*. I thought Arnold's title called for inclusion of such matters, more so now than in his time, since criticism has become so thoroughly institutionalized. As a shortcut to making that point, I mentioned the function criticism had had in advancing the speaker's own career. Well. Old hand though I am at making rude remarks, I can't remember giving such offense, before or since. It was as if I had responded to a theological argument by questioning the theologian's habits of personal cleanliness, so impertinent did our speaker think matters of advancement and reputation to the functioning of criticism in this society.

Second anecdote. Another conference on the humanities, this one at a leading midwestern university. We have spent two days mulling over precisely the institutional questions that the speaker at Wesleyan thought irrelevant. It is the closing session, and I am on a panel that will try to sum up our debates and discussions. Chairing the panel is the vice president of the university, himself a humanistic scholar of distinction, who, however, has the disadvantage of having missed the conference he is summarizing. He expresses much concern about the insecurity of humanistic values in our society and the daunting task before us humanists. He finishes, however, on an upbeat note, with a rhapsody on the great works of which we are the custodians, and the great power they exert for sweetness and light. I demur—politely, since the man *has* missed our deliberations. But then to my surprise, a voice from the audience echoes the vice president's credo, then another, and another. I thought we had discounted that article of faith at the outset of the conference. Reduced to thoughts of one syllable, I say something like this:

Imagine a seventh grade classroom in New York, about 1912. The children of immigrants are studying *Macbeth*. A neatly dressed girl in the third row is learning that the play is great, and that it is about good and evil. She is also learning that she can give answers the teacher likes, that she can get good grades on tests, that the culture of school, though realized via the English language, is not so different from that of her relatively well-educated parents, that she has a future using her mind—that she might become a teacher herself. Next to her, a boy in shabbier clothes is learning that the play is great, and that it is about good and evil, though he cannot understand its lines. He is also learning once again, from the study of *Macbeth* this time, what he has learned each year in school: that his answers are always wrong, that his way of talking makes other kids snicker, that teachers see him as a nuisance, that school is an alien place, that he will be a laborer like his father and older brother, and that this future is what he deserves because he is dumb.

Does my homely example register with the believers in redemptive Literature? Do they think such examples have a place in talk about the functions of the humanities?

I think it belongs there, if the talk is to be consequential and not simply contribute to the discourse of professional justification and morale-boosting. I did not always think so, socialized as I was into the high and disinterested cultural mission of humanities professors during the halcyon post-World War II years. Without the stimulus of the civil rights struggles and the antiwar movement, I doubt that my thinking about criticism and the humanities would have veered toward political and institutional questions about culture, questions about the negotiation of inequality from one generation to the next, about professional interests and careers, about seventh grade classrooms. The events of the sixties were hard on complacency; they provoked self-scrutiny, and an effort to connect the large with the small, the abstract with the concrete.

Like many of my colleagues, I began cocking a more skeptical eye at the humanities. Why, in spite of much good will and intelligence on our part, and in spite of the great works lined up in marching formation on our bookshelves, did the humanities as we practiced them often fail to humanize, or succeed in humanizing a few at the expense of many? Was that so different from asking why the corporate practices of well-trained and well-intentioned doctors do not spread health throughout our society? Or why the work of lawyers does not always make for justice? The answer to all these questions—and how could I have been so dim as not to have known it all along?—is that bodies of knowledge and the people (professionals) who mediate them work through institutions designed to serve in part the self-interest of the practitioners, and that these institutions and practices must respond to the power and needs of dominant groups in the society at large.

In a book published in 1976, I worked this proposition out in some detail, with reference to my own profession. Let me quote one passage that expresses the idea in a way I still endorse:

when George Steiner cites the evidence of cultivated Nazis to prove that the humanities do not necessarily make people humane, or when the more cautious Herbert J. Muller confesses that he does not know whether they do or not, I can only say that the question has been wrongly put. No one should imagine that the humanities always do the same thing simply because their content remains more or less the same. What they do, what literature does, depends on who is doing it. The humanities are not an agent but an instrument. Nazis will make different uses of Goethe and Beethoven than will liberal American professors, and "the" function of literature is almost certain to change within any given society from one century to the next: human values may be eternal, but cultural systems are not. There is just no sense in pondering the function of literature without relating it to the actual society that uses it, to the centers of power within that society, and to the institutions that mediate between literature and people.[1]

Whatever was or is of use in that book, to our thinking about what we do, derived from the strategy of discounting two common angles of vision, and privileging a third. I rejected the view from the timeless and Olympian heights of *The* Humanities, of disembodied texts and values, without human agents who make criticism and literature function for contingent ends, including careers. I included but tried to broaden the view from the trenches, bearing in mind that the seventh grade teacher of *Macbeth*, taking pleasure in the bright spirit of one child and despairing at the dullness or intransigence of another, does not *mean* to be reproducing and accrediting a hurtful class structure. The angle of vision I favored, and still do, is one from the long perspective of history and the whole social process, one that tries to discern alignments of power and fields of force within it. Class, gender, race come into definition, while The Humanities begin to look like a granfalloon.[2]

In adopting this angle of vision, I do so as a would-be historical agent, with projects and values of my own. Those values—equality, the chance of self-actualization for all, empowerment of the powerless—do not differ much from values held by many who profess allegiance to the humanities, in and out of colleges. But I have come to see them as incompatible with the further elaboration of our social order, whether presided over by a Kennedy or a Reagan, and here I differ from most who are likely to read this book. In what follows, I want to spell out, briefly and schematically, the basis of that difference. The next few pages should also serve the purpose of anchoring the essays that follow, and, incidentally, of indicating to those who have read *English in America* how I have carried forward the ideas of that book.[3]

I situate English and the humanities within the long, historical crisis of capitalism. By the 1930s, the productive power of capitalism in the United States had outgrown the capacity of the society, structured as it was and unaided by nonmarket forces, to use that power fully. Intervention by the state has made up the difference, along with three wars and a rapid expansion of U.S. capital into other countries. Subtract the "public" sector from our economy and unemployment would today stand at least at the 25 percent it reached in 1933; some analysts hold that military production alone makes that much difference. But even the combination of Keynesian measures, imperial expansion, the welfare state, and military spending seems inadequate now. The real income of American workers leveled off about 1970. Inflation and unemployment no longer move in a neat reciprocal relationship; both have generally remained higher than in the fifties and sixties. Credit and debt have ceased to promote expansion, and instead hang like a great albatross around our necks. There is a so-called capital shortage, really a capital strike: growth, the sine qua non of capitalism, is halting, and often of no human value, as when Ted Turner tries to buy CBS, or T. Boone Pickens an oil company. The system seems unable to keep on doing what—as even its enemies allow—it did so splendidly for 150 years: expand the material basis of our lives.

Meanwhile, its more vicious characteristics show remarkable persistence, in spite of a thousand liberal remedies. Inequality of income was as great in 1985 as in 1945. A black movement and a women's movement have led to the passage of laws and to some changes of heart, but have had little effect on the relative economic position of these groups; the New Right assaults what gains there were, in the name of freedom and morality. Our educational system, on which we counted so heavily, has not even created equality of opportunity, much less equality itself. We notice again what it was polite to ignore for forty years: that we have a class system. Most people feel and are powerless. They are bored with their work, distrustful of our major institutions, contemptuous of politics as a means of redress and renewal. And the main irrationality of capitalism—that socially produced wealth is privately allocated, and so allocated by the sole criterion of profitability—has produced energy crises, environmental crises, widespread starvation, and so on. The capitalist countries also find, increasingly, that they must either support bloody dictatorships in the third world and perhaps be willing to destroy societies such as those of Southeast Asia and Central America, or watch defection after defection from the system they rule. In support of this imperial house of cards, they have created a military machine that can and may destroy human social life altogether.[4]

Few teachers of the humanities welcome these developments, and a small but increasing number of us have concluded that our liberal values—equality, democracy, civility, full development of each person—cannot be realized in liberal, capitalist society. For I think liberal politics and liberal education have more in common than the accident of a common adjective. The same contradiction that permeates our whole political system also permeates our institutions of liberal education; liberal values are necessary to the maintenance of advanced capitalism, yet advanced capitalism prevents their fulfillment.

Marx and Engels believed that such contradictions would create a revolutionary working class in the industrialized nations, bring down capitalism, and lead to the building of a humanistic socialism. It's been a long time since 1847, and nowhere has this happened according to script. Marxists must ask why the scenario has so often gone wrong in socialist countries, and, as urgently, what in this most advanced capitalist country has held together so unjust and irrational a social order. A repressive state is not the principal answer to the second question, though we can have no illusions, after the Joe McCarthy period and after the revelations since 1965 about CIA and FBI politics, that the state has been or will be a neutral bystander to the formation of a powerful socialist movement. Capitalism owes its durability, I believe, first to its immense productive power, however weakened in recent years; second, to extension of its domain beyond our borders, so that the worst immiseration of workers is put out of sight and out of our political arena; and third, to welfare-warfare state measures.

Still, I cannot believe that even such a combination of remedies would suffice for long, in itself. Something more is needed to conceal the real workings of the society from those most hurt by it, to make it seem inevitable and right to close off alternatives from view. Marx and Engels provided the fundamental explanation, in their notion of a superstructure—laws, institutions, culture, beliefs, values, customs—that rises from the economic base, rationalizes it, and protects its relations. In this century, Antonio Gramsci elaborated this idea through his account of the hegemony of the dominant class: a whole way of life including culture and ideas far more subtle and effective than naked force supported by ideological institutions, which effectively enlists almost everyone in the "party" of the ruling class, sets limits to debate and consciousness, and in general serves as a means of rule—that is, of preserving and reproducing class structure.

The humanities, like the schools and universities within which they are practiced, have contributed through the hundred years of our profession's existence to this hegemonic process. I argued in *English in America* that English teachers have helped train the kind of work force capitalists need in a productive system that relies less and less on purely manual labor. More, we have helped inculcate the discipline—punctuality, good verbal manners, submission to authority, attention to problem-solving assignments set by someone else, long hours spent in one place—necessary to perform the alienated labor that will be the lot of most. And more important still, by helping to sort out those who will succeed in school from those who will not, we have generally confirmed the class origins of our students, while making it possible for a few to rise (and others to sink). The effect—unintended of course—is to sustain the *illusion* of equal opportunity and convince the majority

that their failure to play a significant and rewarding role in society
is a personal failure rather than a systemic one.

What about the Arnoldian claims for literacy and literature and
criticism: their civilizing effect, their preservation of the best values from our history, their offer of a vantage point from which we
may cast a disinterested eye on our society and on the strident fac-
tional jostling of classes within it? I do not wish to put aside this
hope with a cynical gesture. Most of us have experienced in ourselves and seen in at least some of our students the widening of
sympathies, the release from parochial blindness, the refinement
of thought and feeling, the keener awareness of cant, that literature
and criticism *can* nourish.

But the Arnoldians among us—including (strange bedfellows)
those Arnoldian marxists who make up the Frankfurt school—err
by placing faith in the critical force of history, art, literature, and
philosophy, apart from the institutions within which they are mediated at a particular historical moment. Our own profession, as it
has increasingly colonized the experience of literature for American young people, has pretty successfully abstracted it from any
but literary history, muted its social resonance and given it a primary reference point in the individual consciousness, striven to
anchor it in supposedly timeless values and ideas of human nature,
and lately surrounded it with specialist techniques of interpretation and quarrels about theory—New Criticism, myth criticism,
Chicago criticism, structuralist criticism, psychoanalytic criticism, phenomenological criticism, linguistic criticism, feminist
criticism, marxist criticism, reader-centered criticism, deconstruc-
tion, post-structuralism,[5] and no doubt post-every-ism on this
list—quarrels that sometimes enlighten and sometimes do little
more than advance careers and stake out territories. Oddly, it
might seem, the evolution of theory has generated this efflorescence of species just as the old base of our prosperity, laid by the
postwar boom, is crumbling. But maybe that's not so odd.

Let me work back to this subject by considering for a while the
situation that underlies the often-discussed crisis in the humanities, demographics aside. The stagnation of the capitalist economy
seems permanent. There is (as yet) no new Vietnam War to keep it
artificially booming, and the chips have been called in on the Vietnam extravaganza itself, with economic results that are familiar.
The job market is fairly well choked with highly educated workers.
As the subdivision and degradation of labor that has characterized
monopoly capital since its beginning goes forward, and as the per-

centage of Americans doing at least some college study increases (it is close to 60 percent now), a gap widens between the unalienated work and good life that college used to promise and what most college graduates can actually expect.[6] I think that at some level of awareness they know this. Hence their strategy of going for those subjects and techniques that seem to offer the best chance of a decent first job—however disappointed most will be with where that initial job leads, twenty years from now.

We know what that has meant for us. Majors in English and allied fields are down 50 percent or more in two decades. Departments have shrunk. Recent estimates suggest that from 15 percent to 40 percent of job seekers in the field of English find permanent employment there. And the students still in our classrooms are mostly studying composition, which accounted for 40 percent of English enrollments in the late sixties; it accounted for 60 percent in 1985 and for twice the number of literature enrollments.

I see no evidence that students derive less benefit from the study of literature, or are less attracted to that study, now than in 1965. Rather, students will pursue an inherently pleasant and humane activity when there is no penalty for doing so, as in the 1960s when there was a shortage of educated workers and every B.A. got a job; but not so many of them will do so when jobs are short, when there is a premium on marketable skills, and when educational authorities set a course toward vocational training rather than liberal arts. These circumstances underscore the folly of discussing our profession in a historical vacuum. The market determines the use of our work by a calculus of exchange value that need not correspond to our own use values, and right now we—or I should say, our students and younger colleagues—are experiencing one of the irrationalities, a minor but painful one, of the market system.

You may detect a contradiction between what I've just said and my earlier remarks about the uses of our work to capitalists, in helping to reproduce the class system and the ideology that supports it. The contradiction dissolves if we remember that the meaning of our work as *we* understand it is not the same as its structural valence within the society, and that from the social perspective various parts of that work—especially those connected to literature—are more or less interchangeable with tasks of legitimation and class reproduction performed by others: by teachers of accounting or of dry cleaning; by television and the other media; by employers themselves.

If true, this observation suggests that there is not much hope of regaining the position we held two decades ago merely by determining more accurately what our society, as presently constituted, wants of us. In English we know that well enough: our society wants less liberal arts, more grammar, more vocationally useful skills, more emphasis on basic literacy, "higher" standards, generally lowered expectations for our students, a finer and more rigorous sorting out of those who will *have* from those who will *have not*. But acceding to these demands in a servile and unimaginative way can do little, if my analysis is right, to serve even a narrow vision of self-interest, and nothing at all to answer a broader one consistent with the values of civility and democratic culture that most of us hold.

So far I have spoken of the gradually deepening crisis in our economic system and in the humanities as if all of us and all of our students were in the same pickle. This is clearly not true. Worse, it violates one of my own cardinal rules of ideological wariness: whenever you hear someone say *we* or *society* as if we were a homogeneous and conflict-free unity, get your hand on your wallet. And finally, the picture I have sketched does not include some salient features of English (and the humanities) in the United States, 1986: for instance, the efflorescence of theory I mentioned a while back, and those voices exhorting us not to move toward basic skills and vocationalism, but to reassert our dedication to the great books and to a core curriculum based on them. In the remainder of this essay, I turn to these two matters, trying to suggest how the analysis of culture which I have put forward may aid in the understanding of current debates and conflicts.

First, allow me to unpack that bogus *we* by mentioning the single example of my own college, to which little of what I've said about the present moment applies. Wesleyan is one of the dozen most selective schools in the country: applicants jostle and beg for admission, though annual costs for those who pay their own way are approaching $15,000. At Wesleyan (and I suppose at Princeton, at Amherst, etc.) there has been no decline in humanities enrollments. The English major—a fairly traditional one—is overcrowded in spite of my department's efforts to stiffen the requirements in recent years. About one-sixth of Wesleyan students major in English. We put enrollment limits on almost all of our courses, and even when the limit is sixty or eighty or one hundred, the computer usually turns students away. Furthermore, these figures do not reflect a shift in our offering toward composition, though our students would certainly like more of it than we offer. Only about 12 percent to 15 percent of our enrollments, each year, are in writing courses. The rest are in literature and in what I would call cultural studies.

Why? I think the answer is easy. For Wesleyan students (and for those at Yale, Stanford, Wellesley, etc.) there is *still* no penalty for pursuing the humane and pleasant activity of reading good books and trying to understand the world. These students have a reserved place waiting for them in either the professional-managerial class or the ruling class, some by virtue of having made it into an elite college, most by birth and nurture. They will land on their feet, even if they think they are risking downward mobility by studying Shakespeare instead of biochemistry. The class system, I suggest, is becoming more finely etched as the crisis works its way out. This holds true for higher education as for the whole society, and the Reagan administration, in particular, has done what it can to egg the process along, with its tax and student loan proposals.

Meanwhile, in the elite colleges our students' privilege frees their teachers to pursue the activities that attract us, rather than turning our minds and energies to technical writing and the like. Some of us at Wesleyan do traditional scholarship and criticism. There are a couple of post-structuralists, a myth critic, a psychoanalytic critic, and people who ground their research and teaching in feminism, black studies, marxism, cultural studies. We, too, can try to understand the world in our various ways and (yes) try to advance our careers by emulating the leaders in this very heterogeneous field.

Centrifugal tendencies in theory and method over the past fifteen years have a lot to do with a deepening class division in the academy, which parallels that outside of it. Teachers of English in the more expensive private institutions and in some of the most prestigious public ones feel less pressure than before from students' vocational needs and anxieties, whatever the polls say about these matters. And many feel less professional solidarity with those who teach mainly composition to middle-class and working-class students. That division expresses itself not only in recent angry proposals by writing teachers to secede from the uneasy alliance of the English department, but in the freedom of the more privileged academic group to pursue theories and approaches not very directly related to classroom exigencies or to guild traditions. I can't prove any of this, but I ask you to entertain it as at least a plausible explanation, one rooted in class.

Now to the recent voices that call for "excellence," cultural literacy, great books, a core curriculum in the humanities. Here, I will allude mainly to two influentials, very differently positioned in our society, and speaking from very different political orientations, yet in much the same vein. One is Secretary of Education William Bennett, whom I dislike, and fear even more than before, since his elevation to a cabinet post. The other is E. D. Hirsch, whom I like and admire, and whose ideas about cultural literacy have struck me as a sad apostasy, though a tempting one to many liberal humanists.

About the egregious Bennett: probably few of my readers find his position, in "To Reclaim a Legacy,"[7] congenial, so I will not spend time opposing the list of great books he recommends for all our students, whatever their circumstances and goals. (I will note in passing, though, that since most of us *also* think it would be a fine world if everyone had thoughtfully read Montaigne and Melville, Bennett's recommendations have a kind of utopian seductiveness that we must strain to resist.) What I mainly wish to note is the absurdity of his premises about society and history. Their plausibility dissolves as soon as one looks twice at the stirring phrases. (Where is this discourse coming from? Why is anyone listening?)

Bennett begins by asserting that few students get "an adequate education in the culture and civilization of which they are members." If they don't, one might ask, in what sense are they "members" of it? Is a culture something hidden in mysteries? Is it not the practices and beliefs of a people? Immediately we see that Bennett has set culture over and against society, in a way that has very specific historical origins, those traced by Raymond Williams many years ago in *Culture and Society*. Bennett seems unaware of them. Otherwise, he might ask why the culture critique to which he subscribes has generally served to set intellectuals off against the millions on whose behalf we have claimed to speak, and why things should be otherwise in the Reagan epoch.

Perhaps because Bennett's initial position is plainly contradictory, he quickly undertakes a maneuver that projects a unified humanistic culture back into the past. The humanities—"history, literature, philosophy, and the ideals and practices of the past . . . have shaped the society" that our students enter, and to be ignorant of them is to be culturally disenfranchised. Again, he writes: "That our society was founded upon such principles as justice, liberty, government with the consent of the governed, and equality under the law is the result of ideas descended directly from great epochs of Western civilization." Never mind, for now, how well you think Mr. Bennett's society is doing at equality before the law in

Detroit and Grosse Point, or at ensuring government with the consent of the governed in Nicaragua. I am concerned to point out, rather, that Bennett seems to think our society shaped by "the best that has been said, thought, written," and so forth—in short, by the Arnoldian humanities. As a materialist, I believe ideas have a secondary role in shaping this or any other society. But if one subscribes to idealist history, surely the shaping ideas of our society are rendered more accurately in such immortal words from the past as "The business of America is business," and "What's good for General Motors is good for the country," than by the ideas Bennett has in mind.

So if Bennett culture is not constitutive of our society, either now or as a legacy from the past, what makes the humanities an essential study? Bennett's other main rationale, as he slides around the difficulties I have mentioned, is that the humanities well taught can *make* students "become participants in a common culture," not the one they actually have, but one "rooted in civilization's lasting vision, its highest shared ideals and aspirations." In other words, we are to sift out the best (by whose standards?) from the past, and *create* a "sense of community" around that high culture.

Is this not precisely what the professors and schoolmen set out to do in the 1890s (see essay 3 in this book), and have been spasmodically trying to do ever since? And has a good dose of Milton or Goldsmith generally made the farm youth or the Italian immigrant or the recent black arrival in Chicago feel part of a common culture? Or has it more often made her and him feel, precisely, *excluded* from the culture that counts—at best angry about that, and at worst convinced that she or he deserves, because of invincible ignorance, the station of laundress or parking attendant? For the decoded message of Bennett's report is that someone—educational leaders? John Silber? us?—should tell everyone else what the cultural prerequisites are for entry into capitalist elites, that most will fail the test, and that most of these will blame themselves. Either Bennett is a more wicked man than even I think, and understands all this; or, more likely, he is himself invincibly ignorant about culture, history, and power, and has produced this vacuous report out of his own profoundest cogitations, buoyed by the mean-spirited crassness of the Reagan administration—upon whose policies of triage it lays a veneer of resonant clichés.

Briefly, now, E. D. Hirsch, whom Bennett approvingly cites—I hope to Hirsch's therapeutic discomfort. In two articles in *The American Scholar,*[8] which have apparently influenced not only Bennett but the California educators working toward a core reading list for the state's high schools, Hirsch reports the latest discoveries of his long, groping tour through the dark realms of composition and literacy theory. He has now determined that national languages and national cultures are in fact nationalistic. So far so good. But instead of interrogating nationalism as an educational purpose, Hirsch goes on to lament the decline in *our* common culture, as measured by such instruments as the verbal SAT. After working through the implications of the content-neutral theory he developed in his book on composition, he discovered that literacy is *not* after all content-neutral, and that communication works better when both parties know what the discourse is about. Ergo, we must promote "cultural literacy," and shared knowledge; then when we test students on what they know, literacy scores will rise in a most gratifying way—if one finds tautological results gratifying.

Hirsch says that "a certain extent of shared, canonical knowledge is inherently necessary to a literate democracy." This, I believe, is true, and has nothing to do whatsoever with his argument about content and literacy tests. But of course it brings him immediately face to face with what he calls the "political decision of choosing the contents of cultural literacy"—that is, of dictating the terms of literate democracy. Hirsch, unlike Bennett, recognizes this as a problem, and he puzzles who the *we* might be that could make such a decision. But like Bennett, he neglects to wonder how one might legislate democracy in the spheres of culture and education when there is no democracy, no equality, no empowerment for the many outside those spheres.

Interestingly, both Hirsch and Bennett mention along the way an area in which this society does possess a common culture: TV. Hirsch: "Television is perhaps our only national curriculum"; Bennett: "even television and the comics can give us" a national culture. But both theorists drop that subject instantly. That is a mistake. If we already have a cultural center of shared knowledge, why not base the SATs on that, and watch scores shoot up? And if, as most students of the media agree, television expresses broadly shared and historically grounded values and myths, why not accept it as canonical? It would be interesting to hear Hirsch and Bennett on the subject. I imagine they would both say, in different ways, that this truly national culture is shallow and crude. Hirsch might even answer, as would I, that it is undemocratic. But then we would all have to talk together about how this society came to have such a mass culture in the first place. (My answer: it is inseparable from the ways that monopoly capital has in just a hundred years reshaped human life; see part III of this book.) And that would in turn carry us back into the political arena, where Bennett (but not Hirsch, to his credit) scorns to tread.

But to put it in that way is of course to expose the absurdity of such claims. Bennett made the case for the political disinterestedness of culture, in "To Reclaim a Legacy," from his political post at the National Endowment for the Humanities. In preparation for his report, he assembled a conference of mainly right-wing educators whose ideas have gained credence only within the ambience of the Reagan administration, and who gain further legitimacy from their association with Bennett's report. The power of those ideas grows with his political appointment as secretary of education, from which position he can exercise a more direct influence on federal legislation and on state bodies that control public schools. His agenda for the humanities is deeply etched with the New Right's design for our future. All this would be too obvious to put in words, except for the mesmeric power still carried by the idea that criticism, or English, or the great books, or the humanities, or culture, can somehow stand off from the clash of purposes and interests, and serve some higher purpose of its own in a politically neutral way.

The move to reassert the centrality of the traditional canon, seen from the perspective of these essays, contributes to a much broader social strategy. In the economic arena, that strategy calls for freeing up capital to accumulate more or less as it did 125 years ago: in the pockets of the rich, who will presumably invest it in a way that again stokes up the weary engine of production. (Never mind for now the anachronisms entailed by this idea.) Toward that end, the strategy openly demands unraveling the welfare state. Less openly, it authorizes further enrichment and empowerment of the bourgeoisie, consolidation of the professional-managerial class, and a wider spread between these and the working class, with a hopeless underclass—here and abroad—permanently isolated and forgotten. I say "less openly," but this future is fairly evident in the tax "reform" and in many other acts of the Reagan administration.

In the cultural domain, the strategy calls for reestablishment of "traditional" values that link religion and patriarchy to the free market. Bennett's project is a minor skirmish in this battle. Were it to succeed, it would join a kind of cultural authority to the power that schooling must exercise in reproducing class inequality.[9] And of course it would defeat or redirect the more democratic educational movements that arose twenty years ago, in particular those that addressed racism through a multicultural ideal.

Here the question of intent arises. I do not believe Bennett sees his plan for the humanities in this way. (No more does Sen. William Bradley understand his tax "reform" efforts as fostering an even nastier distribution of wealth and power.) Certainly neither E. D. Hirsch nor the many humanists drawn to his idea of cultural literacy and a core curriculum have seen ideological support for inequality as their cause. Of course I may be wrong in my analysis. But if not, the convergence of such different projects and such politically diverse agents, in this attempt to reground English and the humanities, nicely instances the process of hegemony, in a particular moment of capitalist crisis. Ideas from the front lines of capital seep through devious channels back to the ivory towers, joining with and giving momentum to certain ideas that originate there—ideas often motivated initially in quite other ways.

This argument should in no way be understood as identifying the classics or the humanities with domination, transhistorically. If human beings ever achieve a decent world order, I hope that classics from many cultures will have a place of honor in its memory and in its legacy to the young. For now, however, we—and here I mean all those whose allegiance is to equality and justice—should reject the dangerous calls for a spurious common culture handed down from above. In recent years those calls have most often expressed, even if unintentionally, the deepening crisis of our social system, and have represented efforts to patch it up by hardening class lines, calling the result fair, and enlisting us in its behalf under the name of culture.

2 The Social Relations of Criticism

In urging the distinguished speaker at Wesleyan to count among the functions of criticism its role in the careers of those who write it, I was making a broad gesture toward a complex subject. She thought, understandably perhaps, that I was claiming to "see through" criticism in the way a youthful convert to atheism sees through religion, as nothing but a scheme of self-aggrandizement on the part of the priestcraft. Criticism does abet the tenuring and the salary increases of its academic practitioners, and that is far from the least revealing thing one might say about it. But reducing it to that would be unjust, not only to the idealism of many of the critics, but also to the very social and economic relations that conspire with idealism to drive the critical practice. I will briefly consider those relations in this essay, before casting back into history for some of their origins in the essay that follows.

Sartre wrote amusingly on the nature of criticism, and on its social and economic context, almost forty years ago:

It must be borne in mind that most critics are men who have not had much luck and who, just about the time they were growing desperate, found a quiet little job as cemetery watchmen. . . . The dead are there; the only thing they have done is write. . . . The trouble makers have disappeared; all that remains are the little coffins that are stacked on shelves along the walls like urns in a columbarium. The critic lives badly; his wife does not appreciate him as she ought to; his children are ungrateful; the first of the month is hard on him. But it is always possible for him to enter his library, take down a book from the shelf, and open it. It gives off a slight odor of the cellar, and a strange operation begins which he has decided to call reading.

In reading, the critic enters into a kind of "possession" by a book "written by a dead man about dead things," a book that "no longer has any place on earth," does not interest us directly, and whose feelings have "passed on to the status of exemplary feelings and, in a word, of *values*." Sartre's critic considers with equal distance the racism of Gobineau and the humanitarianism of Rousseau (between whom he would have had to choose if he had been their contemporary), because both Gobineau and Rousseau are "profoundly and deliciously wrong, and in the same way: they are dead." Enjoying thus the "well-known superiority of live dogs to dead lions," the critic reduces what were their burning causes and urgencies to "messages" about themselves, often contradicted by their lives. When nothing remains of them but

these capital truths, "that man is neither good nor bad," "that there is a great deal of suffering in human life," "that genius is only great patience," this melancholy cuisine will have achieved its purpose, and the reader, as he lays down the book, will be able to cry out with a tranquil soul, "All this is only literature."[1]

You may judge for yourself whether or not the philosopher is unfair to us. Either way, you will probably want to comment that Sartre's critic occupies a different situation from the one in which we write our criticism: apparently he earns his meager living from it, for one thing; if we had to do that we should find the first of the month a bitter moment indeed. Also, he is emphatically a *man*, and many of us are not. I begin with Sartre, though, because he looks at criticism as the activity of people in particular circumstances, whose criticism responds to those circumstances as well as to literature. Like Raymond Williams, he sees criticism as "a practice, in active and complex relations with the situation and conditions of the practice, and, necessarily, with all other practices."[2] I wish to do likewise, mainly stating the obvious, because sometimes the obvious gets confounded in enigmas of our own making.

Let me insist right away: any enigma that inheres in the question What is (literary) criticism? *must* be partly of our own making. (By *we*, I mean those in this society who profess literature and write about it.) I say this because although Williams adequately shows that "criticism" has become a "very difficult word," it is not a difficult word in our own professional use. Criticism is the formal writing and talking about literature that people like us do. One may wish, for some purpose, to extend the use of the term to cover what the reviewer in today's *Boston Globe* writes about the new novel, or what we say about literature in casual conversation, or anyone's response of any sort to literature. Or one may wish for different purposes to restrict the concept of criticism so that it excludes judgment or interpretation or some other kind of writing. But I believe most will agree that if we examine the way we use the term for easy and natural converse among ourselves, we mean the articles in *Novel* and *Modern Fiction Studies* and do not mean the review in the *Globe* or this morning's argument in class about the ghosts in *The Turn of the Screw* or the applause at the end of the play last night; we do mean the highly judgmental writings of Ivor Winters and F. R. Leavis along with Cleanth Brooks's explications.

So where is the problem? Well, for one thing, the *what* in *What is criticism?* squints; in fact, it has triple vision. The question can mean: what are the various operations that critics carry on—what exactly goes on in critical discourse? That empirical question is difficult, and worth answering in careful detail. But it is no enigma. Nor is there a puzzle in the question read as I have read it in the previous paragraph, where "what" is taken to ask for the extension of the term, its domain. The enigma rises up when we take the *what* as a request to identify the *essence* of criticism, that privileged feature that makes some activities and texts really criticism and others defective criticism or not criticism at all.

Bewitchment. As if one were to ask *What is cooking?* and be satisfied neither with an account of what the word means nor with a descriptive analysis of the various things cooks do nor with an enumeration of the products of cooking, but insist on knowing in addition what cooking *really* is—so as to prove triumphantly, perhaps, that boiling vegetables ("à l'Anglaise") is not cooking at all, or is a travesty of cooking, or is third-rate cooking. Taken this way, the question is an invitation to honor some cooks and excommunicate others. That may be worth doing, but not by the misleading and heavily ideological strategy of trying to derive a value from a fact—*What and how should we cook?* from *What is cooking?* There may be polemical essays titled "What Is Cooking?" gathered from time to time in controversial books, but I doubt it, and not just because we all know that, minimally, to cook food is to heat it. (After all, we all know that criticism is, minimally, formal writing and talking about literature.) I think we have a controversy about what criticism is and not about what cooking is partly because the social relations that surround cooking are fairly obvious and those that surround criticism are opaque. Writing about intellectuals, Gramsci noted the futile effort to find a single feature that characterizes all their activities and distinguishes those activities from the activities of other groups. The error, he said, was to look for such a criterion "in the intrinsic nature of intellectual activities, rather than in the ensemble of the system of relations in which these activities . . . have their place."[3] The same, I think, holds for criticism and critics. I want to examine now the network of relations that surround criticism, putting to work a few basic marxian concepts.

Cooking, done at home, has a clear use value. Done in a restaurant or other institution where one pays to eat, it has that and an exchange value as well. Cooking, in the sense of what has been cooked, is a commodity. In or out of the market, cooking is unmistakably a form of production, and in the market it is the usual sort of commodity. Elementary categories such as these don't embrace criticism so readily. For whom does a work of criticism have a use value? Certainly for some other critics, who use it to inform their teaching and also to "keep up" with their field and to help them produce criticism of their own. It is as if cooking were mainly of use to other cooks, as an aid to further cooking and to instruction in cooking. In addition, criticism has use value for students, but mainly because they have been told to read it by a teacher-critic or because they have been required to write some criticism of their own in a course. This is not to say that critics and students never enjoy criticism or that nobody ever reads it in a disinterested way, but only that as we seek the use value of criticism we find ourselves circling, for the most part, within a chain of uses created by critics themselves.

It might seem easier to pin down the exchange value of criticism. At least some critical essays return a modest fee to their authors, and critical books yield royalties. Yet these payments do not generally flow from the free expression of needs through the market and from the corresponding search for profit on the part of publishers. Most of the few journals that pay for criticism are subsidized by universities or "angels," as are the university presses which print most critical books. And even with subsidy, most of the latter would not be able to survive except for sales to libraries at exorbitant prices, again made possible by university budgets. The few critical books that do remain available in paper covers year after year, and presumably earn their publishers a profit, do so mainly because of sales to other critics or to students required to buy the books for courses or to graduate students apprenticing themselves in the profession. With exchange value as with use value there seems to be no escaping a circle inscribed by critics themselves

and by the institutions where they work. In any event, we are talking of a very small market that is largely an artifact of those who
produce for it.[4] And does anyone doubt that the overwhelming majority of critical efforts, without even counting those of students,
bring no return at all? Criticism is a strange kind of production,
within capitalism, and barely a commodity at all.

In the central situations of criticism—a paper presented at a
conference or published in a journal—critics are at once producers, purveyors, and consumers. Criticism has little value of either
the economic or the personal sort apart from our own needs and
the needs we impose on students and librarians.[5] To go one step
farther, what critics most urgently need is to *produce* criticism not
to consume it. This seems true whether one takes us singly or collectively. Singly, as everyone knows, we want to write it in order to
prove our degree-worthiness, to get jobs, to gain promotions and
tenure, to earn professional status—and also, of course, to win admiration, to gain self-respect, to have the pleasure of discovery, to
celebrate literature, to enjoy argumentative combat, to hold converse with others who have similar interests, and so on. I leave it to
you to decide which set of needs is most formative. Collectively we
need to produce criticism, and create the journals that print it and
the ceremonies of its presentation, in order to confirm our standing
as a profession. For a group of workers will not be recognized as
professionals and granted the special benefits that go with that
status unless it stands guard over and constantly augments a body
of knowledge.[6] Criticism is not the entire body of knowledge that
certifies this profession, but it is the largest one, and for twenty-five
years or more it has been the privileged one. Critics need criticism
in order to hold their place in the university.

But criticism is more than a reason for our exemption from the
worst rigors of the capitalist labor market. When we do it we also
exercise and *express* our professional freedom. In the lingo of our
guild, we distinguish between our jobs and our "work." "How's
your work going?" usually means your criticism or scholarship or
other research, not your teaching. ("I haven't had time for my own
work all semester.") Criticism is our work, but not our job. Our job
is teaching. Its product is education, manifested as grades, credits,
degrees. In our jobs we are directly answerable to our employers.
It's a long way from the secretarial pool or the assembly line to the
university classroom; nonetheless, we too sell our labor power to
our bosses, and they set the broad terms upon which we yield up
our labor—the courses, schedule, rules of instruction. Unlike most

nonprofessional workers, we retain authority over some important areas of planning in our jobs, but the ground rules of teaching are beyond our control. A split between conception and execution exists for us—and of course our control diminishes in times of retrenchment. We are not, technically, exploited, since no capitalist appropriates the surplus value from our labor and no university makes a profit. But we do surrender the product of our labor to our employers, who exact pay from the students or—with diminishing effectiveness, to be sure—from the State. The kinship many of us increasingly feel with other workers has its ground in alienation, no less real for being relatively benign.

But our "work" as critics, precisely because it does not produce a commodity that our employers appropriate, and in fact rarely produces a commodity at all, is not alienated labor. True, many critics must do this labor to survive, and in that respect we are not different from free-lance writers or self-employed physicians. We manage the labor process of criticism, from conception through the more challenging parts of execution. Then we hand over the detail work—typing, word processing, copy-editing, coding, typesetting, proofreading, printing, binding, selling, distributing, mailing—to others. Furthermore, the product belongs to us. Copyright symbolizes this fact, as does the recording of publications and delivered papers on our *vitae*. The critic's name is affixed to the product for good. He or she has performed an act of original creation through (what can only be characterized, at this level of analysis, as) unalienated labor. So, in the practice of criticism, critics come closer than most people ever do to freedom from the usual conditions of labor in capitalist society.[7]

This sounds attractive, so attractive that I should think it would provoke a skeptical question: Why then is criticism not entirely satisfying to those who practice and consume it? Why doesn't criticism appear to us as an area of freedom—both a free exercise of our creative labor and a freely chosen collaboration with others in the exchange and development of ideas? I offer two answers to this question, both of which point to the same kind of structural defect in our freedom.

First, it is not quite true that we do criticism outside the system of exploitation. The university and college managements that employ us make indirect use of criticism and all other research they sponsor, though they do not strictly appropriate these products or sell them for profit. Management demands research in order to keep up the "quality" of the faculty and of the institution. That's to say that the university claims its rank among institutions mainly by citing the research that its faculty carries out, even otherwise useless research like criticism. Research supports its official ranking, and all the more informal measures of repute, such as the flow of promising graduate students, the marketability of those students when they gain Ph.D.'s, and the university's position in the bidding for those same students later on when some of them gain distinction as researchers. This rating system and its values permeate higher education, operating with diminished force "down" through the prestigious colleges, the lesser universities, and the state and municipal colleges. Community colleges and some others may neither reward nor demand research: that fact both reflects and establishes their position at the bottom of the hierarchy.

Management uses the status attained through our research to attract money: gifts from individuals and corporations, grants from foundations and the federal government, and routine funding by states and municipalities—and, in addition to these forms of the social surplus, the tuition that students and their parents pay. Rank turns into money, which, in turn, confirms rank. For students themselves, the rank of their college or university translates into one or another position in the competition for jobs, and for unequally distributed benefits such as income, wealth, prestige, and power. This is just to restate the familiar truth that higher education plays a part in reproducing the class system. Research, including criticism, is one of the media through which class is transmitted. So whatever the aims of the critic, she or he participates through criticism in the processes of competition and of class, as well as that of exploitation. I think we feel at all times the pressure of these social relations, and the tension between them and the free, collaborative exercise of creative labor.

The second reason why the practice of criticism does not measure up to its ideal can be traced through the history of criticism. As Williams points out in *Keywords*, a principal modern sense of "criticism" is *judgment*. As the reception of literature became more isolated, from the seventeenth century on, the reader assumed a position something like that of a consumer, and some readers were able to claim authority as judges. The very idea of judgment implies a division into two groups of people: those qualified by taste, sensibility, or cultivation (later by formal training) to judge, and those disqualified from judging by youth, ignorance, barbarism, or dullness. Furthermore, it implies the existence of external standards by which works are to be judged. Of course there are no such standards: there are only the social processes through which some people are able to win hegemony for their responses. To posit standards is always to engage in an ideological maneuver, to generalize the interests and values of one class or group and present them as the interests and values of all. To the extent that critical practice still disguises response as judgment, critics must feel some insecurity about the concealed power relations that accompany the move from "I like it" to "It is a great work."

It might seem that in the last hundred years, as criticism has become linked to a profession and to a professional emphasis on rigor, method, and objectivity, the class relations of judgment would have drained out of it. And indeed, one now encounters in critical practice much less explicit judgment than formerly; the judgment of works has receded into the background, retained mainly in the form of a tacit and corporate professional judgment as to which works are worth reading, teaching, and criticizing. Judgment is embodied in whatever agreement exists about the canon.

But at the same time and for the same reason—professionalization—that critics have come to judge less, criticism itself has come under judgment more frequently, more formally, and more consequentially. Professionals with the power to grant or deny advancement—graduate professors, editors of journals, referees, reviewers, and others—judge criticism at every stage of a career, and on their judgments depends the passage through college to graduate school to first job, to reappointment, to tenure, and to final promotion. Beyond that, there is the lifelong race to *distinguish* oneself in the judgment of other professionals. Small wonder that the process has led to some rather arcane intellectual gymnastics, to an idea of criticism as an art in competition with literature, to post-this and neo-that, to journals intelligible only to a handful of initiates.

Many will feel that along the way criticism has become an activity in which we exercise our freedom only to be judged and ranked according to what we produce, and in which we can establish our worth only by invidious comparison with others. In this way, and in its tendency to make knowledge inaccessible and private rather than collaborative, the social relations internal to criticism duplicate those very social relations of the larger society from which we try to escape by creating a space for unalienated labor. Nor is this surprising, since the existence of such space contributes to the continuance of just those social relations.

3 Writing and Reading, Work and Leisure

The contrast between *work* and *job* in the casual talk of literary professors (see pp. 22–23) resembles the two oppositions that make up the title of this essay, and for good historical reasons, to be explored herein.

As a profession, we in English spend far more time teaching composition than literature, yet most rewards and most prestige go to those who distinguish themselves in activities related to literature, not to composition. In recent decades there have been loud complaints about this arrangement, and a professional structure has grown within English that is designed to validate work in composition: advanced degrees, journals, professional meetings, a body of theory. Some leaders of the profession have called for a fission of the English department into a writing department and a literature department, holding that only a sharp institutional break can end the subordination of writing. Others have striven to build rationales and practical models for the *unity* of literature and composition. In 1984 the University of New Hampshire sponsored a conference on reading and writing, to advance the cause of unity. There, I looked back to a formative moment in the profession of English, the end of the last century. I argued that bifurcation of the academic subject was and is strongly motivated by social forces outside the profession, as well as by internal needs.

A while back, I was seized by a fascination, or maybe an obsession, with the year 1893, plus or minus one. Let me indulge it for a moment, by mentioning first some events that have a close bearing on our topic here, and then some that are farther afield.

1. Throughout the year 1894, *The Dial* ran a series of articles on programs in English at eighteen American colleges and univer-

sities, written in most cases by the heads of the departments. Imagine such a series appearing today in a national magazine; and imagine a commercial publisher being, as D. C. Heath was then, so impressed by "the great interest aroused in education circles" that it decided to bring the articles out in book form. The interest among *English* teachers was understandable. As William Morton Payne, editor of *The Dial* plausibly argued, the articles "must be admitted to establish beyond question the claims of English as a proper subject of university instruction."[1] That "subject," from Harvard to Berkeley, sidelined a number of older disciplines, and embraced primarily the newer ones of composition and literature.

2. The year before (1893 itself), Harvard University had appointed a Committee on Composition and Rhetoric to examine the writing of its students. The Committee's report deplored the inadequate preparation of these elite students, backing up its indictment with an appendix of comically horrendous themes. The report caused the first national scandal of a type with which we've become all too familiar since then; according to Payne, it gave the English reform movement "its strongest impulse, and made a burning 'question of the day' out of a matter previously little more than academic in its interest."[2]

3. In 1892, the National Educational Association appointed a committee of ten prestigious gentlemen to consider what the curriculum of secondary schools should be. Harvard president Charles W. Eliot was in the chair; the Committee also included the U.S. commissioner of education, four other college presidents, three school heads, and a professor. The Committee of Ten found a chaos in the schools. It determined that nine subjects should make up the bulk of school work (English was one of them), and appointed a "Conference" to make recommendations for each of the nine areas. The Conference on English—seven professors and three schoolmen—met late in 1892, and formulated an elaborate program for grade one through grade twelve. It prefaced its proposals by stating two goals of English instruction:

(1) to enable the pupil to understand the expressed thoughts of others and to give expression to thoughts of his own; and (2) to cultivate a taste for reading, to give the pupil some acquaintance with good literature, and to furnish him with the means of extending that acquaintance.[3]

It went on to insist that although these two goals of communication and appreciation—composition and literature—might be separately named, "yet in practice they should never be dissociated in the mind of the teacher and their mutual dependence should be constantly present to the mind of the pupils." Thus they asserted the unity we are now debating ninety years later. And their assertion came when it counted, for the Report of the Committee of Ten, which appeared in 1894, was probably the most influential one in the history of American education.

4. In 1893, the various professional societies of engineers (civil, mining, etc.) banded together to found the Society for the Promotion of Engineering Education, to regularize standards and maintain their rigor, and to insist that engineering education for undergraduates emphasize basic principles—for example, science—thus more than incidentally grounding their field in a body of unified knowledge that would guarantee it a place in the university.[4]

5. In early 1893 the economy went into a depression, and then into a panic. By 1894, more than 150 railroads had gone bankrupt; in four years, 800 banks failed. Unemployment rose to an estimated 20 percent.[5]

6. Companies responded to the depression in one of their customary ways, by sharply cutting wages. In 1894 a wave of strikes followed, surpassing any previous one in American history, except perhaps that of 1877. In all, 750,000 workers struck that year, more than half in exceptionally bitter, violent, and protracted actions that nearly shut down the coal mines and the railroads, and left many workers dead, injured, or imprisoned.[6]

7. In the middle of the panic of 1893, S. S. McClure brought out his new "quality" monthly magazine, at the unprecedented low price of fifteen cents. John Brisben Walker, editor of the old *Cosmopolitan*, promptly dropped his price to twelve and a half cents. And in October, with much hoopla, Frank Munsey cut the price of his faltering monthly from a quarter to a dime. Its circulation went from 40,000 that month to 200,000 the following February to 500,000 in April 1895. No quality monthly had risen much past a circulation of 200,000 before; by the end of the decade several were close to a million. Historians call this the "magazine revolution" of 1893.[7]

8. In 1893, Sears, Roebuck and Co. was founded; it rapidly became the world's largest merchandiser.

9. In 1892, both the General Electric Company and the United States Rubber Company were formed, by mergers. They represented a new kind of industrial firm—the modern, integrated, corporation. To give an idea of what that means: a few years later the organizational chart of U.S. Rubber showed over eighty divisions,

plants, and subcompanies, comprehending the entire process of production and distribution, from raw materials to the minds of consumers, and rationally arranged in a nine-level tree of command. One of the departments was advertising.[8]

You will not be astounded to hear that I plan to argue more than a coincidental relationship among these nine events. I don't claim any inevitability in their all taking place within a three-year period. Nor do I say that some caused the others. Rather, I suggest that we may understand all of them as belonging to a unified process of historical change, one that transformed our society quite dramatically in a few decades, and that reached a peak of intensity in the 1890s. Though the change came close, for a moment, to revolutionary discontinuity in the national strikes of 1894, it progressed by evolutionary means, catching up every social group and every activity of life. I admit I am not certain just how the separation of reading and writing fit in, but I have some hypotheses—to which I will come after briefly describing the social transformation at its deepest level, the fundamental relations of production and distribution.

In the mid- and late nineteenth century, *competitive* capitalism ran its energetic course, building a huge industrial system with unparalleled speed. The familiar movement from farm and shop to factory, from country to city, can be expressed in any number of statistics. For instance, the value of manufactured goods increased sevenfold in the last four decades of the century, far outdistancing the value of farm products. The number of factories quadrupled, and the number of people working in them tripled. Profits were large, and most of them went into the building of more industrial capacity: industrial capital quadrupled in the last three decades of the century, and the *rate* of capital formation reached the highest point before or since, in the 1890s.[9] Production changed utterly; businessmen were in command of the nation's future.

But, at the same time, they were experiencing that future as a series of shocks. Every decade between 1870 and 1900 brought a major depression, climaxing in the panic of 1893; crises of overproduction were apparently untamable. Within this volatile *system*, individual businesses led precarious existences; competition was fierce, and none of the legal or illegal attempts to restrain it worked. Bankruptcies were endemic. The rate of profit began to decline. And attempts by businessmen to counter these dangers by reducing wages led to all but open class warfare in 1877, 1885,

1892, and 1894. (These conflicts, by the way, sponsored a discourse on "dangerous classes," and what to do about them, just as in England the Hyde Park riots provided an impetus for Matthew Arnold's *Culture and Anarchy*. I will not return to this matter, but it has something to do with the formation of English as a subject.) Businessmen had built an empire, but one they could not govern, one whose anarchy led to great instability, to killing risk, to falling profits, and to social rebellion.[10]

What emerged from this extended crisis—and partially resolved it—was the system I call monopoly capitalism (the adjectives *industrial*, *late*, and *advanced* point to much the same phenomenon). This is no time to characterize it in detail—it is, in any case, the ocean in which we now swim, as familiar to all of us as our bodies. I will only mention a few of its main features, as they bear on my theme. What I'd like you to hold in mind as I do this is that every aspect of monopoly capitalism was in part a response to the crisis of which I have spoken, and an effort to control and rationalize processes that felt—to businessmen as well as to most other people—chaotic and threatening. In fact, one might characterize monopoly capitalism by its powerful drive toward *planning*, by its attempt to replace Adam Smith's invisible hand with the "visible hand" of management.

The phrase "visible hand" is from the title of a book by Alfred D. Chandler (see n. 8), a classic study of monopoly capitalism's main institutional form, the giant corporation, which emerged in the last two decades of the nineteenth century (General Electric and U.S. Rubber were my examples from 1892). Where before entrepreneurs had built factories and concentrated on getting out the goods, from the 1880s on the impersonal corporation became dominant. Characteristically, it brought the entire economic process within its compass, from raw materials through manufacturing through sales. Far too complex for the supervision of a single businessman (and his family), it brought into existence the modern corporate structure, with divisions, subdivisions, and layers of hired management. It attempted to coordinate all stages of making and distributing, so as to eliminate uncertainty from the process. That project never succeeded entirely, of course, but it did establish an economic order that has proved itself quite supple, through our century.

I want now to mention two ways in which the new corporations carried out this design, before turning these thoughts back toward universities and English. First, monopoly capital took control of the labor process, far more precisely and intrusively than had been done before. It developed the approach that came to be known as scientific management, following that magical moment in 1899 when Frederick Winslow Taylor oversaw the work of a "Dutchman" named Schmidt at Bethlehem Steel, and got him to move forty-seven tons of pig iron a day instead of the standard twelve and a half tons. Taylor analyzed a job into its minutest components, divided the process among workers, and created the techniques that culminated in the assembly line. He built on three principles: (1) dissociate the labor process from the vested skills and knowledge of workers; (2) separate conception from execution; and (3) reserve understanding for management and use that understanding to control each step of the labor process. As Studs Terkel's workers said, one way and another: a robot could do my job. Harry Braverman sums up the role of modern management:

to render conscious and systematic, the formerly unconscious tendency of capitalist production. It was to ensure that as craft declined, the worker would sink to the level of general and undifferentiated labor power, adaptable to a large range of simple tasks, while as science grew, it would be concentrated in the hands of management.[11]

The second main movement of monopoly capital was to add control of *sales* to control of production. This was a change of great complexity and unevenness, working through the evolution of department stores, chain stores, mail-order houses (chiefly Sears, Roebuck and Montgomery Ward), the railroads, the telegraph, and the postal system, as well as the new corporate structure and its sales division. The outcome was a universal national market, increasingly managed by the same corporations that produced the goods. To enter national markets successfully they quickly developed a number of new practices: uniform packaging, brand names, trademarks, slogans, jingles, and cartoon characters to penetrate every buyer's mind. They came to rely on advertising as a direct channel of instruction from manufacturer to customer. And piggyback on the new advertising industry arose for the first time a national mass culture, whose main product was not the magazine, the newspaper, the radio program, or the TV broadcast, but the *attention* of the *audience*, sold in blocks to advertisers. The magazine revolution of 1893 created the first really modern channel of mass culture. (Again, see essay 9 of this volume, "Where Did Mass Culture Come From," esp. pp. 139–43, for more of the story.) I can't prove it here, but I assert that this characteristic feature of modern society and of contemporary humanity derives from exactly the same forces that divided and transformed labor. In fact the two are obverse and reverse, in a social mode that has polarized production and consumption, worker and consumer, work and leisure.

Since a society's practices of upbringing and education must somehow mesh with its adult social relations and its productive system, American schools and colleges naturally changed to fit the new conditions, and also helped bring them about. There was no American university in the modern sense of the word, until the last quarter of the nineteenth century, when many sprang up almost simultaneously, as if planned by a national authority—though there was none, beyond the rather empty authorization of the Morrill Act. The old classical, "common" curriculum retreated into the corners of the new institutions, suddenly disestablished by the elective system, and shoved aside by science, professional training, and specialized studies of all sorts—including the new field of English. The university was gearing itself up to be a supplier and certifier of the professionals and managers needed by those integrated corporations and by the other institutions that came into being to monitor and service the corporate social order. In his inaugural address of 1869, Charles W. Eliot forecast the role Harvard and other universities would have in educating specialized *professionals:* "as a people," he lamented, "we do not apply to mental activities the principle of division of labor; and we have but a halting faith in special training for high professional employments."[12] He proposed to remedy that. As for *managers:* there were virtually none in 1869, so Eliot could not have planned for their training, but he understood later that the new university worked to that purpose too. In 1923 he reminisced, "All along Harvard College has produced among its Bachelors of Arts young men who went out into business . . . but it could hardly be said that it was a distinct object in the University to train them for it. Now it has become so."[13]

The new universities came into being along with the professional-managerial class they educated.[14] They developed new structures to accommodate the task: a division between undergraduate and graduate studies; separate "schools" with deans; academic departments, with specialized courses of study that came to be called "majors"; a hierarchy of faculty ranks; administrations above and apart from faculties (cf. the structure of the corporation). Within this format it became crucial for instructors that their field be embodied in a department or school, and that it have its own body of systematized knowledge with graduate degrees leading into its particular profession. Some professions, like the engineers, practiced their discipline mainly outside the university, but all legitimized themselves partly through their standing within it. This is why it was so important, in 1894, to those who taught English, that cultural authorities like Payne and the Committee of Ten accepted "the claims of English as a proper subject of university instruction." No department, no subject, no profession.

For that recognition to occur, the subject must seem to have dignity, a body of knowledge, and if possible, utility as well. That is what English professors—and, with their guidance, schoolteachers—managed to say persuasively in the formative years of the new university. Precisely how that happened is a long story, which others have told. I will simply note that English took its modern shape, in the 1890s, by privileging two of its possible contents—composition and literature—and relegating others to archaism, though those others all had longer traditions: rhetoric, grammar, English language, oratory, elocution. The two newcomers had appeared on the scene sporadically through the century, but had begun to assume a central place only about twenty-five years before the magic year, 1893 plus or minus one.

Eliot spoke of the need for better language training in his inaugural address, and in 1872 brought in Adams Sherman Hill to offer that training. Perhaps that's as close as we can come to spotting the entrenchment of modern composition in the curriculum. It spread like kudzu, mainly because its utility was incontestable—in principle, that is: as already noted, composition barely arrived before it began undergoing crises of perceived effectiveness that have persisted until this day. But all agreed that the young *needed* to write better.

English literature had turned up in this or that college and in some schools, at intervals, but did not gain much credibility until after the Civil War, when professors of English began to be named, and more than a few courses to be offered. One can trace the growing legitimacy of this subject in its emergence as an entrance requirement. Harvard (again) was the first to take an important step, as it proclaimed to the schools in 1873–74 that they should prepare their students in a short list of texts by Shakespeare, Goldsmith, and Scott. But it is important to note that this list appeared under the heading "English Composition," in the requirements: students were to read literature in order to have a subject for their entrance *essays*. That relationship persisted through various attempts at uniform entrance requirements for colleges, in the various regions and finally in the whole country. Only in 1894 did Yale become the first to have an entrance requirement in literature apart from composition, selecting English classics for "their intrinsic importance."[15]

Meanwhile, though, literature had been gaining advocates and prestige *within* the universities at a far more rapid pace than had its more "useful" partner. Why, since few of these advocates claimed for it the kind of utility—beyond virtues of mental discipline that would earn it a place beside the classics—that might admit it into a curriculum for the professional-managerial class? No small part of the answer is that instructors liked teaching it better than they liked reading themes: what else is new? And doubtless students liked studying it. Furthermore, teachers could through literature stake out the necessary claim to a body of scientific knowledge, thanks to the mediation of German philology. Equally important, the Arnoldian ideal of criticism and Culture gained great authority through this period; particularly attractive was Arnold's vision of class harmony through culture, without equality. Professors of literature appropriated this vision, and not, I think, cynically, though at some level of consciousness they probably sensed its ideological appeal to the patrons and clientele of universities, in a moment when class conflict was more and more visible, and frightening enough. Finally, and in hidden contradiction to the Arnoldian justification, English literature carried with it the prestige of the leisured class for whom it had long been a "natural" accomplishment—including in the colleges, where students had pursued literature as a voluntary activity through clubs and societies. It seemed fitting that the birthright of an old elite should be codified and promoted as cultural validation for the newly *credentialed* professional-managerial class.

A strange mixture of forces, then, behind the dynamic march of literature into university and school curriculum. And an even stranger marriage of useful composition and elevating literature, in the subject known as English. But it worked. Only one task of legitimation remained: to convince colleges and presidents that English was *one* subject, not two, so that strong cultural forces behind literature as a field of study could join themselves to the articulate demand for practical composition, and not have to depend solely on the disciplinary and spiritual claims of literature.

In 1894, apparently, the moment had come for a public assertion of the unity of reading and writing, the unity of English. The English Conference of the Committee of Ten spoke with resonance, as did Payne, the editor of *The Dial*, and many of the professors in his collection, when they stated the goals of their departmental programs. Their claims had the backing of a felt historical rightness that did not really need to be stated, a rightness grounded in an emerging social and economic system, the confident growth of a new class, and the transformation of universities in consonance with the needs of that system and that class. By which I do not mean to say that the annunciation of "English" was no more than an epiphenomenon, or a determined outcome of broader developments. The professors and schoolmen voiced genuine convictions and educational purposes. And they not only articulated a rationale for their subject; they also made for it an institutional home that has proved more than durable. We are their direct descendants.

It would be tempting to take their proclamations at face value, and suppose that English won its place in the curriculum with a unity of purpose and practice from which we have been falling away ever since. But I doubt that such unity existed, even in 1894, except as an ideal and an item of professional ideology.

A look at the programs described in Payne's book reveals something close to chaos. Some colleges had separate departments of rhetoric and literature; many taught composition and literature separately within the same department. The balance of emphasis between the two varied extravagantly, from places like Harvard, Amherst, and Michigan, with something like two-thirds of the enrollments (and faculty time) going to composition; to places like Stanford, Berkeley, and Yale, where composition barely existed (though Yale was about to import it from Columbia). And nowhere that I can see were reading and writing integrated in any way more substantial than the use of literary models for student essays, or of literary works as subjects for students to write about.

More telling still, almost all the programs took composition to be the more elementary study, and literature the more advanced. Composition was often required, literature elective. Freshmen and sophomores studied composition; juniors, seniors, and graduate students studied literature. Stanford and Indiana carried this hierarchical division to an extreme, claiming to admit only those students already qualified in composition, and offering no Freshman English (the term already meant composition) at all. Berkeley was attempting to achieve the same result by riding herd over the state's secondary schools, and insisting on three years of school English as an entrance requirement.

Through most of Payne's reports runs a sharp contrast in tone, evidence of this ranking. Professors talk proudly or ecstatically about their literature offerings, while sounding a note of complaint or contempt as they write of composition. Gayley of Berkeley: the "disgust, that frequently attends prolonged indulgence in the habit of theme-correcting." Anderson of Stanford: "the professors were worn out with the drudgery of correcting Freshmen themes,— work really secondary and preparatory, and in no sense forming a proper subject of collegiate instruction." Sampson of Indiana: "the conditioned classes [i.e., remedial composition] make the heaviest drain upon the instructors' time." Small wonder, if the experience of Fred N. Scott at Michigan was typical: he had read more than three thousand themes in the 1893–94 academic year, "most of them written by a class of 216 students."[16] The whole volume reveals less a unity than an unhappy yoking of alienated to unalienated labor. As an anonymous teacher from an eastern university wrote, "I have never done any rhetorical work at _____ except in connection with my courses in literature, and I thank God I have been delivered from the bondage of theme-work into the glorious liberty of literature."[17]

Or, to see it another way, Payne's collection expresses not an articulation of unity but a felt division between work and leisure. Not that teaching literature involved no work, or that the subject had no practical value, but the *goal* of literary instruction was to improve or perfect a self that could exist only in the realm of leisure. Payne makes the connection precise, alluding to Arnold's estimate that "conduct" is three-fourths of life, and claiming "a considerable share of the remaining fraction" for literature (p. 7). A number of professors tie the function of literature to pleasure, extended over the lives of their students.

Anderson, Stanford: "to cultivate a refined appreciation of what is best, and thus to reveal unfailing sources of pure enjoyment" (p. 50).

March, Lafayette: "students come to rejoice in these noble passages, and remember them forever" (p. 77).

Sampson, Indiana: "to give the student a thorough understanding of what he reads, and the ability to read sympathetically and understandingly in the future" (p. 95).

Tolman, Chicago: "An unfailing source of rest and refreshment, a life-long process of self-education . . . through the study of English literature" (pp. 89–90).

They expect literature to become embedded in the higher reaches of their students' being: it is an "aliment of the spiritual life" (p. 39), that can "quicken the spiritual faculties" (p. 61). Clearly it works its benefits in a realm far removed from labor.

Of course these professors were not training a leisure class, by and large. They privilege literature as a spiritual discipline and a mark of cultivation for students who will have a part in the world's work, but whose refined leisure will be in sharp opposition to the struggles of the marketplace. Furthermore, the implied duality of body and spirit hints at another, less philosophical, one: the distinction between those who work with their minds and those who work with their hands. The professors identify their students with the former class, again and again, by speaking of "taste" as a chief goal of literary education. What ladies and gentlemen got from home, tutor, and social milieu, the raw youths of Iowa, Nebraska, and Indiana will get from college instruction in literature.

No such rhetoric springs to the pen when the professors write about the goals of composition. One justifies it by the "grace and skill" it can nurture, thus enabling the graduate to "prove" that he is liberally educated. A few others point to a much-reduced version of its ideal in stating as a goal the ability to write "correct" English. But most don't even attempt to articulate aims for composition: the social context has provided the aim—composition is useful. Again and again the professors speak of their approach as "practical," and their method as "practice." (Along the way, some denigrate *rhetoric* as abstract and theoretical.) Their silence about higher cultural goals is, I think, a tacit acknowledgement that composition fits into the world's work, and so is necessary training for students qualifying themselves to carry out the tasks of the professional-managerial class.

I'm suggesting that from the beginning of English as a fully certified discipline in college and school, its strategic assertion of unity masked a good deal of internal tension, even while expressing a genuine purpose. There was the understandable preference of teachers for literature, buttressed by the fact that they could ground their would-be profession in a growing body of knowledge about literature and of techniques for its study, while—having discarded the discipline of rhetoric—they had left composition without foundation, an amorphous activity that could only be taught through incessant practice. At a deeper level, somewhere in their bones, they regarded composition as preliminary, juvenile, whereas literature was the arena of full maturity. Finally, their conception of English, like that of their daily work, was grounded in institutions that were coming to occupy a key position in a new social order, not yet fully understood. Hence the ideological tensions I have been describing, between manual and mental work, between work and leisure, between an old, more gentlemanly ruling class and a new professional-managerial class that gained its power and privilege from the work it performed on the margins of monopoly capital. This class was developing a conception of itself as *both* vigorous, workful, a progressive historical force, *and* qualified for its social position by its cultural attainments and respectable style of life—including the new museums, symphony orchestras, and libraries, as well as genteel homes maintained by the women of the class. The formation of English as a university subject both cast up and built upon a justification that was homologous in its inner tensions to the ideology of the class itself.[18]

This was a poignant moment, with the new profession poised for growth, yet full of unresolved contradictions. These were to break out most sharply in relations between the colleges and the schools. English literature already had a firm position in many schools, but beginning with Harvard's first list of required literary works, in 1874, the colleges came to exercise a strong influence over high school curricula in English, as teachers sought to prepare *some* of their students for admission to the most prestigious colleges, rather than looking directly to the needs of *all* their students. This hegemony expressed itself in the effort to establish uniform entrance requirements, through the last quarter of the century, climaxing in the formation of the College Entrance Examination Board, which administered its first test in 1901. During this period the colleges sent out mixed signals, indeed. Most notably, first, they told schools that composition and literature were equal, and one. In the same breath, the Committee of Ten report recommended twice as much secondary class time for literature as for composition. And out of the other side of their mouths, professors were saying: teach your pupils to write correct English, so *we* can teach them the more advanced and elevating subject of literature. Second, the Committee of Ten spoke resoundingly against tracking: *all* students, whether bound for liberal arts or technical education, or for office and shop, should receive the same training in their "mother tongue." Yet the message communicated in every other way was: a *few* of your students will use their mother tongue to manage the others, to certify their own superiority, and to cultivate their spiritual selves.

Furthermore, this divided message came just as the public high school was about to assume an entirely new place in American society. Not until 1888 had the number of students in public high school passed the number in preparatory schools and in the academy divisions of colleges and universities. And though the ratio was shifting rapidly, even in 1894 only 40 percent of college students had gone to public high school. Besides, the total numbers involved were small: in 1890 less than 7 percent of the age group was in *any* kind of secondary school.[19] Not only were colleges, prep schools, and academies all elite institutions, but the public high school itself represented the aspirations of the professional-managerial class, more than it did equal opportunity for all classes.

The Committee of Ten framed its policies with an old, aristocratic ideal of the cultivated, unified self in the back of its collective mind. It adapted that ideal to a moment in which college was becoming the central institution for training and promoting a new professional-managerial class. And it proclaimed the idea to high schools that were about to expand into institutions of socialization for everyone; they would inevitably take on missions of vocational training, Americanization, and class reproduction very different from anything envisioned by the Committee of Ten in 1894.

Ironically, for the nascent high school, the Committee's recommendations carried enormous weight and influence, just when they were about to become archaic. The schools took seriously this instruction from above, the more so since they had in effect asked for it (the NEA, which created the Committee, was dominated by school superintendents). By 1904, almost all schools required three or four years of work in English. They tried harder than the colleges themselves to achieve a unity of reading and writing. And they struggled to give all of their increasingly diverse students—middle-class children, immigrants, rural youths, rural blacks newly arrived in the city—uniform instruction in the "mother tongue."

Needless to say, the effort could not and did not overcome the reality of new social conditions and new functions for school training. No more could it work in colleges, which expanded in direct proportion to the high schools and which faced many of the same tensions. And the colleges, apparently, did not even try that hard, as professional ideology continued to privilege literature and to relegate composition and its teachers to second-class status.

Even as books about the teaching of English first began to appear, a note of resignation began to sound in them. In 1903, George R. Carpenter and Franklin T. Baker of Columbia and Fred N. Scott of

Michigan (he of the three thousand themes) linked the teaching of speech and writing to "the necessary demands of business, professional, or social life," while they saw literature as on the defensive against that very "world of fact," against business, science, "the practical life surrounding" the student.[20] In 1909, Percival Chubb acknowledged a dual role for the school: "preparation for social and personal life," and "aid in the choice of, and advance toward, a vocation." He admitted the value of writing in the latter cause ("the practical importance of the art of the ready writer; its sheer business value"), even while urging "higher motives" for the teaching of composition.[21]

This division, implicit in social reality, led in time to overt pleas for the separation of writing and reading in the curriculum. An editorial in *The English Journal* in 1916 *celebrated* this trend, in language coincidentally close to that of my title:

the separation of the teaching of English as a training for work from the teaching of it as a preparation for the enjoyment of leisure is rapidly growing in favor and will mark the present decade, as the union of rhetoric and literary study did that which closed the last century.[22]

Exactly so; though I've already expressed my skepticism about the reality of that union in the 1890s.

I will close with two other dicta from this later time. First, on a lighter note, John B. Opdycke of Julia Richman High School, in New York City, wrote in *The English Journal:*

The language of work is to the language of leisure very much as labor is to capital. The one serves; the other conserves. The one accumulates; the other perpetuates. The one is currency; the other is investment. The one is concerned with immediate use, more or less regardless of form and feature; the other is always conscious of the close relationship between content and form for ultimate purpose. As labor creates values for capital to maintain, so the language of work crystallizes into beautiful expressional forms maintained by the language of literature.[23]

And here is Mervin Curl, author of a 1919 textbook on expository writing:

"The Anglo-Saxons," Emerson said, "are the hands of the world"—they more than any other people, turn the wheels of the world, do its work, keep things moving. . . . [W]e may safely assert that Expository Writing is the hands of literature.[24]

We can't take Opdycke and Curl to represent a professional consensus. But we might pay some attention to their analogies. Those suggest an underlying unity of reading and writing more dialectical and truer to our world than that proposed in the halcyon moment of 1894, and one that will somehow have to be understood if we are to bring our two practices together.

II THINKING AND TEACHING ABOUT AMERICAN LITERATURE

4 A Case Study in Canon Formation: Reviewers, Critics, and *The Catcher in the Rye*

On the day *The Catcher in the Rye* was published, on Monday, July 16, 1951, the *New Tork Times* reviewed it; a review in the Sunday *Times* had appeared the day before, and a rush of other reviews followed. Through the later fifties and on into the sixties, *Catcher* engaged academic critics, and it still does, although the novel generates criticism at a slower rate today than it used to. By 1963 Warren French supposed that critics had written more on *Catcher* than on any other contemporary novel, and in 1965 James E. Miller, Jr., claimed, reasonably enough, that Salinger had stirred more interest among the public and critics alike than any writer since Fitzgerald and Hemingway. By 1961, *Catcher* had sold 1 million copies; by 1965, 5 million; last year the total of its sales stood at more than 9 million.[1]

The Catcher in the Rye arrived to stay; it is older than most of its audience were when they read it for the first time. That quarter century is time enough to allow us to generalize not only about the book's reception in 1951 but about the consensus of critical opinion that developed afterward. We are concerned, in brief, with how *Catcher* became a classic: this is a case study of capitalist criticism. And in it, we shall have in mind the distinction Raymond Williams makes in *Culture and Society* between the lives books lead in the minds of readers and the lives their readers (and writers) live in particular historical times.

To return to July 16, 1951: on that Monday, the front page of the *Times* carried eleven news stories. The largest headline, with the text beneath breaking into two parts, concerned the war in Korea, then a year old: one part told that peace talks between United Nations negotiators and Communists had resumed in Kaesong (they would, of course, be unsuccessful), and the other reported with extensive quotation a speech Secretary of State Dean Acheson made in New York to book and magazine publishers on the meaning of the Korean conflict; the State Department had released the speech "at the request of a number of those" who were present to hear it. An account of the fighting itself with maps and communiqués from the field and a list of casualties appeared on page two. The front-page news was not, in other words, of the combat and its immediate consequences but of verbal maneuvering in the conflict between Communism and the Western world and of the ideological interpretation the leading U.S. spokesman in foreign affairs wished to give to events in Korea. Apart from stories on a flood in Kansas City, the weather in New York (hot, dry, and hard on the water supply), and a request for funding for new schools in the city, all the other articles on the front page bore on the struggle between East and West, of which events in Korea were simply for the moment the most dramatic and costly example: in Teheran, 10,000 "Iranian Reds" rioted to protest the arrival of Averell Harriman, who had come as Truman's special assistant to talk with the shah's government about the Iranian-British oil dispute; Adm. Forrest P. Sherman, chief of naval operations, left for a week in Europe, which would include discussion in Spain about possibilities of "joint military cooperation"; the United States asked for the recall from Washington of two Hungarian diplomats in retaliation for the expulsion of two American officials from Budapest; a Republican congressman protested that his party's opposition to Truman's proposal for continued price, wage, and credit controls was not "sabotaging" those controls but aimed at stopping "socialistic power grabs" on the part of the administration.

The front page of the *Times* on July 16, 1951, serves to outline, quickly enough, the situation of the world into which *The Catcher in the Rye* made such a successful and relatively well-publicized entrance. The main action of the world, the chief events of its days, were occurring within a framework of struggle between two systems of life, two different ways of organizing human beings socially, politically, economically. The opposition between East and West, between socialist and capitalist, was determining what happened in Kaesong, Budapest, Madrid, Teheran, Washington, New York. Name-calling the administration, Republicans threw out the

term *socialist,* and the bid for millions to build schools in the five
boroughs of New York would finally have to dovetail with alloca-
tions of taxes for defense.

The review of *The Catcher in the Rye* in the back pages of the
Times made no mention of any of this. The kind of reality reported
on the front page belonged to one world; the new novel was about
to be assimilated into another, into the world of culture, which was
split from politics and society. And this separation repeated itself in
other reviews: typically, they did not mention the framework of
world history contemporary with the novel; they did not try to relate *Catcher* to that framework even to the extent of claiming that
there was only a partial relationship or complaining, however sim-
plistically, that there was none. Our concern from here on will be
to try to sketch what reviewers and what academic critics after
them did see in the novel and what they might have seen in it. We
are interested in the conceptual frameworks, the alternatives to
history, they used to respond to and interpret *Catcher* as they
passed it on to its millions of lay readers.

Before turning to the world of culture, though, it seems useful to
turn back one last time to the news of July 16, 1951, for even as it
was being reported it was, of course, already being interpreted.
The secretary of state's speech in New York and the lead editorial
were especially rich in interpretive intent. Acheson placed the
Korean War in the perspective of an *ongoing* conflict between the
United States and Russia, and urged Americans to prevail in that
conflict: "Korea's significance is not the final crusade. It is not finally making valid the idea of collective security. It is important
perhaps for the inverse reason that in Korea we prevented the
invalidation of collective security." Even if peace were made in
Korea, we should not relax, because further dangers resided in the

awakening of the vast populations of Asia, populations which are beginning to feel that they should have and should exercise in the world an
influence which is proportionate to their numbers and worthy of their cultures. We must manage our difficulties so prudently that we have strength
and initiative and power left to help shape and guide these emerging
forces so that they will not turn out to be forces which rend and destroy.

What Acheson implied to be the eventual happy ending of our
present and future efforts is obvious and familiar: we would not
only retain our present advantages economically and politically
but augment them. Nations emerging in Asia would do so in ways
compatible with rather than antagonistic to our hegemony, hence

to our own well-being. The fundamental value to which Acheson appealed in his speech, the goal and the sanction of all that he urged, is comprehended in the phrase "national interests." Nationalism was not, in the language of his argument, aggressive but defensive. "A blow has been struck at us in Korea." Another might be struck in a year elsewhere if we slackened in our defense effort; Asian nations would rend and destroy us if we did not guide them otherwise.

The lead editorial supported Acheson's policies and yet at the same time shifted the mode of justifying them:

We would be less than humane if we did not urge and support any course of action that can spare the loss of life. No honest person wanted a war in Korea and all right-minded persons want to see it ended. Nevertheless, we are not willing to sacrifice honor and morality to our will to peace. The United Nations was right in the first place to resist aggression, and that rightness has not been changed. Obviously, the aggression that will have to be resisted now is political rather than military. Our defenses need to be as strong in one field as in the other.

The fundamental appeal here was to a timeless, extranational morality transcending particular interests. Sparing lives and living peacefully are good—everyone right-minded and honest and honorable believes that—but, regrettably and inexorably, the defense of freedom must come first. The United Nations was fighting for a self-determining, united Korea independent of foreign intrusion, and would go on fighting if that end was not achieved at the conference table in Kaesong.

In appealing to "national interests," Acheson offered a justification, a definition of right, congruent with the historical moment; "national interests" fittingly named, though it certainly did not spell out, a clear-sighted interpretation of politico-economic realities in 1951: the United States, having determined the policy of the United Nations, was fighting in Korea to protect and eventually to extend America's post–World War II domination of the world's economic system. The editorial writer obscured the historical moment and mystified the Korean War: as an honorable nation, the United States was fighting north and south of the thirty-eighth parallel to preserve morality. The transformation worked on historical fact between the front page and the editorial parallels, we think, the transformation reviewers and critics worked on *The Catcher in the Rye*. The novel does not, of course, mention the conflict between East and West. It does mirror a competitive, acquisitive society, where those who have, keep and press for more—the same society that put half a million troops on the field in Korea and sent Harriman to Teheran and Sherman to Madrid. *Catcher*, to anticipate our argument at this point, is precisely revealing of social relationships in midcentury America, and motives that sustained them, and rationalizations that masked them. In the hands of reviewers and critics, though, its precision and its protest were blurred and muted, masked not quite white but grayed by a steady application of interpretive terms that tended to abstract and merely universalize its characters and its action, dimming the pattern of their own historical time. As Acheson spoke of interests and the editorial writer of morality, Salinger wrote about power and wealth, and reviewers and critics about good and evil and the problems of growing up.

From the *Times* directly or from other daily papers and from radio and television broadcasts purveying the same news, reviewers turned to *The Catcher in the Rye*. They were fairly consistent in their estimates of the novel; either they praised it or, finding some fault with it, they allowed that it was nonetheless brilliant or a tour de force or at the very least lively. What concerns us here, though, is not how the reviewers rated it but the categories under which they apprehended it. They viewed the novel as a novel, commenting especially on its most striking formal feature, Salinger's choice of a seventeen-year-old personal narrator and his matching of syntax and idiom to that choice. They were also concerned to label *Catcher* generically; they saw it as satire or comedy or tragicomedy, or at their most casual they called it funny or sad or both at once. And in a rudimentary way at least they positioned the novel in the history of fiction; it reminded them of Twain's work and Lardner's and Hemingway's. In other words, neither surprisingly nor inappropriately, the reviewers described *Catcher* as a literary work and placed it vis-à-vis other works similar in genre and style. What they were concerned to do mostly, though, was to relate *Catcher* to life, and upon that relationship they hinged their estimates of its quality far more than they did on its stylistic or generic features. They assumed that a novel's most important function is mimetic and that insofar as it succeeds as representation, it succeeds as fiction. Theoretically, this standard might have integrated the two worlds we have spoken of as separate. But in fact it did not because of the way the reviewers defined, and circumscribed, *life*.

They were, first of all, concerned to describe Holden Caulfield as a person, and, doing that, they emphasized his youth; usually they went on to diagnose what ails him and, some of them, to prescribe a cure and to guess what would happen to him next, beyond the point where the novel itself ends. In the *Times*, Nash K. Burger wrote: "Holden's mercurial changes of mood, his stubborn refusal to admit his own sensitiveness and emotions, his cheerful disregard of what is sometimes known as reality are typically and heartbreakingly adolescent." Phrases similar to "typically and heartbreakingly adolescent" recur in other reviews: "[Salinger] charts the miseries and ecstasies of an adolescent rebel" (*Time*); "[Holden is a] bright, terrible, and possibly normal sixteen-year-old" (Harvey Breit, *Atlantic*); "Holden is not a normal boy. He is hyper-sensitive and hyper-imaginative" (S. N. Behrman, *New Yorker*); "the reader wearies of this kind of explicitness, repetition and adolescence, exactly as one would weary of Holden himself" (Anne L. Goodman, *New Republic*). The kind of typing implicit in these quotations is laid out plain in Ernest Jones's review: "[*Catcher*] is a mirror. It reflects something not at all rich and strange but what every sensitive sixteen-year-old since Rousseau has felt, and of course what each one of us is certain he has felt. . . . its insights . . . are not really insights; since they are so general, 'The Catcher in the Rye' becomes more and more a case history of all of us" (*Nation*). The reviewers differed on certain points: Holden is normal or he is not, but even those who say he is not or possibly not, have a norm in mind. They type Holden according to a timeless developmental standard. They do not fully agree on how to define adolescence, or on how far Holden fits the category (is he *hyper*sensitive? is he *especially* bright?), but they do agree that there is a norm or model and that Holden more or less matches it.

We would exaggerate if we said the reviewers had no awareness at all of Holden Caulfield's time and place. They did address themselves to Salinger's representation of his hero's society, although much less emphatically than they set about describing the hero himself, but here again, they showed a common disposition to typify or to categorize and to do so in remarkably similar ways. Harvey Breit called *Catcher* "a critique of the contemporary grown-up world" (*Atlantic*). Harrison Smith referred to the "complexity of modern life" and "the spectacle of perversity and evil," which bewilder and shock Holden as they do so many youths (*Saturday Review*). Both these reviewers alluded at least to the time of the novel's time. But Breit did not enlarge upon his point save to say that Holden is not a good observer, that we do not see the world through his eyes, only himself; the phrases Smith employed are very far from specific, and this disposition to abstraction is even more pronounced in some other reviews.

In S. N. Behrman's words, "[Holden] is driven crazy by 'phoniness,' a heading under which he loosely gathers not only insincerity but snobbery, injustice, callousness to the tears in things, and a lot more"; he is faced in the novel with "the tremendously complicated and often depraved facts of life" (*New Yorker*). Burger had attributed Holden's difficulties to "a world that is out of joint." In Virgilia Peterson's opinion, Holden "sees the mixtures, the inextricably mingled good and bad, as it is, but the very knowledge of reality is what almost breaks his heart" (*Herald Tribune Book Review*). To say that modern life is complex is to say very little indeed about it, and to speak of "the tears in things" and "a world that is out of joint" and "reality" is to move *Catcher* altogether out of its contemporary setting, to see Holden's difficulties as everywhere and always the same. Even the reviews that make no explicit mention of modernity or of Holden's "world" imply by typing him as an adolescent that a sixteen-year-old's problems have been, are, and will remain the same.[2]

In the March 1957 issue of *The Nation*, David L. Stevenson remarked, "It is a curiosity of our age that J. D. Salinger . . . is rarely acknowledged by the official guardians of our literary virtue in the quarterlies."[3] That was accurate, though not perhaps so curious if, as we suppose to be the case, our official guardians then as now work primarily in our prestigious institutions of higher learning and work over a canonical list of English and American and other Western writers passed on down by those institutions. Although *The Catcher in the Rye* continued to be very much read through the fifties, there was a lag between its date of publication and the appearance of much professional or academic criticism about the novel. Two years after Stevenson's comment, however, *The Nation* carried an article by George Steiner titled "The Salinger Industry." "[Stevenson,]" Steiner wrote, "can now rest assured. The heavy guns are in action along the entire critical front."[4] What were they booming? In Steiner's opinion, they were not only noisy but off target. He was concerned both to note the critical energy being expended on Salinger and to correct its aim. At the very time *Catcher* was being assumed into our literary canon, he was suggesting what bounds criticism should keep within and what conclusions it ought to be reaching. Salinger was a "gifted and entertaining writer with one excellent short novel and a number of memorable stories to his credit."

But criticism, Steiner complained, was busy comparing Salinger to *great* writers and speaking of his work in "complex" and "sublime" terms. Why so much activity, more than Salinger's merit (in Steiner's opinion) deserved, and why such exaggeration and pretension? Steiner gave two reasons, and to his mind they exposed what was wrong with criticism written in contemporary America: first, critics had grafted New Critical jargon onto Germanic scholarship and could no longer speak plainly; second, our academic institutions turned out too many critics, too many assistant and associate professors in need of promotions and fellowships and constrained to publish to get them. "Along comes a small though clearly interesting fish like Salinger and out go the whaling fleets. The academic critic can do his piece with few footnotes, it will be accepted by critical reviews or little magazines, and it is another tally on the sheet of his career."

Steiner's piece is in certain ways inaccurate. It tells what one might have expected to happen if one were predicting the nature of Salinger criticism in the later fities from an exclusive and judgmental point of view of American academic institutions (too many critics on their way up the ladder, "too many critical journals, too many seminars, too many summer schools and fellowships for critics"); but it is skewed in its description of Salinger criticism as it actually did happen in the fifties. Still, Steiner did remark on the arrival of the "Salinger industry" and the prejudices he brings into the play *are* commonly leveled against academics. But we want to distinguish our quarrel with the critics from Steiner's. As we see them, they were generously intentioned and more sincere, less dominated by New Criticism or any other "school" and more subtle, than they appeared to be in Steiner's account of a "vast machine in constant need of new raw material." If, as we go on to argue, they underestimated or overlooked or misread Salinger's rendering of contemporary American life, they do not appear to have done so because they were time-serving drudges fattening their bibliographies for promotion.

It is true that critics exercised their professional training in writing on Salinger; so they might be expected to do. They spoke of the novel's style; an article in *American Speech*, for example, scrutinized Holden's vocabulary and grammar, noting how far they conformed to teenage vernacular in the 1950s.[5] They clustered its images in significant patterns, interpreted its symbols, explained its literary allusions, brought to light principles of narrative repetition and variation that govern its structure, spoke of its time scheme, saw Holden in California as a novelist of sorts himself, looking back on his experience and shaping it to try to understand it. They paid, unsurprisingly, more precise and lengthier attention to the novel as a work of art than its reviewers had in 1951. And they cared much more than the reviewers about positioning *Catcher* with reference to other literary works, discovering generic and literarily historical lodgings for it. In a particularly influential article in 1956, Arthur Heiserman and James E. Miller, Jr., identified *Catcher* as belonging to "an ancient and honorable narrative tradition" in Western literature, "the tradition of the Quest."[6] Other critics reiterated the idea of the quest, or they spoke of Holden's trip to New York as a journey to the underworld or through the waste land, or they called his series of adventures picaresque. And yet, academics though they were, the critics as a whole were less concerned, really, with typing the novel and less employed, even, with explication as an activity in itself than they were with elucidating the novel's rendering of human experience and with evaluating its moral attitudes. In this they were close to the original concerns of the reviewers. And they give the impression less of being elaborately trained professionals eager to display their learning and methodological expertise (while hungering after advancement) than they do of being serious common readers approaching *Catcher* for what it reveals of life and offers in the way of wisdom.

We shall lower here a very plain but, we hope, serviceable grid on a number of critics and ask how they saw *Catcher* answering two questions: what went wrong with Holden, propelling him from Pencey Prep to New York to a psychiatrist's couch in California, and what, if anything, could have been, or could be, done about it?

One group of critics located the causes of Holden's predicament altogether or mainly in himself, in his soul or in his psyche. Flunking out of his third prep school, Holden is responding to inner rather than outer pressures; "he is a victim not so much of society as of his own spiritual illness," which forbids his discarding any of his experiences and condemns him to carry the burden of indiscriminate remembrance.[7] Or else he is saintly in his sensitivity, suffering and yet blessed in his inability to withhold either empathy or compassion.[8] Or else Holden is immature or spoiled, an adolescent too absolute in his judgments, too intolerant of human failings, or an "upper-class New York City boy" who is a "snob."[9] For his spiritual illness, there can be no cure unless he grows into spiritual perfection, finding God and living by the divine injunction to love. His immaturity calls for growth, for maturing into an acceptance of things as they are, and so does his snobbery.[10] These critics differed as to whether or not Holden is left arrested in his difficulties or moved toward or even through redemption or initiation or acceptance or adjustment. But, in any case, these views of his predicament all imply that the answer, whether realized in the action of the novel or not, lies in some inward movement of the soul or psyche, a kind of resource that might be available to anyone any time and just as timelessly necessary to saints and sinners as to bewildered young men.

More often than they held Holden responsible for his fate, for his breakdown and the events that led him to it, critics saw it derived more emphatically from external causes; they were disposed to blame the world instead of or along with the hero. For some, Holden collides with an unchanging set of antagonists, which they speak of in religious or philosophical terms. Holden confronts "evil," an "immoral world," a "mutable and deceitful world";[11] his is, as everyman's always is, the existential condition. Like Hamlet, he "stand[s] aghast before a corrupt world." He is "sickened by the material values and the inhumanity of the world."[12] In other readings, his antagonists are more particularly named American and modern. Holden is seen facing, and breaking on, forces characteristic of American life and, more particularly, twentieth-century American life. The people he meets are "innocently imperceptive and emotionally dead"; they impose standards of conformity, as they did on Thoreau and Henry Adams.[13] Or, Holden's society, worse than Thoreau's, and Adams's (and Huck Finn's), is complex, urbanized, dehumanized and dehumanizing; his condition is that of "contemporary alienation."[14] Holden is encircled by "phoniness, indifference and vulgarity"; "as a 'neo-picaresque,' [Catcher] shows itself to be concerned far less with the education or initiation of an adolescent than with a dramatic exposure of the manner in which ideals are denied access to our lives and the modes which mendacity assumes in our urban culture." Contemporary America is afflicted with "neurosis and fatigue." Society is "sick"; "our national experience hurtles us along routes more menacing than the Mississippi."[15] The critic who cast his net widest, aiming at both the enduring and the timely explanation, drew in the most reasons for

Holden's fate, for the fact that his retrospective narration issues from a California institution for the mentally ill: "Holden could not face a world of age, death, sickness, ugliness, sex and perversion, poverty, custom, and cant."[16]

Most of these terms, we need hardly emphasize, conceptualize Holden's world in a general way. Many have a moral frame of reference (evil, deceit, corruption, inhumanity, mendacity); many have a psychological or emotional frame of reference (the individual feels the pressure to conform, or society is tired and disturbed). In all cases, they tend away from precise description of the society Salinger renders in *Catcher*.

When *Catcher*'s society did draw pointed comments from critics, they were apt to be negative. Maxwell Geismar, for example, admired Salinger's creation of Pencey Prep, with "all the petty horrors, the banalities, the final mediocrity of the typical American prep school," but faulted his portrayal of Holden's family and class as vague and empty. Holden, he argued, comes to us from "both a social and a psychological void"; Salinger makes no reference to the "real nature and dynamics" of the hero's urban environment.[17] And Ihab Hassan conceded that *Catcher* is not a "sociological" novel: "No doubt social realities are repressed in the work of Salinger—note how gingerly he handles his Jews."[18] There is an assumption here that a novel that is satisfyingly realistic mirrors society sweepingly and fully, follows Mr. Caulfield into his corporate office and introduces the maid who lives in the room behind Phoebe's. And that assumption, we think, worked to obscure how much Salinger did represent of the contemporary world, and how far he understood what he represented.

And when Holden's predicament *was* given external cause, at least in part, what could be done about it? What resolution if any did these critics see the novel reaching or at least implying? For certainly a difference in diagnosis would seem to entail a difference in prescription, especially when critics invoked historical time and place to account for Holden's misadventures. They did not, however, differ very much from the critics who addressed themselves primarily to the state of Holden's soul. Holden was searching, as they saw it, for truth or for wisdom or for personal integrity. And beyond reaching understanding and achieving his own identity, he needed to communicate and to love or to find an object for the love he was able to feel at least as the novel ended if not before. Salinger showed that "the resources of the personality are sufficient for self-recovery and discovery."[19] Or they saw

Catcher posing Holden's predicament without offering or even implying its solution. More rarely, they touched on the question of how society itself might change along with or apart from any change Holden might manage within his own psychic territory. America had lost its own innocence and, like Holden himself, needed to "face [the] problems of growing up." Although facing them was more likely to lead to "despair" than to "hope."[20]

Of this common intellectual strategy, we can take James E. Miller's criticism as typical. In 1965, almost ten years after his article with Heiserman appeared, Miller wrote again about *Catcher*, this time in the Minnesota pamphlet series on American writers, where his responsibility was in part to voice the critical consensus that had developed. He did so in language by now familiar. Holden is on a threefold quest: for "the innocence of childhood," for "an ideal but un-human love," and for "identity." His is "the modern predicament." He is up against "the world as it is," and "the fundamental physicality of the human predicament," which is "a phenomenon of all human relationships, all human situations, by their very nature of being human." In spite of the word "modern," and some references to the atom bomb ("contemporary horrors"), Miller's language takes the novel out of real history and makes it an eternal story of "death and rebirth."[21] This critical transformation, evidently, was what it took in the academic American fifties and sixties to claim for a literary work the status of a classic.

We fix on Miller, not because he was an inept critic, but because, on the contrary, he was one of the best. In 1965, had we written the Minnesota pamphlet, we surely would have written it in the same ideological key—and less well than Miller. But through another decade of history the book has come to lead a different kind of life in our minds.

For us, as for almost all readers, Holden's sensitivity is the heart of the book, that which animates the story and makes it compelling. Events are laden with affect, for Holden. He cannot speak of an experience for long in a neutral way, apart from judgment and feeling. And of course those judgments and feelings are largely negative. Not so entirely negative as Phoebe says—"You don't like *any*thing that's happening"—but this novel is first the story of a young man so displeased with himself and with much of the world around him that his strongest impulse is to leave, break loose, move on. From his pain follows rejection and retreat.

But what exactly is it that puts Holden out of sorts with his life?

What does he reject? The critics answer, as we have seen, in phrases that universalize: an immoral world, the inhumanity of the world, the adult world, the predicament of modern life, the human condition, the facts of life, evil. But the leap is too quick and too long. Holden lives in a time and place, and these provide the material against which his particular adolescent sensibility reacts.

Holden has many ways of condemning, and an ample lexicon to render his judgments. Some people are bastards, others jerks. The way they act makes you want to puke. What they do and say can be—in Holden's favorite adjectives—depressing, corny, dopey, crumby, screwed-up, boring, phony. *Phony* is probably Holden's most frequently employed term of abuse, definitely his strongest and most ethically weighted. For that reason his application of the word is a good index to what he finds most intolerable in his life. And Holden is quite consistent in what he calls phony.

Holden says he left Elkton Hills, one of the schools he attended before Pencey, because he was "surrounded by phonies," in particular Mr. Haas the headmaster, "the phoniest bastard I ever met in my life." Haas earned this label in the following way:

On Sundays [he] went around shaking hands with everybody's parents when they drove up to school. He'd be charming as hell and all. Except if some boy had little old funny-looking parents. You should've seen the way he did with my roommate's parents. I mean if a boy's mother was sort of fat or corny-looking or something, and if somebody's father was one of those guys that wear those suits with very big shoulders and corny black-and-white shoes, then old Haas would just shake hands with them and give them a phony smile and then he'd go talk, for maybe half an *hour*, with somebody else's parents. I can't stand that stuff.[22]

In a word, snobbery. Haas toadies to those who comfortably wear the uniform of their class—some register of high bourgeois—and snubs those with padded shoulders and unfashionable shoes who have come lately to their money, or not at all. His gestures to the latter are inauthentic, and such contempt can wound. But only because class does exist; Haas is not just personally mean; his phoniness and his power to hurt depend on an established class system that institutionalizes slight and injury.

Just a bit later Holden tells of another phony, an old Pencey grad named Ossenburger, who has "made a pot of dough" through a chain of "undertaking parlors all over the country that you could get members of your family buried for about five bucks apiece." Holden has little respect for Ossenburger's enterprise: "He probably just shoves them in a sack and dumps them in the river." None-theless, Ossenburger is an eminence at Pencey, to which he has given "a pile of dough," and where Holden's dormitory is named after him. On a football weekend Ossenburger comes to the school in "this big goddam Cadillac," receives an obligatory cheer at the game, and gives a speech in chapel "that lasted about ten hours." It is a pious affair, making obliquely the Calvinist connection be-tween wealth and virtue. Ossenburger extols prayer:

he started telling us how he was never ashamed, when he was in some kind of trouble or something, to get right down on his knees and pray to God. . . . He said *he* talked to Jesus all the time. Even when he was driving his car. That killed me. I can just see the big phony bastard shifting into first gear and asking Jesus to send him a few more stiffs (pp. 16–17).

Holden demystifies in the telling, better than if he had said, "this man claims legitimacy for his money, his Cadillac, his business ethics, his eminence and class privilege, by enlisting religion on his side." Again, phoniness is rooted in the economic and social ar-rangements of capitalism, and in their concealment.

But a second motif in these scenes also deserves comment. The clues to phoniness lie in outward forms of conduct. Haas's phony smile follows an external convention, but accords poorly with emotional reality. His handshakes imply equality, but thinly hide the reverse of equality. Ossenburger talks within a framework of conventions: he is in chapel; he gives a sermon; he speaks of prayer. Holden's revulsion attends, in part, on ceremony itself: on pre-scribed forms that shape the flow of our words and movements. A smile, a handshake, a chapel assembly with boys seated in rows, a sermon, a prayer: none of these is a spontaneous expression of the self; all impose limits and bear conventional meaning. Holden re-sents these constraints, and delights in release from them. Hence:

The only good part of [Ossenburger's] speech was right in the middle of it. He was telling us all about what a swell guy he was, what a hot-shot and all, then all of a sudden this guy sitting in the row in front of me, Edgar Marsalla, laid this terrific fart. It was a very crude thing to do, in chapel and all, but it was also quite amusing. Old Marsalla (p. 17).

We won't offer a disquisition on old Marsalla's fart, but these things may be noted: a fart is the antithesis of ceremony (in this society, anyhow). It asserts the body, assaults manners and convention. Here, it shatters Ossenburger's hypocrisy and boastfulness. But it also strikes at the social idea behind a "*speech*" itself. It mocks the

meaning of "sitting in the *row.*" It is a "crude thing to do, in *chapel
and all.*" In brief, it is commendable ("quite amusing") because it
challenges, not only Ossenburger's false ideology but also the very
existence of social forms.

These twin themes run through the book. When a situation or act
seems phony to Holden, it is evidence of bad class relationships, or
public ritual, or both. The first theme is foregrounded when Holden stigmatizes the word "grand," or the phrase "marvelous to see
you"; the second when he notes the hollow formality of "glad to've
met you." The first theme unites the Wicker Bar at the Seton Hotel,
ambitious lawyers, the fashionable opinion that the Lunts are "angels," Spencer's deference to headmaster Thurmer, the nightclub
set's public affection for pseudoculture (cute French songs), the
"dirty little goddam cliques" at boys' schools (where "all you do is
study so that you can learn enough to be smart enough to be able to
buy a goddam Cadillac some day"), Andover, "Ivy League voices,"
men in "their goddam checkered vests, criticizing shows and books
and women in those tired, snobby voices." The second theme is
foregrounded in Sally Hayes's *letter,* inviting Holden to help trim
the *Christmas tree;* in the black piano player, Ernie, and his "very
phony, *humble*" *bow* to his philistine audience; in that audience's
applause; in *actors'* conventional representation of people; in min-
isters' *sermons* ("they all have these Holy Joe voices. . . . I don't see
why the hell they can't talk in their natural voice"); in Stradlater's
hello to Ackley; in Holden's *handshake* with Ackley; in phony *parties* and smoking for show and *conversations* about art.

Holden rounds on mores and conventions that are a badge of
class. He also revolts against convention itself. Although these two
feelings often blend they have quite different origins. Society is
imaginable without privilege, snobbery, unequal wealth. To banish
all convention would be to end society itself. More of that later.

For now, we want to underline the first of the two conclusions we
have reached by looking at what Holden calls phony. The novel's
critique of class distinction may be found, not just between the
lines of Holden's account, but in some of his most explicit comments on what's awry in his world. We quote from his digression
on suitcases. When Holden meets the two nuns in the sandwich
bar, the sight of their suitcases prompts him to say,

It isn't important, I know, but I hate it when somebody has cheap suitcases. It sounds terrible to say it, but I can even get to hate somebody, just
looking at them, if they have cheap suitcases with them. Something hap-

pened once. For a while when I was at Elkton Hills, I roomed with this boy, Dick Slagle, that had these very inexpensive suitcases. He used to keep them under the bed, instead of on the rack, so that nobody'd see them standing next to mine. It depressed holy hell out of me, and I kept wanting to throw mine out or something, or even *trade* with him. Mine came from Mark Cross, and they were genuine cowhide and all that crap, and I guess they cost quite a pretty penny. But it was a funny thing. Here's what happened. What I did, I finally put *my* suitcases under *my* bed, instead of on the rack, so that old Slagle wouldn't get a goddam inferiority complex about it. But here's what he did. The day after I put mine under my bed, he took them out and put them back on the rack. The reason he did it, it took me a while to find out, was because he wanted people to think my bags were his. He really did. He was a very funny guy, that way. He was always saying snotty things about them, my suitcases, for instance. He kept saying they were too new and bourgeois. That was his favorite goddam word. He read it somewhere or heard it somewhere. Everything I had was bourgeois as hell. Even my fountain pen was bourgeois. He borrowed it off me all the time, but it was bourgeois anyway. We only roomed together about two months. Then we both asked to be moved. And the funny thing was, I sort of missed him after we moved, because he had a helluva good sense of humor and we had a lot of fun sometimes. I wouldn't be surprised if he missed me, too. At first he only used to be kidding when he called my stuff bourgeois, and I didn't give a damn—it *was* sort of funny, in fact. Then, after a while, you could tell he wasn't kidding any more. The thing is, it's really hard to be roommates with people if your suitcases are much better than theirs—if yours are really *good* ones and theirs aren't. You think if they're intelligent and all, the other person, and have a good sense of humor, that they don't give a damn whose suitcases are better, but they do. They really do. It's one of the reasons why I roomed with a stupid bastard like Stradlater. At least his suitcases were as good as mine (pp. 108–9).

The source of Holden's feeling could hardly be clearer, or related with more social precision. He belongs by birthright at Elkton Hills; Dick Slagle presumably does not. Their situation—living together—calls for an equality of human beings. (School itself, the American institution that most supports our myth of equal opportunity, carries the same hope.) Likewise, Holden's desires point him toward a world in which human qualities like intelligence and a sense of humor, rather than Mark Cross luggage and the money that stands behind it, would be the ground of relatedness.

Both boys are deformed by what they bring with them to their room from the social order outside. Holden is depressed, and wishes to find the right gesture (throw the suitcases away, trade with Slagle) to deny their socially imposed difference. He is hurt by Slagle's resentment, when it becomes more than kidding, and he finally gives up on the relationship. Slagle, naturally, suffers more. Shame over his suitcases is one thing, but worse are the contradictory feelings: he hates the class injustice, and strives through the word *bourgeois* ("He read it somewhere") for the ideas that would combat it; yet at the same time he longs to be on the *right* side of the barrier, to *benefit* from class antagonism by having others think he owns the Mark Cross suitcases. Clearly Holden understands all this; we can only suppose that Salinger does too.

It was the nuns' suitcases, and their straw baskets, that reminded Holden of Slagle; the nuns also stir in him reflections about money and the expression of social feeling. He tries to imagine women from his own class "collecting dough for poor people in a beat-up old straw basket," but it's "hard to picture." His aunt is "pretty charitable," but always dressed in a way that emphasizes her condescension. "I couldn't picture her doing anything for charity if she had to wear black clothes and no lipstick." As for Sally Hayes's mother: "Jesus Christ. The only way *she* could go around with a basket collecting dough would be if everybody kissed her ass for her when they made a contribution." If they didn't, she'd get bored and "go someplace swanky for lunch. That's what I liked about those nuns. You could tell, for one thing, that they never went anywhere swanky for lunch. It made me so damn sad" (p. 114). At the root of Holden's sadness are lives confined by poverty, the loss of human connectedness, the power of feelings distorted by class to overcome natural bonds of affinity and friendship. In the end, one chooses to room with "a stupid bastard like Stradlater," whose suitcases are as good as one's own.

So we hold that the text of this novel, and the experience of it, warrants a formulation of what wounds Holden quite a lot more precise than the one given it by phrases like "the complexity of modern life," "the neurosis and fatigue of the world," or "our collective civilized fate." These epitomes are in fact strongly ideological; they displace the political emotion that is an important part of Salinger's novel, finding causes for it that are presumed to be universal.

Likewise, the majority opinion on what Holden yearns for— ideal love, innocence, truth, wisdom, personal integrity, and so forth. Let's examine one such idea in detail. James Miller writes, "Perhaps in its profoundest sense Holden's quest is a quest for identity, a search for the self." Holden tries various disguises, but "the self he is led to discover is Holden's and none other. And that self he discovers is a human self and an involved self that cannot, finally, break with what Hawthorne once called the 'magnetic chain of humanity.'"[23] Miller writes of the self as if it were innate, genetically coded, yet somehow repressed. When Holden does rediscover it, it is "human" and "involved."

These rather vague characterizations lack social content. Yet we doubt that Miller or anyone else believes the identity of a person to lie beyond social influence, not to say, definition. Any society provides identities for its members to step into; Holden's is no exception. We can hardly consider his quest for identity apart, for instance, from the fact that his father is a corporation lawyer ("Those boys really haul it in") on the edge of the ruling class, who has tried, however fruitlessly, to open for Holden the way to a similar identity by apprenticing him in a series of private schools. For Holden, such an identity is imaginatively real, and coercive. He gives it a reasonably concrete description when Sally Hayes refuses his invitation to go live by a brook in Vermont. She says there will be time for such pleasures later, after college. Holden:

No, there wouldn't be. There wouldn't be oodles of places to go at all. It'd be entirely different. . . . We'd have to go downstairs in elevators with suitcases and stuff. We'd have to phone up everybody and tell 'em good-by and send 'em postcards from hotels and all. And I'd be working in some office, making a lot of dough, and riding to work in cabs and Madison Avenue buses, and reading newspapers, and playing bridge all the time, and going to the movies and seeing a lot of stupid shorts and coming attractions and newsreels (p. 133).

Holden understands well enough that such an identity is incompatible with the spontaneous feeling and relatedness he wishes for.

But what vision can he entertain of some alternate self? Here imagination darkens. Holden has no idea of changing society, and within the present one he can see forward only to the bourgeois identity that awaits him. So he fantasizes another identity which fulfills desire by escaping society almost entirely. He would hitchhike out West to "where it was pretty and sunny and where nobody'd know me," get a (working-class) job at a filling station, and build a cabin at the edge of the woods. He would "pretend I was one of those deaf-mutes," thereby ending the necessity of having "goddam stupid useless conversations with anybody." If he married, it would be to a beautiful deaf-mute, and if they had children, "we'd hide them somewhere . . . and teach them how to read and write by ourselves" (pp. 198–99). No corporate structure and no Madison Avenue; but also no social production, no school, and no talk. In short, an identity for Holden that erases human history.

Here is the main equivocation of the book, and it seems to be both Holden's and Salinger's. We argued a while back that the force of Holden's severest judgment is divided. *Phony* stigmatizes both the manners and culture of a dominant bourgeoisie—class society—and ceremonies and institutions themselves—any society. But when we listen to those hints of something better, of alternative futures, of reconstruction, it makes a great deal of difference. Given Salinger's perception of what's wrong, there are three possible responses: do the best you can with this society; work for a better one; flee society altogether. Only the second answers to the critical feeling that dominates the book, but Salinger omits precisely that response when he shows Holden turning from that which his heart rejects to that which has value, that which commands allegiance and invites living into the future without despair. So, when Holden imagines an adult self, he can think only of the Madison Avenue executive or the deaf-mute, this society or no society.

And what does he like in the present? Phoebe accuses him of not liking anything, but he likes much: his dead brother Allie, for inscribing poems on his baseball mitt; Jane Gallagher, for keeping her kings in the back row at checkers. Both violate convention, and show a disdain for winning. Richard Kinsella, who broke the rules of the Oral Expression class, and digressed upon his uncle's brace when he should have been telling about his father's farm. The nuns with their straw baskets, poor but outside competitive society. James Castle, who refused even the minimal compromise with society that would have saved his life. The Museum of Natural History, where the Eskimos remain as changeless as figures on a Grecian urn, and so defy historical process. For Holden, images of the valuable are generally images of people withdrawn from convention—people who are private, whimsical, losers, saints, dead. Holden's imagination cannot join the social and the desirable. At the beginning and again at the end of the novel he has the illusion of disappearing, losing his identity altogether—both times when he is crossing that most social of artifacts, a street.

So long as the choice is between this society and no society, Holden's imagination has no place to go. He wants love and a relatedness among equals. These do not thrive in the institutions that surround him, but they cannot exist at all without institutions, which shape human feeling and give life social form. When Phoebe retrieves Holden from nothingness and despair she draws him, inevitably, toward institutions: the family, school, the Christmas play, the zoo in the park, the carousel where "they always play the same songs." In short, toward the same society he has fled, and toward some of its innocent social forms, this time magically redeemed by love.

Holden returns to society, the only one available. It is unchanged; he has changed somewhat, in the direction of acceptance. To go the rest of the way back, he requires the help of another institution and of a psychoanalyst. Society has classified him as neurotic—a fitting response, apparently, to his having wanted from it a more hospitable human climate than it could offer. He will change more. Society will not. But that's all right, in the end: the very act of telling his story has overlaid it with nostalgia, and he misses everybody he has told about, "Even old Stradlater and Ackley, for instance. I think I even miss that goddam Maurice. It's funny. Don't ever tell anybody anything. If you do, you start missing everybody" (p. 214). In a word, *Art* forms the needed bridge between the desirable and the actual, provides the mediation by which social experience, rendered through much of the story as oppressive, can be embraced.

The Catcher in the Rye is among other things a serious critical mimesis of bourgeois life in the eastern United States, 1950—of snobbery, privilege, class injury, culture as badge of superiority, sexual exploitation, education subordinated to status, warped social feeing, competitiveness, stunted human possibility. The list could go on. Salinger is astute in imaging these hurtful things, though not in explaining them. Connections exist between Holden's ordeal and the events reported on the front page of the *Times*, and we think that those connections are necessary to complete Salinger's understanding of social reality. Iran and Korea and the hard-pressed New York City school system express the dominance of Holden's class, as do Broadway and Pencey and Stradlater. Salinger's novel makes no reference to the economic and military scope of that class's power, but the manners and institutions he renders so meticulously are those of people who take their power for granted, and expect their young to step into it.

We say, further, that these themes are not just discernible to the eye of an obsessed political reader, as one might strain to give *Catcher* an ecological or existential or Seventh-Day Adventist reading. They are central to the book's meaning and to the impact it has on us and other readers. Its power is located, all agree, in Holden's sensitivity, keen observation, and moral urgency, and in the language with which he conveys these in relating his story. For all his perceptiveness, though, he is an adolescent with limited understanding of what he perceives. Readers (adults, at least) understand more, and in this gap a poignancy grows. Most readers share or are won to Holden's values—equality, spontaneity, brotherhood—but sense that these values cannot be realized within extant social forms. The novel draws readers into a powerful longing for what-could-be, and at the same time interposes what-is, as an unchanging and immovable reality.

It does so in a way that mirrors a contradiction of bourgeois society: advanced capitalism has made it imaginable that there could be enough "suitcases" for everyone, as well as spontaneity and brotherhood, and it feeds these desires at the same time that it prevents their fulfillment. Only a few can hope for suitcases and spontaneity, at the expense of the many, and enjoyment of them depends on shutting out awareness of the many. Furthermore, even the few are somehow blocked from enjoyment by the antagonistic striving required to secure one's suitcases, by the snotty human relationships of the Wicker Bar and Madison Avenue, by what Philip Slater calls "our invidious dreams of personal glory." In short, the aesthetic force of the novel is quite precisely located in its rendering a contradiction of a particular society, as expressed through an adolescent sensibility that feels, though it cannot comprehend, this contradiction. Short of comprehension, both Holden and Salinger are driven to a false equation—to reject this society is to reject society itself—and a false choice—accept this society or defect from society altogether.

It is here that the novel most invites criticism, informed by history and politics. But the critics have instead, with few exceptions,[24] followed Salinger's own lead and deepened the confusion of the novel with the help of mystifications like "the adult world," "the human condition," and so on. Pressing for such formulations, they have left history and the novel behind. They have failed both to understand its very large achievement—for we consider it a marvelous book—and to identify the shortcomings of its awareness and its art. And in this way they have certified it as a timeless classic.

We have been speaking of *readers*, *critics*, and *criticism*. This is itself, needless to say, a mystification. Most readers and almost all the critics belong to the professional and managerial strata between the high bourgeoisie and the working class. Almost all the critics have been college teachers, and at a time when their (our) lives were affected dramatically by the course of American capitalism. Specifically, in the fifties and the sixties, these conditions wrought a significant change in the position of academic intellectuals: (1) the United States preserved, with great success at first, the world hegemony of capitalism through a policy of "containment" (Korea, etc.). (2) This achievement, along with rapid technical development and corporate expansion, allowed unprecedented use of the world's markets and resources (e.g., Iranian oil) for the enrichment of the U.S. economy. (3) U.S. higher education responds very directly to the needs of the economy: both the new imperialism and new technical development (television, computers, military hardware, etc.) resulted in a rapidly increasing demand for college-trained people and for research. Hence the enormous expansion of the university system. (4) This happened just when new teachers had to be recruited from the small cohort of depression babies, while the *student* population began to swell as the much larger cohort born after the war reached school and college. In short, there was a sharp increase in demand for college teachers, and a corresponding improvement in our absolute and relative position in the society. Not great wealth, to be sure, but modest prosperity, quick advancement, more prestige, confidence, and a new self-esteem.

Here we must leave the argument without perfect closure. It would be vulgar determinism to hold that from these economic conditions followed a "bourgeoisification" of the academic mind, and from that a capitalist misreading of *The Catcher in the Rye*. For one thing, this picture ignores the McCarthyism of the time, the pressure toward liberal conformity in the university, and the sweet, secret inducements proffered to intellectuals by the CIA through the Congress for Cultural Freedom, *Encounter*, and all the instruments of cooptation.[25]

But common sense and a belief in real connections between people's ideas and their material lives are enough, we think, to make it seem natural for a critical establishment so located in U.S. capitalism to interpret and judge literary works in a way harmonious with the continuance of capitalism.

We need hardly say that the world is a different place in 1976 than it was in 1951 or 1971. Even from the American academy, capitalism now seems a less inevitable and less friendly part of the landscape. Academic criticism and, indeed, literary study hold a less favored position than they did even five years ago, and all indications point to a further decline. As thousands of people in our field join the unemployed or ill-employed, it will be surprising if most teachers of English maintain a separation of culture from society, and keep on writing the kind of criticism that mediated *Catcher*'s acceptance as a classic.

5 The Shaping of a Canon: U.S. Fiction, 1960-1975

Categorical names such as The English Novel, The Modern American Novel, and American Literature often turn up in catalogues as titles of college courses, and we know from them pretty much what to expect. They also have standing in critical discourse, along with allied terms unlikely to serve as course titles: *good writing, great literature, serious fiction, literature* itself. The awareness has grown in recent years that such concepts pose problems, even though we use them with easy enough comprehension when we talk or write to others who share our cultural matrix.

Lately, critics like Raymond Williams have been reminding us that the categories change over time (just as *literature* used to mean all printed books but has come to mean only certain poems, plays, novels, etc.) and that at any given moment categories embody complex social relations and a continuing historical process. That process deeply invests all terms with value: since not everyone's values are the same, the negotiating of such concepts is, among other things, a struggle for dominance—whether between adults and the young, professors and their students, one class and another, or men and women. One doesn't usually notice the power or the conflict, except when some previously weak or silent group seeks a share of the power: for example, when, in the 1960s, American blacks and their supporters insisted that black literature be included in school and college curricula, or when they openly challenged the candidacy of William Styron's *Confessions of Nat Turner* for inclusion in some eventual canon.[1] But the gradual firming up of concepts like, say, postwar American fiction is always a contest for cultural hegemony, even if in our society it is often muted—carried on behind the scenes or in the seemingly neutral marketplace.

Not only do the concepts change, in both intension and extension, but the process of their formation also changes. The English, who had power to do so, admitted *Great Expectations* to the canon by means very different from those used to admit the *Canterbury Tales* by earlier generations of tastemakers. Again, the process may differ from genre to genre even in a particular time and place. For instance, profit and the book market are relatively unimportant in deciding what will be considered modern American poetry, by contrast with their function in defining modern American fiction. As a result, in order to work toward a serviceable theory of canon formation, it is necessary to look at a variety of these processes and at how they impinge on one another.

Here, I attempt to sketch out one of them, the process by which novels written by Americans from about 1960 to 1975 have been sifted and assessed, so that a modest number of them retain the kind of attention and respect that eventually makes them eligible for canonical status.[2] I am going to argue that the emergence of these novels has been a process saturated with class values and interests, a process inseparable from the broader struggle for position and power in our society, from the institutions that mediate that struggle, as well as from legitimation of and challenges to the social order. I will then try to be more specific about the representation of those values and interests in the fiction itself.

Reading and the Book Market

People read books silently, and often in isolation, but reading is nonetheless a social act. As one study concludes:

Book reading in adult life is sustained . . . by interpersonal situations which minimize the individual's isolation from others. To persist over the years, the act of book reading must be incorporated . . . into a social context. Reading a book becomes meaningful when, after completion, it is shared with others. . . . Social integration . . . sustains a persistent engagement with books. Social isolation, in contrast, is likely to lead to the abandonment of books.[3]

Simone Beserman found, in her study of best-sellers around 1970, that frequent reading of books correlated highly with social interaction—in particular, with the desire to rise in society. Upwardly mobile second- and third-generation Americans were heavy readers of best-sellers.[4]

As you would expect, given the way reading is embedded in and reinforced by social relations, networks of friends and family also contributed in determining which books would be widely read. In her survey, Beserman found that 58 percent of those who read a particular best-seller did so upon recommendation of a friend or relative. Who were these people, so crucial to a book's success? Beserman found that they were of better-than-average education (most had finished college), relatively well-to-do, many of them professionals, in middle life, upwardly mobile, living near New York or oriented, especially through the *New York Times*, to New York cultural life.

These people were responsive to novels where they discovered the values in which they believed or where they found needed moral guidance when shaken in their own beliefs. Saul Bellow's remark, "What Americans want to learn from their writers is how to live," finds support in Philip H. Ennis's study, *Adult Book Reading in the United States*.[5] Ennis determined that three of the main interests people carried into their reading were a "search for personal meaning, for some kind of map to the moral landscape"; a need to "reinforce or to celebrate beliefs already held, or, when shaken by events, to provide support in some personal crisis"; and a wish to keep up "with the book talk of friends and neighbors."[6]

The values and beliefs of a small group of people played a disproportionate role in deciding what novels would be widely read in the United States. (Toward the end of this essay, I will turn to those values in some detail.) To underscore their influence, consider two other facts about the book market. First, if a novel did not become a best-seller within three or four weeks of publication, it was unlikely to reach a large readership later on. In the 1960s, only a very few books that were slow starters eventually became best-sellers (in paperback, not hardback). I know of three: *Catch-22*, *Call It Sleep*, and *I Never Promised You a Rose Garden*, to which we may add the early novels of Vonnegut, which were not published in hard covers, and—if we count its 1970s revival in connection with the film—*One Flew over the Cuckoo's Nest*. To look at the process the other way around, once a new book did make the *New York Times* best-seller list, many other people bought it (and store managers around the country stocked it) *because* it was a best-seller. The process was cumulative. So the early buyers of hardcover books exercised a crucial role in selecting the books that the rest of the country's readers would buy.

Second, best-sellerdom was much more important than suggested by the figures for hardbound sales through bookstores. *Love Story*, for instance, the leading best-seller (in all forms) of the decade sold 450,000 hardback copies in bookstores but more than 700,000 through book clubs, 2.5 million through the *Reader's Digest*, 6.5 million in the *Ladies' Home Journal*, and more than 9,000,000 in paperback—not to mention library circulation or the millions of people who saw the film. Books were adopted by clubs, paperback publishers, film producers, and so forth, in large part because they were best-sellers or because those investing in subsidiary rights thought them likely to become best-sellers. As Victor Navasky rather wryly said:

Publishers got out of the business of *selling* hardcover books ten or fifteen years ago. The idea now is to publish hardcover books so that they can be reviewed or promoted on television in order to sell paperback rights, movie rights, book club rights, comic book rights, serialization rights, international satellite rights, Barbie doll rights, etc.[7]

The phenomenon of the hardbound best-seller had only modest economic and cultural significance in itself but great significance in triggering reproduction and consumption of the story in other forms.

A small group of relatively homogeneous readers, then, had a great deal of influence at this preliminary stage. But of course these people did not make *their* decisions freely among the thousands of novels completed each year. They chose among the smaller number actually published. This fact points to an important role in canon formation for literary agents and for editors at the major houses, who belong to the same social stratum as the buyers of hardbound books, and who—as profitability in publishing came to hinge more and more on the achievement of best-sellerdom for a few books—increasingly earned their keep by spotting (and pushing) novels that looked like best-sellers. Here we have a nearly closed circle of marketing and consumption, the simultaneous exploitation and creation of taste, familiar to anyone who has examined marketplace culture under monopoly capitalism.

But, it is clear, influential readers chose not among all novels published but among the few that came to their attention in an urgent or attractive way. How did that happen? As a gesture toward the kind of answer that question requires, I will consider the extraordinary role of the *New York Times*. The *New York Times Book Review* had about a million and a half readers, several times the audience of any other literary periodical. Among them were most bookstore managers, deciding what to stock, and librarians, deciding what to buy, not to mention the well-to-do, well-educated east-coasters who led in establishing hardback best-sellers. The single most important boost a novel could get was a prominent review in the Sunday *New York Times*—better a favorable one than an unfavorable one, but better an unfavorable one than none at all.

Ads complemented the reviews, or perhaps the word is *inundated:* two-thirds of the space in the *Times Book Review* went to ads. According to Richard Kostelanetz, most publishers spent more than half their advertising budgets for space in that journal.[8] They often placed ads in such a way as to reinforce a good *Times* review or offset a bad one with favorable quotations from reviews in other periodicals. And of course reviews and adds were further reinforced by the *Times* best-seller list itself, for the reason already mentioned. Apparently, the publishers' faith in the *Times* was not misplaced. Beserman asked early readers of *Love Story* where they had heard of the book. Most read it on recommendation of another person; Beserman then spoke to *that* person, and so on back to the beginning of the chain of verbal endorsements. At the original source, in more than half the instances, she found the *Times*.[9] (This in spite of the quite unusual impact, for that time, of Segal's appearance on the "Today" show the day of publication—Barbara Walters said the book made her cry all night; Harper was immediately swamped with orders—and of the novel's appearance in the *Ladies' Home Journal* just before book publication.)

The influence of the *Times Book Review* led publicity departments to direct much of their prepublication effort toward persuading the *Book Review*'s editors that a particular novel was important. It is hard to estimate the power of this suasion, but one thing can be measured: the correlation between advertising in the *Book Review* and being reviewed there. A 1968 study concluded, perhaps unsurprisingly, that the largest advertisers got disproportionately large amounts of review space. Among the large advertisers were, for instance:

	Pages of ads	Pages of reviews
Random House	74	58
Harper	29	22
Little, Brown	29	21

And the smaller ones:

Dutton	16	4
Lippincott	16	4
Harvard	9	"negligible"

During the same year Random House (including Knopf and Pantheon) had nearly three times as many books mentioned in the feature "New and Recommended" as Doubleday or Harper, both of which published as many books as the Random House group.[10]

To summarize: a small group of book buyers formed a screen through which novels passed on their way to commercial success; a handful of agents and editors picked the novels that would compete for the notice of those buyers; and a tight network of advertisers and reviewers, organized around the *New York Times Book Review*, selected from these a few to be recognized as compelling, important, "talked-about."

The Next Stage

So far I have been speaking of a process that led to a mass readership for a few books each year. But most of these were never regarded as serious literature and did not live long in popularity or memory. Books like *Love Story, The Godfather, Jonathan Livingston Seagull*, and the novels of Susann, Robbins, Wouk, Wallace, and Uris would run a predictable course. They had large hardback sales for a few months, tapering off to a trickle in a year or so. Meanwhile, they were reprinted in paper covers and enjoyed two or three years of popularity (often stoked by a film version). After that they disappeared or remained in print to be bought in smaller numbers by, for instance, newly won fans of Wallace who wanted to go back and read his earlier books. There was a similar pattern for mysteries, science fiction, and other specialized genres.

But a few novels survived and continued (in paper covers) to attract buyers and readers for a longer time, and they still do. Why? To answer that the *best* novels survive is to beg the question. Excellence is a constantly changing, socially chosen value. Who attributed it to only some novels, and how? I hope now to hint at the way such a judgment took shape.

First, one more word about the *New York Times Book Review*. I have argued that it led in developing a broad audience for fiction. It also began, I believe, the process of distinguishing between ephemeral popular novels and those to be taken seriously over a longer period of time. There was a marked difference in impact between, say, Martin Levin's favorable but mildly condescending (and brief) review of *Love Story* and the kind of front-page review by an Alfred Kazin or an Irving Howe that asked readers to regard a new novel as literature, and that so often helped give the stamp of highbrow approval to books by Bellow, Malamud, Updike, Roth, Doctorow, and so forth.[11] Cultural leaders read the *Times Book Review* too: not only professors but (according to Julie Hoover and Charles Kadushin) 75 percent of our elite intellectuals.[12] By reaching these circles, a major *Times* review could help put a novel on the cultural agenda and ensure that other journals would have to take it seriously.

Among those others, a few carried special weight in forming cultural judgments. In a survey of leading intellectuals, just eight journals—the *New York Review of Books*, the *New Republic*, the *New York Times Book Review*, the *New Yorker*, *Commentary*, *Saturday Review*, *Partisan Review*, and *Harpers*—received almost half the participants' "votes" in response to various questions about influence and importance.[13] In effect, these periodicals were both a communication network among the influentials (where they reviewed one another's books) and an avenue of access to a wider cultural leadership. The elite, writing in these journals, largely determined which books would be seriously debated and which ones permanently valued, as well as what ideas were kept alive, circulated, discussed.[14] Kadushin and his colleagues concluded, from their studies of our intellectual elite and influential journals, that the "top intellectual journals constitute the American equivalent of an Oxbridge establishment, and have served as one of the main gatekeepers for new talent and new ideas."[15]

A novel had to win at least the divided approval of these arbiters in order to remain in the universe of cultural discourse, once past the notoriety of best-sellerdom. The career of *Love Story* is a good example of failure to do so. After some initial favorable reviews (and enormous publicity on television and other media), the intellectuals began cutting it down to size. In the elite journals, it was either panned or ignored. Styron and the rest of the National Book Award fiction panel threatened to quit if it were not removed from the list of candidates. And who will read it tomorrow, except on an excursion into the archives of mass culture?

In talking about the *New York Times Book Review*, I suggested a close alliance between reviewing and profit, literary and monetary values. The example of the *New York Review of Books* shows that a similar alliance can exist on the higher ramparts of literary culture. This journal, far and away the most influential among intellectuals (in answer to Kadushin's questions, it was mentioned almost twice as often as the *New Republic*, its nearest competitor),[16] was founded by Jason Epstein, a vice president of Random House, and coedited by his wife, Barbara Epstein. It may be more than co-incidental that in 1968 almost one-fourth of the books granted full reviews in the *New York Review* were published by Random House (again, including Knopf and Pantheon)—more than the combined total of books from Viking, Grove, Holt, Harper, Houghton Mifflin, Oxford, Doubleday, Macmillan, and Harvard so honored; or that in the same year one-fourth of the *reviewers* had books in print with Random House and that a third of those were reviewing other Random House books, mainly favorably; or that over a five-year period more than half the regular reviewers (ten or more appearances) were Random House authors.[17] This is not to deny the intellectual strength of the *New York Review*—only to suggest that it sometimes deployed that strength in ways consistent with the financial inter-est of Random House. One need not subscribe to conspiracy theo-ries in order to see, almost everywhere one looks in the milieu of publishing and reviewing, linkages of fellowship and common in-terest. Together these networks make up a cultural establishment, inseparable from the market, both influencing and influenced by it.

If a novel was certified in the court of the prestigious journals, it was likely to draw the attention of academic critics in more spe-cialized and academic journals like *Contemporary Literature* and by this route make its way into college curricula, where the very context—course title, academic setting, methodology—gave it de facto recognition as literature. This final step was all but necessary: the college classroom and its counterpart, the academic journal, have become in our society the final arbiters of literary merit, and even of survival. It is hard to think of a novel more than twenty-five years old, aside from specialist fiction and *Gone with the Wind*, that still commands a large readership outside of school and college.

I am suggesting that novels moved toward a canonical posi-tion only if they attained both large sales (usually, but not always, concentrated enough to place them among the best-sellers for a while) and the right kind of critical attention. On the one side, this hypothesis conflicts with the one most vigorously advanced by Les-lie A. Fiedler—that intellectuals are, in the long run, outvoted by the sorts of readers who keep liking *Gone with the Wind*.[18] On the other side, it collides with the hopes or expectations of critics such as Kostelanetz and Jerome Klinkowitz, who promote an avant-garde fiction called postmodernist, postcontemporary, antinovel, or whatever.[19]

Clearly, I need an independent measure of precanonical status, or my argument closes into a circle. Unfortunately, I don't have a very good one, in part, because it is still too early to settle the issue. But let me offer two scraps of pertinent information. First, the editors of *Wilson Quarterly* polled forty-four professors of American literature (in 1977 or 1978, apparently), asking them to rank in order the ten "most important" novels published in the United States after World War II.[20] The editors printed a list of the twenty-one novels rated highest in this survey; eleven of them were published in or after 1960. In rank order, they are *Catch-22, Gravity's Rainbow, Herzog, An American Dream, The Sotweed Factor, Second Skin, Portnoy's Complaint, The Armies of the Night, V, Rabbit Run,* and *One Flew over the Cuckoo's Nest.* All easily meet the criterion of attention from intellectuals. (Again, it doesn't matter that Norman Podhoretz *hates* Updike's novels, so long as he takes them seriously enough to argue with his peers about them.) As for broad readership, all of the novels except *Second Skin* and perhaps *The Sotweed Factor* have sold over half a million copies—and one may be sure that many of those sales occurred through adoption in college courses.[21]

My second cast of the net is much broader. *Contemporary Literary Criticism* abstracts commentary on recent world literature, mainly by American professors and intellectuals. Its coverage includes critical books, respected academic journals, taste-forming magazines, quarterlies, and little magazines. It claims to excerpt from criticism of "work by well-known creative writers," "writers of considerable public interest," who are alive or who died after January 1, 1960. So it constitutes a sampling of the interests of those who set literary standards, and it monitors the intermediate stage in canon formation. During the ten years and twenty-two volumes of its publication, up through 1982, it has run four or more entries (maximum, nine; and the average entry includes excerpts from four or five critical sources) for forty-eight American novelists of the period in question:[22]

Auchincloss	Capote	Gardner
Baldwin	Cheever	Gass
Barth	Condon	Hawkes
Barthelme	de Vries	Heller
Bellow	Dickey	Higgins
Berger	Didion	Jong
Bradbury	Doctorow	Kesey
Brautigan	Elkin	R. MacDonald
Burroughs	Gaddis	Mailer

Malamud	Porter	Sorrentino
McCarthy	Pynchon	Styron
McMurtry	Rechy	Theroux
Oates	Reed	Updike
Percy	Roth	Vidal
Piercy	Salinger	Vonnegut
Plath	Selby	Walker

Most of these meet my two criteria. All but a few (Bradbury, Condon, MacDonald, perhaps Auchincloss and Higgins) have received ample consideration by influential critics. Yet most novelists promoted by postcontemporary advocates such as Klinkowitz (Sloan, Coover, Wurlitzer, Katz, Federman, Sukenick, etc.) are missing, while the list includes only a few writers who have had elite approval but small readerships (Elkin, Hawkes, Sorrentino, maybe two or three others). In fact, at least thirty-one of these novelists published one book or more between 1960 and 1975 that was a best-seller in hard or paper covers.[23] On the other hand, the list excludes the overwhelming majority of the writers who regularly produced large best-sellers: Puzo, Susann, Wouk, West, Robbins, Wallace, Michener, Krantz, Forsyth, Chrichton, and so on and on. I conclude that both the *Contemporary Literary Criticism* selection and the *Wilson Quarterly* survey give modest support to my thesis. Canon formation during this period took place in the interaction between large audiences and gatekeeper intellectuals.

Class and the Canon

To return to the main theme, then: I have drawn a sketch of the course a novel had to run in order to lodge itself in our culture as precanonical—as "literature," at least for the moment. It was selected, in turn, by an agent, an editor, a publicity department, a review editor (especially the one at the Sunday *New York Times Book Review*), the New York metropolitan book buyers whose patronage was necessary to commercial success, critics writing for gatekeeper intellectual journals, academic critics, and college teachers. Obviously, the sequence was not rigid, and some steps might on occasion be omitted entirely (as I have indicated with respect to *Catch-22* and *One Flew over the Cuckoo's Nest*). But one would expect the pattern to have become more regular through this period, as publishing was increasingly drawn into the sphere of monopoly capital (with RCA acquiring Random House; ITT, Howard Sams;

Time, Inc., Little, Brown; CBS, Holt, Rinehart & Winston; Xerox, Ginn; and so on throughout almost the whole industry). For monopoly capital changed this industry much as it has changed the automobile and the toothpaste industries: by placing much greater emphasis on planned marketing and predictability of profits.[24]

This shift brought publishing into the same arena as many other cultural processes. In fact, the absorption of culture began almost as soon as monopoly capitalism itself, with the emergence of the advertising industry (crucial to planned marketing) in the 1880s and 1890s, and simultaneously with mass-circulation magazines as the main vehicle of national brand advertising.[25] With some variations, cinema, radio, music, sports, newspapers, television, and many lesser forms have followed this path, with books among the last to do so. The change has transformed our culture and the ways we participate in it. It demands rethinking, not only of bourgeois ideas about culture but of central marxian oppositions like base and superstructure, production and reproduction.[26] Culture cannot, without straining, be understood as a reflex of basic economic activity, when culture is itself a core industry and a major source of capital accumulation. Nor can we bracket culture as reproduction, when it is inseparable from the making and selling of commodities. We have at present a relatively new and rapidly changing cultural process that calls for new and flexible ways of thinking about culture.

My account may, however, have made it sound as if in one respect nothing has changed. Under monopoly capital, even more than when Marx and Engels wrote *The German Ideology*, the "class which has the means of material production at its disposal, has control at the same time over the means of mental production." But does it still follow that, "thereby, generally speaking, the ideas of those who lack the means of mental production are subject to" the ruling class?[27] The theory can explain contemporary reality only with an expanded and enriched understanding of "control" and "subject to." For although our ruling class owns the media and controls them formally, it does not exercise direct control over their content—does not now use them in the instrumental and ideological way that Marx and Engels identified 140 years ago. Mobil "idea ads" are the exception, not the rule.

To return to the instance at hand: neither the major stockholders of ITT and Xerox and RCA nor their boards of directors played a significant role in deciding which novels of the 1960s and early 1970s would gain acceptance as literature, and they certainly established no house rules—printing only those books that would advance their outlook on the world. (If they had done so, how could they have allowed, e.g., the Pantheon division of Random House virtually to enlist in the New Left?) They exercised control over publishing in the usual abstract way: they sought a good return on investment and cared little whether it came from a novel by Bellow or by Krantz, or for that matter from novels or computer chips. And very few of the historical actors who did make critical decisions about fiction were members of the haute bourgeoisie. Was class then irrelevant to the early shaping of a canon of fiction? Alternatively, did the working class make its own culture in this sphere?

My argument points toward a conclusion different from both of these, one that still turns upon class but not just upon the two great traditional classes. Intuitively, one can see that literary agents, editors, publicity people, reviewers, buyers of hardbound novels, taste-making intellectuals, critics, professors, most of the students who took literary courses, and, in fact, the writers of the novels themselves, all had social affinities. They went to the same colleges, married one another, lived in the same neighborhoods, talked about the same movies, had to work for their livings (but worked with their minds more than with their hands), and earned pretty good incomes. I hold that they belonged to a common class, one that itself emerged and grew up only with monopoly capitalism. Following Barbara and John Ehrenreich, I call it the professional-managerial class.[28] I characterize it by the affinities just mentioned; by its conflicted relation to the ruling class (intellectuals managed that class's affairs and many of its institutions, and they derived benefits from this position, but they also strove for autonomy and for a somewhat different vision of the future); by its equally mixed relation to the working class (it dominated, supervised, taught, and planned for them, but even in doing so it also served and augmented capital); and by its own marginal position with respect to capital (its members didn't have the wealth to sit back and clip coupons, but they had ready access to credit and most could choose—at least at an early stage in their careers—between working for themselves and selling their labor power to others).[29]

People in the professional-managerial class shared one relation to the bourgeoisie and another to the working class: they had many common social experiences and acted out similar styles of life. I hold that they also had—with of course many complexities and much variation—a common understanding of the world and their place in it. In the remainder of this essay, I will look at some of the values, beliefs, and interests that constituted that class perspective, by considering the novels given cultural currency by those class members who produced, marketed, read, interpreted, and taught fiction. My claim is that the needs and values of the professional-managerial class permeate the general form of these novels, as well as their categories of understanding and their means of representation.

For my examples I will draw upon such works as *Franny and Zooey, One Flew over the Cuckoo's Nest, The Bell Jar, Herzog, Portnoy's Complaint*, and Updike's *Rabbit* series. But what I say of these books is true of many other novels from the postwar period that have as yet a chance of becoming canonical.[30] To glance ahead for a moment: these novels told stories of people trying to live a decent life in contemporary social settings, people represented as analogous to "us," rather than as "cases" to be examined and understood from a clinical distance, as in an older realistic convention. They are unhappy people, who move toward happiness, at least a bit, by the ends of their stories.

A premise of this fiction—nothing new to American literature but particularly salient in this period—is that individual consciousness, not the social or historical field, is the locus of significant happening. In passing, note that on the level of style this premise authorizes variety, the pursuit of a unique and personal voice.[31] But on the levels of conceptualization and story, the premise of individual autonomy has an opposite effect: it gives these fictions a common problem and drives their material into narratives that, seen from the middle distance, look very similar. I suggest that much precanonical fiction of this period expresses, in Williams's term, a particular structure of feeling,[32] that that structure of feeling was a common one for the class in question, and that novelists explored its contours before it was articulated in books of social commentary like Philip Slater's *The Pursuit of Loneliness* (1970) and Charles Reich's *The Greening of America* (1970), or in films like *The Graduate*, and certainly, before that structure of feeling informed a broad social movement or entered conversational cliché, in phrases like "a sick society," "the establishment," and "the system." (More avant-garde writers, outside the circuit of best-sellers, had given it earlier expression: the Beats, Mailer in *Advertisements for Myself*, Barth in *The End of the Road*, etc.)

This structure of feeling gathered and strengthened during the postwar period. It became rather intense by the early 1960s. After

1965 it exploded into the wider cultural and political arena, when black rebellions, the student movement, the antiwar movement, and later the women's movement made it clear, right there in the headlines and on television, that not everyone considered ours an age of only "happy problems."[33]

In retrospect it is easy to understand some of the forces that generated this consciousness. To chart the connection, I will take a broad and speculative look at the historical experience of the class that endowed fiction with value and suggest how that experience shaped that class's concerns and needs, before I turn at greater length to the fiction that its members wrote, published, read, and preserved.

Like everyone in the society, people in the professional-managerial class lived through a time when the United States was enjoying the spoils of World War II. It altogether dominated the "free world" for two decades, militarily, politically, and economically. Its power sufficed to give it dominance among its allies and to prevent defections from the capitalist sphere, though the "loss" of China and Cuba gave cause for worried vigilance. Its products and its capital flowed freely through most parts of the world (its very money was the currency of capitalism after the Bretton Woods and Dumbarton Oaks agreements). U.S. values also flowed freely, borne by advertising, television shows, and the *Reader's Digest* more than by propaganda. The confidence one would expect to find in the metropolis of such an empire strengthened the feeling of righteousness that came from having defeated one set of enemies in war and having held at bay another set in peace. Both the war and the cold war fostered a chauvinistic and morally polarized conception of the world. *They* were totalitarian monsters; *we* were an open society of free citizens pursuing a way of life superior to any other, past or present.

Furthermore, that way of life generated a material prosperity that was historically unprecedented and that increased from one year to the next. The pent-up buying power of the war period (never before or since has the broad working class had so much money in the bank) eased the conversion from war production to production for consumers by providing capitalists with an enormous and secure domestic market, and they responded with rapid investment and a flow of old and new products. Affluence, like victory in war, made people confident that they and their society were doing things right.

On top of that, social conflict became muted. Inequality remained as pronounced as it had been before, but no more so, and the working class participated in the steady growth of total product.[34] Though workers could not see any narrowing of the divide between themselves and higher classes, the postwar generation experienced an absolute gain, both from year to year and by comparison with the 1930s; many *perceived* this gain as a softening of class lines. The sense of economic well-being that results from such an experience of history promoted allegiance to the social order, as did the tightening bonds between unions and management, amounting to a truce in class conflict within the assumptions of the welfare state. Cold war propaganda helped make it possible— especially for those who managed the new arrangements and lived in suburbs—to see our society as a harmonious collaboration.

Developments in business additionally gave support to this image of harmony. There was a rapid growth and sophistication of advertising, which not only sold products but continued to shape people into masses, for the purpose of selling those products and advancing a whole way of life whose cornerstones were the suburban home, the family, and the automobile. Leisure and social life became more private, drained of class feeling and even of the feeling of interdependence.

Politics seemed nearly irrelevant to such a life. Moreover, the boundaries of respectable political debate steadily closed in through the 1950s. On one side, socialism was pushed off the agenda by union leaders almost as vigorously as by Truman, McCarthy, the blacklisters, the FBI. On the other side, businessmen gradually abandoned the tough old capitalist principles of laissez-faire and espoused a more benign program of cooperation with labor and government. The spectrum of discussable ideas reached only from corporate liberalism to welfare-state liberalism; no wonder some thought they were witnessing the end of ideology.[35]

Consider the experience of the class that creates the canon of fiction in such an environment. Not only were its numbers and its prosperity growing rapidly along with its institutions but every public voice seemed to be saying to intellectuals, professionals, technical elites, and managers: "History is over, though progress continues. There is no more poverty. Everyone is middle class. The state is a friendly power, capable of smoothing out the abrasions of the economic system, solving its problems one by one through legislation that itself is the product of your ideas and values. You have brought a neutral and a humane rationality to the supervision of public life (exemplified beautifully by that parade of Harvard intellectuals to Washington in 1961). Politics is for experts, not ideologues. You are, therefore, the favored people, the peacemakers, the technicians of an intelligent society, justly rewarded with quick promotions, respect, and adequate incomes. So carry forward this valued social mission, which in no way conflicts with individual achievement. Enjoy your prestige and comforts. Fulfill yourselves on the terrain of private life."

But because the economic underpinnings of this consciousness were of course *not* unchanging and free of conflict, because material interdependence was an ever more pervasive fact,[36] whether perceived or not, because society cannot be wished away, because freedom on such terms is an illusion—for all these reasons, the individual pursuit of happiness continued to be a problem. Yet myth, ideology, and experience assured the professional-managerial class that no real barriers would prevent personal satisfaction, so it was easy to nourish the suspicion that any perceived lack was one's own fault. If unhappy, one must be personally maladjusted, perhaps even neurotic. I am suggesting that for the people who wrote, read, promoted, and preserved fiction, social contradictions were easily displaced into images of personal illness.

The Illness Story

This fiction of illness locates the experience of personal crisis somewhere in the passage from youth to maturity. This is easy to understand. Within the configuration of social forces I have described, maturity is equated with independence, in fact with a kind of invulnerability to the intrusion of social tension, an invulnerability to society itself. But even though one may push social conflict and historical process out of sight, one cannot really cease to be social: at a minimum, social *roles* are indivisible from selfhood. To put the contradiction another way: the ideal calls for a self that is complete, integral, unique; but in actual living one must be *some*thing and *some*body, and definitions of "somebody" already exist in a complete array provided by that very social and economic system that one has wished to transcend. Society comes back at the individual as a hostile force, threatening to diminish or annihilate one's "real" self. Furthermore, society has the power to label one as sick, if one is unable to make the transition into a suitable combination of adult roles. So the representation of malaise and neurosis in the favored novels of the period incorporates an ambiguity, sometimes explicit and sometimes latent: I seem to be crazy, but again, possibly it's *society* that's crazy. The balance tips sometimes toward one construction of the ambiguity, sometimes toward the other, but the polarity is always there.

It will be convenient to take Plath's *The Bell Jar* (first published obscurely in Britain in 1963 but an American best-seller after its 1971 publication here) as a paradigm. Esther Greenwood's achievements are supposed to make her the "envy" of everyone, but as she puts it, "all the little successes I'd totted up so happily at college fizzled to nothing outside the slick marble and plate-glass fronts along Madison Avenue."[37] In those windows, she cannot see the self she wants to be. An insistent imagery of alien reflections in mirrors, of frightening photographs, of makeup and clothes that conceal the self, of fade-outs and disappearances and false identities makes it clear that Esther is unwilling to equate the person she feels herself to be with the person presented to the world in these various guises. "I knew something was wrong with me that summer" (p. 2), she thinks. Patricia Ann Meyer Spacks calls Esther's malaise "negative narcissism"—a helpful diagnosis, though it obscures the way social roles and power relations translate into personal illness.[38]

Esther is on the threshold of maturity. A transition will be forced upon her, but a transition to what? Nothing so simple as winning all the prizes at school. Her summer in New York is a trial run for her in one possible adult role, that of "career girl," and she feels desperately estranged. She puts on a series of acts that humiliate and confuse her and ends by casting her New York wardrobe into the night, "like a loved one's ashes," from the sunroof of her hotel (p. 124). She is holding rites for a possible grown-up identity prepared for her by her past, her gender, and her society.

It is not the only one, of course. The main alternative role that awaits her adult self is that of wife and mother. She can make womanhood itself her identity, as womanhood is constituted by her society and her class. Yet she feels both inadequate to and oppressed by this possibility—marriage would make her "numb as a slave in some private, totalitarian state" (p. 94). Through the course of the story she systematically attempts or witnesses the main activities linked to this role and finds them at best distasteful, at worst ruinous. Courtship: a cold ritual with Constantin, a humiliating deception with Buddy, a brutal assault with Marco. Sex: detached from feeling, whether in Buddy's clinical version or Irwin's suave one. Birth: appropriated by men, their institutions, their technique. Motherhood: Dodo Conway and her "paraphernalia of suburban childhood" leave Esther musing, "Children make me sick" (pp. 130–31).

Other roles exist, some presented in the very explicit image of the fig tree, with "a wonderful future" at the end of every branch, and Esther starving because to choose one future is to renounce all the others. The identities available to her are destructive, confining, partly because identities are, partly because of the extra divisions that gender adds to the division of labor, partly because Esther is endowed with the class ideal of being unbounded and autonomous. Casting about for solace, she remembers the time when she was "purely happy"—up to age nine. Skiing joyously, she thinks of herself as aiming back through her past at an image of both purity and happiness, "the white sweet baby cradled in its mother's belly" (p. 108). But in present life she can gesture toward purity, toward exemption from adult being, only through madness and a suicide attempt. Her female psychiatrist may guide her back to a hesitant reentry into the social world, but since that world presented her with the impasse that made her mad in the first place, the end of the novel resolves its crisis at best only tentatively.

With a few mutations, Salinger tells the same story in *Franny and Zooey*. Franny Glass's neurosis has patently social origins: the class snobbery and male privilege of Lane Coutell, who represents one future for her; and the appropriation of art and knowledge for competitive self-advancement by the professors and poets and theater people, who represent another. Like Esther, Franny seeks a purity that she cannot envisage in adult life as given by class and gender. Like Esther, she tries to annihilate her social self, not literally but through the spiritual discipline of the Jesus prayer, through the "way of the pilgrim" and its denial of all discriminations between social classes—just as her brother Buddy would have us unlearn the "illusory differences, between boys and girls."[39] And like Esther, Franny returns to sanity and—we are to expect— the untransformed social world, where she will be able to go on toward her adult role of actress, healed through Zooey's agency and through the image of the Fat Lady who is Christ who is all of us: a perfect symbol for the refusal to take society as real.

These novels tell a version of *the* story of the postwar period, a story firmly established earlier in one of the two securely canonical works of the 1950s, *The Catcher in the Rye*.[40] But not much of the acclaimed fiction from 1960 to 1975 is literally about adolescent rites of passge. To make my claim more adequate, I need to posit one transformation of the story: the person hanging onto childhood as the only defense against capitalist and patriarchal social relations is most often a man or woman already implanted in an adult role but only masquerading as a productive and well-adjusted member of society. In other words, the rite of passage marked by illness and movement toward recovery may be, and usually is, an adult crisis, of the sort popularized later by Gail Sheehy in *Passages*.

As an example, consider Alexander Portnoy, who, at thirty-three, is the assistant commissioner of human opportunity for the city of New York; but he feels like a fraud—he cannot love; he cannot act or feel grown-up toward his parents. As he puts it: "A Jewish man with parents alive is a fifteen-year-old boy, and will remain a fifteen-year-old boy till *they die!*"[41] Masturbation is an apt image of his arrested growth, for it joins pleasure to internalized parental disapproval, fixes it on objects (liver, an apple, his sister's underwear) rather than people, and detaches sex from any social function. Why this refusal of adult participation? For one answer, think of the few idealized images Alex retains from childhood of the adult life that might await him: the Turkish bath, for instance, or the men playing baseball. Significantly, these are scenes "without *goyim* and women" and exempt from the pressure toward competitive individual achievement. I suggest that in this, one of the most politically sophisticated fictions of the period, it is rather explicit that "maturity" entails acceptance of distorted social relations: male supremacy, class domination represented as rule by the gentiles ("These people are the *Americans*, Doctor" [p. 145]), and the compensatory drive to best others in school, sport, moral righteousness, public recognition. Even Alex, talking wildly from the analyst's couch, can see beyond the peculiarities of his own parents and Weequahic culture to broad social configurations that make growing up a betrayal of integrity.

We can read this story over and over in the precanonical novels: a man (occasionally a woman) is doing pretty well by external measures; yet somehow the tension between his aspirations and his quotidian social existence grows unbearable. He stops doing what people expect of him and enters a period of disorientation and disreputable experiment. Bellow's paradigmatic hero, Moses Herzog, thinks, "If I am out of my mind, it's all right with me," and his students realize that in their class on Romanticism "they would see and hear odd things."[42] This is the condition of Bellow's heroes, from Eugene Henderson through Charlie Citrine. Updike tells the story too—three times so far in the *Rabbit* novels alone—though his character is no would-be hero of the intellect. Running, space flight, a plane trip to the Caribbean, image, Harry Angstrom's three excursions into adventurous abnormality, breaking the "stale peace" of marriage, paternity, and work.[43]

Even those precanonical novels that depart from a realistic convention tend to thematize bad social relations as the illness of ordinary people. A car dealer loses his bearings in Vonnegut's *Breakfast of Champions*, a housewife, in Pynchon's *The Crying of Lot 49*, a businessman, in Heller's *Something Happened*. An established classic of the period, Kesey's *One Flew over the Cuckoo's Nest*, takes the problematic to its logical extreme, where normality is submission to totalitarian madness and those who don't fit are shut up in a lunatic asylum. And the same total inversion of socially defined sanity and madness appears, though less thoroughly developed, in the few acclaimed novels that locate their exploration of American social reality in an earlier time: Heller's *Catch-22*, Porter's *Ship of Fools*, McCarthy's *The Group*, Doctorow's *Ragtime*, even Morrison's *Song of Solomon*.

Let me now sketch in a few other lineaments of this story. Against the threat that the project of happy selfhood may shatter into the fragmentations of capitalist production (the division of labor) and reproduction (the family as a separate sphere of consolation and fulfillment), most of these novels offer at least a glimpse of a more integral way of being. Plath gives us those images of childhood happiness and of skiing back to the perfect moment of conception. Roth has Portnoy remember not only the prehistoric world of the Turkish bath but those temporary idylls of oceanic love with his mother. Herzog finds sustenance in images of his childhood family, as does Harry Angstrom—especially the recurring one of himself protecting his sister Mim as they go sledding. Salinger's idealization of childhood needs no commentary. Even McMurphy and Chief Bromden recall times when life was simple and spontaneous. Almost always, these visions of a better way point us toward the past, and most often toward an individual childhood past when the self was engulfed in familial love and society stood at a distance, unperceived.

Such visions of wholeness linger in memory and animate desire, but they collide with the main experiences of adult life. I'll mention three such experiences, beginning with work. Most often, it is a scam: Pynchon, Vonnegut, and Updike, for example, locate it in car lots and salesrooms, where one needs a measure of cynicism to peddle the American dream on wheels. Salinger's Zooey deplores the fake world of television work. Plath gives us the hype of the woman's magazine, Heller, the mutual- and self-deception of the corporate headquarters. Kesey and Pynchon render brief, nightmarish visions of factory and corporation. Occasionally there are images of nonalienating work, but: Rabbit loses his rather satisfying job as a linotypist (this old-fashioned work disappears entirely, with automation); Moses Herzog can't get back to his great book; Esther Greenwood has no idea how to become the poet she imagines; Kilgore Trout is indeed a writer, but he is ignored and savagely lonely; Alexander Portnoy's city bureaucracy defeats the humane purposes his work is supposed to achieve; Chief Bromden knows that a big dam has made salmon fishing all but impossible. Only Salinger, in what strikes me as a sleight-of-hand, manages to retrieve a sense of wholeness in work, taking it quite out of the system of commodity relations through the spiritual device of the Fat Lady.

The experience of sexuality, no more than of work, can offer a reintegration of the self. When these authors take advantage of the new freedom to represent sexual encounters, what they disclose is remarkable for its botched eroticism. Esther Greenwood sees male genitals as turkey parts; she hemorrhages uncontrollably when she discards her virginity. Dotty Renfrew, of *The Group*, fails to get her diaphragm in, watches with horror as it rolls across the floor of the clinic, and later undergoes a clinical deflowering. For Portnoy, sex emerges from the bathroom only to take shape as exploitative orgies with the "Monkey" and an attempted rape in Israel. Rabbit Angstrom's fantasies barely take him past impotence with his young housemate Jill. And Vonnegut aptly expresses the objectification of sex by providing us with the penis measurements of his male characters and drawings of girls' underpants and a "wide open beaver." Only Kesey offers an uncritical fantasy of the erotic, and his liberated ladies are compliant whores while his proper women are "ball cutters." In virtually none of these novels is there an arena of erotic playfulness uncontaminated by bad social relations, in which one might recover a childlike unity of body and spirit.

Finally, the experience of objects—of the socially produced physical world—runs from the banal to the terrifying. Characters live among and by commodities but experience commodities as antagonistic, destructive to one's individuality, vulgar and homogenized, or full of factitious variety. Characteristic scenes in these novels are Rabbit's drab homes, organized around the TV set; Herzog's farmhouse filled with things that don't work; the cultural hodgepodge of Pynchon's Fangoso Lagoons; the paraphernalia of beauty and fashion in *The Bell Jar*. At a monstrous extreme are Kesey's sterile ward with its hellish machinery and Vonnegut's plastic river. Only Salinger's Zooey is truly at home with commodities, and then only in the sanctified retreat of the Glass apartment, where bought objects have become saturated with love and memory. For most of these writers, the things produced by cooperative human labor are as alienated as the labor itself and the mechanics of *re*production.

Through the story of mental disorientation or derangement, then, these novels transform deep social contradictions into a dynamic of personal crisis, a sense of there being no comfortable place in the world for the private self. These books are narratives of illness.

I want now to touch on the form of the story they tell about it. We might see that story as a version of the comic plot, with society itself as the tyrannical older generation; but these stories do not point toward a new society built around the values of the young or to the marriage feast that solemnizes it. They end, at best, in mere recovery—in the achievement of personal equilibrium vis-à-vis the same untransformed external world. Not all the central figures become whole again, but the movement into illness and toward recovery is the basic story on which the novels play variations.

What are the means of recovery? I think the medical theme asserts itself in the plethora of healers who figure in these stories. Some, of course, are bad therapists, like those who misunderstand or bully Esther Greenwood before the good Dr. Nolan assumes charge of her welfare, or like the timid hacks manipulated by Nurse Ratched in *One Flew over the Cuckoo's Nest*. Some are shadowy Germanic stereotypes like Dr. Hilarius in *The Crying of Lot 49* and the silent listener Spielvogel in *Portnoy's Complaint*. Almost never does the professional healer effect a cure, and the same holds true for the many self-appointed counselors and prophets who proffer guidance or wisdom. There are the innumerable "reality instructors": those who bedevil Bellow's heroes with well-intentioned or self-serving advice; Rabbit's young educators in new thought, Skeeter and Jill; Kilgore Trout, the unintentional wise man whose book pushes Dwayne Hoover off the deep end; the kooks and true believers who confuse and eventually desert Oedipa Maas.

Yet the central characters of these novels do not heal themselves: if they recover at all, it is with the help of someone who takes on the role of therapist but who does so out of love and personal commitment. Zooey is the archetype here, marshaling all his Glass family wit, backed by his mother's chicken soup, his brothers' anthology of wise sayings, and the saintly presence of the dead Seymour. Contemptuous of psychiatrists, he is able to be one for Franny on her couch because he has the techniques that love and family provide. Likewise, Willie Herzog, just by caring and being there, helps Moses back to sanity—as does Rabbit's sister Mim, by offering him the simple revelation that "people want to be nice." And of course Randle Patrick McMurphy becomes Christ to the men on the ward, choosing his own death, in effect, to restore their health and autonomy.

But if I am right in this analysis, the ministrations of these healers should not produce altogether convincing resolutions. If these novels thematize social contradictions as personal neurosis, one would expect any recovery to be a problem, for individual cures cannot address the causes of the illness. At best, they can produce a kind of adjustment. And indeed, some of the novels acknowledge this impasse. Vonnegut, whose story never really departs from the social, offers no hope for his individual creations, only for the whole human race in a distant future through the somewhat magical agency of more "humane ideas." None of the four possible solutions to Oedipa Maas's puzzle will afford her much personal repose. Roth leaves Alex Portnoy on the couch, ready only to *begin* his therapy under the tutelage of the dubious Spielvogel.

Where the hero does return to health, a strange diminution usually occurs, signaling, I think, a disengagement from the issues that generated the story in the first place. Chief Bromden heads off to see how some men from his tribe have managed to go on spearing salmon on the spillway of the new dam, carrying on the old ways in a preindustrial pocket that the "Combine" has overlooked. Esther Greenwood steps into a room filled with eyes that will judge her sane; her triumph is simply that she can face them. Franny Glass is able, finally, to sleep. Herzog, also lying on a couch, in an isolated farmhouse in the Berkshires, knows he has recovered because he has "no messages for anyone." Harry Angstrom and his wife Janice, provisionally reunited, curl up together in a motel-room bed and, like Franny, fall asleep. Nothing has changed "out there," but our heroes are now "O.K.?"

In this essay I have barely outlined an intricate social process and a sizable body of fiction. I have ignored vital distinctions: for instance, I have said nothing about the value attributed to these works by different fractions of their readership. Obviously, young people and older people experience class and history differently and have different literary tastes. The same holds even more strongly for men and women. Neither have I spoken of changes in the form and tone of the illness story through fifteen years of rather turbulent history. I have omitted consideration of the balance between explicit and implicit—or even unconscious—criticism in the novels; an analysis that equates Kesey's fiction and Plath's clearly needs refinement. And of course I have neglected even to mention many novels that may come to reside in the canon.

What I hope to have accomplished, nonetheless, is to have given concrete enough form to the following powerful yet vague ideas about culture and value, so that they may be criticized and perhaps developed.[44] (1) A canon—a shared understanding of what literature is worth preserving—takes shape through a troubled historical process. (2) It emerges through specific institutions and practices, not in some historically invariant way. (3) These institutions are likely to have a rather well-defined class base. (4) Although the ruling ideas and myths may indeed be, in every age, the ideas and myths of the ruling class, the ruling class in advanced capitalist societies does not advance its ideas directly through its control of the means of mental production. Rather, a subordinate but influential class shapes culture in ways that express its own interests and experience and that sometimes turn on ruling-class values rather critically—yet in a nonrevolutionary period end up confirming root elements of the dominant ideology, such as the premise of individualism. I hope, in short, to have given a usable and attackable account of the hegemonic process and to have added content to the claim that aesthetic value arises from class conflict.

6 Style and Ideology

Tracing the "illness story" as figuring the historical experience and needs of a particular class, I wrote of many novels as if they constituted a sort of collective mimesis, a monomyth. To see their stories as versions of *one* story, I stepped back many paces from the novelistic surface, to let the outlines of a structure come into relief. If the general argument (see essay 5) has force, one should be able to look closely at verbal texture and find there, too, shapes that would please the inner eye of a canon-making class. After all, a reader or critic of "serious" fiction does not go to it—not consciously—for repetition of an already-known formula. Such a person may on the contrary seek an unrepeatable experience, valuing a given narrative partly for the distinctness of its form and idiom.

On the heels of that thought follows an obvious caveat against searching the pages of these novels for *a* PMC style. In fact, as Fredric Jameson has suggestively argued, the capitalist epoch itself is more or less coterminous with the emergence of stylistic individuality as a literary value, by contrast with the privileging of socially funded *rhetoric* (Jameson's term) in earlier periods.[1] This makes intuitive sense. And one would certainly expect the culturally oriented part of a professional-managerial class, with its dream of autonomy on the terrain of private life, to ratify and extend the bourgeois values of originality, innovation, and individual personality.

To call the roll of leading novelists from the 1960s and early 1970s is to bear out this hypothesis. What does Salinger's style have in common with Kesey's? Bellow's with Pynchon's? Each writer has a distinct verbal signature; difference itself would seem a minimal criterion for being taken seriously. But if there is no shared PMC rhetoric in fiction, no preferred syntax or reservoir of tropes, perhaps we can nonetheless scan the styles of these writers for analogous mimetic strategies. I propose raising questions about verbal texture: How do styles in this fiction present material and social reality? And how do they respond to the authors' distress or concern about that reality? The kind of answer I suggest here, by carefully examining only one style and glancing briefly at another, is that we might find, in most of the precanonical novels, styles that one way or another evade or mystify political questions—and questions that, often, the novels explicitly thematize. To put it another way: as the conclusion of the illness story tends to channel social conflicts into personal solutions, its verbal style tends either to make the same move, or at most to leave those conflicts hanging in dazed incomprehension.

I imagine that of all contemporary novelists, John Updike has drawn the most attention to his prose. It demands notice *as* prose, and noticed it has been. Scanning the covers of a few paperbacks, I pick up these phrases: "crystal-bright prose" (*Washington Post*), "surest writing in years" (*Time*), "Prose that is . . . always held under impeccable control" (*Kansas City Star*), "angel-tongued" (*Washington Post*), "subtle, superbly written" (*Newsweek*), "language as lyrical as any written in America today" (*Washington Post Times Herald*), "brilliant in language" (*New York Herald Tribune*), "a dazzler in prose" (*Pittsburgh Press*), "a rare verbal genius" (*Time*). Updike's public reputation is pinned on his style, more than on any other quality.

Academic critics are more reserved in their adjectives, but, in general, agree with the reviewers about the salience of Updike's style. And the dissenters, those with a low estimate of his fiction, are also likely to fix on its style. Norman Podhoretz, for instance, writes of Updike's prose as "overly lyrical, bloated like a child who had eaten too much candy," and wonders if his "rhetorical virtuosity" has the purpose of assuring "the reader that he is in the presence of a writer who is very sophisticated indeed and who therefore cannot possibly be so callow and sentimental as he seems to be and in fact is?"[2] This, at least, is to reckon style as purposeful, rather than ornamental. Yet Podhoretz is not much different in outlook from the reviewers: they treat style as a separate category of excellence; he sees it as a disguise.

I'd prefer to adopt the organic hypothesis, until it proves inadequate. Even the briefest displays of "rhetorical virtuosity" seem motivated, generally, by more than an irrepressible angel-tongue or a wish to hide callowness. At the end of *Rabbit Redux*, as Rabbit and Janice try a fumbling and tentative reconciliation, a stretch of banal dialogue is interrupted by this sentence: "The slither of sheets as she rotates her body is a silver music, sheets of pale noise extending outward unresisted by space."[3] The abrupt transition from halting speech to gorgeous image reminds us that Rabbit—the narrator speaks here as through most of the novel from Rabbit's consciousness—can still hear and see the loveliness in ordinary things. It hints that Janice's affair and his anomie have not spoiled this gift in him, that the couple may resume a marriage that is commonplace yet for him not cut off from transcendence. The equation set up by the syntax—slither=music=sheets=noise—is a flight of associations, recalling the flights through inner and outer space that are a main motif of the novel. Likewise the synaesthetic metaphors, "silver music," "pale noise"; these also emphasize the mind's freedom from routine categories of language and experience, and reassert light as a medium of grace. The sentence is knit into the plot of the novel, and consonant with its theme and pattern.

Still, Updike's appeal as a stylist cannot rest mainly in the aptness of such passages, however fine a bouquet of them one might gather. Updike himself may have come to realize this gradually. His earlier novels were richly laced with such passages, sometimes almost making readers forget context and design. He has disciplined himself in later works, holding in the free display of his great verbal talent, and bending his style more snugly to the shapes of his fictional worlds. What *does* it do to readers, then? For me, its initial effect is to link the transcendent inner world of the novel to narrow experience. Updike works with commonplace materials—bedsheets and television sets, banalities and irritations—rooted in all of our lives. The task he sets for style is partly just to rescue the humdrum from being perceived as such by use of new language and offering of new vision that might revive the freshness obscured in the deadness of our perceiving. It is a familiar role for literature, from haiku and Williams's red wheelbarrow to the metamorphoses of Wilder's *Our Town* or Woolf's *To the Lighthouse*. The Prague Circle's notion of foregrounding is pertinent here, or Conrad's determination to make us "see." Updike, too, presses us to notice, really notice, the ordinary, reminding us of what we've seen or felt before but also getting behind the screen of easy categories, the habitual filing systems we carry in our heads, which mediate in daily life between percept and act, saving us from paralysis. But they also close out what is not to some pragmatic purpose. "Oh yes, sunlight again, a house, wind, kids playing."

Updike's style brings memory and perception alive, makes connections that are surprising but right, and loads percept with feeling drawn from the relationship of people to things and to each other. In the first paragraph of *Rabbit Redux* Updike gives us the "stagnant city" of Brewer at four o'clock on a summer afternoon, as men leave their work at a printing plant. Outside, the granite curbs are "starred with mica," and the texture is made new, as sunlight sorts granite out into its bright elements and a curb is something more than an undifferentiated obstacle at roadside. The houses are alike except for their "speckled bastard sidings"—an instant reminder of maroon and gray-green composition shingles in a thousand old towns and cities. But more than a reminder of the sight, too, for the metaphor hints at honest old wood covered by artificial new materials, themselves now old; at the pathetic attempt of each owner to distinguish his house from the nearly identical one next door; at the tired lives in ill-fitting, dowdy homes. Likewise the "hopeful small porches with their jigsaw brackets," the adjective "hopeful" permeating architectural detail with the modest but defeated aspirations of builders and occupants. Curbs, houses, gingko trees, "baking curbside cars," all "wince beneath a brilliance like a frozen explosion"—just right for dull objects caught in bright sun, and for the ill-relatedness, almost random, of things in a seedy downtown. "The sky is cloudless yet colorless, hovering blanched humidity." This does more than evoke the familiar gray-white color; "hovering" captures the sky's lack of depth on a day like this; "blanched" neatly gets the combination of heat and warmth, and projects into the atmosphere the feeling of being half-cooked, a happy pathetic fallacy.

The speech act in this present-tense narration bears notice. One would not say "the sky is colorless" or "men emerge pale from the little printing shop" to an equally privileged observer. This is a mode of reporting we use when the other person is not there (as with radio narration of a baseball game) or is blind or inattentive. The privilege of Updike's narrator is gained partly through his ability to add that the men are "ghosts for an instant, blinking, until the outdoor light overcomes the look of constant indoor light clinging to them," or to render the sky's "hovering blanched humidity." He lays claim to being our guide, through a fineness of perception, imagination, and language beyond the capacity of most of us, but to our benefit if we use it to augment and reanimate our own perceptions. The language often warrants this claim, I think. Updike establishes a way of looking at the ordinary that reaches into our own fund of memory, knowledge, and feeling, and renews it. This way of perceiving, and of talking about perceiving, is not decorative, but is central to what the novel communicates.

When a reader allows Updike—as I and most readers seem to do, though a minority, including Norman Podhoretz, do not—this privileged status, that reader in effect gives up for a while his or her pragmatic and habitual strategies of perception. A relaxation of hardened categories: we become more flexible in our imagination of things, more open to reshaping and novelty. This relaxation prepares us to see the mica in the curbstone or the pinched lives in the composition siding, but of course it also opens us to more systematic reorganization of sensing and conceiving. Or, to look at this from Updike's side, a style can do (and generally does) more than reanimate discrete bits of experience. It may arrange them as a totality, screened and shaped by a particular way of seeing. I want now to look at a longer stretch of Updike's prose, watching for this kind of reshaping.

[1] He walks back through the West Brewer side streets toward Weiser, through the dulling summer light and the sounds of distant games, of dishes rattled in kitchen sinks, of television muffled to a murmur mechanically laced with laughter and applause, of cars driven by teenagers laying rubber and shifting down. [2] Children and old men sit on the porch steps beside the lead-colored milk-bottle boxes. [3] Some stretches of sidewalk are brick; these neighborhoods, the oldest in West Brewer, close to the river, are cramped, gentle, barren. [4] Between the few trees, city trees that never knew an American forest, they brought them in from China and Brazil, there is a rigid flourishing of hydrants, meters, and signs, some of them, virtual billboards in white on green, directing motorists to superhighways whose number is blazoned on the federal shield or on the commonwealth keystone; from these obscure West Brewer byways, sidewalks and asphalt streets rumpled comfortable as old clothes, one can be arrowed toward Philadelphia, Baltimore, Washington, the national capital, New York the headquarters of commerce and fashion. [5] Or in the other direction can find Pittsburgh, Chicago, mountains of snow, a coastline of sun. [6] But beneath these awesome metal insignia of vastness and motion fat men in undershirts loiter, old ladies move between patches of gossip with the rural waddle of egg-gatherers, dogs sleep curled beside the cooling curb, and children with hockey sticks and tape-handled bats diffidently chip at whiffle balls and wads of leather, whittling themselves into the next generation of athletes and astronauts. [7] Rabbit's eyes sting in the dusk, in this smoke of his essence, these harmless neighborhoods that have gone to seed. [8] So much love, too much love, it is our madness, it is rotting us out, exploding us like dandelion polls. [9] He stops at a corner grocery for a candy bar, an Oh Henry, then at the Burger Bliss on Weiser,

dazzling in its lake of parking space, for a Lunar Special (double cheese-burger with an American flag stuck into the bun) and a vanilla milkshake, that tastes toward the bottom of chemical sludge (p. 105).

Rabbit walks through West Brewer at twilight, then makes two stops to buy food. The passage recounts a sequence of acts within (perhaps) a square mile of city and lasting the amount of time it takes for dusk to become dark. The story could be told that way (as acts), or as a series of phenomena (he saw this, then he heard that), or through analysis and explanation, or in a stream of conscious-ness—there are many choices. Updike chooses none of these pos-sibilities, but has Rabbit enter both the material streets of West Brewer and a surreal medium where lights and sounds and ob-jects are in ontological parity. This happens in the first sentence, with its spatial complement ("back") and series of spatial prepo-sitions: "through," "toward," and again "through." Since all the prepositional phrases modify "Rabbit walks," they establish an in-terchangeability among the things he walks through and toward: side streets, Weiser, dulling summer light, and a variety of sounds. This is what I mean by a surreal medium. In it, ontological catego-ries and distinctions are suspended. Updike creates the effect, here, mainly through a combination of spatial prepositions, seriation, and metaphor. These three structures are crucial to the style of the whole passage.

Seriation. When two or more words are in the same syntactic re-lation (either direct or mediated) to a single word, the structure calls attention to similarities that link their meanings and refer-ents (if any). It invites us to level their conceptual and material dif-ferences.[4] A game, for instance, is an event; dishes and cars are objects; television, in the sense Updike uses here, is amplified elec-tronic impulses. Putting them in a series, identically related to "sounds of," levels these sharp ontological distinctions, takes us away from causes, sources, and material reality, and puts us in a world of epiphenomena. In the surface structure of sentence 3 there are two series. In the deep structure, all adjectives—"old," "close," "cramped," "gentle," and "barren"—stand in the same relationship to "neighborhoods" (*neighborhoods* + *Be* + adj.). The structural parallel plays down semantic differences: "oldest in West Brewer" gives the neighborhoods a history; "close to the river," a place; "cramped" is configurational; "gentle" seems to refer to both archi-tecture and the lives of the people; "barren" points most literally to sparseness of vegetation, and probably also to such things as eco-

nomic and social stagnation. These diverse and complicated relations reduce, through syntax, to rather nebulous *qualities,* a kind of
emanation given off by the city. Similarly, sentence 5 equalizes two
cities (proper-named) and two fairyland constructions, "mountains of snow, a coastline of sun." That series is joined indirectly
(both of them related to "one") to the one in sentence 4, which adds
social and political conceptions (commerce, fashion, capital) to the
spatial and geographical. For a last example, sentence 7 equates, in
a prepositional series overlaid by an appositional structure, dusk,
"smoke of his essence," and neighborhoods, on whose conceptual
incompatibility I won't elaborate. There are many other series in
the passage (e.g., "hydrants, meters, and signs") that do not re-
shuffle our perceptions and ideas. Taken together with those that
do, they add up to a major grammatical strategy. It represents for
the author, and encourages in the reader, a perceptual and idea-
tional strategy as well. The senses and mind are like nets, cast into
the ambiance of West Brewer, and recovering from it catches of fish
that are sometimes all of a species, but sometimes neither of the
same species nor from the same order of reality. The effect is hazy,
disorienting, a little psychedelic, to me quite seductive, though
vaguely disturbing too.

Spatial prepositions. "Through," "between," "beside," "toward,"
"on," "in": these words are sprinkled through the passage. Along
with conjunction (the series), spatial prepositions take the leading
role in joining the elements of the prose. Some of the effects I described above owe partly to the way Updike spatializes things: for
example, Rabbit's eyes sting *in* dusk, smoke of essence, neighborhoods; and he walks *through* streets, light, and sounds. But beyond
that, reliance on these links creates a spatial network that dominates other kinds of relatedness.

To move straight to the main instance: about half the passage
(sentences 4–6) is tied together in such a network, with the road
signs as its hub. They, along with meters and hydrants, are *between*
the few trees of West Brewer. They point motorists *to* highways; the
highway numbers are *on* federal shield and commonwealth keystone, which of course are on the green signs. So are arrows: one
can be arrowed (by the signs—"signs," I take it, is the deep structure
subject of "arrow") *from* West Brewer streets *toward* Philadelphia
and the other eastern cities, or, *in the other direction,* Pittsburgh and
the rest. Meanwhile, *beneath* the "insignia," men, ladies, dogs, and
children are located. In other words, the main elements of this section—trees, superhighways, West Brewer streets, the cities of east

and west, and the people and dogs of the neighborhood—are directly linked by a network of prepositions to the signs (= billboards) and the insignia, shields, arrows, that they display.

By this spatial mediation, syntax also relates the signs less directly to a different range of meaning: to China and Brazil, entirely outside the society, where the trees came from; to "an American forest," with the suggestion of the continent's ecology before white men and commerce intervened; to the more vaguely delineated "headquarters of commerce and fashion" and "mountains of snow"; to old clothes and undershirts; to abstract "vastness and motion"; to "patches of gossip" *between* which old ladies move and the cooling curb *beside* which dogs sleep; to imagined rural egg-gatherers from quite a different milieu; to sticks and bats and balls and wads; and finally, as space and time merge, to (*"into"*) the next generation. The network brings town and country and wilderness, past and present and future, progress and decay, national industrial society and neighborhood culture, all into relations that are primarily spatial and associative. More of this later.

Metaphor. Most obviously, the mingling of levels and categories I've been finding goes on through metaphor—most obviously, because metaphors are constituted by violations of syntactic or semantic rules,[5] which violations ask us to see or conceptualize a bit of reality in a way not sponsored by the set of categories that language has made normal for us. In effect, metaphor glosses reality by shaking it up, introducing new relations into it. When Rabbit walks through light and sounds, Updike materializes these nonmaterial things by putting them on a syntactic and conceptual par with West Brewer side streets. The same thing happens to sound in "a murmur mechanically laced with laughter and applause." The metaphor "patches of gossip" spatializes talk. Equating the dusk to "smoke of his essence" and both to "harmless neighborhoods" creates a blend of nonmaterial dusk and soul with material smoke and city. (I might add that the paragraph after this one is built almost entirely on metaphors that treat light as a material medium—and this is a main motif of the whole novel.)

Another conceptual boundary Updike denies is that between living and inanimate. The neighborhoods are gentle, harmless, and have gone to seed; they are humanized by streets; there is a "flourishing" of hydrants, meters, and signs, like rumpled old clothes, between the trees; the signs actively "arrow" motorists. Abstract and concrete interact, not only when Rabbit's "essence" is joined to smoke, but when love is "rotting us out, exploding us like dandelion polls," and when vastness and motion are embodied on "metal insignia." A few of the metaphors spatialize time. I've mentioned the children whittling themselves "into" a future generation. When Rabbit walks "through dulling summer light," for another example, the temporal change—nightfall—is frozen into a static aura. Again, the sound of television programs interrupted from time to time by laughter and applause is pictured as an artifact, laced together as if by a stitching machine. Time, space; abstract, material; human, inanimate: all fuse in Updike's metaphors.

This passage presents a moment of heightened consciousness. Rabbit, in a dead end of tedium, and recently deserted by Janice, has just deferred adultery with Peggy Fosnacht, and is on his way to a rendezvous in a tavern mostly frequented by blacks, where he will enter a strange culture and a new, frightening life for himself. He is open to experience, his perceptions laden with feeling. The gorgeousness of Updike's prose gives a kind of endorsement to Rabbit's perceptions here; there is no suggestion that Rabbit is obtuse, muddled, blind to what he sees. So as Updike reanimates his (and our) experience, we can take it that his ordering of it carries authority—that of the whole novel, and of the novelist.

The worldview I have found in his seriation, spatial organization, and metaphor is one that subdues temporal relatedness and blends it with the spatial and the subjective. It denies the borders between material and nonmaterial, living and inanimate. In the process, it mystifies social connections, and virtually eliminates causation as a way of understanding things. It creates what I have called a medium—sensory, spatial, personal, and associative—in which all things flow and merge. Elsewhere in the novel, this medium swallows up television, politics, the moon landing, sex, Rabbit's loss of his job. In effect, the style of the novel turns the world into an aggregate of unmoored percepts, available for fluid patterning by the imagination.

I need hardly insist that other patterns may offer more understanding than the pattern Updike imposes; nor does one have to be a marxist to imagine them. The events reported here are historically and socially specific: they take place in a run-down Pennsylvania city, in 1969. The elements of the scene—seedy neighborhoods, working people on the margin of a wealthy society, signs that relate Brewer to a national highway system, the corner grocery and the national fast-food chain—assume another configuration if one allows history and economic forces a shaping role. The dowdiness of the city and Rabbit's nostalgia have something to do with an indus-

trial revolution that has moved on, with the impact of the automobile on cities, with New York as headquarters of commerce *and*
capital and a logic of development that abandons human lives
when the criterion of profitability so dictates, with the always increasing concentration of power that eliminates corner grocery
stores and makes Burger Bliss prosper, and that eliminates Rabbit's job in a technologically backward printing plant. The disorientation Rabbit experiences has much to do not only with the
Vietnam War, the "sexual revolution," and the black rebellions of
the sixties—Updike includes these symptoms in his purview—but
with alienation in the strict sense and with the intolerable burden
placed on the family, in this society, as a remedy for or refuge from
all the injuries of class and failures of organic community that
seem endemic to late capitalism.

In saying this, do I import an external criterion for style? In part,
yes. Whatever may be said for the "autonomy" of art (not much, I
think) we do, and should, value literature partly for the guidance it
gives us in understanding and in living. But each writer sets the
terms within which to seek insight. And in *Rabbit Redux* Updike
quite explicitly takes on Vietnam, the malaise of "middle America"
(our supposedly affluent working class), inequality, racial conflicts,
and stress in the bourgeois family. These are the givens of the novel.
The question it poses is how can one—one sensitive, moderately
capable, working-class man—live well in this setting? I'm arguing
that Updike gives his answer partly through style. One should
make a sacrament of the mundane. One should arrange experience
in noncausal patterns that point to no action. At best, one may become a monarch of perception, safe in a world one controls, and
insulated from historical process. To me, this does not seem an adequate answer. In short, I think the critique I have made of his style
is "fair"—it takes into account the challenge Updike himself sets
for his art in *Rabbit Redux.*

Furthermore, though I cannot argue it here, the answer given by
style is quite compatible with the answer given by the story and
form of the novel as a whole. Rabbit, launched unwillingly out of
the "stale peace" of his life with Janice, comes into touch with a
much more varied section of American life than he knew before. In
the central part of the novel he receives a kind of education: from
Jill, about noncapitalist ethics of the flower-child sort; from Skeeter,
about race, history, power; from Charlie Stavros, about Vietnam;
from his neighbors, about the limited decency of other patriotic
Americans like Rabbit himself. But the learning both enlarges and

dazes Rabbit. He retreats from the books on Skeeter's shelf—"history, Marx, economics, stuff that makes Rabbit feel sick, as when he thinks about what surgeons do, or all the plumbing and gas lines there are under the street" (p. 201). His last instructor is the best: his sister Mim, who has made her peace with American society, and who teaches that "people want to be nice, haven't you noticed? They don't like being shits, that much; but you have to find some way out of it for them." (p. 326). Rabbit narrows his scope, shrinks back from society to the personal and familial. His partial victory— so I take the end of the novel—is in a small room with just one other person, Janice. They begin to rebuild the family, this time redeemed by tolerance, affection, and lower horizons. Their peace is certified by sleep at the novel's end. This is a novel that sets aside or begs the question it poses. Its style is part of that process.

I want to take the briefest look, now, at style as mimetic strategy, and as strategy for coping with life in contemporary American society, in one other novel. I cannot elaborate on or prove my case, but hope to suggest that the perspective I have adopted toward Updike's style may be useful elsewhere. With Kurt Vonnegut, I will stick to main features of style that have been widely noted by critics and ordinary readers, and need not be described in detail: specifically, the deadpan tone and childlike rhetorical structure of *Breakfast of Champions*. And I want to relate this style to the book's purpose of criticizing the entire culture of industrial America, and finding an adequate stance toward it.

The book works with two veins of material, one a fiction about Dwayne Hoover and Kilgore Trout, the other, the condition of the human race in the real world, circa 1970. The first is bizarre, and obviously invented. The second is factual, and subject to reality testing by any reader of the book. Yet both are made to seem equally fantastic by Vonnegut's selection from the latter, and this effect is supported by the equalizing, matter-of-fact tone. That Celia Hoover committed suicide by eating Drano, and "became a small volcano, since she was composed of the same sort of substances which commonly clogged drains" is no crazier than that "the people in a country called Germany . . . built factories whose only purpose was to kill people by the millions." The style seems to say "this is how it was," to stand without the aid, or need, of rhetoric in the face of the incredible; in so doing, it spreads the aura of unreality from invented facts to actual ones.

A second strategy to which style contributes is telling the story from a galactic perspective ("the planet Earth," "a planet that was dying fast"), from a point in the future, and from what seems to be a different cultural epoch, to whose people the United States of 1970 is an unfamiliar place in need of much explication. To this imagined audience, Vonnegut (I do not say "the narrator," because Vonnegut himself refuses the distinction) recites the facts of our culture in the past tense and in the most elementary way, as if describing to school children the way things were in a vanished civilization:

A hamburger was made out of an animal which looked like this:
[crude drawing of cow]
The animal was killed and ground up into little bits, then shaped into patties and fried, and put between two pieces of bread. The finished product looked like this:
[drawing of hamburger][6]

Vonnegut as future historian of our times is free from involvement, and can render his descriptions with a minimum of polemics and editorializing.

Hence, rather than insist that industry has wantonly ravaged the landscape and poisoned the streams, he writes, of West Virginia,

The surface of the State had been demolished by men and machinery and explosives in order to make it yield up its coal. The coal was mostly gone now. It had been turned into heat.
The surface of West Virginia, with its coal and trees and topsoil gone, was rearranging what was left of itself in conformity with the laws of gravity. It was collapsing into all the holes which had been dug into it. Its mountains, which had once found it easy to stand by themselves, were sliding into valleys now (p. 119).

The distance and understatement help readers to see our world without blinders of routine, myth, Ideology. It's an achievement not to be dismissed; partly through the agency of its style, this novel renders a strong critique of our social arrangements, and restores our sensuous grasp of many irrationalities.

But the style has its limits. In a critical novel, I want to see how particulars connect. Failing this, criticism can itself be a form of insanity, which meets every depressing fact with a shrug, or registers it as yet another instance of human ineptness. We need explanation, some sense of how facts are tied together, or we are left paralyzed.

Now of course Vonnegut is constantly offering explanations. Of assassination: "Sometimes people would put holes in famous people so they could be at least fairly famous, too." Of drug addiction: "People took such awful chances with chemicals and their bodies because they wanted the quality of their lives to improve. They lived in ugly places where there were only ugly things to do. They didn't own doodley-squat, so they couldn't improve their surroundings. So they did their best to make their insides beautiful instead" (p. 71). Of private property: "Because of the peculiar laws in that part of the planet, Rockefeller was allowed to own vast areas of Earth's surface, and the petroleum and other valuable minerals underneath the surface as well" (p. 106). But each explanation accounts for one insanity with another—a process of pseudoexplanation giving the prose and the associated worldview a veneer of rationality.

Take the matter of industrialism, central to Vonnegut's critique. We have already seen how he describes the demolition of West Virginia, for heat. What was the heat for? "It boiled water, and the steam had made steel windmills whiz around and around. The windmills had made rotors in generators whiz around and around. America was jazzed with electricity for a while. Coal had also powered old-fashioned steamboats and choo-choo trains." And so on to the whistles of the choo-choo trains, activated by steam, which "made harshly beautiful laments, as though they were the voice boxes of mating or dying dinosaurs" (p. 122). Nothing here about conversion of energy for social reproduction, nothing about market forces or the competitive search for profit or accumulation of surplus. Vonnegut is talking of energy and manufacturing in one two-hundred-year historical epoch, driven by one kind of economic system. A complex set of events, to be sure, but not impossible to explain. The style trivializes the task, and makes the effort seem absurd.

Vonnegut makes only a couple of sallies at deeper explanation. There is the oddity of the Rockefellers and Rosewaters owning so much land and power. But why? How did they come to own so much? Here the chain of explanation reaches an end in greed— "the arbitrary lust for gold"—which, along with lust—"a glimpse of a little girl's underpants"—is the driving impulse of all this social disorder. In short, the economic and historical causes derive in turn, through childlike logic and style, from causes of a different order: human nature, and two of the seven deadly sins. And ideas. Bad ideas propel Dwayne to his demise, and place human beings generally in their sorry fix: "there was no immunity to cuckoo ideas on Earth." Ideas, along with greed and lust, cause material history, not the other way around.

Vonnegut's approach—mixing all facts together on one level, exploring causes haphazardly and in isolation—blocks off such a line of analysis, much less anything as complex as dialectics. His style is part of a method that creates a fictional world with a foreground of dazzlingly perceptive nuttiness, and a background of the most nebulous and jejune concepts: greed and lust, susceptibility to bad ideas, human beings as machines, the inevitability of things being as they are. It is half a moral vision. And the absence of the other half cripples any search for a way out. Kilgore Trout, in a time after the present of the story, will show humanity that "we can build an unselfish society by devoting to unselfishness the frenzy we once devoted to gold and to underpants." That is, good ideas might be as mysteriously implanted in us as the bad ones are now. This is a slender hope, and Vonnegut himself can hardly hang onto it. Much more natural "solutions," in this fictional world, are the tear in the author's eye, Trout's hopeless cry to "make me young," and the great "ETC" with which the novel concludes.

A simple style and an ornate one. Both writers release us, through style in part, from routinized perception and the easy categories and explanations of bourgeois life. Updike does so by blurring edges, mixing levels of apprehension, and building a world of subjective association. Vonnegut does it by saying the unthinkable in small, separate bits. Both styles erect barriers to systematic understanding.

The novels ask, in effect, why life is so unsatisfactory for their central characters. Their styles collaborate with other features of plot, conception, and technique to give answers that mystify, by personalizing and by directing attention away from the social. Rabbit's malaise is dealt with, finally, as a kind of neurosis that can be cured by more sensitivity and lower expectations—good goals for individual therapy, but not I think for the host of social disorders that invade Rabbit's life. Vonnegut's answers—bad ideas, bad chemistry, and the like—are correlates of a style that almost precludes making integrated sense of things.

As for solutions—by which I mean only ways of acting that answer to the factuality which these novels admit? For Updike, acceptance and inner transformation. For Vonnegut, despair, and the rather unconvincing hope for redeeming ideas. Updike said somewhere that he was "sort of elegiacally concerned with the Protestant middle class," and that captures the quietism I feel in his books. Vonnegut places his hope in artists, especially writers, who will "poison the minds" of the young, make them unwilling to fight unjust wars, and "give them . . . myths" that will become potent for change when the young mature.[7] A good aim for an American writer, but a little divorced from material history. In the cleft between ideas and history, there is plenty of room for the despair *Breakfast of Champions* leaves me with.

I am aware that I ask a lot of these writers, their styles, and their visions. But they are two of our most influential novelists, and two whose talents and humane instincts I admire. It is not surprising, but it is saddening, that these talents and instincts are directed into pathways so little likely to create a new consciousness, and help lead us out of the bourgeois reality that both writers powerfully render, and that apparently causes them as much distress as it does me.

7 Politics and Genre in Nonfiction Prose

I want to consider a familiar kind of book, and my starting point is Northrop Frye's notion, "radical of presentation," on which he grounds the theory of genres in *Anatomy of Criticism*. Or rather, he claims to do so, saying that "the basis of generic criticism . . . is rhetorical, in the sense that the genre is determined by the conditions established between the poet and his public." This idea directly sponsors his initial division of literature into four genres. In *epos* the poet recites directly to his audience. In *fiction*, audience and author are hidden from each other, with the book mediating. The poet of *drama* is concealed, while characters speaking the poet's words directly confront the audience. By contrast, in the *lyric* radical of presentation, the audience is concealed from the poet and, as it were, overhears him. Frye's two terms—an author and an audience—and his one two-valued relationship between them—concealment/confrontation—neatly define four main genres.[1]

Fair enough, as an abstract beginning. But Frye breaks off this line of inquiry before long (at least *I* lose track of it), and when he comes round to discussing the specific forms of epos, lyric, drama, and fiction, he pretty much ignores "the conditions established between the poet and his audience," except for some remarks in the section on drama which are among the most illuminating of the whole essay. There he speaks of the audience's *status*, relative to poet and characters, and of the relation of all three to the society's history. I wish he had done likewise in discussing the other genres, for I suspect that only by being historically and socially specific can one build an understanding of genres on the connections between poet and public.[2] Perhaps that is why the essay on genres seems to many readers the least satisfactory in the *Anatomy*.

Anyhow, I want to press Frye's initial point somewhat further, in discussing what I take to be one genre of nonfiction prose. In violation of the first rule of genre theory, I won't coin a name for it—though it *could* be called, by someone with a taste for naming, social exploration, or mediated speech, or discourse of plural authorship. I refer to works that present to a reading audience the lives, and especially the spoken *words*, of someone other than the author or editor. The author has sought out, become familiar with, perhaps lived with, certainly interviewed, one or more persons, using note pad or tape recorder. Then she transcribes, selects from, arranges, and edits their words, and frames them somehow with words of her own. At one extreme, she may simply introduce their edited speech, and retreat into the background: close to this extreme are Studs Terkel's *Working*, Nancy Seifer's *Nobody Speaks for Me*, Theodore Rosengarten's *All God's Dangers*, and Ronald Blythe's *Akenfield*. At the other extreme, the author knits their words, as evidence, into an argument or meditation of his own: examples are Richard Sennett and Jonathan Cobb's *The Hidden Injuries of Class*, George Orwell's *Road to Wigan Pier*, Andrew Levison's *Working Class Majority*, James Agee's *Let Us Now Praise Famous Men*. In between are books like Robert Coles's *Children of Crisis*, Alan Bullock's *Watts: The Aftermath*, and Oscar Lewis's *La Vida*. I pick these examples by a simple, if not scientific, criterion: they are books I've recently used in courses. But anyone can think of many other books that fit my definition. The genre seems a popular one in America. And since I wish to be historically and socially specific, I'll exclude the two English examples from my list, and base my remarks on the American works.

Now it seems to me that in defining the genre as I have, I've gone as far as Frye's rhetorical geometry allows. In his terms, both the initial speaker (or speakers) and the mediating author are concealed from the audience, and vice versa, whereas speaker and author confront each other. That is the radical of presentation, a bit more complex than those of lyric, fiction, epos, and drama, because there's an extra term in the relationship.

But I think it's possible to say a good deal more than this about the "conditions established between the poet and his public." One might start in this direction by asking why such a genre exists at all and where it came from. I suppose it could be granted a lineage going back to the Gospels, and even to the Platonic dialogues, if they are what they purport to be. In any case, there are many preindustrial examples right up to what is perhaps the epitome of the genre, Boswell's life of Johnson. This suggests an obvious reason for the genre to have developed: the public has a natural interest in the talk of the great (or notorious), and a mediating author can supply a vicarious intimacy, give us insight from close up, into the distinction we have remarked from a distance.

Already, however, the inquiry seems to have run aground. The audience's relationship to Jesus or Dr. Johnson is hardly the same as its relationship to Agee's tenant farmers or Lewis's Puerto Rican family. Far from being famous, the latter are entirely unknown to the audience, and I would suggest that their anonymity comes close to being the cause of the work. The authors of the books on my list bring us the words of their speakers, not because we have a prior interest in the speakers, but because we know nothing of them except generically. Boswell brought to his audience hidden aspects of a famous life; Coles and Terkel and the rest put us in touch with hidden lives. This difference also radically affects the rhetorical relationship of author to audience, I think; but I'll save that subject for later.

The point is that if we stick with Frye's terms—the parties to the literary encounter, and the dimension of concealment or confrontation—we do not approximate closely enough the "conditions established between the poet [and speaker, I would add] and his public." And we find ourselves including two quite different kinds of work in the same genre.

Those two kinds exist alongside each other now; we have *Playboy*'s interview with Jimmy Carter, the *Paris Review* interviews, a host of lives of X as told to Y, in addition to the work of Terkel and his kin. But I don't know that the second kind has much of a history in preindustrial—which is the same as saying precapitalist—times. With capitalism we begin to run across it: Cobbett discovering rural desolation; Engels, the workers of Manchester; Mayhew, the London poor; and so on. The reason, I think, is to be found in Marx's observation that of all social forms, capitalism is the most opaque. Not only do the detailed division of labor, urbanization, and the enormous complicating of social and economic relations conceal from one class or group the way that another lives. In addition, the market becomes the only universal connection among people. Relations of objects—and especially of money—substitute for more immediate human relations. The dynamic of historical process becomes obscure. And power and victimization are mystified. In this situation it is easy for the privileged to be ignorant of the basis of their own affluence, or of how the oppressed live, or of what work is like for others, or of what a historical episode like the integration of southern schools or the Watts rebellion means for those involved in it. Yet perhaps because of the democratic ideology we are supposed to live by, many of the privileged are not content to write off the majority as beneath notice, but maintain a reformist, or a guilty, or at least a voyeuristic interest in them. Meanwhile, as the chance to know other lives directly is diminished, capitalists create new media—mass circulation magazines and newspapers, radio, television—that offer a vicarious intimacy.

I believe that this much social context is necessary to establish the genre to which my books belong and distinguish it from the neighboring one that includes Boswell's life of Johnson. The relation of poet to public, on which I've agreed (with Frye) to base the establishment of genres, can't lead us to more than the crudest discriminations if it is abstracted from history. After all, real relations of authors and publics have changed beyond recognition, with the development of writing and then printing, and perhaps even more with the emergence of capitalist society, as Raymond Williams has shown us.

Let me try now to delineate my genre more adequately, admitting history and an analysis of society into the picture. First, the dimension of concealment. We can note immediately that the speaker is concealed from the audience (and at first from the author), not just by literary convention but as a matter of social fact. People who buy and read books make up a small and relatively affluent part of the population, and do not live next door to or mingle with sharecroppers, day laborers, new arrivals from San Juan, residents of Watts, or even working-class women.

Nor do we have other means of approaching their lives, as we do with the celebrities who are the speakers in the other, closely related genre—the Jimmy Carters and Saul Bellows and Elizabeth Taylors and so on. Some of the anonymous people are illiterate or barely literate, and even if literate they have no skills of writing, no access to print, no TV coverage, and so on. In Marx's terms, they own none of the means of mental production, and have no access to them. Nor do they belong to the professional stratum that staffs the media or does free-lance writing. The *audience* is by definition conversant with books, though it may not write them, and is centered in professional and managerial groups. This means that the genre is grounded in a rather specific power relationship: author and audience are relatively well off, educated, and possessed of the skills that go with power or at least with influence in our society. The speaker is generally inferior in power and status to both.

The audience's relative privilege extends further: a reader has leisure and the tranquility to think and appropriate other people's experience vicariously. The speaker, by contrast, may endure a lifetime of hardship, like Nate Shaw in *All God's Dangers* and the Gudgers, Ricketts, and Woods in *Let Us Now Praise Famous Men*, or be exploited and emotionally oppressed like the blue collar workers that Levison or Sennett and Cobb interview. Or we see a segment of the speaker's life that is close to bondage, as with Terkel's workers; or a time when the speaker endures turmoil and danger through conflict with greater powers than his or her own, as with the civil rights workers and parents and segregationists in *Children of Crisis*. It is part of the author's job to make real and sensuous for the audience some trouble or hardship ordinarily glossed over with a label such as *desegregation*, or *work*, or *riot*. The author does this by individuating the experience, through the voices of those who directly undergo it.

And this brings me to a final point about the "conditions established between the poet and his public." Both author and audience belong to a range of the society that "we" think of as individuated: people with careers rather than jobs, and with enough education and ability to give them some life choices and a measure of control over circumstance. But most of the speakers belong to that part of the society often seen as undifferentiated *masses*. Sennett and Cobb usefully point out that in a society that places such value on individual achievement, being part of a mass is a psychological burden, a stigma that few can remove by distinguishing themselves in the way prescribed by the ideology of equal opportunity and class mobility. The author sees this and thinks it unfair. She also knows that, as Raymond Williams put it in *Culture and Society*, you cannot think of "relatives, friends, neighbours, colleagues, acquaintances, as masses. . . . Masses are *other* people."[3] The author has made acquaintances or friends of her speakers: part of her task is to individuate them for the audience, and so remove them from the mass. Almost every book of this genre is written as if to shatter some stereotype or class term, some term that puts us at a distance from the people to whom it applies. Bullock does this for *ghetto black*, Agee for *tenant*, Rosengarten for *black sharecropper*, Levison for *blue collar*, Coles for *the South*, Lewis for *Puerto Rican*, Seifer for *working-class woman*, and so on.

In sum, the underlying social relations of the genre are quite specific to capitalist, industrialized society, where an ideal of equality exists in the presence of the most blatant inequality, and an ideal of individual fulfillment alongside an actual proletariat divided into various stigmatized or anonymous groups. And since books in the genre confront the idea of equality with individual voices and lives of the oppressed, they are to this extent intrinsically critical of the society in which they are written, whether the author is consciously anticapitalist or not.

So much for the defining characteristics of the genre. I turn briefly now to the rhetorical situation created by these characteristics, and to the ways in which the genre is, in Claudio Guillén's words, "an invitation to form,"[4] as well as in my own, an enemy of form.

Note first that the genre's radical of presentation itself implies that reading a book within it will be a challenging or distressing experience for the audience. It's partly just that the audience will be let in on lives far less fortunate than its own, and in this process there is an obvious potential for feeling discomfort, guilt, and frustrated sympathy. Beyond that, the genre works against a background of liberal democratic ideology. It assumes that the audience believes in equality (of opportunity, at least) and in freedom. But the speakers are *not* equal to the audience (or author), and their freedom is patently limited. So a book in the genre not only tends to make the audience uneasy about its privilege, but also undermines whatever reassurance the audience might get from believing the whole society just and rational. The book is at least a disturbing intrusion into the reader's well-being, and maybe even an invasion, an aggression. (If, by the way, a particular reader adheres to an older form of capitalist ideology, believing that anyone can make it in America and that the poor are poor because they deserve to be poor, the book will challenge this reassuring idea too, just by humanizing its speakers, presenting them as individuals and in their own voices.)

In showing the audience that the ideology which rationalizes privilege is faulty, the book leaves the audience naked, defenseless. Beyond that, it tends to demystify power relations in the society, and in showing that oppression and exploitation exist, it makes the audience question where *they* stand in the power dynamic. The answer for most will be, not that they are themselves exploiters and oppressors, but that they are *shielded by* a system founded on exploitation—shielded by birth, education, suburbs, police, money. In this way, too, the book assaults the audience's complacency, the more so since it may seem to accuse the audience of ignorance, of not knowing what it should have known.

Finally, in removing individuals from masses and giving them human qualities, the book inevitably makes them seem worthy of respect, more admirable at least than the audience might have thought—and perhaps, given their hardship, more admirable than the relatively sheltered audience. The author usually encourages this attitude—Coles by arguing that his southerners are not "sick" but courageous; Terkel in saying that his interviewees "perform astonishingly to survive the day"; Rosengarten in saying "Nate Shaw was—and is—a hero to me"; and so on. The audience may agree, but even so there is a potential for judging itself harshly by comparison.

All these likely responses are generic problems for the author. Remember that he too is educated, privileged. He has come to know his speakers and identify to some extent with them by leaving behind for a while the comforts of his class. He stands, therefore, in an ambiguous position vis-à-vis the audience. He is like them, but in a sense has "gone over" to the other side of a class line. How shall he address the audience? Shall he emphasize his similarity to them, as Coles does, and so try to ease them across the line? Shall he rage against them and accuse them as Agee does ("you cannot for one moment exchange places with her, not by any such hope make expiation for what she has suffered at your hands, and for what you have gained at hers")? Shall he merely recede into the background, letting the speakers' words do the work? How much interpreting and shaping shall he do? And what claims can he make of objectivity, given the social distance from which he has approached the speakers? How much shall he tell about himself and the emotional difficulty he had in crossing the lines of race or class? There is risk that the book will become an indulgence, more about the author than the speakers, but a contrary risk also that without being able to know, trust, and identify with the author as mediator, the audience will reject the emotional risk *it* is asked to take. These are all questions of strategy that rise from the nature of the genre itself, all "invitations to form." You can readily think of others, and I won't prolong the list.

My point, of course, is that the genre is not politically neutral. I doubt that any genre is, if defined in terms of real relations between "the poet and his public" rather than timelessly. And to conclude, I want to make one more observation along the same line. An invitation to form is normally an invitation to some kind of closure; a form resolves the matter that it contains. What would closure be for the genre I am discussing? Perhaps simply the completeness of understanding the speakers, and a book like *All God's Dangers* comes close to letting things rest there. But I think that the genre releases energies that resist such closure, and the repose or resignation that would go with it. The authors of these books—if I may overstate a bit—have become traitors to their own class, and in some measure to the society itself. Understanding and resignation would not satisfy *them*, as their having written the books bears witness. A book in this genre implicitly or explicitly poses the question, whose side are you on? It invites the audience to forego the isolated comfort of reading and the satisfaction of closure. It asks them to take a critical stance toward the society; it poses anger and action as the only alternatives to guilt or smug ignorance. And it does this whether the author intends it or not.

But what action can the audience take against so complicated a thing as injustice? There is no easy answer. Hence, the books cannot take the form of a simple exhortation, and any more self-contained form would betray the terms of the genre. This is why, I believe, the genre tends away from resolution, why it ultimately subverts form, and cannot contain the energies it provokes.

8 Teaching as Theoretical Practice

The foregoing essays on literature all had their origins in my teaching of undergraduates. Like many of us, I take on a course assignment or invent a course of my own, think my way through texts and issues in the late night or early morning, scramble to prepare for class, test and often alter my ideas in the exchange with students, and sometimes have the serendipity of a good new thought, adrenalin-driven, in the middle of a class. After the semester is over, along may come an invitation to lecture, give a paper, or contribute an article to a book; often, then, I send my mind back into that confusing but exhilarating process, look over lecture notes that fed into good classes, and begin working up those half-formed ideas for an audience of peers. The working-up may include more research; it will involve the tightening of arguments and concepts. Very likely it will also prompt a movement toward more theoretical language, and even the introduction of theoretical issues that were nowhere explicit in the course. Pedagogical thrusts and sallies have now undergone a transformation into the discourse of professional intellectuals.

How do we transport theory in the other direction, back to the classroom? As theory has become the privileged discourse in our major journals and at our conferences, a gap has widened between the language we use in those arenas and the language(s) we use in our daily practice. To be sure, some of us can and do teach unmediated theory, in seminars or advanced classes. But most of us spend most of our time teaching composition or literature—and that mainly to undergraduates. Should theory enter into that discourse? My answer is: Yes, sooner or later, one way or another; or the theory in question is void. I'm suggesting that theory "for its own sake" is a self-indulgent project of distinguishing ourselves from the ignorant laity. If anyone wants to reply that theory is the advancement of knowledge, I ask, "for whom"? Transmission of knowledge to students is no demeaning or special test to which humanists alone must submit; theoretical physics has the same goal. We all try to know the world, and keep that knowledge alive and growing by teaching it.

To my mind, we differ from the physicists mainly in the sort of thing we call theory, and in how we connect it to phenomena. Our theory is softer—I would be happier if we used the word *ideas*, most of the time, instead of *theory*—and it is harder to detach from the things it is about, as is evident by the absence from it of mathematics. But in a way, those differences make it easier to teach. We can integrate it with the practice of reading texts, which is our equivalent of doing experiments and making observations. And I think we must do so, not just for the sake of theory, but for the good of our students. They cannot test the implications of one way of reading against those of another without some kind of theoretical grid. Nor can they easily interrogate ideas about culture and history that they have taken in from the capitalist milieu, unless the alternatives show forth in clear outline. In fact they may not even notice that the leftist professor is inviting them to read with a different set of interests and commitments in their ten o'clock class from those brought by the Christian humanist professor to their eleven o'clock class.

The question is not whether to incorporate theory; it is how, and how explicitly, to do so. I approach this question in words addressed in the first instance to my students, in a course titled Modern American Fiction, 1918–1940, and by reflecting on those words. Just as cultural and literary theory resist autonomous formulation, so do theories of the pedagogy of theory; I can best get at what seem to me the issues by saying what I try to do.

Specifically, I encourage students to read and ponder literature as part of the historical process, and in engagement with some ideas about how history happens and how consciousness and culture interact with material life. My framework of ideas is marxist (and feminist—but I'll limit myself to the former, here). And of course I can assume no prior knowledge of these ideas, any more than I could if I were drawing upon semiotics or the theory of myth. Furthermore, Modern American Fiction is a period course, with the usual commitment to a fairly long list of novels, as well as readings in social, literary, and economic history. So there is no time for a leisurely study of theory. I have to invoke it as a kind of counterpoint to other activities.

Needless to say, this stretches my attention and that of the students. I make it clear to them that we are embarked upon a large, messy project rather than a neat, encompassable one. For instance, at the beginning of the course, when I have assigned a brief excerpt from Terry Eagleton's *Marxism and Literary Criticism*, I say to them—in writing, for reasons I'll explain later:

As Eagleton says, literature—and more broadly, consciousness—is part of a whole way of life built on and around the economic forces and relations that propel any society. So "To understand literature . . . means understanding the total social process of which it is part" (5–6). He soon acknowledges that "this may seem a tall order to the student of literature" (7); and I would drop the word "seem." It's not just a tall order, in fact; it's impossible. You can't comprehend a "total social process"; neither can I or anyone else. But this only means that we (you and I) are in the situation that *always* holds in humanities classrooms: we are trying to understand something infinitely complex—a world in which everything is connected to everything else. We are trying, that is, to do something we can never complete, or maybe even do very well. That's cause for modesty, but not for giving up the effort. Whatever we accomplish is better than nothing, certainly better than the blank ignorance about culture and history that is the air we breathe in this society.

Yet I do not begin by striving for the totalizing comprehension to which Eagleton refers. I start with something like close reading, but directing it toward an exploration of social and historical consciousness, working up to the point where I can bring Eagleton's discussion of ideology into focus. For instance, this is how I move into Wharton's *The Age of Innocence*, our second novel:[1]

To make the challenge less intimidating, it may help to start small, with some particulars about *The Age of Innocence*, taking it on (what seem to me) its own terms. This is not a general method—I *have* no general method—but a handy way to proceed at the beginning. So let me start by asking what consciousness the novel establishes, what kind of experience it asks you to become involved in.

You enter a world tightly circumscribed. The narrator calls it "the world of fashion" on p. 3, "society" on p. 5 ("never appearing in society without a flower . . . in his buttonhole"), and "New York" on pp. 1 and 8. The second and third of these names make clear what an exclusive consciousness you have come into. For these people, society *is* this small elite; New York *is* the "brilliant audience" assembled at the Academy of Music. (Have you heard of "the 400"? That was roughly the number that could fit into the ballroom of Mrs. William Backhouse Astor in the 1870s, so "the 400" became a nickname for the only people who counted.) You will not meet many people from outside this group, in *The Age of Innocence*. In Chapter 1, for instance, only one is mentioned, and that generally: "the cold-and-

gin congested nose of one's own coachman" (4). A servant, a non-person—
there only because he is needed by the people who count, and referred to
contemptuously. As you read the novel, notice how—and how rarely—
people outside the group appear.

And think about the other exclusions. The special world of the novel is a
few square miles of Manhattan, along with a few places where "New York"
goes for recreation: the great houses on the Hudson, Newport, St. Au-
gustine, Paris, London. In between, there is nothing, just as there are no
workers, no immigrants (though there are "foreigners"), no farmers (check
out the one exception to this). There is virtually no *work*—we find out only
on page 84 what Newland Archer's job is (some job!). Food, houses, dresses,
silver, draperies, are just magically there, when needed by the wealthy.
Think about what is and isn't included in the consciousness of the novel, in
its "world." The scope is narrow.

Within that scope, values are also narrow, and rigid. Preserving "society" is high on the list, "keeping out the 'new people' whom New York
was beginning to dread and yet be drawn to" (3). That has to do centrally
with marriage and money, as you will find out in exquisite detail, and also
with the usually-unspoken rules that govern the conduct of society. It is
"not the thing" (4) to get to the Opera early; Newland understands the
"duty" (5) of using two monogrammed brushes to part his hair; Lawrence
Lefferts, the expert on "form," can "tell a fellow just when to wear a black
tie with evening clothes and when not to" (8). More consequentially, the
elaborate rules which govern relations between men and women are a
main theme of the novel.

Given this consciousness and these values, you can predict that action
itself will be narrowly defined in the novel, even before you discover that
the climactic action of the first chapter is the appearance in Mrs. Manson
Mingott's box of a young woman with the "Josephine look," and the reaction her entry provokes: "Well—upon my soul!" and "My God!" from Lefferts, and "I didn't think the Mingotts would have tried it on" from Siller-
ton Jackson. That such shock waves emanate from the Mingotts' decision
to appear in public with a family member who has left her husband shows
what small events count as big actions in this narrative. That this is the only
significant event in eight pages suggests that the *meanings* of an action are
more central to this novel than the action itself; and that ratio of act to commentary will hold throughout the novel—probably to the considerable
impatience of some of you. By other standards, nothing much happens in
this novel: invitations, visits, refusals, words said and not said, a wedding,
a bank failure. Yet these are presented as tremendously meaningful.

Of course there's another part of the novel's consciousness, right from
the start—the narrator's humor and satire. (Try to figure out how distinct
this is from that of Newland Archer, whose point of view the narrator generally adopts.) It's quietly there from the outset: "remote metropolitan distances above the Forties'"; "excellent acoustics, always so problematic a

quality in halls built for the hearing of music"; "democratic principles."
It's a little more pointed in reference to the affair that had nearly ruined
Mrs. Rushworth's life, and "disarranged [Newland's] own plans for a whole
winter" (7). It supplies a steady perspective on the small moral universe of
these people: Mrs. Manson Mingott, the boldest of them all, had "put the
crowning touch to her audacities by building a large house of pale cream-
colored stone . . . in an inaccessible wilderness near the Central Park," a
house that remains as "visible proof of her moral courage" (13).

But we can't take this satire as the novel's main perspective. If we did,
the novel would have only the slightest interest for most of us: OK, so
these are trivial, self-important people with quaint mores; is that enough
to keep us reading for 350 pages? (Not me.) Wharton's gentle mockery isn't
the final word, because the novel's main characters are more generous and
intelligent than what the satire mocks, and because the ethos of "New
York" causes them pain and deprivation. One can mock the "system" (8),
but one can't dismiss it, because it damages human beings. For instance:

1. It represses sexuality—for women more than men, but for men too;
and even within marriage, since preparation for marriage desexualizes
women and teaches men to expect the erotic only from "bad" women. This
is too obvious for commentary. I'll just mention that one intelligent critic
(Elizabeth Ammons, *Edith Wharton's Argument with America*) holds that
"the subject" of this novel is "fear" of female sexuality, in the person of
Ellen Olenska. I think that's too specific, but not bad.

2. The system deforms *all* relations between men and women. Again, no
need for commentary, because after Newland's outburst—"Women ought
to be free—as free as we are" (42)—Chapter VI begins with several pages
of a devastatingly acute and explicit critique of patriarchy. (Read it now, if
you haven't: do you think Wharton fully endorses it? Is this a feminist
novel? Why does Wharton give these insights to a *male* character?)

3. The system destroys honesty, because so much of human life is labeled "unpleasant" and hence undiscussable: "Does no one want to know
the truth here, Mr. Archer?," asks Ellen (78). And Newland himself recognizes that he lives in a world "where the real thing was never said or done
or even thought" (45). Very often, the key part of a dialogue is what Newland thinks, and wants to say, but does not (145, 232, 237, 295, and dozens
of other examples). Several times, he is on the edge of saying the "real
thing" and taking some responsibility for his life, but he can't, and when
he can it's too late.

4. In short, the system badly impairs the self. Ellen wants to be "free"
(e.g., 109, 111), but can't. No more can Newland. May not only can't, but
"had not the dimmest notion that she was not free" (195). It's futile for
Newland to burst out at her: "Original! We're all as like each other as those
dolls cut out of the same folded paper. We're like patterns stencilled on a
wall" (83). The rules and the power behind them have made the possibility
of an untrammeled self as unattainable as it is desirable.

So the novel appeals to values far deeper than the sophisticated, "modern" ones carried along by the satire and humor. It appeals to values that are undoubtedly important to many of you, and if so, you have to care about what's at issue in the novel, that is, much more than a silly stuffiness that one can brush aside with a knowing gesture.

Well, if "Society" crushes its most decent members, is the presiding attitude of the novel one of resentment, rage, and good riddance? Pretty obviously not: the narrator (and Wharton, I'd say) finds this social milieu fascinating, even noble, as well as restrictive and foolish. Why? You'll find lots of answers as you read, but for an important one, please turn for a minute to the middle of p. 265, and read to the end of the chapter. The extraordinary translation, in the long paragraph on p. 266, of May Archer's brief sentence makes it as clear as anything in the book that the "hieroglyphic" code of this world is more than "a set of arbitrary signs" (45): it is a subtle instrument for expressing—and *living out*—the most complex meanings. The culture is not just hollow and fraudulent. It is a rich though flawed achievement of human beings living together over historical time. Its passing can occasion the same kind of sadness we might feel at the passing of any traditional society. Human variety and possibility have been diminished, and the loss is irretrievable.

Wharton explicitly encourages an anthropological perspective. Right at the beginning, New York's code of conduct is compared to "the inscrutable totem terrors that had ruled the destinies of his forefathers thousands of years ago" (4). We find (45) that people of "advanced culture" are beginning to read "books on Primitive Man"; Newland finds that "his readings in anthropology" (69) give him insight into the workings of his society. The wedding of Newland and May—the structurally central event of the novel, both in that it occurs just halfway through, and that all other events either lead up to it or proceed from it—is "a rite that seemed to belong to the dawn of history" (179), and secrecy about the location of the bridal night (sex, get it?) is "one of the most sacred taboos of the prehistoric ritual" (180). The language of totem and taboo, rite and ritual, tribe and clan, matriarch and patriarch, runs through the whole narration, climaxing in a terrifyingly polite ceremony at the Archers', which Newland understands as "the tribal rally around a kinswoman about to be eliminated from the tribe" (334). Of course most of this vocabulary suggests an unenlightened way of life; still, the loss of any culture diminishes us, and as Newland muses years later, "there was good in the old ways" (347).

Where does this anthropological consciousness come from? Is it the icily neutral distance of science? I think not. Partly, it comes from the historical distance Wharton and her readers (1920) would naturally feel, looking back on the early 1870s. More about that in the next non-lecture. But within the novel, too, this consciousness has perceptible links, not to a supposedly objective science, but to a way of life apart from that of New York society, and with claims and values of its own. Think again of the books on Primitive Man: who reads them? People of "advanced culture"—intellectuals? *Newland* reads them, and reads much else that is "advanced" (George Eliot, George Meredith, Nietzsche), as well as much that is old and beautiful. Why is Newland Archer fit to be the hero of this novel? He may flatter himself a bit in feeling superior to other members of the club, because of his having "read more, thought more, and even seen a good deal more of the world, than any other man of the number" (8), but again and again his Culture, capital "C", of poetry, fiction, philosophy, music, and art seems to qualify him for more refined feelings, and a broader perspective than the others. What has made Ellen Olenska so much wiser and freer and deeper a person than the other women? Her suffering, of course, but mainly her roots in the high culture of Europe, by comparison to which New York is a provincial backwater. What keeps "New York" that way? Partly its isolation from artists and "people who write," the people among whom Ellen chooses—unfashionably—to live, on 23rd St. A cosmopolitan awareness is woven through the book, affording a breadth of vision to which New York society appears narrow, like a tribe at the dawn of history.

That awareness gains authority, also, from the only two characters in the novel who, though outside Society, are given some attention: Winsett, with his sad irony and his decent family life; and, much more important, M. Rivière. The latter's part is small, but he comes through as the only person in the novel who is—within limits set by his circumstances—both entirely honorable and his own free self. Check out the passage on p. 200, where Rivière articulates his philosophy: I don't think there's another passage in the book that gives such a glimpse of autonomy and liberation—and this good life is entirely bound up with books, ideas, the arts.

I'm suggesting that the ideal behind the anthropological view of New York, and behind the narrator's voice, is that of the free intellectual or artist, bound to no class or country, citizen of the republic of letters. (If so, that's not too surprising: such a person was Edith Wharton, or she tried to be; and after all, a novel is written by a novelist, who more than likely has her own professional ideology!)

Now, back to the beginning, and let me wind this up fast—it's already too long. I set out to explore the consciousness that we enter when we read *The Age of Innocence*. That turned out to be fairly complex. How might it be related to the "total social process" that Eagleton asks us to consider? Literature, he says, following Marx, belongs among the "forms of social consciousness" which overlay the productive base of a society. It is part of "ideology," that complex of beliefs and values and habits which makes the existing power relations of the society seem "natural," or invisible (4–5). He qualifies this in two ways: an ideology is a complicated and contradictory phenomenon (6–7), appearing differently in different classes and individuals; and art is not *just* ideology, but often a critical or subversive force, too (17–19).

Here's how I suggest viewing *The Age of Innocence*, against this background of ideas. On one level, the fiction stays within the ideology of New York's (capitalist) dominant class, *c.* 1875—accepts as limits its definition of people who count, its values, its customs, all the blinders that allow it a serene confidence in the propriety of its wealth, privilege, and power. But of course Wharton also permits us to "feel" and "perceive" this ideology, "thus revealing to us (its) limits" (Eagleton, 18–19). She does this through the satire of her narrator, through the troubled consciousness of Newland Archer, through the "anthropological" perspective, through the suffering that "New York's" ideology brings to characters we are supposed to care about. In spite of the nostalgia that enters the novel, I doubt that anyone reading it would come away thinking the Mingotts, Van Luydens, Leffertses, etc. a fit set of rulers for a society the reader would want to live in.

But beyond that is another level still, where the values reside by which that ruling class is found wanting. The free, untrammeled, unique, "original" individual, expressing itself freely (including sexually), above or outside of any particular society or set of institutions, free through ideas and literature and art and conversation: this is the ideal that the novel privileges—even though Wharton and her narrator concede that it is all but impossible to achieve. I've called this an ideology of writers and intellectuals, who stand apart from bankers and industrialists and stockbrokers and often bitterly criticize them. But this romantic ideal of the free self, I suggest, is critical of the capitalist world order only from a point of view internal to it; it is itself a form of capitalist ideology—of individualism, specifically, which has its base in the ideology of the free market and of free competition.

Think about it, and let's debate it in class.

Ideology is a key concept, and a notoriously vexed one; I have trouble with it; so do students. I return to it again and again through the course. It is the bridge between fictional texts and the historical process, impossible to understand through merely synchronic analyses like the one just excerpted.[2] Students need to know something about economic and social history, and about class. To repeat, I ask them to read a variety of materials to help ground our discussion of novels and consciousness. But those readings would add up to little more than fragments, without something like a historical overview. I attempt that, from time to time, fully aware of how crude the attempt must be.

I do not reach that level of analysis until the fifth week of the course. After commenting about awareness of historical change on the part of Newland Archer, Jim Burden (in Cather's *My Ántonia*), Amory Blaine (in Fitzgerald's *This Side of Paradise*), and Frederic Henry (in Hemingway's *A Farewell to Arms*), I turn to fictions whose leading characters have little or no such awareness (James T. Farrell, "A Jazz-Age Clerk"; Katherine Brush, "Night Club"; and the first hundred pages or so of John Dos Passos, *The Big Money*), a fact that I try to connect to their lack of privilege and education—their different class position. But what is historical awareness an awareness *of?* Since we are discussing fictions that claim to be mimetic of American life, I believe it legitimate, indeed necessary, to see them as all signifying in one way or another the process of history as it actually happened (!) in this society. (Without some partly independent account of history, there is no way to consider fiction as mimesis—one of many unpleasant results of dissolving history into "textuality.") By this time in the course students have heard and read several empirically based discussions of the great transformation of American society between about 1875 and 1920. Now I try to make my premises clear about the forces behind that transformation, and I gather my energies to a high level of abstraction:

What brings about historical change, especially epochal change? Why does history happen? Marxists locate the answer to this question in *production*, the fundamental relationship of human beings to nature and to one another. To explain why, I return to the idea of *forces* and *relations* of production, mentioned all too briefly by Eagleton.

Forces of production include materials used in growing and making useful things; tools, machines, and (in our epoch) factories; and also skills, techniques, and knowledge—all the accumulated capabilities of the producers. Relations of production are the social structures and processes within which production takes place. In our epoch, for instance, they include the legal relationship of private property, processes for exchanging money and commodities, the boss-worker relationship, and many others. A central relation, almost the defining characteristic of capitalism, is that of the labor market, in which most people sell—as a *commodity*—their labor power, to an employer who will then extract their labor during the specified time of work. Another crucial relation concerns the social *surplus:* everything that is produced beyond the minimum necessary to maintain a stagnant society from one generation to the next. (In every non-stagnant society, there is conflict over possession and use of the surplus, sometimes muted and sometimes intense.) Most past societies have produced a surplus, but the ways in which it emerges and in which it is controlled differ sharply from one epoch to another. In capitalism, uniquely, the surplus emerges in the form of *profit*, and control of it partly defines the bourgeoisie, or capitalist class. This is another relation of production.

All right, change: forces of production are generally dynamic, as individuals and groups devise ways to produce more things or new things, or to cut down the labor required, and thus to better their material lives. Relations of production, by contrast, are conservative. Laws and institutions, for instance, fix in place relations of power and privilege, which the beneficiaries will hang onto in every way possible. So within any mode of production, a tension grows between new forces and old relations. Eventually, the class allied with the new forces asserts its dominance. This may happen gradually and without full-scale class war, as, in the Northern states, industrial capitalism outpaced the old "domestic" mode of production, and capitalists took control of the future from landowners and small farmers. Or it may happen suddenly and violently, as the Civil War abruptly ended the slave mode of production in the American South. (Need I add that every term and every sentence in this thumbnail sketch could be elaborated and disputed endlessly?)

From here I edge back toward the main subjects of the course, tying historical materialism to the transformation of American life in "our" period. Then I attempt to indicate how marxism, as a totalizing theory, reaches with explanatory power into areas of experience directly rendered by the fictions themselves. I touch on the new domination of country by city, on life among strangers as a new and intimidating condition, on the mimesis of alienated labor, and on the antagonism of work and leisure, all with brief reference to the fictional texts of the week. Here is one example of such a movement from theory into text:

In capitalist society, almost all production is for exchange, not for use by the producers. The product disappears from the ken of workers, goes into the universal *market*, and there confronts the same workers as a commodity available for purchase. One lives by commodities, hence what one can purchase, hence money. Money in the form of wages also measures one's worth; one's labor power is itself a commodity with a certain value in money terms.

Notice how these stories linger on commodities, as signifiers of personhood. Money itself becomes a daily concern, a focus of desire, an inescapable adjunct to fantasy. Mrs. Brady accepts the slights and insults of the evening so that her seventy cents of "decoy money," arranged "in four-leaf clover formation" (!-308) will accumulate more; obsessed with money and the dreary work she does for it, she fails even to notice the human conflicts and crises that rage around her. For Jack Stratton, investing a hard-earned dime in a shoeshine might transform him into a big shot in the lobby of the Potter Hotel, and magically win a "ritzy queen" for him (355–56). Charley Anderson also sits in a hotel lobby, making the connection between money and sexual fulfillment; the silk stockings, high heels, and fur-coats give off an "expensive jingle and crinkle," and he starts "counting up how much jack he had" (37). Jim's and Hedwig's money-grubbing disgusts him, but he heads back to New York dreaming of success and an expensive woman (67–68). I think it's interesting how often, in the fiction of this time, money ties in with the most fundamental of all fantasies, sexual ones. Money also defines the free, satisfied self; all these

*characters identify their unfreedom with the lack of it. People must go shop-
ping to survive, they are also coaxed and lured into markets.*

After these and a few more bridges between theory and text, I
angle back toward my point of departure, the consciousness of our
fictional characters. I point out that in the world of the giant corporation, key areas of human activity and the exercise of power recede from view, and elude understanding:

In effect, both the human activities of making things and the centers of
social control became invisible. (Compare an eighteenth-century village,
where practices of farming and craftsmanship were visible to all, and
where, to the extent that a few men had power, other men and women
knew exactly where it lay and how it was being used.) Monopoly capitalism is the most opaque mode of production and form of society, ever. Its
workings are hidden. Ordinary people cannot see the springs of its power,
though they know themselves not to share it.

*In fiction, especially fiction about "little" people, this fact of the social order
often appears in a sense of diminished scope and freedom for characters. We
have "heroes" with little power to act, and with a narrow grasp of their situations. A trapped feeling emanates from the text in what Northrop Frye called
the "ironic mode." We've seen this—even in the relatively well-positioned heroes of the first four novels: Jim Burden, drawn almost unwillingly into urban
life; Newland Archer, enmeshed by the rules of "Society"; Frederic Henry, reduced to doing what feels right, but discovering that "they" will destroy you
anyhow; Amory Blaine, stripped of his romantic illusions. The feeling is
much more overwhelming with characters like Jack Stratton and Mrs. Brady;
their freedom of action hardly extends beyond getting a shoeshine or arrang-
ing coins in a saucer. They don't act; circumstances act through them.*

*Dos Passos conveys this helplessness pointedly; most of his characters get
bumped along by forces within and without, which they barely understand,
much less control. Look at p. 63 of* The Big Money, *for a fairly typical example. Charley has been prisoner of his emotions at and after his mother's
funeral. The next day, Emiscah asks him for a date. "Before he knew what he
was doing, he'd said he'd come." He dislikes her and her life, but when she
cries and asks for a kiss, he kisses her. He goes up to her apartment even
"though it was the last thing he'd intended to do." She talks despondently, and
Charley "had to pet her a little to make her stop crying"; then, aroused, he
"had to make love to her." Charley is often on automatic pilot, when he's not
yielding to someone else's will. He has a vague goal for himself, but no plans
for achieving it; when his break eventually comes, it feels like magic.*

This sort of argument can—with much amplification and refinement in class discussion—give substance to the idea that literature
doesn't happen in an autonomous realm of culture, but responds to
and participates in the *whole* of history. The theory promotes, un-

abashedly, the view that fiction is about something. It is a form of discovery, critique, and creation, even though also determined in certain ways by forces beyond the artist's ken. With luck, the approach demystifies literary art without disrespecting it. Here is how I wind up this written lecture:

I'm saying that many of these writers imaginatively render, through individual lives, some of the deepest and most abstract features of their social system, including precisely those features new to it. Some of the characters themselves are aware of their personal lives as part of historical change. Others are not. The very lack of historical perspective—that narrowness of vision that can't look beyond the next lunch hour or the next work break or the next drink—often signals that the character is one of the little people,—a member of the working class without class consciousness, a non-participant in history.

Of course the *writers* of these fictions know more than their little people; the reader is supposed to share that knowledge. One thing to ask yourself, as you read these and other fictions of the period, is what attitude writer and implied reader (intellectuals, of a sort) have toward these characters. It can range all the way from amused condescension to pained sympathy and even admiration. Tracing such attitudes can tell us a lot about the position of writers themselves within American society, and how they felt about that position.

I hope the connections I make between literary representations and movements of history help both to promote critical reading of the texts and to animate the theory. That last is very difficult: I don't know how well I succeed. Doubtless, some students skim past the broad terms (*surplus, relations of production,* etc.), fall back on empiricist habits of understanding, and thereby render the marxist concepts familiar, sapping their explanatory power. I may make that risk greater by incorporating the theoretical terms in a relaxed, conversational style. But I think it important to fix my discourse in that key. For one thing, I want to project in the lectures my own appropriation of these ideas, their integration into my whole outlook, which the students encounter in my impromptu relations with them, too. Second, I want to contest the routine segmentation of academic discourse into special languages, a segmentation that often expresses itself in students' tacit or overt feeling that they should not have to think about "economics" or "sociology" in a literature class. Those are my rationales; I leave it to the reader to decide how well or badly I have done in this matter.

In any case, the idea is to encourage making connections, thinking holistically. I hope students will try to see an epoch in an image. I'd like them to read a narrative as a system of meanings, a response to history, and an intervention *in* history. That is hard, given the ahistorical premises of our culture, and of the literary instruction many students have had.

This brings me to the matter of students' own relations to texts, their involvement in reading, and their perceptions of the course itself as an institution. I think it important to problematize all these things. On the one side, they need to see their own responses as themselves social and historical, not as unassailably individual, much less as objectively professional (apprentice scholars, learning a Method). Here's the kind of thing I say to remind them of this aim, from time to time:

> *Digression: you have to care about the issues, but obviously you don't have to like the novel's way of representing them in a fiction. No one has to like any book, no matter how many critics and teachers say it's "great" or a "classic." The point of this course is not to get you to appreciate/like all the novels; there are some I don't much like myself. But what do you do with your reaction when you find yourself bored or contemptuous or antagonistic? I suggest making that the subject of inquiry. Remember that very many other people, in the nineteen-twenties and after, have hugely admired each of these novels. Ask why; and ask why you don't. Remember that boredom, like admiration, is a relation: a novel isn't simply boring—it bores you; a novel isn't simply great—people (who?) admire it. Exploring these relations is an important part of historical thinking about literature. If you find yourself hating a novel, take that as an invitation to learn something about yourself, as an historical being, with a class, a gender, a race, a particular background, as well as about other people who loved the same novel. (Also, keep reading; you've got to pass this course.)*

Marxist teaching cannot leave the student reader outside of society and history; to do so would be by default to privilege the bourgeois self whose autonomy marxism challenges. No more can teaching, within this theoretical framework, take the syllabus or the literary canon as inevitable. Although canon formation is not my main emphasis in this course, I try to keep alive an awareness that we have received novels of the 1920s and 1930s through a complex social process that assigns value to certain books and shunts others aside. The politics and economics of canon formation become a subject for me when I teach about novels that were quickly forgotten and later rediscovered, like *Daughter of Earth, Their Eyes Were Watching God, Miss Lonelyhearts,* and *Call It Sleep.* Why the "neglect"? What historical shifts prompted the rediscovery?

I also remind students of this process when teaching about novels that were celebrated when new. Celebrated by whom? Here is a digression on novel buying and reading, from my nonlecture on *This Side of Paradise:*

Digression: Success is success, by the irrefutable measures of sales figures and profit. But it's important to keep in mind that "the book-buying public" was and is a small minority of the whole population. Wharton's novel was a blockbuster with sales of 115,000. This Side of Paradise, a novel that "every-one" read and talked about, sold 40,000 copies in the first year and 70,000 by 1924. (Similar figures can put a novel on the hard-bound Best Seller List to-day, with the U.S. population more than twice what it was in 1920.) Suppose that each copy of a novel was read by three people, on average. Then a novel with sales of 100,000 had an audience consisting of three-tenths of one per-cent of the population. A tiny fraction, compared to the forty million who tuned into Amos'n'Andy each night on the.radio, by the end of the decade. Yet from such publishing successes, along with critical acclaim, novels like these have become "classics," and, as part of "Modern American Fiction," appear on college syllabi in 1984. Think about this cultural process, and about the authority in it of a relatively few people. Who were they?

And how did novels enter into the arena of cultural discourse in the first place? I try to touch on this question, too, *en passant.* For instance, while discussing the pertinence of *The Age of Innocence* to its time, I work back to the decisions that brought it into being, and into print:

It may seem that *The Age of Innocence* was an anachronism in 1920—not really *of* that time. A curious incident supports such a view: although Wharton's novel won the Pulitzer Prize in 1921, the *jury* had actually named another novel, Sinclair Lewis' *Main Street*, feeling that it had more contemporary relevance than *The Age of Innocence*. But the trustees (of the Pulitzer fund and of Columbia University) overruled the jury, apparently on grounds that *Main Street* gave offense to "a number of prominent per-sons in the Middle West" as Wharton put it in response to a sportsmanlike letter that Lewis wrote her. (This and much other information I'll draw upon comes mainly from R. W. B. Lewis' fine biography of Wharton.)

Still, Wharton did win the prize, and readers of 1920 gave a more telling verdict by buying over 100,000 copies of the book and making it a major best seller, while critics and reviewers praised it. The book was very much part of the cultural and commercial scene in 1920; in fact, its very genesis was commercial. In April, 1919, the editor of *Pictorial Review* offered Whar-ton $18,000 for serialization of her next novel. She jumped at the money (though she was hardly poor, with an inherited annual income of about $25,000 a year), and offered her novel-in-progress, *A Son at the Front*. Both the magazine editor and her publisher discouraged this, feeling that the public was tired of war novels. So she cooked up a scenario for a novel to be called "Old New York" (in which "Langdon Archer" and "Clementine Olenska" would spend a "few mad weeks" together in Florida, before returning to their routine lives). Publisher and magazine editor said fine, Wharton got the $18,000 plus a $15,000 advance on royalties, and she set to work. So the story had "contemporary relevance" in a crucial sense: men with the cultural and financial power to make such decisions bet that it would please the public, and they were right. Something in it spoke to the experience and needs of book-buying Americans in 1920.

For the last century, culture itself has been importantly a commercial process. To take note of that fact helps complicate crude ideas of base and superstructure within marxist theory. At the same time, it demystifies the academic category of modern American fiction, and my syllabus itself.

For marxism demands critical reflection on the processes of its own transmission, as on everything else. Hegemony exists in course catalogs, in syllabi, in the conventions of teaching, in the architecture of the classroom, in the institution of college. If critical theory leaves these things unexamined, it falls short of its purpose, whatever insights it may promote into literature and history. To question one's own profession and practices is, of course, the hardest task of all. I don't know how successful I have been in this. But— without opening up, here, the educational controversies of the 1960s and after—I want to say how I tried to interrogate the lecture system in Modern American Fiction.

I have mentioned that these lectures were written out. I called them nonlectures, because I never delivered them orally. Instead, I distributed each one, a week or so in advance of the date on which I might have given it. When the class met, I did not begin the proceedings. There were six TA-led discussion and study groups (total enrollment was fifty-five once, a hundred another time). One of the groups was responsible for a presentation, for initiating a dialogue, for somehow making the class happen. I was there, to participate in whatever role the TA group designated, or to respond to and develop what it had done. Sometimes I ended up being little more than an observer, as when one group did a well-researched demonstration of twenties radio, music, dancing, and advertising. Sometimes I turned out to be a main participant, when, for instance, a group decided to formulate questions about and challenges to my nonlecture—or, more amusingly, when they cast me as Miss Lonelyhearts, and delivered me a small packet of letters like the ones in West's novel, to which I had to respond extempore. There were surprises; there were classes that floundered. But we persisted, and I think most students gained confidence that they could take some responsibility for their education even in a so-called lecture course. And as Marx would have it, the educator got educated.

I have addressed four related questions in this chapter: how to bring theory into the teaching of literature; how to find a register of discourse that naturalizes theory—marxism, in this case—without neutralizing it; how to speak about history; and how to devise classroom practices that bring academic institutions and pedagogical habits under critical self-reflection. The first two of these questions arise for anyone who would make his or her commitment to theory explicit. The third (history) is a challenge only for those whose theory allows history to exist; alas, some do not. The fourth is an issue especially for marxists and for the few others, like feminists, who seek not only to understand the world but to change it. Marxism and feminism will not simply teach themselves, via the conventions of the traditional classroom. We must work out ways of mediating them that estrange those conventions and hint at alternatives. The language we use and, yes, the arrangement of the chairs, can make a difference.

Those last thoughts point toward the uneasy position of marxism and marxists in American universities, and I want to continue with the theme for a while without specific reference to the relations of theory, pedagogy, and American fiction which have been the main subject of this essay.

We who took part in sixties movements and became socialists, feminists, and (some of us) marxists along the way can take satisfaction from the renewal of American marxism since then. Those who do marxist scholarship have no cause to feel lonely now. There are thousands of us, at least according to a scandalized bourgeois press: the *Wall Street Journal*, the *Boston Globe*, *Business Week*, the *National Enquirer*, and other publications have run articles on marxists in academe, and whether we are likely to go away soon. Accuracy in Academia, a right-wing group, has said there are ten thousand of us whose classrooms need to be monitored for untruth and bias. We have our conferences and our journals, but are not ghettoized in these. We also give papers at meetings of established professional groups. Many of the more prestigious journals are open to our work, even solicit it. Mainstream publishers contend with left presses for our books, and there are even successful marxist *textbooks*, like Edwards, Reich, and Weiskopf's *The Capitalist System*. Academic marxist celebrities (I confess myself to be among them) go on the lecture circuit and get paid moderately well for our efforts at subversion. Perhaps the number of us getting tenure for such efforts has even exceeded the number being fired for them—though surely the most prudent course is the one I inadvertently pursued: get tenure first; become a marxist afterward. Many departments, even conservative ones, want to have a (token? polite?) marxist on board. And more to the point, some would say, we have persuasively reinterpreted wide areas of experience, and in some academic fields have so established the power of historical materialism that it must at least be attacked, rather than simply ignored as in the intellectual darkness of the early 1960s.

The danger I see in our present situation, after such a long string of gains, is a *new* kind of isolation. Acceptance in the academy came to us just as the movements that had fueled our thinking were breaking up, losing steam, or changing direction. So our respectability—precarious and partial, of course—coincides with our greater distance from vital popular movements; cynics might say that the latter explains the former. Trustees and administrators can congratulate themselves on harboring critical thinkers, so long as they produce scholarly articles and an enhanced reputation for the university rather than strikes and sit-ins. I am concerned that we may become *harmlessly* respectable. I am also concerned that our marxism may become attenuated and abstract, one theory among many, a new marxology.

An obvious antidote is to involve ourselves in campus activism, happily on the rise in the mid-1980s. Another (please excuse the platitudes) is to connect with struggles outside the university, as many have done and are doing. In this chapter, I have tried to explore some implications of a third platitude: that what universities pay us to do—teach—is our main political praxis. That holds true whether we remain conscious of it or not. And since the entire context of our work—disciplinary structure, pedagogical traditions, classroom conventions, professional goals, university regulations, students' life plans, and the mass culture that surrounds all the above—since all this conspires to deflect us from a political conception of our labor, it requires constant effort, so I find, even to keep that conception alive. It is a worthwhile effort. To be sure, teaching is not organizing—usually. But it is engagement with people other than ourselves, many of whom are open to new (and old) ways of understanding the world.

Jim Merod calls them "provisional intellectuals," expanding on Gramsci's categories of "organic" and "traditional" intellectuals;

the idea seems helpful because it suggests both the structural position of students as "intellectuals-in-process" and the uncertain end of that process. Merod is well aware of the forces aligned to draft students into contemporary North American roles analogous to that of Gramsci's traditional intellectual: places "in the professional hierarchies that wait for the most competent." Those who turn up in our classes in the more prestigious or expensive four-year colleges and universities come with an "already well-engrained sense of urgency and self-worth within the hierarchical order where success means accepting what authorities of different kinds demand, where 'playing the game' without much dissent or antagonism seems necessary."

But Merod believes it a reasonable goal for the oppositional teacher to "promote an intellectual identity in students who would otherwise remain almost wholly vulnerable to the common culture which organizes capitalist reality," to spark in them

a freely constituted, self-directed desire which, in the process of questioning received assumptions and conventional practices, challenges authority not by temporary (and mostly futile) rebellion but by working where one works in the long drawn-out effort to create resistance to domination and cultural indoctrination.

Students can come to see themselves as intellectuals, who, as Foucault suggests, can make a difference in the world by knowing how to examine specific work-regimes to advance human solidarity over capitalist hierarchies and professional cynicism.[3]

I think this a reasonable goal, too, for those of us teaching students entitled by birth, or by the occasional, semirandom successes of "equal opportunity," to a place in the professional-managerial class.[4]

III THINKING AND TEACHING ABOUT MASS CULTURE

9 Where Did Mass Culture Come From? The Case of Magazines

To my knowledge, it was Daniel Lerner who most formally brought mass culture into the scope of modernization theory. In *The Passing of Traditional Society* he outlined a model that presented developing societies as systems, in which four processes work together: more people move to cities; more people learn how to read and write; more people buy newspapers, listen to radios, and so forth; and more people vote. Furthermore the system evolves in that order: urbanization, literacy, "media participation," and "electoral participation"—to give these processes the names Lerner used. Lerner set out to formulate "correlational hypotheses which can be tested," in order to avoid "the genetic problem of causality."[1] Yet regular stages do hint at causality, and Lerner accepted the hint. Urbanization, he said, was the "key variable" in the system, for "it is with urbanization that the modernizing process historically has begun in Western societies" (p. 58). And his language gravitated toward the causal: urbanization "stimulates the needs" for participation in society: "Only cities require a largely literate population"; they also "create the demand for impersonal communication" (p. 61)—that is, for media; in turn, "a communication system is both index and agent of change" (p. 56) and so on through the steps toward political participation.

Of course neither a communication system nor cities nor the process of urbanization can literally be an agent, so Lerner needed a premise about the human agents behind these abstractions, and why they act as they do. That premise, implicit throughout his exposition, was clearly stated at the end: "the great dramas of societal transition occur through individuals involved in solving their personal problems and living their private lives" (pp. 74–75). Thus ur-

135

banization is a "movement by individuals, each having made a personal choice to seek elsewhere his own version of a better life" (pp. 47–48). A plain truth. Yet one need only recall Midland farm laborers deprived of subsistence by enclosure, Lancashire hand-loom weavers starved out in competition with power-loom owners in the 1820s and 1830s, or Irish peasants driven by repression and famine to Liverpool and New York, to want to add Marx's qualification: "not under circumstances they themselves have chosen." Likewise, it is a bit misleading, not to say callous, to think of a peasant robbed blind by his landlord and squatting in a shack town on the edge of Adana or Ankara, in Lerner's much-admired Turkey, as "having made a personal choice to seek elsewhere his own version of a better life."

But I wish to challenge the theory at another point—its account of mass culture, an area where it is more plausible to think of millions of people making real choices. People do choose to buy a newspaper or a magazine or a radio, and not sheerly out of desperation. "Media participation" is mainly voluntary (you can even stay away from Muzak if you are dedicated to the project), and it is chosen in pursuit of a better life, or at least a better Tuesday evening. What I think to be unhelpfully vague in modernization theory's account of mass culture is its undifferentiated treatment of the people and the choices that are at work. Thus Lerner writes: "when most people in a society have become literate, they tend to generate all sorts of new desires and to develop the means of satisfying them." They do so, he says, through media participation, which in turn "tends to raise participation in all sectors of the social system"—for example, in the economy, in the "public forum," in politics. The generating force here is, simply, "people" and their desires "to which participant institutions have responded" (p. 62). In other words, people get what they want; suppliers merely meet their demand.

Modernization theory may be defunct, but this combination of free market theory and functionalism has persisted as a main strand in the debate over mass culture.[2] I believe it defective because it says virtually nothing about the desires and choices of those who *produce* mass culture, or about the way "supply" and "demand" actually work. In effect, it puts CBS and a viewer tuning in "Dynasty" on an equal footing.

Needless to say, the main competing theory of social change, marxism, assigns very different roles to CBS and to that viewer. Taking off from Marx and Engels's suggestion that those who own

the means of material production control the means of mental production as well, and so make their ideas the ruling ideas of the age,
this theory has yielded much valuable work, often under titles that
dramatize its polemical force: for example, Herbert I. Schiller's
The Mind Managers and Hans Magnus Enzensberger's *The Consciousness Industry.*[3] As Enzensberger captiously puts it, "The mind
industry's main business and concern is not to sell its product: it is
to 'sell' the existing order" (p. 10). Although this theory is much
more helpful than the other, I believe it is defective because it under-
estimates the practical task of selling mass cultural products (if CBS
does not sell its product it is out of business, and thus unable to
shape anyone's consciousness), and because, unlike Lerner's theory,
it gives too little place to the choices and needs of the people who
buy mass cultural experiences. They tend to become poor suckers
who passively take subliminal commands from their rulers and believe what they are told. Lerner's theory is naïve, but any adequate
theory will have to account for the individual choices he emphasizes (although it must not, as he does, make them the sole driving
force of history).

Against this background of ideas (*theories* is really too grand a
word for them) I want to consider the way mass culture actually
came into being in the United States. I have two purposes in doing
so. First, to drive another nail into the coffin of modernization theory: I think many people hold that it collapsed because poor societies in the twentieth century could not, in their dependence on
rich, industrialized societies, follow the same path that those societies had cut in the nineteenth. This may be true, but I hold that
modernization theory also fails to explain what happened to begin
with in Britain, the United States, and elsewhere. Second: going
back to origins is a much more direct route to an outlook on cause
than a "latitudinal" study like Lerner's. By looking back we can see
what needs led some people to produce mass culture and others to
consume it. We can see that it appeared as the result of competing urgencies and projects, not of conflict-free strategies that all
adopted in concert. And we may also see *why* this kind of society
adopted mass culture (in the only sense of *why* that makes sense to
me—one that refers us to the social process in which human beings
create lives, institutions, a society).

When did mass culture arise in the United States? Not all at
once, of course, any more than the industrial revolution began on
the day Watt got his steam engine to work. Historians of cultural
forms are fond of pushing back to firsts. One traces printed adver-

tising in English back to a 1480 poster by Caxton, offering to sell rules for the guidance of clergy at Easter.[4] The first book in the Colonies was published in Cambridge in 1640, the first newspaper in 1690, the first magazine in 1741. But for nearly one hundred years after the last of these dates there was nothing in the Colonies or the new Republic that even distantly resembled modern mass culture. There were beginnings in the decades before the Civil War. In the 1820s, a crowd of over fifty thousand watched the horse race between Eclipse and Sir Henry on Long Island, and an equally large one saw a regatta in New York Harbor. Most literate households had a Bible. Tens of thousands visited Barnum's American Museum after it opened in 1842. A vigorous penny press developed in New York after 1835. There was a paperback revolution of sorts in book publishing in the 1840s. But despite these and other events, I contend that a national mass culture was not firmly established in this country until the 1880s and 1890s.

I cannot fully develop that argument here. But the point is important because I am talking about historical explanation, and social forces at work in 1830 will no more account for what happened in 1890 than vice versa. At both times people were meeting particular historical challenges. So I shall enumerate quickly some reasons for fixing upon the latter date.

First, sporting events were not regularized and repeated daily or weekly for large paying audiences until a decade or so after the National Baseball League was founded in 1876.

Second, newspapers were big but mainly local phenomena before the Civil War. Only after that time did the Associated Press spread nationally reprinted dispatches (aided of course by the telegraph); syndication of features became common in the 1880s; the comics arrived in the 1890s. That was the first moment when Americans had available a homogeneous national experience of "the" news, of opinion, of household helps, and of entertainment through newspapers. It was also the time when newspapers began to get more than half their revenue from ads, and when ads for national brands took a prominent place along classifieds and ads for local merchants.

Third, a handful of books spread through the national consciousness before the Civil War. In addition to the Bible, Webster's speller must have been almost everywhere, since 30 million copies of it were sold by 1860. Stowe's *Uncle Tom's Cabin* became a prototype for the modern best-seller, when it almost immediately sold 300,000 hard-bound copies in 1852, and then 3 million of various editions in the next eight years. But these were isolated publishing phenomena; they did not build a stable mass readership for a dependable succession of "hits." The explosion of paperbacks (really novels printed in newspaper format) in the 1840s was a move in that direction: printers drove the price of a novel down from half a dollar to a quarter, then to twelve and one-half cents, and finally to six cents.[5] A series of bankruptcies ended the scramble, but a precedent was set for the dime novels of the sixties and seventies and the cheap libraries of the seventies and eighties. But these remained essentially wildcat operations, with piracy and price-cutting as their strategies, and without habituated audiences. Only in the eighties and nineties did book publishing become a business with regular methods of hype, with many dependable outlets across the nation, and with a conscious program for replicating big sellers like *Trilby* and *Ben Hur*. The establishment of a best-seller list in 1895 can serve as an indication that the book industry took something like its modern form at about the same time as newspaper publishing and the business of sports.

The same was true for magazine publishing. I choose magazines for my case history because their transformation was dramatic, and obvious to all. A typical magazine of the 1830s, to take a starting point, claimed a circulation measured in hundreds for a few pages of solid columns of print, with few or no ads. These magazines rarely made a profit, usually died young, and reached audiences that were regional at most. There were no national magazines before 1850. Even after the railroad linked the two coasts in 1869 and even (for a while) after the Postal Act of 1879 made cheap distribution possible, magazines were not a main feature of American culture, and they barely resembled mass magazines of today. Yet shortly after 1900 they very much did, and the total circulation of monthlies alone was 64 million. How did this happen?

Magazine historians generally focus on the "magazine revolution" of 1893. And although I think it bears a different kind of scrutiny than they have given it, it was indeed a kind of revolution. The leading respectable monthlies—*Harper's, Century, Atlantic,* and a few others—sold for twenty-five or thirty-five cents, and had circulations of no more than 200,000. In the middle of the panic of 1893, S. S. McClure brought out his magazine at an unprecedented fifteen cents. John Brisben Walker, editor of the old *Cosmopolitan*, quickly dropped his price to twelve and a half cents. And in October, with much hoopla, Frank Munsey cut the price of his faltering monthly from a quarter to a dime. Its circulation went from 40,000 that month to 200,000 the following February, then to 500,000 in April, and finally by 1898 to the largest circulation in the world (so Munsey claimed, anyhow).[6] These entrepreneurs—Munsey most consciously—had hit upon an elegantly simple formula: identify a large audience that is not affluent or particularly classy, but that is getting on well enough, and that has cultural aspirations; give it what it wants to read; build a huge circulation; sell a lot of advertising space at rates based on that circulation (Munsey's rate was one dollar per page per thousand of circulation); sell the magazine at a price *below* the cost of production, and make your profit on ads.

But if this is the principle behind the mass magazines of our century—and it is—the historians' decision to fix 1893 as the critical moment is only a narrative convenience. Not only had at least one of the elite monthlies (the *Century*) built up a large advertising business during the 1880s, but other magazines had also built mass audiences during that decade. One such group was the women's magazines. Even before Munsey's "revolution," but after improvements had been made on the formulas of earlier magazines like *Godey's Lady's Book* and *Peterson's*, the *Delineator* was selling half a million copies and the *Ladies' Home Journal* 600,000; the *Journal*, furthermore, cost only five cents through the eighties and ten cents when Munsey made his move. The historians' emphasis on 1893 seems to discount magazines for women (Munsey himself, for some reason, never regarded the *Journal* as a magazine). It also dismisses another group of pioneers, with what amounts to cultural snobbery if not class contempt: magazines called *The Youth's Companion*, the *People's Literary Companion*, and *Comfort* all had circulations of more than half a million at some time before 1893. These printed fiction and features, but were given over (primarily) to ads: in effect, they were mail-order catalogs dressed up as magazines to meet postal regulations, and were often sent free to "subscribers" with little or no actual effort to gather in renewals.

In short, in the 1880s editors and publishers first succeeded in basing their business on low prices, large circulations, and advertising revenues. And the great editors of the 1890s, who turned this principle into even greater profits, understood it well. Edward Bok of the *Journal* served his apprenticeship under Frank Doubleday in the advertising department of Scribner's in 1884, and was head of advertising for two Scribner's periodicals at the time when he was sensing the untapped market for a national women's magazine. Frank Munsey had drawn the right conclusion from his earlier troubles with a youth magazine: he had built up a large circulation among young people for the *Golden Argosy,* but later saw that his audience was of little value to advertisers, since it had little money to spend. Both Bok and Munsey were quite consciously looking for a mass readership not served by magazines, but attractive to advertisers.

What actually happened in 1893, then, was an extension of a revolution already underway. Munsey, McClure, and Walker fused two business practices that were already working well, but separately. They took from the women's magazines and the cheap weeklies the idea of delivering a large group of consumers to advertisers, and from the leading monthlies they took the idea of appealing to people who wanted, as Lerner puts it, to "participate" in the new national society that was evolving. How they accomplished this second thing, I shall briefly relate at the end of this essay. For now, suffice it to say that their magazines gave a very large group of readers the sense of participation in a mainstream of culture rather than in an elite tributary identified with family, old money, universities, the past.

So magazines rather suddenly took on a central role in national life. I have mentioned only a few of the leaders, but the phenomenon was quite widespread. At the end of the Civil War the total circulation of monthlies seems to have been, at most, 4 million. It was about 18 million in 1890, and 64 million in 1905.[7] To bring those figures down to scale a bit, in 1865 there may have been one copy of a monthly magazine for every ten people in the country. By 1905 there were three for every four people, or about four to every household. And for a contrast, while monthly magazine circulation was more than tripling between 1890 and 1905, the total circulation of newspapers and weekly magazines rose only from 36 million to 57 million—less than that of all monthlies.[8] By this measure, monthly magazines had become the major form of repeated cultural experience for the people of the United States.

But not for *all* of its people. Who were magazine readers? I would like to know of some careful research on that. Without such research, we are left with conjecture based on content, and (perhaps better) on what readership the editors were trying to reach, and what readership they thought they had succeeded in reaching. McClure, for instance, derived his idea of what "people" wanted by peddling kitchenware and trinkets through Indiana, Illinois, Michigan, and Ohio during his summer vacations from Knox College, about 1880. He wrote: "My experience had taught me that the people in the little towns . . . were just like the people in New York or Boston. . . . I felt myself to be a fairly representative Middle-Westerner. I . . . printed what interested me, and it usually seemed to interest the other Middle-Westerners."⁹ These were people who had cash to buy coffee pots, clothes, and knick-knacks, who owned homes, who had what McClure called "business affairs" (farms, shops, trades) and who were eager for more contact with the wider society. (Note that McClure regarded them as much like their eastern counterparts: "people" were the same everywhere.)

Cyrus Curtis, the most adroit businessman of them all, intentionally shaped the *Ladies' Home Journal* as a "high class magazine" for people aspiring to respectability. He and Bok carried out some rudimentary market research in the early days, studying some neighborhoods where the *Journal* was read; Curtis claimed in 1893 that "the majority of *Journal* readers lived in the suburbs of large cities . . . and that his small-town readers belonged to the professional ranks in their communities."¹⁰ Since he was advancing this claim in order to attract tony advertisers, I suspect he overstated it. But I would also guess he was right in thinking his readers *wanted* to be professionals and suburbanites, and shaped their working and domestic lives with that in mind. In short, the main audience for these magazines was what was called then, as now, the "middle class": people in small businesses, professionals, clerks, tradespeople, farmers, and significantly, wives and mothers from this same stratum.

To put the point negatively, the readership was not "people," not the entire population (magazines were not a universal medium like television). It was not the 20 percent who were immigrants or children of immigrants; not the 12 percent who were black; not the poorest Anglo-Saxon farmers and workers; but probably a full half of the white "native" stock and something like a third of all the people. It is worth emphasizing this point, both to counter the vagueness of modernization theory and to oppose an implication carried by the categorical term *general magazines* in use among historians that some magazine audiences had no social definition. They may not have grouped together as cycling fans or young boys or farmers, but *Atlantic* spoke to an audience grouped by class perspective, and *Munsey's* addressed another one. Then as now, magazine audiences were segmented, organized around particular interests or strategies for living in society. And the segments were organized by interest (in both senses of the word) *for the purpose* of selling their attention to advertisers.

As I turn to the question of why magazines became a form of mass culture when they did, I want to keep the idea of purpose clearly in mind. Purpose has no place in the classic formula of Harold Lasswell upon which almost all bourgeois communications research has built; that formula includes who says what, how, to whom, and with what effect, but not *with what intent*. And, in Lerner's model, purpose appears only as a need expressed by participants and suppliers in the neutral market place. I will try to be a good deal more specific than that, if still too vague for my own satisfaction.

Why magazines? Why then? First, it may be wise quickly to dismiss one frequent answer: technology. Indisputably, the rise of mass magazines could not have happened without certain mechanical and chemical innovations, notably the rotary press, stereotype plates, and photoengraving. But the rotary press had been around since 1847, and the other two since the 1860s. As with most media techniques, all were developed gradually, and *in response* to commercial needs, not in advance or independent of them. (New rotary presses of record capacity, for instance, were built to order for *Century* in 1886 and *Munsey's* in 1898).[11] All the necessary technology depended on simple and well-known principles, and was applied as capital would have it.

If technology must be cited, we had better note a much broader set of developments after the Civil War: electric lights and motors, trolleys, the telephone, and a sixfold expansion of railroads by 1890. Most crucial, I think, was a huge increase in manufacturing generally. The total value of manufactured things passed that of farm products in 1850, and doubled every ten or fifteen years through the 1890s.

Consider this transformation still more abstractly: in the 1880s and 1890s, capital expanded faster than at any other period in our history; in fact, capital formation climaxed precisely in the years 1889–93. But I do not wish to make too much of that conjuncture. The point is that the progress of competitive capitalism reached a crescendo during the period just before and during the growth of the new magazines.

The facts and events are well known. As capitalists raced ahead without external check, making fortunes and transforming the society, they were experiencing rather painfully the *internal* contradictions of the new system:

1. For the system as a whole, there were crises of overproduc-

tion, boom and bust. Between 1873 and 1897, there were fourteen years of recession or depression.

2. For individual firms, there was great instability. The free market was an intolerably dangerous environment, and remained so in spite of ingenious efforts to make it less free: bribery, rebates, pools, trusts, outright monopoly. Nothing worked well for long.

3. Profitability fell off. Marx's theory of the declining rate of profit may not apply to later phases of capitalism, but it worked as he predicted in the competitive capitalism of the American nineteenth century. The worst period was 1889 to 1898.

4. Attempts to cope by reducing wages and taking more control over the labor process led to all but open class war. Indeed, it became quite open at intervals throughout this period: 1877, the "Great Upheaval"; 1886, Haymarket; 1892, Homestead, the Idaho mine wars, the New Orleans streetcar strike; 1894, 750,000 workers on strike at one time or another.

By concentrating their energies on production and on price competition, businessmen had supervised the building of a tremendous productive system, but a system whose advance they could not well control, either as a class or as individuals; it was a system whose chaos led simultaneously to killing risk, diminishing profits, and social rebellion. The challenge for them was to create an environment in which they could carry on the process of accumulation with less uncertainty and resistance. Their attempt to do so through monopoly was never more than a temporary success, even before the federal government began its half-hearted and feeble interventions. Other corporate strategies that later proved effective, such as tacitly agreeing not to compete through prices, getting the government to regulate competition, or enlisting the cooperation of unions to administer industrial peace, were for one reason or another not yet available.

In this fix, capitalists began to hit on the idea of controlling not output or prices, but *sales*. I do not suggest a conscious, classwide blueprint for the future. Individual capitalists made specific business decisions to solve immediate problems, and the sum of those decisions was to emphasize marketing rather than production. Looking around, businessmen of the postwar period would have had no trouble noticing that, year by year, a lot more people had a lot more money. Looking back, we can put what they sensed into numbers. For instance, the number of white collar workers increased sixfold from 1870 to 1900 (and at that time the distinction

between white and blue still translated into cash, not just gentility).
Per capita income, adjusted to stable dollars, nearly doubled from
1880 to 1900. And because of the rapid growth in numbers of workers, the total amount of "discretionary" income available grew
even faster. We can gather an idea of the magnitudes involved by
noting that even though industrial workers lagged behind others,
the total wage paid to them quintupled, from $380 million to $1.9
billion, between 1860 and 1890.[12] Not only was there vastly more
cash circulating; in addition, a larger and larger portion of the
people were dependent on purchases in the market to satisfy needs
once met through home production. So there were many new purchasing dollars to be claimed, and also a broad area of life for
businessmen to colonize and shape.

They responded to the opportunity—and to the crisis—with supple ingenuity, developing a variety of practices and institutions
that are commonplace now, but were unprecedented then. One
group of businessmen specialized in marketing on a large scale,
and created systems through which producers had to work: department stores (Wanamaker's and a few others were large operations
before the end of the 1870s); chain stores (A&P and Woolworth's, for
instance, were firmly established by 1890); and, about the same
time, mail-order firms (Sears and Montgomery Ward). While merchants were assembling and presenting these arrays of commodities, the railroads and the postal system allowed distribution of
them to people all over the country.

Markets became national. In an effort to establish their products
among many others in those markets, businessmen hit on some
practices that take us back toward the origin of mass circulation
magazines. Notably, they developed uniform packaging, to replace
bulk sales of anonymous crackers or cereal or soap. They gave their
products brand names to help buyers form habits of loyalty, and
trademarks to link a second sign to the product and so enhance its
symbolic aura. They further mythicized consumption by connecting slogans and jingles and cartoon characters to commodities. In
short, they came to depend upon advertising.

As with newspapers and magazines, it is important to see that
modern brand advertising has little in common with forerunners
like Roman signs or seventeenth-century handbills, or even the
prolific ads of the early nineteenth century. Those ads promoted a
particular service, like the stage coach from New York to Philadelphia; or a unique opportunity to buy, as when a Main Street
merchant had received a new shipment of clothes from England;

or an exchange not far removed from barter as when Mr. Robinson was prepared to sell or trade his bay mare. Those early ads were local and tied to the instant, not to a commodity that one could buy in identical form in Baltimore or St. Louis, next week or next year. And their format was austere (a few discursive lines of small type) even if their claims were often flamboyant.

It is clear that national brand advertising could not develop without transport and media, but those were not its causes. Its causes were the needs of capitalist production:

1. With high fixed costs and a low marginal cost, it made sense to keep the machines running, and therefore to strain for higher sales.

2. Production for exchange was production apart from a known use of the thing made, and apart from a guaranteed purchase; thus it made urgent sense to reach out and influence anonymous buyers in the aggregate.

3. Markets were an impersonal medium of human relationship. Manufacturers had to overcome buyers' uneasiness at dealing with complete strangers.

At early stages, human intermediaries helped solve these merchandising problems: the local shopkeeper who would vouch for the product; the peddler who at least returned each year; the drummers for particular lines who overspread the country a hundred years ago. People originally experienced impersonal markets as a kind of con game, and the huckstering during the early phase of product advertising (patent medicines, sex aids, books that would renew your life) did little to change that image. Only gradually did advertisers learn to seek and obtain confidence in particular goods and in the whole commodity-based way of life.

That did not happen until advertising arose as a separate business, with specialized techniques and knowledge. The first agency was founded in 1841, but again, "firsts" are always misleading. The early agents were no more than space brokers for manufacturers or merchants who wrote their own copy. That copy was plain, even when deceitful, and virtually unadorned with pictures. Only after the Civil War did some agents take on the writing of copy. Only then did they create visual displays (first engravings and paintings, then photographs) to which, by the 1890s, color could be added. Gradually they learned to reduce the ratio of prose to picture, of information to aura, creating the iconic links that most strikingly characterize advertising today.

Most important, not until the eighties and nineties did they light on the idea of a nationwide advertising *campaign* to launch a new product or to claim a leading share of national sales for an old one: Ivory Soap, the Royal baking powder, the Waltham watch, Heinz 57 varieties. It was at that moment, too, that they tried out what are known as "primary appeals," pushing not just a brand, but the idea of bringing into one's daily routines a whole new genre of commodity, the idea of changing one's life: bicycles, canned goods, sewing machines, gum, eventually automobiles, Nabisco crackers, Kodak cameras, Coca Cola. If it did not create new needs, such advertising certainly did channel present needs into new habits and dependencies. More broadly still, advertising became a strategy for creating a new social order beyond the workplace, and for shaping people's social identities in leisure time, as consumers. Advertisers strove to organize home life around commodities and turn the home itself into a sanctuary away from work, a place where what was remembered as human caring and closeness could survive, mediated by products.

One can abstract this complex historical process into figures. Advertising expenditures were 22 cents per capita in 1865, but $1.13 in 1890.[13] This was the only period until after World War I when advertising revenue grew rapidly as a portion of the gross national product. And if it were possible to sort out brand advertising from merchant advertising, the shift would appear even more striking. In just three decades advertising had metamorphosed from a small and primitive activity into a skilled practice central to economic and cultural life.

Magazines played a central role in this change from the start. By the 1870s J. Walter Thompson had seen them as a likely vehicle for national brand campaigns. By the 1890s, all the major agencies had entered the magazine field. In this they showed a fine harmony of purpose with new magazine entrepreneurs like Cyrus Curtis and Frank Munsey who had no genteel scruples to prevent them from seeing themselves as in the advertising business. From the perspective I have adopted, then, it is hardly too much to say that modern magazines were an outgrowth of advertising which, in turn, was a strategy of big capitalists to deal with the historical conditions in which they found themselves.

Of course this is one perspective only. I have adopted it to underscore my point that mass culture first arose as an adjunct to the circulation of commodities and as a partial solution to problems encountered by early capitalists. In itself, though, this way of looking at things is undialectical. Like manipulation theory, it credits or blames the bourgeoisie for everything, the workers for nothing. I need to restore wholeness to the picture—though all too sketchily— by bringing Lerner's "people" back into it—not, however, just as individuals who moved to cities in pursuit of a better life and there expressed a need to participate in media.

By the 1890s a substantial majority of adult men were selling their labor power to somebody else for wages. This much-studied transition from an earlier system of work meant a great loss of autonomy for workers. Clock in, clock out, follow the pace of the machine, give over to your boss the tasks of conceiving and planning. With this degrading of work came a loss of authority at home. As major kinds of production moved from farm and village to factory, the economic basis for the old patriarchal family was eroded. And as the man gave up autonomy and authority, so did the woman, in that the new system devalued the kind of work she did, since it was outside the money economy and thus outside the main calculus of value. Finally, because the family no longer produced what it used, its members had to go out into the market to satisfy their basic needs. The new system brought many comforts, too; I don't want to label it "bad" according to some ahistorical ethic, but only to insist that it confronted wage earners with a drastic change in the terms of their existence.

Advertising helped people negotiate this way of life. It helped them feel at home with commodities and their uses. It helped them trust the distant strangers who made commodities. It showed them a way to use commodities as a sign of competence and status, evidence that one knew the sophisticated and respectable way to do things. For women, consumption was at the center of their new role. They could show new skills as purchasers and users of commodities; they could show care for their families with products; they could give the home social standing by placing the right things in it. They could make it a secure and loving place where those who went out to work returned to a sphere of dignity and autonomy, a place where alienated products were brought under psychic control.

If ads helped wage earners and wives to create such a space, so did the rest of what magazines contained. After all, though subcribers may have welcomed advertising messages and symbols into their homes, they bought one magazine rather than another for its editorial content; here is where the ingenuity and intuition of the new editors came into play. This is a big subject. I will elaborate upon it in essay 10, and simply note here that dramatic changes took place in the content of magazines.

For instance, just before the 1893 "revolution," *Harper's* featured articles and stories such as "Street Scenes of India," "Agricultural Chile," "The Social Side of Yachting," and "The Young Whist Player's Novitiate," whose titles are enough to adumbrate the class appeal of this leading journal. It scanned the whole world from a tourist's perspective. It nurtured the habits and interests of a moneyed readership, along, no doubt, with a readership that *wished* it had money and could run the world. Some of the new monthlies preserved this upper-class base; most did not. But during this period all shifted their emphasis toward daily life and contemporary American society. I will mention three such emphases:

First, magazines told people how to live (as magazines do today). The *Ladies' Home Journal* offered readers in 1893 moral guidance and inspiration from wives of famous pastors. It presented memoirs by exemplary men, often writers with cultural and moral authority like Garland and Howells. It gave practical advice to girls and women on proper conduct and on practical tasks like shopping, sending packages, giving parties, trying new recipes, and wearing new fashions. The *Journal* cultivated a very personal relationship with its readers, that of a friend and counselor. (Before Bok discontinued the practice during World War I, the *Journal* staff had individually answered millions of inquiries and appeals.) And it made itself a bulwark of middle-class values against the dangerous classes (blacks, immigrants) on one side and decadent classes on the other.

Second, magazines helped readers understand how things work, and that was something one could no longer learn through daily work and community life. *Cosmopolitan* ran a "Progress of Society" section, and explained in detail how men had harnessed Niagara to produce electricity. Magazines helped middle-class people feel competent and at home in the world through a *mediated* comprehension of human action upon nature, and of nature itself as represented through science.

Third, magazines told how society works. For *society*—as opposed to *Community* and *hierarchy*—was a new object of apprehension (the word itself did not take on its present meaning until the eighteenth century, nor was there another word to express that way of looking at ourselves). And as soon as society became visible, it grew opaque. Market relations replaced direct personal relations. It was hard to tell why depressions and progress happened. The social process, like production, was invisible, but it could be investigated and reported in words. This emphasis sometimes took the form (as in *Cosmopolitan*) of laudatory articles on business and its achievements, sometimes the form (as in *McClure's*) of muckraking. But most or all of the monthlies tried to present to their public a reconstruction of contemporary society and its springs and levers.

In these ways the magazines restored to readers a sense of at-homeness in the distanced and puzzling world that capitalism had made. The extravagant use of photographs, which was one of their main appeals, seems just as related to a recognition of this need as to a fascination with a new gimmick. In sum, the contents of magazines spoke to the deepest sort of socially created needs. Magazines helped ease the passage into industrial society for working people of moderate means just as, on the other side of the class divide, they helped capitalists make that society a less menacing environment for their project of development.

I hope this account has shown modernization theory, in Lerner's version, to be of little use in explaining how mass culture arose in the United States. Urbanization was not a cause; along with mass culture, it was an effect of the way businessmen took over and reorganized production. Magazines met important needs for millions of people, but those needs were themselves historically specific and generated by the new system. To label them needs for "impersonal communication" or for "participation" is to cloud understanding, not sharpen it. Above all, magazines grew up in response to the capitalist manufacturers' power to shape consumer publics. Supplying a "people's" need for media had no place in the purpose of those capitalists nor in the intent of the advertising entrepreneurs who helped them achieve their ends; its only place was in the purpose of publishers and editors who, creative though they were and prosperous though they became, were small fry whose ingenuity would have come to nothing had they not been in a position to help the big fish control the circulation of commodities and accumulate capital. *Modernization*, it seems, is another term for *capitalist development*. It is a term that obfuscates.

What about Marxian media theory? A final word, now, about that version of it which explains mass culture as an attempt by the ruling class to control ideology. Magazines did arise from needs of the ruling class, and successful publishers themselves did quickly join the ruling class. But what the capitalists needed was to control and stabilize growth; what the publishers needed was to sell magazines to the right audiences. The former did not make ideological control an issue, and probably could not have done so. The latter had some ideological goals, but of divergent sorts, and if an editor's ideology did not correspond closely to that of his potential readers, he would fail anyhow.

Nonetheless, magazines did and do, in my opinion, contribute notably to ideological domination. How? Within the limits of the conditions given, a magazine editor's overriding aim must be the building and holding of large audiences for regularly repeated experiences. Let me say, again with draconian brevity, how I think they have done that:

1. Magazines have to be predictable (though always "new" at the same time, of course). That necessity drives their representation of life into formulas that simplify, regularize, and smooth out the contradictions of social existence. Predictable formulas also convey to readers the comfortable feeling that things are after all much the same from month to month, year to year: they tend to deny history.

2. Magazines must help readers live as they want to, must address their problems. Since magazines are read by individuals and families, they tend to show people how to live *as* individuals and families; but, especially, they show people how to improve, how to rise. With this aim, they generally take for granted everything not susceptible to private amendment. The market, property, profit, inequality, the whole base of capitalist society, all these are accepted or ignored—a backdrop for the life of individuals. And this is even more true now than it was in 1900.

3. Magazines must project a strange mixture of anxiety and optimism. If people have no anxiety they will not need magazines. If magazines offer no hope of solutions, accommodations, improvement of the self or reform of society, they will be too depressing to read. Perhaps I may make further commentary unnecessary by noting that the most successful magazine of all time, the *Reader's Digest*, is one that has beautifully managed that combination.

4. Magazines must shape a mass public that is valuable to advertisers. Readers with money count for more. Magazines speak to a group's common experience of the world, but common experiences like poverty, age, and unemployment will not support a mass circulation magazine. So magazines express the perspective of people to whom our society has been reasonably kind.

Mass magazines are a gatekeeping medium. They admit ideas and feelings into the arena of the discussable. But they work within invisible hegemonic limits, not primarily by the design of the capitalist class but because, to succeed, they must treat their readers precisely *as* masses of consumers.

10 Advertising and the New Discourse of Mass Culture

By 1890 some North American manufacturers had recognized their need to bring more order into the unruly scramble of production, and had begun developing a strategy for such control, which I touched upon in the preceding essay.[1] Seen most broadly, that strategy was to build the large, integrated corporation, which rationalized a particular kind of production by encompassing most or all of its stages within one company, creating a regulated flow from the gathering of raw materials all the way through to final sales of the product. From the viewpoint of corporate leaders, then, direct access to the minds, desires, and anxieties of a national audience was so urgent a need that they were bound to satisfy it in one way or another. And since they also had by this time great social and economic power to pursue their ends, I have assigned a causal priority to the actions of these businessmen in the forging of a national mass culture.

But as things happened, they did not themselves actually found the advertising industry or the mass circulation monthlies. Editors, publishers, and ad men did so, pursuing their own projects within limits set by the needs and power of manufacturers, as well as by the needs of people who read the magazines and bought the goods. Out of this complex agency, a new set of market relations grew. I believe that what filled the pages of the mass magazines can best be understood as an expression of those relations, though a coded one that takes some effort to perceive, so "natural" has it become in the intervening years.

In this chapter I try to read what I am calling the "discourse of mass culture," at a time when it had just begun to establish itself as a dominant idiom in our social life.[2] I begin with advertising, both because of its pivotal place in the market relations with which I am concerned, and because it expressed a core system of meanings within the new discourse. The advertising of the 1890s was sharply different from that of the 1830s, or even of the 1870s. Its words and images would have been at least as opaque to readers of earlier decades as the Maidenform ads would have been to readers of 1895. Both ad men and consumers had to create and learn a new language; in doing so they became new human beings.

To clarify this claim, I turn first to the ads reprinted here. The first example is a page from the *Atlantic Monthly* of November 1880, included here to give an idea what most ads were like on the eve of the transformation (fig. 1). I'll not comment on them, except by implication as I register a few points about the three full-page ads for breakfast foods (figs. 2–4). *They* all come from *McClure's Magazine* of October 1899, an issue that contained, rather typically, about 160 pages of ads to 90-some of editorial matter—a proportion unthinkable even fifteen years earlier.

Note, first, that these ads are for permanently available, national name brands, not for transitory, local opportunities to make a particular purchase. They appear, with variations, in issue after issue of magazine upon magazine—a discourse of *repetition* whose instances are unimportant as against their cumulative weight. This is not information, or even discourse, in the conventional sense, but part of a series of subrational assaults on memory and habit.

In accord with that principle of communication, image overrides verbal text, claiming a residual place in memory even if the reader (viewer?) skips the text entirely. *Should* she proceed into the verbal message, she will find little specific information there: the cereals all taste good; they are all healthful. These are texts intended to familiarize and soothe and reassure, not to enumerate the actual qualities of the product.

Furthermore, the product itself makes no visual appearance, except for an obscure one on the stove in the Pillsbury's ad. What saliently appears in all three is the product's arbitrary sign—its trademark—claiming all visual attention in the Cream of Wheat ad, prominently displayed on packages in the other two. The packages themselves are arbitrarily related to the product: they might as well be larger or smaller, cylindrical, made of other materials. The point is to establish the commercial *image* of the cereal, as it may be seen on the shelves and in innumerable other ads.

Through another arbitrary connection, the product is embedded in a whole way of life, full of social meaning. All three ads, two of

Figure 1. Ads from *Atlantic Monthly,* November, 1880

them strongly, link the product to the home. This is not surprising, since that's where most people eat breakfast; but the *kind* of home commands interest, however quietly. An elegant sideboard, china, silver, and an ample bowl of fresh fruit fix the social level of the Quaker Oats home. Pillsbury's Vitos adorn a modern kitchen in a house with a yard, and the cook is a maid, as her uniform shows. Cream of Wheat eaters also have servants, or are invited to imagine themselves in that condition ("ask your chef . . ."). These cereals are cheap to buy, though not so cheap as the old bulk cereals. The ads, through magical juxtaposition, associate them with affluence, respectability, and a well-regulated home establishment—a large return on a few pennies of extra cost.

And it goes without saying that these homes run on commodities: even if one has no chef or maid, one will find it easy to heat up this highly processed food. Home production is retreating into the corners of daily life, replaced by the work of strangers under corporate direction. This change goes under the sign of modernity, as the ads proclaim their products to be part of a new and progressive way of life.

Into the home, so constituted, and into the ear of the housewife addressed as *already having* such a home, comes a voice, speaking in a new key. It is conversational, familiar, sometimes humorously nagging ("How foolish to keep on eating meat . . ."). Yet it carries authority, too, like the figure of the Quaker looking out of your mirror. It knows about the gluten in wheat; it knows what "dietary experts" have said; it knows what makes an "ideal" food in the autumn. It is not the voice of the brazen huckster (P. T. Barnum), or that of the direct testimonial (an enthusiastic letter from Dr. So-and-So), or that of the haughty aristocrat—though all these earlier advertising voices may still be heard in ads of the 1890s. It is a voice *like ours*, reaching across the gap between anonymous corporation and anonymous readership, establishing in that gap a chatty, humorous, reliable, *neighborly* helper, as if to stand in place of the grandmothers and mothers who no longer live with or near the young wife or pass on to her their generational skills and wisdom.

An imagined social relation is in the process of erasing real ones. Vestiges of the real ones remain. All three ads include a corporate address: the company may be located on the map of the Republic. (How rarely this happens today, except in direct-mail ads.) Cream of Wheat retains the grocer as an intermediary, distributing free gravures to the customer. Quaker Oats mentions grocers and invites the housewife to write to the company for Mrs. Rorer's cook-

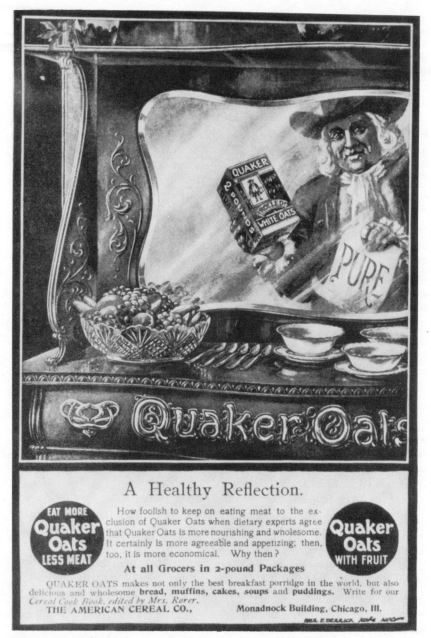

Figure 2. Quaker Oats; *McClure's Magazine,* October, 1899

An Autumn Morning Dish.

Pillsbury's VITOS, the ideal Wheat Food, can be prepared in the form of fried mush, but fried mush of unusual delicacy and ease of digestion. Fried mush made of Pillsbury's VITOS is neither greasy nor heavy. Served with maple syrup it is an ideal breakfast dish for cool autumn mornings

PILLSBURY-WASHBURN FLOUR MILLS CO., Ltd., MINNEAPOLIS, MINN.
MAKERS OF PILLSBURY'S BEST FLOUR.
Please mention McClure's when you write to advertisers.

138

Figure 3. Pillsbury's Vitos

Cream of Wheat

A Dainty Breakfast Dish, made solely of the gluten of the wheat, literally the "cream." Pure, healthful, nourishing. If you want a breakfast dainty or an ideal dessert dish ask your chef to serve Cream of Wheat, you will not be disappointed.

You should also ask your Grocer to show you those elegant Cream of Wheat Pictures which he will give you

FREE

They are not common prints but artistic Gravures which you will want to hang in the finest room in your house. You will m᷄ it if you do not look them over. **CREAM OF WHEAT CO., Minneapolis, Minn.**

Figure 4. Cream of Wheat

book. The Pillsbury ad, more modern, eschews such reminders of the chain of production and marketing, leaving the reader with the voice from nowhere and the image of her own desire—as projected by someone whose address and name are not to be found.

That someone—the Other who predetermines the field of this discourse and constructs its reader—is in fact several employees of an advertising agency. Such employees were a new species. Advertising goes back as far as periodicals, but earlier ads conveyed a direct message from seller to potential buyer. Even after the first agency was founded (1841), for decades agents were only buyers and sellers of space in periodicals. Gradually some of them stumbled on the idea of writing copy for their clients, as a a kind of free, extra service. Only after 1880 did this practice come forward as a necessary, specialized trade, and agencies took on the job of creating tailor-made images still later.

Also in the 1880s and 1890s, the more advanced agencies created the practice of the total, nationwide *campaign* to launch a new product or claim for an old one a leading share of national sales: Ivory Soap, Campbell's Soups, Remington Typewriter, Heinz 57 Varieties, Uneeda Biscuits. At that moment, too, they tried out what are now known as "primary appeals": pushing not just a new brand, but the need to incorporate a whole new genre of commodity into one's daily routines, to reorganize one's life around bicycles, canned goods, cameras, soft drinks, gum, eventually cars. The discourse they devised was a powerful agent for change, channeling old needs into new habits and dependencies, fostering new needs, pointing toward a new social order of home and leisure apart from the workplace, and surrounding commodities with the myths and ideologies of mass culture.

Some of this was quite conscious, as I've meant to suggest by reproducing the N. W. Ayer ad, from the same issue of *McClure's* (fig. 5). (A rarity in that place in 1899, such ads would later appear only in trade journals, as the actual *business* of advertising receded from the view of its mass audience.) Ayer assumes, rightly, that the trademarks and slogans it devised for the National Biscuit Company are already (after six months) embedded in the minds of every reader. It boasts of its autonomy in planning and executing the campaign— the military metaphor is fitting. It knows that ad agencies have nearly vanquished "the evils of the old way of marketing goods" (the generic crackers in a barrel, the unreliable shopkeeper, etc.). And it boasts of its reputability, though still feeling the need to dissociate its modern business from the unsavory image of older adver-

The advertising success of the century is that of "Uneeda Biscuit" and "Uneeda Jinjer Wayfer."

The name "Uneeda" was coined by us. The name "Uneeda Jinjer Wayfer" was produced by us.

The popular catch phrases, "Do You Know Uneeda Biscuit", "Everybody Knows Uneeda Biscuit" and "Now Uneeda Jinjer Wayfer" were originated by us.

The advertising campaign was planned, and is being executed in all its branches by us.

We are not in the general scramble to get an advertising order regardless of the interest of the advertiser.

We do not accept advertisements relating to vile diseases, disreputable business or intoxicating drinks.

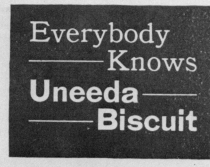

We are anxious for all the first-class advertising that can be made profitable to the advertiser and to ourselves— and only such.

Our long experience (thirty years) and our large business (the greatest in our line), should give us unequaled advantages and facilities for doing *good* advertising.

Advertising would open a profitable field to many a manufacturer who to-day is fretting over the evils of the old way of marketing goods, little dreaming of the opportunities that might be his. We are specially glad to talk to thinking men of this class.

N. W. AYER & SON,

Newspaper Advertising.
Magazine Advertising.

PHILADELPHIA.

Figure 5. N. W. Ayer & Son

tising (patent medicines, sex aids, get-rich-quick schemes, booze). It proclaims and offers for sale its mastery of consciousness.

In early issues of the advertising trade journal *Printer's Ink*, and in the archive of the J. Walter Thompson Co.,[3] one can find bolder announcements of this project. The ad men are gaining, through the 1890s, a boisterous confidence in their ability to write the copy that will strike the candid, friendly note and stick in memory (avoid "high-sounding language" *and* slang), to create the images that will rivet attention, to get these displays in the right media, to repeat and vary them through vigorous campaigns. Thompson speaks of "successful attacks on the public," leading to "quick surrender" and "complete victory." More specifically, he offers the public to his clients in segments, often explicitly in *classes:* through market research he can know exactly how one man supports a family on ten dollars a week and another on a thousand dollars a month, and what dreams and commodities may be inserted into the lives of each. He lays out quite cheerfully the goal of advertising: it "aims to teach people that they have wants, which they did not realize before"; likewise a *Printer's Ink* author defines advertising, in 1891, as "the artificial creation and stimulation of wants." It's all there in the open, as ad men talk to their clients and to one another.

They understand much, too, about the historical changes for which their labors were catalytic. Thompson knows that while the industrial revolution "solved the vast economic problem of production," it left unresolved the problem of distribution and that the latter demanded a discourse between capitalist and "consumer," so as to subjugate those unreliable agents, the country storekeeper and city shopkeeper. He knows that on the other side of the market there is a greenhorn in the city, newly dependent on commodities and fearful of dealing with strangers at a distance; advertising must implant trust, as well as desire, in this new human being. By 1909 he sees this world-historical change as essentially completed: his profession is "part of the existing commercial universe. It could not be abolished or reduced to any noticeable degree without changing the entire economic aspect of life." J. Walter Thompson wrote this just one year before the date upon which, according to Virginia Woolf, human nature changed.[4]

Of course ad men puffed their own product, just as they puffed cereal and soap. Doubtless they worked fewer miracles than they took credit for. Yet they did have spectacular successes with many consumer products, and I believe they were instrumental in facilitating the great transformation to our own kind of society. Certainly they persuaded businessman after businessman to adopt the new methods: brand names, trademarks, distinctive packages, slogans, the discourse of advertising. That success in turn put irresistible pressure on retailers to *stock* the famous goods for which their customers were clamoring. The president of a soap company described the change thus, as he looked back to the 1880s:

> Twenty-five years ago the manufacturer went to the jobber, related the merits of his goods, and arranged the terms. . . . The jobber then went to the retailer and told him that he had goods of exceptional quality, stated the terms, and the retailer ordered several cases. When the consumer came to the retailer, she asked for an article but did not specify the brand. She relied upon the retailer, who supplied her from his stock on hand. The method of twenty-five years ago is reversed today. The manufacturer goes first to the consumer. By advertising he burns it into the consumer's mind that he wants a certain brand. . . . At tremendous expense the manufacturer educates her to ask for Fels Naphtha, Ivory, Rub-No-More, Arrow collars, etc., as the case may be. The demand created, the retailer goes to the jobber asking him to furnish the articles called for. Then the jobber goes to the manufacturer.
>
> Our company sells through the jobber, and we do the rest. We create the desire for our product through advertising.[3]

Obviously this businessman welcomed the access to "the consumer's mind" offered by the ad men.

Perhaps more surprisingly, J. Walter Thompson and others also persuaded many magazine editors to take the leap into dependence on advertising, explaining that they could thereby pay writers and artists more and improve the quality of their journals—this in the face of much resistance: in the 1880s, William Curtis, editor of *Harper's*, threatened to resign lest that staid publication become a "circus magazine," through a proffered contract for only one hundred pages of ads per *year*.

I don't want to claim too much for the ad men. Publishers like Cyrus Curtis, Frank Munsey, and S. S. McClure needed no one to tell them that their enterprise depended upon advertising. And many capitalists were reaching out for imperial marketing methods, even as the ad men were seeking their trade. If J. W. Thompson had not been there, cajoling and explaining and encouraging, Pillsbury and Armour and Procter and Gamble would doubtless have invented him and put him on their own payrolls. This was a complex and integrated process. But it does seem to me important that a new group of entrepreneurs, *specialists* in consciousness, took the lead, creating a discourse that served not just one or another business interest but the entire market universe, enveloping capital, labor, and the new professional-managerial class in a ghostly monologue of consumption and social aspiration.

Let me add that, for all the controversy over the effects of advertising, its dynamism through this transformation of American society finds expression in one very concrete fact: advertising expenditures per capita grew sixfold from the end of the Civil War to the end of the century; moreover, they grew more rapidly as a percentage of gross national product through this period than at any time since, including the 1920s and the 1950s. If it were possible to isolate expenditures on *national brand* advertising from merchant advertising, the growth would be more striking still. No one can prove that advertising restructured consciousness and social life, but clearly those with the capability were paying lavishly to make it a dominant discourse. This is *not* to say that they imposed it on an unwilling or helpless audience. As I suggested in the last chapter, great shifts were taking place in the terms of social existence. People in cities needed both commodities and a discourse that would help mediate commodities, by reconstituting and imaging a social life organized around them. No more democratic discourse than advertising was universally available to them.

I turn now to the other portions of magazine discourse; high time, the reader might say. After all, people bought one magazine or another for its articles, pictures, features, and stories, not for its ads, and the genius of Bok, McClure, Munsey, John Brisben Walker of *Cosmopolitan*, and the rest expressed itself in editorial matter, not ads. Yet if we stand back far enough, we can see these two parts of the magazine as integrated—as bait and hook. One uses different bait for different fish, and for the same fish at different times. The *Ladies' Home Journal*, in the 1890s, invited its readers to share hints and secrets about social decorum, cooking, shopping, the making and wearing of new fashions, along with moral guidance and stories of exemplary men and women. *Munsey's* struck a more rakish note, with departments on women of the stage, on current fads and celebrities, on sport, on art, tricked out with innumerable photographs and engravings. *McClure's* ran on a higher track—a kind of *Harper's* for the million—with fiction by Kipling, Howells, Stevenson, and the like, and extravagant serialized works such as Ida Tarbell's life of Napoleon.

To be more specific, the October 1899 issue of *McClure's* included articles on Admiral Dewey, Mark Twain, the Dreyfus case, and the America's Cup yachts and yachtsmen. We can get a helpful perspective on this kind of magazine fare—for which readers seemed to have an insatiable appetite—by referring to Theodore Greene's study *America's Heroes*. Greene surveyed magazine biographies and profiles over more than a century. His chapter on the years 1894–1903 is titled "The Hero as Napoleon"[6] and that title suggests his thesis. The typical subject of a biography at this time is a man (almost always) characterized above all by his power, of thought and of will. His achievement flows from extraordinary personal qualities and especially from his strength and determination. He has risen from humble origins. The main criterion of his success is fame, not wealth or a contribution to human betterment, though he is often credited with the latter as well.

Greene argues, I think persuasively, that we should see this typical hero as a response to the growing dominance of American life by corporations, a dominance that seriously called into question the Horatio Alger ideal of entrepreneurial individualism and of success readily available to all. The new form of capitalism made power remote and mysterious. Magazine writers and editors responded with real-life stories that reasserted the empowerment of individuals, who, through their own efforts, placed their stamp on history, rather than serving as agents of larger historical forces. (Theodore Roosevelt explicitly raises this question in his article on Dewey in the October 1899 *McClure's*.) One can conjecture that the biographies attained their extraordinary popularity because they offered to salvage the ideal of individualism in new circumstances that made it more and more problematic as a guide to one's life.

In this issue of *McClure's*, the articles on Dewey and Twain fit this pattern, as does the piece on yachts and yachtsmen. They all project a feeling of wonder at the great and exotic men who walk the earth, but they also employ a confidential, knowing tone—we are getting the inside story on a world grown opaque. All the magazines encouraged this celebratory gaze (muckraking came later), re-presenting to readers their own world, managed by leaders who deserve their leadership.

The fiction carries a complementary message: stories brimming with heroism, but tempered by sacrifice and sentimental reconciliations. The heroes resemble us more than they do Admiral Dewey or Napoleon. They bring noble achievement within our horizons, while downplaying the opposition between great man and ordinary person. Let Booth Tarkington's novel *The Gentleman from Indiana* be the example: its concluding episode appeared in this issue of *McClure's;* it was a terrific success; and it is the only one of the fictions in this issue that is still read today.

But since it is probably not a common bedside companion, I will quickly enumerate the main elements of its story. John Harkless, a taciturn, upright young man from "the East," arrives at the outset in the sleepy town of Plattville, Indiana. He has bought, sight unseen, the town's weekly newspaper, which turns out to be at best moribund. Harkless grimly sets to work and surprises the people of Plattville by both his quiet competence and his modest courage in fighting entrenched evil—in the person first of a corrupt politician, then of a clan of rural thugs called the White Caps. Meanwhile he falls (taciturnly) in love with a tiny bright spirit named Helen Sherwood, also an outsider to Plattville. Leaving her one night, he is ambushed by a horde of White Caps, who leave him for dead (though not until he has given a good account of himself with his fists). During his slow recovery in a distant hospital, Helen Sherwood bravely and pseudonymously takes over the newspaper and thoroughly modernizes it. She also engineers the nomination of Harkless for a seat in Congress, unbeknownst to him. When he finally returns to Plattville, certain that things have gone all wrong, his train ride turns into a triumphal parade, as thousands of loving townspeople and farmers give him a hero's welcome.

Now consider some of the meanings that are advanced through the medium of Tarkington's buoyant style, and through a narrative that can only be characterized as heartwarming, one designed to make readers feel good about themselves and their society. First, Tarkington quite explicitly identifies the people of Plattville, Indiana, with the United States as a whole. Helen Sherwood is "Americanly capable";[7] the narrator tells us, with reference to her and another member of the party of goodness, that the "genius of the American is adaptability" (p. 313); in his acceptance speech Harkless, almost overcome with feeling, says "oh, we are all Americans here!" (p. 369). We note that John, Helen, and John's friend Tom Meredith, have all blended easily into this archetypal American town, even as they have renewed its energies.

So the community becomes a mirror in which readers see an ideological image of themselves. The people have qualities we would expect. They are simple, kind, instinctively good, neighborly. They "know that God is good" (p. 261) and will take care that Harkless, the best among them, will recover. They are "less artificial" than people elsewhere and do not try "to be somebody else" (p. 139). In short, here the social somehow dissolves into the natural. Distinctions and hierarchies don't exist; leadership (John and Helen) rises naturally out of individual merit and the unanimous affection of the people. The only social category used to characterize this town—and it appears again and again—is that seemingly natural one, the *family.* Plattville is "just one big, jolly family" (p. 105). Significantly, Tarkington explicitly rules out class as a category of understanding at one point, attributing to fat, rich women rocking on eastern piazzas the idea that rural people are "the lower classes." "How happy this big family is," says Helen, "in not knowing it is the lower classes!" (p. 106). Plattville is a classless society of common folk, which, magically, assimilates Helen, who has summered at Winter Harbor, and John, who went to a college remarkably like Princeton. Readers, then, are invited to see themselves (represented by the hero and heroine) as simultaneously part of a natural meritocracy and yet just ordinary folks. The harmony includes women (people are *surprised* at Helen's achievement but don't resent or block it). And it is even condescendingly biracial, with a place in the community for a much-loved "darky" who insists on calling John "Marse Harkless."

Now this Edenic vision of the United States would probably have been too shallow to arouse interest and affection, were there no representation at all of conflicts and processes that troubled the complacency of *McClure's'* actual readers. And indeed those disturbances are in the novel. Plattville itself is classless, but we hear about classes elsewhere and know that the rest of the country has not quite attained the Plattville ideal. There is an upper class, but those of its members who cannot easily shed their distinction in Plattville as Tom Meredith does are a distant joke—the fat women on the piazzas and those snobs who, unable to "set up crests in the face of an unimpressionable democracy," drift off to villas in England. More threatening are those *other* "excrescent individuals," the "foreign-born agitators," who, happily, "find themselves removed by the police to institutions of routine" (p. 313). So much for immigrants.

But the novel also confronts the fact of a working class directly, and eloquently, through the part it gives to the White Caps of Six-Cross-Roads, a surly mob of Jukes and Kallikaks who go around terrorizing the countryside in white hoods that foreshadow the ascendency of the Klan in Indiana and who nearly kill Harkless in revenge for his having put some of them in jail. Their image is ideologically sharp: they are poor because they are bad, and bad because they are poor. Tarkington stirs loathing for them as much by images of their shanties and ragged clothes as by their violence. He has Helen draw the moral: "Six-Cross-Roads is entirely vicious, isn't it; and bears the same relation to the country that slums do to a city?" (p. 46). Scary, but we can feel all right about this unruly proletariat because it is no organic part of Plattville (Six-Cross-Roads lies some miles off), and of course because Harkless and the people of Plattville utterly defeat it—not really by violence so much as by colonizing the whole countryside with goodness. Once bested, the White Caps are in fact forgiven, their rebellion attributed to ignorance.

The other threat to complacency is change. How can the pre-eminence of America be fixed to the ideal of a sleepy, preindustrial town, where the old organic community remains undisturbed, when as every reader knew, the United States was actually pushing toward hegemony in the world through the power of industrial capitalism? The novel answers that question quite simply and quite magically. Plattville does change. Through the agency of its most forward-looking citizens it acquires a modern daily newspaper (with AP dispatches and a women's page) that brings it in touch with national and international markets; its main street is paved; its dreary center turns into a commercial hive. An oil boom fuels all this growth. Yet all these developments are entirely controlled by the best people in town, infused with the old values of the country village and so rendered harmless. The new order will retain all the qualities of the old. Modernization will in no way set exploiters against exploited. Here we have a powerful legitimation of capitalist change, one calculated to put at ease the main concerns of the professional-managerial class. It equates the present with the past, in ways that retain their power even today (the suburb, Marlboro ads, "The Waltons," etc.).

These ideological reconciliations didn't just happen to turn up in the showcase of *McClure's Magazine*. Tarkington had been struggling for several years to establish himself as a writer, with no luck. But when his manuscript found its way to *McClure's* (his sister sent it in), Hamlin Garland and S. S. McClure instantly recognized it as the stuff of American dreams. Garland pronounced his verdict: "You are a novelist." McClure, who claimed to have learned what all Americans like by peddling housewares through the Midwest during college vacations, summoned Tarkington to the New York office for a triumphal welcome resembling that of Harkless in Plattville. McClure promised, "We are going to push you and make you known everywhere—you are to be the greatest of the new generation, and we'll help you to be." Introducing the young man to the most famous writer on his staff, he said, "Miss Tarbell, this is to be the most famous young man in America." He undertook to serialize *The Gentleman from Indiana*, an honor he was currently granting only to Kipling. And he personally supervised and encouraged Tarkington through weeks of revision, much of it done at McClure's own home. In effect, he *made* Tarkington "the greatest of the new generation," almost overnight.[8]

This cultural entrepreneurship should not, however, be seen as manipulation. McClure, who knew what he liked and what his readers would like, was confident that the two coincided. More a weathervane than a propagandist, he stumbled into muckraking a few years later and wholeheartedly rode its popularity. Indeed, the values that supported Plattville's homely oil boom could easily turn against the Standard Oil trust: John D. Rockefeller did not act like just ordinary folks. But in 1899, McClure's intuition favored stories and articles that proclaimed, in effect, "the society is in good hands; ordinary people are decent people doing worthwhile deeds; it is quite all right for readers to live out their lives on that private terrain where social relations dissolve into commodities." The other magazines had other ways of conveying similar reassurances. Their content harmonized with and supported advertising images of modern kitchens and happy families, making a seamless though quite incoherent world.

The last two visual exhibits afford a neat instance of this new, mystifying unity, of the discourse that we now call mass culture. This issue of *McClure's* celebrates the battle of Manila Bay; its two lead articles capitalize upon and help create a celebrity, the great patriot and liberator, Admiral Dewey. The cover (which, of course, helps sell the magazine) features his portrait, flanked by three sisters of liberty, Pre-Raphaelite echoes of the one in Delacroix's painting (fig. 6). Turn the page, and there inside the cover, verso to its recto, is the good admiral once again, this time at his lavabo, flanked now by warship, merchant ship, missionary, grateful savage, and Pears' Soap (fig. 7).

Figure 6. Cover of *McClure's*, October, 1899

The first step towards lightening

The White Man's Burden

is through teaching the virtues of cleanliness.

Pears' Soap

is a potent factor in brightening the dark corners of the earth as civilization advances, while amongst the cultured of all nations it holds the highest place—it is the ideal toilet soap.

Figure 7. Inside cover: Pears' Soap

11 TV and the Sterilization of Politics

In the last essay I held that the discourse of mass culture in 1890s magazines managed to construct, between advertisements and editorial content, a "seamless though quite incoherent world." New media emerge, new idioms arise; but that "mystifying unity" tends to persist, a subtext that whispers reassurance beneath the cacophony of images and messages that dazzle our eyes and minds. I skip over eighty years now, to look at a mass cultural production of the 1970s that reached an audience in the tens of millions, not the hundreds of thousands of the 1890s. It got there by a technology only vaguely imagined in the heyday of *McClure's Magazine*. And politics was its theme, not its subliminal counterpoint. Yet the interplay within it of "content" and advertising was similar.

Politics. In this country the term has come to mean little more than elections. And the election that really counts is the one that delivers us a president every four years. As almost everyone complains, the big contest starts up in earnest a year or more before the final vote, bores on through months of caucuses and primaries, reaches a false climax with the conventions, then bores *on* through more months of debating whether to debate, and other such entertainments. No one seems to want it. Yet it's there, in the middle of our public culture, jostling with sports and the weather for a share in small talk and the Evening News. What does it add up to? For the shape of an answer, I look at how the 1976 campaign ended, not at the polls but in the arena of public discussion and public consciousness.

The Way It Was   fine

Election eve, 1976, 7:00 p.m., CBS Evening News. A purposeful clatter in the newsroom, brought to order by Walter Cronkite's comforting presence.

The show begins with a brief story on the eleventh-hour embarrassment that Jimmy Carter's church has caused him by turning away a group of black worshipers: Carter himself, we hear, deplores the act and the policy of his elders.

Then a longer story, on the final day of the campaign in Michigan. That state is critical for Gerald Ford; it "could make the difference between victory and defeat." He has the home-state advantage, but it may be offset: there is a big drive for Carter by organized labor, a potent force in a state with so many blue collar workers and with a 9 percent unemployment rate. Throughout this report the screen is busy with movement: a crowd of workers leaving a plant at the end of their shift, a hectic scene at Republican campaign headquarters, and other visual signs of the drama in Michigan.

Next, a brief item on the unusually large number of absentee ballots being cast this year. These take a while to tally, and could delay the verdict in a close election. Close it will be, for CBS tells us next that the latest Barnes-Roper poll gives Carter 47 percent and Ford 43 percent, with the rest still undecided.

Now a commercial for Momentum—a backache remedy with three ingredients—and one for the Wearever Cookieshooter, described as "revolutionary."

Back to news, and a story about the running mates. Senator Mondale, the vice-presidential candidate, is in New York, in Philadelphia (with Mayor Rizzo), in Buffalo, in Gary, in Michigan. He has made more than two hundred appearances during the campaign: has he helped or hurt the Democratic ticket? Now we shift to Mondale's counterpart, Senator Dole, touring several midwestern states. He remarks upon the erosion of the Democrats' early lead in the polls, and condemns his opponents for (desperately, unsportingly) fixing on Watergate in these last days. To sum up: he, like Mondale, has by now done his ticket all the good or harm he can do.

A brief note on the weather. Expected to be good in most of the nation on election day. A bit confusingly, a weatherlady comes on screen, yawning over her weather report. But she turns out to be fictional; it's a commercial for Nytol, followed by an elegant one for Karastan carpets, foundation for the decor of a chic, gallerylike apartment that will also display art deco and a Calder.

Settle in now for a lengthy and serious analysis of the issues. Unemployment. The economy. Taxes. Welfare. Energy. Defense. Abortion. We learn Ford's and Carter's positions on each, and they do differ. There is a choice.

Next a series of compact stories:

—many voters will use a new, experimental punchcard system at their voting machines tomorrow;

—Ford is a 4 to 5 favorite in British betting, and winner by 238 to 236 at Harry's Bar in Paris. Tass-the-Soviet-newsagency says there's no difference between the two candidates;

—will the new peace hold up in Lebanon?

—no progress in the Geneva talks on Rhodesia; the Rhodesian government has attacked Mozambique;

—averages were higher today on the New York Stock Exchange.

After commercials for Fresh Horizons bread and FTD Green Ribbon (plants by mail), Eric Sevareid rather morosely occupies the screen, to wrap up the show and the campaign. It's "all over but the muttering and the wondering," he reflects. People are down on this campaign, confused. The election does make a difference, issues *were* presented, the people listened. Yet they are still confused. Why? It is a time of "national uncertainty" and "ambiguity." Their "whole picture is blurred . . . and naturally so," because it reflects the times we live in.

No uncertainty or ambiguity on the part of Pat Boone, who is now praising the West Bend coffeemaker, or in an Ex-Lax commercial which assures us that "people know what's good." After the CBS News logo, a final pair of commercials: one for Good Seasons and one for Gerald Ford. 7:30. The show is over.

It has been as probing and steady a look at politics as we ever get on the Evening News. And it has beautifully organized our political reality into safe and familiar patterns. I want to explore three of them.

The most obvious one is that of the sporting contest. CBS didn't invent it; it is stamped into our most habitual political vocabulary. Ford and Carter are having a "race" for the presidency, running for office. Each had a "running mate," a kind of sturdy, colorless blocking back. And the stars are supported by their teams, the Democratic and Republican parties. But these participants, who show up in this edition of the news as organized labor and Republican campaign workers, are massed together on the screen, without a voice, anonymous. All attention fixes on the chief contestants. It is for them that Michigan will spell "victory or defeat," not for their voting constituencies, not for the multinational corporations, not for the poor. (No more do we say that Cleveland *fans* have scored a victory when the Indians win.) An election, like a sporting contest, goes on within set boundaries by made-up rules, and is terminated by a final whistle. On television, it seems apart from real life. When it ends, one candidate has won, the other lost, and the rest of us slide back into our old routines as quickly as we do after a Steeler victory in the Superbowl.

Our elections are spectacles, and increasingly TV puts its audience in the role of fans and connoisseurs rather than agents. Guided by the expert announcer, we puzzle whether this or that strategy is a blunder, whether the running mates have played well, what caused the latest shift in the polls. The polls themselves, like the eventual vote with its running totals and computer projections, resemble the penumbra of statistics that surround the big game and often displace the event itself from the center of our attention. (Polls also offer us a rare chance to talk back: I wonder how many of the surprises in the 1980 primaries—Kennedy's landslide in Massachusetts, the Anderson vote in Connecticut, and others— represented a kind of Bronx cheer from voters to pollsters, a way of saying "you can't take us *completely* for granted.") Television's image of the election sets politics apart from real history and from our own lives, trivializing the contest even beyond its inherent triviality but at the same time loading it with vicarious excitement. And that, of course, is necessary so that politics and the Evening News may compete with the big game itself and with TV's innumerable bouts between good and evil—for our time, for Nielsen ratings, and for advertising dollars.

The second pattern is that of problem and solution. Horace Newcomb, in *TV: The Most Popular Art*,[1] showed that almost every type of TV series—cop show, sitcom, medical show, and so forth— follows this pattern. The CBS news show as a whole bears traces of it, with twenty minutes of chaos and moral disorder subdued by Eric Sevareid in three minutes of mournful but comforting resolutions and balanced judgments. More telling is the fact that each segment of the political news on November 1, 1976, fell into the problem-solution form. His church's bigotry is a problem for Carter, which he tries to solve by his disapproval. The voters of Michigan, standing for all voters, are presented as a problem for both candidates and their organizations. What ingenious stratagem will capture them? CBS reflects on formulas for swaying the blue collar workers, the unemployed. The story on Dole and Mondale uses the same framework. Their problem has been to help their running mates; our problem is to figure out, along with CBS, whether they did so.

In the long analytic segment, each campaign issue is a problem in itself. Inflation, energy, abortion: all disturb the smooth, untroubled flow of social life which is assumed as normal. And to each problem, each candidate has a solution. On taxation: Carter favors reform, Ford a cut. On the economy: Ford wants steady growth with no inflation; Carter would attack unemployment by having the government provide jobs. And so on through the list. CBS frames the issues as technical ones, in whose solution we all share a common interest. The solutions are equally technical and, in spite of CBS's heroic efforts, opaque in their meanings and uncertain in their results. But complexity aside, the problem-solution approach drains issues of their politics, by (1) artificially separating each from the others and detaching them all from a full picture of our society and its history; (2) presenting them as technical challenges, like taking out an appendix or repairing a carburetor, and in this way (3) suppressing what I take to be the main fact of politics: conflict. Unpack any political issue in real life—even, alas, that of peace—and you find one group contesting with another for power, for the goods of our productive system, for the future. A given solution is *not* in everyone's interest, like rain after a drought. Every political solution creates winners and losers. One camp's solution is another's problem.

The problem-solution form, like that of the sporting event, casts us as onlookers rather than as what we really are: participants in or victims of the process. This is especially clear in the emphasis CBS gives to another set of problems. Will the absentee ballots delay resolution of the contest? Will the new voting machines work? Will the good weather favor Carter or Ford? Is Carter's lead in the Barnes-Roper poll statistically meaningful? Attention to these purely formal matters puts us deeper in our spectator chairs, at two removes from conflict over the direction of American society, fussing about administrative details.

I've already hinted at the third pattern: a splintering of the political world and of society itself into discrete "issues." Pro or con; more or less; a law here and an amendment there; take a stand. Where in this bazaar full of patent medicine hawkers can we even glimpse a vision of the history we are making? In forty years our society has changed almost beyond recognition: freeways, McDonalds, TV, the bomb, the death of cities, multinationals. When did we vote on this transformation? Surely we are in the midst of another such, as the postwar boom finally dies and we run out of the resources that fueled it and the American dollar becomes just another currency. The course of history is up for decision, and those who mediate politics for the "public" can do no better than a cafeteria of separate issues. Not even a blue plate special.

Look more closely into this political darkness. The fragmentation of history into issues hides the more basic splits and alignments in American society, and shifts attention to supposedly neutral questions of policy. The very names that issues bear in our political discourse are saturated with false neutrality. Take *unemployment*. The term presents a complicated *process*, full of conflict and hard knocks, as if it were a *thing,* a symptom, a static fact. In this way it conceals a major crisis of our economic system: that as it produces more things more efficiently, it wastes and impoverishes more human beings.

Furthermore, the concept of unemployment masks the play of class interests in our society. It encourages us to think of those 9 percent unemployed in Michigan as a separate group (if as people at all) and to be concerned whether the percentage goes up or down a point. In this scheme of ideas, unemployment is an issue for workers in only a personal way. I have a job and may lose it; someone else has none and wants one. But unemployment is not just a risk for individuals or for "the economy." It is a handicap to workers in general. A reserve army of the unemployed weakens the bargaining position of the employed, too, and strengthens that of employers. This basic fact gets lost in the idea of unemployment (which also undermines class unity by fostering antagonism between "hardworking Americans" and "freeloaders").

Inflation used to be the flip side of unemployment, shifting wealth toward workers and away from the wealthy. The new inflation of the last few years has tipped the other way, hitting the poor especially hard. A tricky matter, to be sure. The point is that all such questions vanish when our politicians and commentators strip the issue of conflict, presenting inflation as "public enemy number one," looking for technical solutions. A final example, *defense*. That this is a euphemism has long been clear. More seriously, the term preempts any discussion of the United States's power relationship to the rest of the world, setting in its place a "nonpolitical" debate about budgets and hardware. And so on through our vocabulary of issues. No coherent politics emerges, only bundles of "positions." TV didn't initiate the atomization of politics, but it has driven it to dizzying extremes. A agrees with B on defense; they are at odds on the environment; they will compromise on abortion. How can a voter penetrate this labyrinth? No wonder elections are won and lost over one man's five o'clock shadow and another's smile.

This last pattern effectively sets hidden limits to our debate. Within its terms one cannot even speak about the organization of society or about structural change. A candidate must take a "stand" on "crime": in doing so he will accept as background— invisible, undiscussable—the basic form of our laws and the property relations they embody. He will tell us instead of his ingenious scheme to catch or hang a thief. When he takes his "stand" on "the environment" he takes for granted private control over wealth, investment, and the major decisions that will decide whether the environment is still here fifty years from now. Pass the bottle bill. (And pass the bottle. And dispose of properly.)

All three of these patterns conceal the dynamics of American society, smooth over real antagonisms, narrowly confine political thought and argument, and so support the existing order. It is easy to forgive Eric Sevareid, trapped in this universe of discourse, for being unable to leave his audience with any political explanation more lucid than "national uncertainty," "ambiguity," a "blurred picture," "the muttering and the wondering," and for blaming the whole muddle on "the times." We can appreciate and maybe even welcome the news team's effort to lighten the supposedly serious news with comic relief from British bookies and Harry's Bar and Tass. CBS gives us a problem-solving framework, but no solution other than the trivial one of casting a vote and waiting for the results tomorrow night. It's only a show. And not our show, at that.

For viewers of the Evening News on that November 1, though, Eric Sevareid's was not the only commentary. At frequent intervals throughout the thirty minutes, commercials offered a far more succinct and telling commentary on politics in the U.S. Commercials share with the news the pattern of fragmentation into separate issues (back pain, obesity, loneliness, boredom). And in commercials as in news, the problem-solution pattern organizes each segment of air time. But with a remarkable difference: do you have a painful muscular backache? Momentum's three ingredients *will* banish it, and no ambiguity or blurred picture about it. Falling asleep on your job because you had insomnia last night? Take

Nytol. Intestines not working? Ex-Lax. Weight and health problems? Fresh Horizons bread will make you as trim as the Kabuki actor in the commercial. Which of three coffeemakers? No national uncertainty here—Pat Boone has the facts you need, to choose West Bend. Each problem *actually has one surefire solution.*

Other commercials address the broader problems of social isolation and empty lives, offering the promise of invigoration and meaning through purchases. The revolutionary Wearever Cookie-shooter can change the way you make cookies: on the screen, a table heaped with goodies, a party about to begin, no sign of anomie here. Achieve at home the self-worth and security denied you out in the world, by "investing" in (not simply buying) a Karastan carpet. Vary your routines (and recapture the creativity that has vanished from most work) by using Good Seasons to glaze the chicken tonight. Wire FTD Green Ribbon plants to a distant friend—the gesture may rekindle a feeling of community that is hard to come by in a society where people move every four or five years. Whenever the news takes a two-minute vacation, images of the good life chase one another from the screen: health, abundance, conviviality; friendly rural scenes, elegant apartments; people being happy with each other through products. And everywhere the vibrant, dynamic family, knit together by kindness and commodities beyond any possible threat of dissonance or breakup.

In effect, the election eve news show had two parts. One concerned politics, a clutter of technical issues and dubious remedies, a muddle, with no hint of how one might improve his or her life through any conceivable choice, certainly not through the choice of Ford or Carter. The other part concerned products, their purchase a sure way to amelioration of hard circumstance. Juxtapose these two parts, and you, viewer, got a message of adequate clarity: stay well clear of politics except as a spectator sport; leave the social order alone; attend to family, home, and your metabolism; address every hurt or lack in your life by purchasing something.

In *The Hidden Injuries of Class,* Sennett and Cobb argue that workers in this society have few ways to validate themselves as people, to earn dignity and respect, other than the indirect one of buying things.[2] Stanley Aronowitz goes further: for workers in the United States "all relations appear as object relations. . . . People become identical with their occupations, consumption styles, and social prestige, and the self has no autonomy apart from its exchange value."[3] Commodities are the alternatives our society offers to community and to human relationships. A look at the TV news

suggests the corollary that for us, things are also the alternative
to—and a welcome refuge from—politics. There is no support, in
the way CBS patterns reality, for satisfaction through politics, or
for the idea that this is _our_ society, or for anything but individual
achievement and commodity relations.

Things against politics, things against ideas. The network news
and its commercial accompaniment are a daily blitz on the minds
of the audience. Edward Jay Epstein points out, in _News from No-
where_, that the dinnertime audience is relatively low on the scale
of affluence and education.[4] The _makers_ of the news show are of
course professional people of good income. And higher up, those
who control the networks and the local stations, like the advertisers who are the customers of the networks, are people of great
wealth and power with a large stake in the status quo. The media
they own and run urge a fragmented, classless, nonpolitical awareness on those who might have something to gain by changing the
status quo through a genuine politics.

Brainwashing?

Those last few sentences are only a description—not controversial, I think—of the class relations that surround television news.
But to describe them in this way is strongly to imply an explanation. And many readers will identify the explanation waiting in the
wings as a standard marxian one. I would like to sketch it briefly—
for it has both power and plausibility—before going on to suggest
that it cannot without adjustment explain the peculiar way our
media image politics.

A good starting point is a fine essay called "The Industrialization
of the Mind," by the German poet and social critic Hans Magnus
Enzensberger. Once a society has achieved industrialization and its
people are no longer wholly occupied with bare survival, he says,
"material exploitation alone is insufficient to guarantee the continuity of the system." The people will want more than bread and
shelter, and are likely to be fired by the enlightenment ideals of liberty, equality, and democracy, which have never been fully realized. Enzensberger goes on: "Real democracy, as opposed to the
formal facades of parliamentary democracy, does not exist anywhere in the world, but its ghost haunts every existing regime.
Consequently, all the existing power structures must seek to obtain
the consent, however passive, of their subjects."[5]

They may do that by naked coercion, of course. Historical ex-

amples abound. And even in societies not terrorized by some ge-
stapo or other, the power of the state to imprison or kill stands as a
last, quiet warning to the rebellious. But for obvious reasons the
powerful would rather hold onto their privileges by "consent" than
by coercion, rather have their power be seen as legitimate than as
backed by guns alone. Better a respected Rockefeller than a de-
spised Somoza. (Better yet, perhaps, to sit on your billions and not
be noticed at all.) Capitalist democracy is most secure when it uses
force least, preferably only to restrain those who are generally
viewed as criminals, or to defend the "national" interest. The alternative to force, in this account, is manipulation: the few must influence or control the minds of the many, so that the many either
acquiesce in their exploitation or are quite unaware of it.

How do the few accomplish this? The most direct answer is that
of Marx and Engels in *The German Ideology:* "The class which has
the means of material production at its disposal, has control at the
same time over the means of mental production, so that thereby,
generally speaking, the ideas of those who lack the means of mental production are subject to it."[6] Marx and Engels passed over a
lot of hard questions with that "thereby," but their idea has gained
plausibility in the 130 years since they wrote, as the means of mental production have grown vast and expensive beyond anything
in their ken. In the United States the rich do own and control
television, radio, the movies, major newspapers and magazines,
books, advertising, foundations, research institutes, elite universities, virtually all of what Enzensberger calls the "mind industry,"
except for the public schools—and many would argue that the
dominant class controls the schools without owning them.

The greater the impact of a particular mind industry, and the
wider its reach, the more likely is it to be controlled by the few.
Television is of course the prime example. It reaches 92 percent of
the population in an average day, and 98 percent in a week. Just
three networks claim most of this huge audience—94 percent of it
in the fifty largest markets; across the whole country, on the average, the networks send out the images on 65 percent of all TV
screens at a given moment.[7] This in turn means that the few who
control the networks also create much of what people see as political reality: most Americans have no direct experience of politics,
and draw their vicarious experience more from TV than from any
other medium. (In the 1960s, TV took a lead it has not given up as
the source to which most people turn for news, and the source they
consider most reliable.) There can be no dispute about who owns

this means of mental production in the United States. And in a formal sense they also control it.

To what end do they use their formal control? Marxian theory has a straightforward answer; I'll quote Enzensberger one more time for a statement of it: "The mind industry's main business and concern is not to sell its product: it is to 'sell' the existing order, to perpetuate the prevailing pattern of man's domination by man."[8] Now marxism is a theory of history that makes class conflict the dynamo of change, casts workers as the bearers within capitalism of a new order that will replace it, but claims that workers cannot exercise their historical role without attaining class consciousness. Given such a theory, to "sell" the existing order means to prevent workers from understanding their exploitation, their unity as a class, their antagonistic position toward the capitalist class, and their historical power. In short, it means obfuscating and subverting politics, if politics is the arena of conflict and change. I have tried to show that television news accomplishes just that, by making politics a trivial, confused, and distant spectacle.

So far, so good. But this version of marxism leaves a rather big gap between, on the one side, the needs and intentions of those who control the means of mental production and, on the other, the achievement of their aims. The theory vaguely implies that mind industry capitalists set out to sell the existing order, then hire media workers to carry out details of the propaganda scheme. Now, this theory explains pretty well what happens in "idea advertising" like that of Mobil Oil, U.S. Steel, Allied Chemical, ITT, and others, wherein it is explained that profits are good for us all, that "free" markets are the neatest arrangement ever devised for making and distributing the good things of life, that industry is hard at work solving the energy crisis on our behalf, and so on. It also offers a good account, in my view, of the "public service announcements" broadcast free by the Advertising Council (see pages 198–204). And, ironically, it may be a true enough picture of the way news is prepared in the Soviet Union. But it falls short of explaining why U.S. network news is the way it is.

News for Sale

First, the news is not propaganda, as are the Mobil ads or the series of commercials made by Phillips Petroleum to be sponsored by local firms around the country—each commercial guaranteed to meet "performance norms in positively influencing viewer attitudes toward free enterprise." If my analysis is right, sale of the status quo through news is much more subtle and indirect than any such effort could be. And there is, to start with, a simple reason why the main content of TV (as of radio, newspapers, and most of the other media) *cannot* be direct propaganda: these means of mental production are themselves businesses in the United States, run for profit. And although with enough hype one can sell many worthless or harmful things, it is doubtful that any but a small and unprofitable mind industry could exist if propaganda were its main stock in trade. Would almost 100 percent of our families buy TV sets in order to hear preached, over and over again, the benefits of free enterprise? If our mind industry does sell the existing order, to do so is a far greater challenge for it than for, say, the mind industry of North Korea. It must hold voluntary audiences and sell its product for profit, while plugging the status quo between the lines.

What exactly is the product that television networks sell? Not the programs themselves (e.g., the news), nor our viewing experience, nor the television sets that make that experience available to us, nor the soap and toothpaste advertised on the air. What the networks sell, directly or via their affiliate stations, is *our attention*, as Todd Gitlin puts it, "and the market to which it is sold is advertisers."[9] This is why networks rise and fall by Nielsen ratings, which purport to measure exactly how much of our attention they can offer for sale, and determine what they can charge for it. As Gitlin's helpful analysis continues, "the corporate advertiser will buy only a *mass* audience; the more mass the better. You get a mass audience by, in a sense, manufacturing it. That is, you manufacture an audience that is reliable: that watches reliably, that thinks and feels . . . reliably, and finally, that buys . . . reliably." To build an audience you must of course attract their interest. To make that audience come back again and again, and keep it feeling secure, comfortable, and receptive, you have to do more. You must convince it that tuning in will guarantee it familiar and undisturbing pleasures. From this principle derive the main TV forms: the series, the serial (soap opera), the game show, the sporting event, the talk show, and so on. Each in its way builds on repetitions and formulas. Each has one or more stars who accumulate loyal fans. Each comes at a dependable time. Even post-"Roots," consoling repetitions fill nearly all TV time. They work.

Needless to say, the TV networks must and do sell our attention to advertisers through news broadcasting, just as through "Three's

Company" and "The Dating Game." This urgency is most evident in "60 Minutes" and its imitators, which present only stories chosen in advance for audience appeal, and in the local news—"happy news," as it's called—with its personalities and slick banter. (One study found that most people watch the eleven o'clock news to relax before bed, secure in the knowledge that things are OK for another night. And in *The Newscasters*, Ron Powers tells of a booming news consultancy group called Entertainment Response Analysts that measures galvanic skin responses of viewers to advise local news directors on the most seductive formats, writing styles, and weathercasters.)[10] But even the more dignified network news must operate within the same logic of reliable mass audiences and profitability. So it should surprise no one that network news programs create their own repetitions, formulas, dependable patterns. I have tried to identify just three of these, from CBS's wrap-up of the 1976 campaign: the sporting contest, the problem-solution frame, the array of separate issues each with its pros and cons. All flow naturally enough from the need of network programs to build and hold audiences.

Turning Events Into News

Of course the news show of November 1, 1976, was not typical. I picked it to examine political coverage on the Evening News at its fullest and most analytical—at its sorry best, from my perspective. Watch on any ordinary night, and you will see the formulas even more plainly. The main one: that of the "story" itself. Everything a news team selects as newsworthy must be shaped into a story through choice of events and nonevents to film, of sources, of commentary, of the footage that will actually be shown. This much is conscious policy. For instance, when NBC went to a half-hour version of the evening news in 1963, producer Reuven Frank wrote in a memo to his staff: "Every news story should, without any sacrifice of probity or responsibility, display the attributes of fiction, of drama. It should have structure and conflict, problem and denouement, rising action and falling action, a beginning, a middle and an end."[11] Edward Jay Epstein found this formula crucial, as did Herbert Gans in his research on CBS and NBC: "Every story must always include a lead, a narrative, and a closer."[12]

This three-part structure wedges every kind of news, from an earthquake to the staged announcement of a candidacy, into a mold that also shapes our response. The lead reveals something new and perhaps unsettling; the narrative develops it, often by balancing off "both sides" if the news is in any way controversial; and the closer achieves at least a temporary resolution, if not a solution. The newscaster's authoritative voice, his falling cadence as he signs off, his serious or wry expression, all convey the message that something has been settled. Or if not, at least wiser heads than ours are in charge. Gans notes that an item with no pointed ending is likely to be dropped out, so urgent is it that each story reach closure. And of course the whole program itself normally takes this reassuring form, with the dangerous and perplexing news at the outset, and with a light or funny "capper" at the end. (And that's the way it is.)

This form sterilizes politics, and in that way promotes the existing order. But clearly it does not do so by some grand ideological design handed down from big stockholders and board chairmen to boost corporate power and secure the free enterprise system. Network news divisions are indeed responsible to their corporate managements, but with rare exceptions—playing down Edward R. Murrow's exposés of Sen. Joseph McCarthy, scotching CBS coverage of the 1966 Senate hearings on Vietnam—the political aims of the higher-ups have apparently had little effect on news decisions. News journalists prize their autonomy, and a Fred Friendly will quit when pushed too hard. The directive from top management that counts most in shaping TV news, far more than ideological interference, is the directive to make the news itself popular enough to claim the attention of millions each night. And it is this directive that leads, by the route I've sketched, to formulas that turn politics into story.

Alongside this cause, and also quite important, are some that have to do with who puts the news together, and how.

1. The news journalists themselves are ambitious and successful. They got where they were going partly because their employers saw them as politically neutral. Neither do they have strong religious or other beliefs. They have left their local and class origins behind. They make good salaries and live in suburbs. They take upper-middle-class values for granted.

2. They are also *professionals.* They see themselves as objective, serving the public like doctors. They are in the midst of events, but not involved. And they had better maintain that posture, because any signs of activism, ideology, or commitment will probably get them fired.

3. Their time is short and they need the "inside" story; thus they depend heavily on sources who are well placed, authoritative, powerful—and, in a neat reciprocal arrangement, eager to get *their* version of events out to large audiences. So when we watch the news, we tend to see the world from the outlook of those who make it run. (On top of this, celebrities draw audiences and ordinary people don't, so there's an irresistible motive to get famous political personalities on camera.)

4. The FCC requires, through the Fairness Doctrine, that when TV represents one view on a controversial matter it must air the other side too. To admit positions outside the mainstream would open the news to an expensive cacaphony of rebuttals from all sides. (As the FCC says, its aim does not include making time "available to Communists or to the Communist viewpoints.") Thus political discussion gravitates always toward the center. Two and only two sides to every question.

5. Historically, TV news grew out of movie newsreels blended with radio commentary. But since pictures are what draw people to the tube, there's a premium on stories that carry visual excitement. Analysis fades into the background, and in any case must be brief because there is little place for it in a two-minute "story."

In these and other ways, the history and structure of television news broadcasting have created a form that highlights the factual and visual, removes events from history, presents them as disconnected stories complete in themselves, divests politics of ideas as well as of ideology, and pictures the world from a perspective of natural hierarchy and upper-middle-class values. It is a world in which conflict and disorder make news, but only as aberrations from the underlying moral order and harmony of interests. No classes, no power structure, no unfolding war of haves and have-nots. In this world, things would be all right if it were not for shortages, nuclear accidents, rebellions, dictators, corruption, strikes, hurricanes, oil spills, Cuba, and other unwelcome departures from the tranquility of the existing order.

The product, in short, is much like what the most conspiratorial version of marxism would predict, and even more effective because more subtle and more subliminal. But the process by which TV builds this worldview is extraordinarily complex and hardly conspiratorial at all. In fact, the worldview gains credibility because it is so obviously *not* the intended, manipulative vision of a ruling class, but rather the natural perspective of honest, independent news professionals. Thus it strikes the viewer as reality it-self, not as reality from a particular outlook, and certainly not as propaganda forced down our throats. The whole image- and myth-making apparatus of the news division becomes nearly trans-parent, visible only in the persons of correspondents and commen-tators, serious men and women who help us to be there.

During his years in Mussolini's prisons, Antonio Gramsci, founder of the Italian Communist party, elaborated an idea of hegemony that has lately gained force among marxists, and that aptly de-scribes the kind of process I have been discussing.[13] Hegemony is a kind of domination different from both force and manipulation. The hegemony of a class is a total way of living and thinking and feeling spread throughout a society. It is not exactly the "consent of the governed," for neither the governed nor the governing need be aware of the power relations between them. Indeed, best not. When powerless people do become aware of power, as lately in this country millions have come to see themselves as in thrall to big oil companies, resentment and political action follow. But a hegemonic sense of reality feels like simple common sense, not like a prison. The personal and political habits that go with it feel like choices *we make.* The Evening News helps in a small way to strengthen and broadcast this sense of reality.

How well does the process work? Summarizing a lot of social scientific research, David Sallach finds that while "the political views of influentials are relatively ordered and coherent," those of the majority are rudimentary and splintered. Working class people are less consistent in their beliefs and values than are the affluent. Their "compliance with the political order is based on a *lack* of consensus and a lack of internal consistency that prevents that class from translating its experience into a political framework."[14] Well, maybe. But even if so, no one knows much about the impact of television on political beliefs and actions, certainly not on class consciousness, which is what I have really been talking about. So let me settle for my hunch that television news is bad for most of those who rely on it. What I am sure of is that it grotesquely mis-represents political reality.

Not believing much in top-down reform, I have no advice for the networks or the Federal Communications Commission. My advice is for unions, community groups, minority and women's organiza-tions, consumer groups, the unorganized. It is so traditional and obvious and democratic that I'm almost embarrassed to say it: take back the airwaves. They belong by rights to us.

12 Worldthink

Television news helps shape and naturalize an aberrant sense of political reality. Part of my argument in the last essay was that TV journalists do that as a consequence of carrying out their professional routines, in a context determined by the need to hold large, profitable audiences, rather than by the dictates of wealthy men who would use their control of the networks to propagandize audiences on behalf of the ruling class. A striking example in support of this claim was Ted Turner's challenge to ABC, CBS, and NBC. When he founded the Cable News Network, he declared openly his intention of combating the liberal bias he saw in the news divisions of the big three, thus assuming a sort of historical agency more in keeping with Marx and Engels's account of ideology—and with the behavior of the mid-nineteenth-century newspaper publishers they were in a position to observe. But Turner, rich as he was, could not afford to run his twenty-four-hour-a-day show forever at a loss. In trying to make it profitable he had to make it entertaining, had to appeal to a mass audience's already-funded expectations about TV news, had to hire professional journalists well schooled in network conventions, had to let them run the show with relative independence, and so on. The result: CNN quickly assumed a profile barely distinguishable from that of its "liberal" competitors.

But in saying that mind-industry moguls do not directly take on the role of class ideologists, I don't want to imply that their class in general stays aloof from ideological combat. In this chapter and the next, I look at two of the many ways in which its representatives try to organize fields of public discourse. Here, the agents are principally high officials of the Reagan administration, whose credentials as ideologues for U.S. capital are authentic enough. Yet even this clear instance is more complicated than most domestic opponents of the New Right would allow. Mainstream representations of the world—my subject in this essay—are rich in ideological words, concepts, and images that a gradual historical process has familiarized for most people in this society. Reagan's gladiators could send up new extravagancies of word and thought (*freedom fighters* as a term for right-wing murderers and mercenaries), but they did so within a semantic field already bent and smeared, over decades of imperial rhetoric. In my view, the accepted language of U.S. foreign policy is even more corrupt and dangerous than the crass jingoism of the particular Reagan moment.

Not that it's unimportant to expose and ridicule the blatant distortions, euphemisms, and lies. Critical intellectuals, who do have at least a small public voice, have thereby a responsibility to resist every new act of linguistic cynicism or legerdemain. To fix on some nuclear examples: we should make a disrespectful noise when the Emperor of the Free World decides to call the MX missile system the "Peacekeeper," no question. But the world doesn't need us to keep watch over such murderous tomfoolery: a hundred journalists and politicians will cry halt, and the new usage will go the way of the late fifties coinage "clean bomb," with its radiation measured in "Sunshine Units"—laughed out of the lexicon. In front of me as I write is Nicole Hollander's comic strip, "Sylvia," a neat example: "The Reagan Administration announced that since the renaming of the MX missile 'Peacekeeper' has proved acceptable to the American public, it will now refer to unemployment figures as 'worker vacation statistics,' and to the recession as 'doing the hokey pokey.'"[1] A widely read book like *Nukespeak*,[2] simply by assembling a collection of these terms, can discredit them. To read through the tough-casual lexicon of "megadeaths," "nuclear umbrellas," "clean, surgical strikes," cities as "bargaining chips," and so on is to perceive this as a code facilitating the zany death games of smart asses from Rand and the Pentagon and Harvard, boys who have somehow graduated from fraternity pranks to a deadly and irresponsible preeminence without having grown up. Or a fine piece of reportage like Robert Scheer's *With Enough Shovels*[3] can provoke a healthy terror mainly by quoting the night thoughts of those who have the power to end all our lives.

The limit on this remedy is that it promotes a vision of our leaders as Dr. Strangeloves, and hence a hope that we might regain sanity in public discourse merely by turning out a particular group of maniacs. But any new set of leaders, short of a government genuinely oriented toward peace, would inherit the death machine and

the generals, the think tanks and the lobbyists, as well as the accumulated legacy of concept and language that has been left us by
forty years of carrying on daily life with the bomb in our midst,
and of learning not only to think the unthinkable but to forget that
it *is* unthinkable. The language of military policy is a structure of
quiet, deadly euphemisms beneath the veneer of blatant, deadly
euphemisms like *Peacekeeper*. Conservatives and liberals, doves
and hawks alike, wear this vocabulary like a comfortable old hat.
Getting rid of the Reagan administration, with its policies drawn
from the lunatic Right, would not purify this deeper stratum of
language and thought.

Thus, it is easy to mock a supposedly reassuring term like *nuclear exchange, and* insist on substituting the more blunt *nuclear
war*. Yet *war* itself soothes and deceives in this context. A war is a
military conflict between nations through the engagement of their
armed forces, with civilians pretty freely killed along the way, and
with territory and power to be won or lost That's bad enough, but
in no significant way does the definition apply to the events that
would take place were the Soviet Union and the United States to
cut loose with their missiles. Every term in the definition is inap-
plicable. This would not be a *conflict*, but a technological spasm
beyond the control of either side. It would not be *between nations*,
but would annihilate all nations, at least in the Northern Hemi-
sphere. The *armed forces* of the United States and the USSR would
never *engage* with each other. The very distinction between *civilians* and armed forces would vanish, except that some of the higher-
ranking military men, ten stories underground, would probably
survive for a while longer than any civilians. No nation could retain its identity as a society, much less *win;* none would be able to
occupy the uninhabitable *territory* of another, and no *power* of human institutions, including government, would remain. The term
war masks all this, and makes the unprecedented and abominable
seem routinely horrible.[4]

Likewise, nuclear weapons are not weapons (you can't use them
to fight, or wage a battle).[5] "Strategic" nuclear missiles could implement no strategy, if fired, and in fact would obliterate the very
relationship of means to ends that makes strategy a meaningful
concept. The word *defense*, already a sick joke for other reasons
in the phrase *Department of Defense*, implies in a nuclear context
something that cannot be the case, for there is no defense against
missiles carrying nuclear bombs. (The fond hope that there might
be, a hope latent in the misused word, has helped make the Strate-

gic Defense Initiative politically viable though almost all scientists think it technically absurd.) _Security,_ as in _national security_ and _collective security_, refers to a condition of mortal danger. And _disarmament_, as used by the negotiating "teams," refers to a process by which the two superpowers would retain enough bombs to destroy each other and everyone in between.

How do the illusions and lies behind terms like these escape serious challenge? In part because they fit easily into a conception of our world that is thoroughly familiar. In this conception, good and evil stand opposed across an iron curtain that girdles the globe— two systems of belief and two eschatologies that can unstably coexist but never change. One or the other must finally rule. So high are the stakes in this transhistorical opposition that it requires weapons and strategies that might end history. Our defense is not the defense of people and a productive system and a set of human interests, but of an eternal principle. A war almost no one survived could still be a victory, if evil were itself destroyed. Naturally, in a battle of such proportions ordinary citizens have nothing to contribute; they must deed over their futures to a handful of leaders grown godlike through the power they command. Naturally, too, societies on the margins of this confrontation have no standing except as they can be deployed in the positional jockeying of good and evil; their people do not exist as beings with their own history and needs, but only in relation to the Manichaean struggle. To be sure, few see the world in just this way, or see it this way all the time. But the picture is there as a ready referent in political debate, and its taken-for-grantedness places the burden of seeming rational upon those who would contest it.

This picture connects the semantics of nuclear confrontation to those of more mundane discourse about foreign policy. Take a little thing, like the names of countries. When Alexander Haig said (while still secretary of state), "more help to El Salvador is needed," what could he possibly have meant by "El Salvador"? The junta, of course,[6] and its military cadres of the right, who had killed 15,000 to 20,000 citizens of the country in the previous two years. And when Haig went on to say, "they're going to continue to need security support,"[7] plainly his pronoun did not refer to the opposition in this civil war, nor to the peasants, for whom U.S. "security support" means only the secure knowledge that there will be more bodies to bury tomorrow morning. Yet his use of the name "El Salvador" reassures us that we are helping a whole people, rather than helping one faction—and a faction that by all accounts has

set some kind of record for viciousness, even among our "authoritarian" friends. The deception is possible only because it accords with a world picture that constitutes El Salvador and other nations as counters in a transcendent moral opposition,[8] so that what goes on inside the country really doesn't matter as long as the rulers are on "our" side.

The semantics work the same way when the U.S. government wishes to harm, not help: Haig once referred to Libya as "a cancer that has to be removed."[9] Does this not encourage his hearers to think beyond opposing the Quaddafi government, and imagine with equanimity the wholesale destruction of Libyan society? (By what means could one "remove" a whole country? Only, one assumes, by one of those "surgical strikes.")[10] And when a country is beyond both harm and help, its name may cease to refer to its government *or* the majority of its people, as when an unnamed U.S. official said, "Barring a miracle, Nicaragua is a lost cause."[11] Lost to whom? And did we lose it in the same place we lost Vietnam? (These small countries are apparently easy to misplace.) The lost cause was not Nicaragua, but what the U.S. government took as its right to control the future of that society—though it must be added that years later our leaders have not given up on finding Nicaragua again, through support of the same bloody killers who used to run it.

In each of these instances a U.S. official appropriates the name of a country, along with the feelings most of us have about whole peoples and sovereign nations, attaching the name and the feelings to some construct that answers only to the needs of the U.S. government as its policy makers see them. In this lexicon, societies disappear, to be replaced by tallies on some global score sheet.[12] This inverted telescopic view of other societies, incidentally, permits a close connection between intervention and nuclear force. Thus Richard Perle, assistant secretary of defense for international security policy (!), commented on the "effect that the nuclear balance has on our willingness to take risks in local situations."[13] He meant that if the Soviets are more afraid of us than we are of them, we can more cheerfully mine the harbors or assassinate the leaders of small societies—indeed, invade them outright if the war of good and evil calls for that. "Local situations" derive their meaning from the global struggle, not from the wishes of local human beings. Needless to say, this attitude makes the bomb an implement of routine foreign policy, in its use as a standing threat to any power that would impede our imperial will by supporting popular revolutions.

If the humble names of countries serve so readily the imperial outlook of the evangelists, abstractions are understandably more pliable. President Reagan said to the International Monetary Fund, "We who live in free market societies believe that growth, prosperity, and ultimately, human fulfillment, are created from the bottom up, not the government down." One who considers the United States a free market society will naturally see no contradiction in going on to say, "Unless a nation puts its own financial house in order, no amount of aid will produce progress."[14] Just how are nations to do this, unless their governments intervene in the operations of the market (with the benign aid of the International Monetary Fund or the World Bank), to starve their citizens? *Free market* is a term without a referent in the real world, but with a heavy freight of value in the system of polarities that constitutes the apocalyptic world image. It may be applied as one wishes, usually to advance the freedom of large corporations in making markets and people unfree.

Again, *terrorism* used to be a handy word, meaning, roughly, the advancement of political aims by the threat or use of indiscriminate violence. I don't know what it means any more: our officials apply it not only to IRA or PLO street bombings, but to a range of events from sabotage to mob rampages to assassination of political enemies—but not to similar actions by right-wing governments or paramilitary death squads. And the media accept without comment Menachem Begin's practice of referring always to the PLO, and indeed the whole Palestinian people, as "terrorists," even at times when his own government is destroying refugee camps and killing thousands of civilians. The word floats free, a bundle of affects to be attached wherever those with access to the media can slap them.

Ditto for *human rights*. The administration has found that these do, after all, count for something in circles like Congress and the court of world opinion. So a State Department memo, approved by Secretary Haig, declared that "human rights is at the core of our foreign policy because it is central to what America is and stands for."[15] (America?) Whatever human rights are, they must have been flourishing at that time in Chile, Argentina, Uruguay, and Paraguay, because the U.S. government had recently supported loans to the regimes that presided over these countries, indicating that they measured up to the human rights provisions of the International Financial Institutions Act of 1977.[16]

Fortunately, Haig gave us a map to this part of the semantic field by defining the one word in terms of the other: "International terrorism . . . is the ultimate abuse of human rights."[17] Nothing remains of meaning here, other than a moral polarity that may be applied in whichever way the purposes of the great demand. And indeed, the main administrative use of all these terms in foreign policy discourse is to destroy their referential meaning, saving the moral feeling that used to accompany it for opportunistic purposes of the moment. Of course any vocabulary is a battleground. The opposition can always contest or try to rehabilitate the heavily freighted words, as I am doing now. But virtually the whole public debate is carried on in this debased verbal coinage, while a few intellectuals buzz away in books or journals with at most a few thousand readers.

This is the crux. For if the world picture behind U.S. foreign policy were the sudden, Machiavellian invention of a few leaders, they would have little chance of establishing it. Instead, it has evolved through a complex process of interaction among leaders, intellectuals, media professionals, and millions of ordinary citizens. One can see the power dynamics of the process more nakedly by looking back at an earlier stage, when the image of the United States as bearer of righteousness among nations was not broadly accepted, and when leaders like Theodore Roosevelt had to argue for it openly:

The simple truth is that there is nothing even remotely resembling "imperialism" or "militarism" involved in the development of that policy of expansion which has been part of the history of America from the day she became a nation. The word means absolutely nothing as applied to our present policy in the Philippines: for this policy is only imperialistic in the sense that Jefferson's policy in Louisiana was imperialistic; only military in the sense that Jackson's policy toward the Seminoles or Custer's toward the Sioux embodied militarism.[18]

Plain expression of sentiments like these, today, would stamp the writer as a racist and a hypocrite. Yet the discourse of world politics that I have been discussing has slowly naturalized and neutralized these same premises—except that *expansion* no longer entails the formal annexation of territory by our government. The terms and meanings of that discourse gain wide circulation, of course, through the media, and I now return to that subject. The boundary between Pentagon-talk and the news is naturally permeable: journalists must report what important officials say. But in what ways do they mediate its transmission? They may hold a new usage up for analysis, even object to it. They may blankly convey it, within quotation marks. Or they may, as it were, remove the quotation marks and ease the term from novel speech into routine language. Just as mainstream journalists refused to swallow *Peacekeeper* for the MX missile, most of them kept a critical distance between themselves and the Reagan usage of *freedom fighters*. Yet there is a tendency for Pentagon-talk to become media language over a period of time.

A personal experience will illustrate the point. Sometime around 1968 I complained in writing to the *New York Times* about that paper's repeated use of the word *enemy*, in news reporting, to refer to the Vietnamese National Liberation Front. A staff member actually troubled to write back, explaining that the *Times* used this word only in a descriptive, not in a pejorative, sense. I suggested to him that the nonpejorative use of *enemy*, like that of *kike* or *wop*, was difficult to achieve. That terminated our brief correspondence. The point is that somehow, between perhaps 1964 and 1968, government officials' conception of the South Vietnamese opposition as enemy of the American people had slid comfortably into the standard lexicon of our newspaper of record. Thus did the *Times* help naturalize the war, even while becoming more critical of it on the editorial page.

As I pointed out in the last chapter, journalists' habit of depending on inside sources tends to align their basic conceptions with those of high officials, and make their language porous to official words. The professional doctrine of journalistic objectivity offers no defense against such leakage, over time. And other journalistic routines and attitudes (see pp. 183–85) abet the distortion of international news as they do that of domestic politics. For instance, television's requirement that each news segment take the shape of a "story" urges correspondents toward narrative closure. In coverage of international events, this drive toward resolution, even when no actual resolution is in sight, tends to return a story at its end to the perspective of American policy makers, whose plans and ideas serve as a bulwark against disorder. Again, the demand for exciting visual images to hold viewers' attention increases the likelihood that when foreigners turn up on the screen they will appear marching or demonstrating or conducting guerrilla attacks or enduring them or being bombed or holding hostages. Foreigners, by pictorial definition, are violent and irrational, quite different from us.

It is worth mentioning three other ways in which the exigencies of TV journalism foster worldthink. Whatever else it is, the news must be habit-forming entertainment, to keep ratings and revenue up. Producers of the news, as of other shows, work toward this end partly by staying with dependably popular subjects. Happenings in other countries are not normally among those subjects. Daily coverage of Brazil or India does not appeal to mass audiences, so news divisions hold foreign coverage down to a barely respectable minimum—except when events abroad impinge on the stability of the world order, as perceived by U.S. leaders. News is by definition that which disturbs the status quo. For that reason, and because networks don't have the staff or the air time to cover the slow unfolding of the social process in other parts of the world, Iranians, Palestinians, Filipinos, and so on appear on our screens mainly when they become unruly, when they threaten "collective security," when they do something unwelcome to the authorities. After the disruption ends, they recede back into nonexistence.

Second, because TV news sells itself as right up to the minute, it feeds on what is happening *now*, and tries to hold its audience by presenting brief, dramatic segments of event. Thus it virtually excludes history, which appears only as hastily assembled "background" for a current outrage. (Perhaps the most egregious example in recent years was the pathetic attempt of newspeople to remedy their ignorance about Grenada when it suddenly became news in the fall of 1983.) We do not see on our screens the long infusion of multinational capital into third world countries, the gradual development of expectations and grievances, the rise of indigenous movements, or the evolution of local politics—nothing that would humanize the mob on the screen and make its actions predictable or comprehensible.

Finally, like other shows, the news organizes reality around famous persons. Consider how the image of domestic politics is narrowed to the doings of a few candidates and officeholders, most of the time. Likewise, the news tends to present a handful of leaders—Arafat, Khomeini, Castro, Walesa, Aquino—as synechdoches for their entire societies. History, economics, politics, the complex struggles of a people, all dissolve into personality and celebrity.

In all these ways the institutions and people who picture the world for television watchers create a systematic ignorance of Latin America, Asia, Africa, and the Middle East. These parts of the rest of the world are supposed to stay out of sight, and in fact not exist, other than as a field for the normal cultivation of U.S. projects and a stable weight in the balance of good and evil. Think of the way Latin American societies appear and disappear. Nicaragua exists on the screen at the moment for obvious reasons, though its realities run a poor second to talking heads from our government, fitting Nicaragua into *their* reality. El Salvador has receded into the shadows, now that things are going "well" there. Honduras is only a place where Contras hang out and where U.S. forces maneuver. Panama is just one name in the list of "Contadora nations." Belize is a total blank. And so on.[19] In addition, the homogenizing process I have described blends these societies together, and indeed tends to make them indistinguishable from Arab societies, African societies (South Africa excepted), and the rest. All merge into a general type of the *other*. *why lower "o"*

If that is correct, it helps explain why public rage over the taking of hostages in Iran was so undifferentiated. I mention that because I remember vividly the sight (on TV) of a spontaneous demonstration on the streets of Washington, soon after the hostages were taken. A man was shouting repeatedly, "we're *tired* of other countries telling us what to do," and then he led the crowd in a wholehearted rendition of "God Bless America." (Given the last thirty years of U.S.-Iranian relations, I wonder how Iranian viewers would have responded to this scene, and what in particular they would have thought to see a black man venting such sentiments.) The United States is the only society that really exists as a society— however distorted—on television. The way Americans experience it, of course, depends in good part on subordination of other societies, but we can't see that process and the dominated are not available to be perceived, except as people who suddenly, incomprehensibly, and irrationally appear on the screen, cause some trouble, then are eventually taken care of and recede back into nonbeing.

This is one of the forms hegemony takes, mediated by the peculiarly complex social relations of the consciousness industry. Capitalism is indeed the most opaque of all social forms, and far more opaque today than when Marx made this observation. In it, human beings and whole societies vanish behind market relations and market culture. We cannot know our interdependence. Exploitation appears as freedom, conflict as an abnormality rather than as the engine of history. The discourse of foreign affairs takes place in a near vacuum of knowledge and understanding, where other peoples, their histories, and their aspirations are momentary distractions.

To sum up these reflections, I suggest that the deeper and more dangerous lies implicit in this discourse derive from and support a picture of the world as organized around two great moral forces. This picture expresses in a broad way the interests of those with power. When it is generally accepted or only weakly challenged, it gives legitimacy to their projects by making their interests seem the interests of "us" all. The words, concepts, and images I've discussed can seem valid only from a perspective of power, from which most people and their needs appear as problems to be solved. And this perspective is inseparable from a flagrantly undemocratic structure of communication,[20] which endows a few with the power to speak, and casts the others as masses to be spoken about and to.[21] Yet the structure of domination persists not because our ruling class uses the media, that some of its members own, as organs of propaganda, but because its hegemony saturates the practices and beliefs and feelings of most Americans, including those who staff the media.

If I am generally right in this analysis, the world picture and the language that accompanies it will change significantly only when the power of the rulers is challenged by broad social movements, when new voices are admitted to the central arena of discourse, *new way* and when the majority of the people become leading actors in the historical process. Until that happens, however—and to help *make* it happen—critical intellectuals have a responsibility to expose and attack the underlying concepts and images of foreign policy discourse.

13 Free Messages, Messages of Freedom

In the last two essays I have stressed obliqueness of control. The ruling class's conception of reality saturates the discourse of mass culture, but the channels through which it arrives in our living rooms are complex and crooked. That's not the *whole* story, however. Right-wing foundations do underwrite programs and publications; some multimillionaires do buy air time for themselves or their pet ideologues; corporations do run "idea ads" that directly solicit our belief. Here I focus on such an effort, a venerable one.

Power is the great American secret. That it exists and where it exists are subjects that have, at least until recently, been met with reticence or silence in American public discourse, as if to speak openly of them were a breach of etiquette—like opening a conversation with a stranger by asking, "Sir, what is your precise income?"

Here are four slogans on the power Americans have—slogans that, since millions of dollars have been spent to implant them in minds, are probably familiar.

America. It only works as well as we do.

People start pollution. People can stop it.

Remember, only you can prevent forest fires.

The United Way. Thanks to you it's working.

I suggest, first, that these slogans share a common theme: the remedy of social ills begins with individual action—even as, generally, individuals caused the ills in the first place. The notoriously sickly economy, slogan 1 tells us, can only be mended if we work harder (I picture malingering hod-carriers, long coffee breaks at the office, fat-cat union bosses). A litter problem in America? Dispose of your bottle properly. (But don't vote against disposable containers—*that's* not how "people" can stop pollution.) And so on. Our social power lies in behaving well as individuals to clean up our messes.

Aside from this root political idea, the slogans communicate, by various semantic strategies, a number of ideas that are at best debatable and at worst silly, and that bear directly on questions of power in and over our lives. Some simple analysis of words and ideas will show what I mean.

1. "America. It only works as well as we do." What *is* America, here? Clearly not our political system, for that can work all right whether or not people go full tilt on their jobs. Not our social institutions. Not America as a social contract or a metaphysical entity. No, the slogan equates America with its economic system. America means, here, all present employers and employees, in their present relationship. If that changed, apparently America would be no more. This effort to attach all our patriotic feeling to the economic status quo strikes me as a clearly political move. Yet the slogan is written so that it will sound like a truism; it is billed as nonpolitical and noncontroversial (a "public service message").

2. "People start pollution. People can stop it." Another truism. But are the same people in both sentences? And do we stop pollution just by refraining from our individual guilty acts? Plainly not. If people all stopped driving motor vehicles that would be good for the air but incompatible with continuing to live, once food ran out. And what about industrial pollution? It's a 150-year-old story— think of Coketown in *Hard Times*—that pollution gets started as a by-product of the scramble for profit, and gets stopped only when the pollutees organize against the power of the chief polluters. So in the slogan something very common happens with the word "people": it is used, quite without justification, to imply that all of us are on a par: just folks, equally powerful, equally responsible for social ills. And the pairing of "start" and "stop" implies a totally false notion of social process; it directs our eyes away from the real mechanics of pollution and remedies for it, and toward the simpler matter of the cast-off beer can—I discard it, you pick it up.

3. What about Smokey Bear, reminding us since 1946 that only we can prevent forest fires? This slogan creates—forgive me— a smoke screen. Leave aside the belief, increasingly widespread among foresters, that forests *need* periodic burning off, which in the absence of rampaging picnickers would be accomplished by divine intervention in the form of lightning. Allowing that it's good to

be careful with fire in the woods, Smokey's campaign is nonetheless deceptive because by dramatizing Man as predator upon the forest, and individual campers as Man, it draws attention from the main relationship of people to woods—that of the wood and paper industries. Recreational users of the forest are relatively powerless to determine the future of this resource; industry and government have a great deal of power. The "only you" formula camouflages this imbalance by pointing a finger at individuals. Paradoxically, the tactic overstates our personal responsibility and guilt, while ignoring the latent power we do have to control and conserve natural resources—by banding together politically.

4. What about the United Way? Well, anyone mean-spirited enough to bad-mouth Smokey Bear will surely not have a kind word for charity—right? I do happily grant that the United Fund is an aggregation of worthy causes pursued by good people. But what does the *slogan say* about the United Fund? "Thanks to you it's working." In the word "working" lies a neat equivocation. The United Fund campaign works in the unilluminating sense that it collects money. The other meaning of the slogan is more airy: the United Way "works" in meeting the social needs for which the money is collected: namely, the amelioration of poverty, ill health, malnutrition, unemployment, family and community breakdown, anomie—in short, most of the disorders of our economic and social system. In *that* sense, it perhaps works well enough for those who hold power in and are the main beneficiaries of the economic and social system, but does it work for those on the other side of the tracks? My own answer, plainly, is that it does not: that it works more or less the way aspirin works for a broken leg. But whatever your answer, I hope you'll agree that this slogan, like the others, uses language to conceal relationships of power in America—even while congratulating us on our supposed power to make the United Way work.

Four semantic processes, then:

    narrowing the meaning (America)

    suppressing distinctions (people)

    distraction (Smokey)

    equivocation (it's working)

And each confirms much the same beliefs about power, and the same dispersion of our citizenship and energy into individual pack-

ets. I believe that one cause, and an important one, of the gentleman's agreement in America to avert our eyes from power is the
way that those eyes—and ears and brains—are saturated with un-
asked-for messages of the kind I've tried to explicate here.

Furthermore, I contend that these messages are sent by design,
and by the design of very powerful people. Many of you will know
that I have lifted my four slogans from campaigns of the Advertising Council. You hear them on radio, read them in every sort of
publication, see them on TV and on billboards and on subways.
But I doubt that most people know just what the Ad Council is and
how it works, in spite of some good recent articles on it, and in
spite of its own boastfulness.

First, then, the Ad Council presides over most of the free advertising in America. For instance, radio and TV stations are under
pressure from the FCC to run some "public service announcements,"
PSAs as they are called. And in fact just less than 3 percent of total
air time goes to PSAs. Of that, the bulk belongs to the Ad Council—
80 percent on network TV, less on radio and local TV. Each year
now, the Ad Council receives well over half a billion dollars worth
of free time and space for its messages.

And who makes up the Ad Council? As Bruce Howard points out
in "Selling Lies" (*Ramparts*, December/January 1974–75), exactly
the same people who send us *paid* commercial messages: industry,
advertising agencies, the mass media. Their executives make up
the Ad Council's board, and their companies contribute the relatively minuscule amounts of money necessary to produce the Ad
Council's materials.

So picture the situation thus: through paid advertising, business
sells its products and ideas directly to the American people. Furthermore, by paying to do this it supports the media, and gains
much influence over reporting, entertainment, and other such messages. Now on top of that, business observes that the government
strongly encourages some "public service announcements"; business would like to control these free messages, too—and in the process get credit for being selfless and civic minded. It hits on this
happy combination of ideas in 1942, and beginning with the war
bond campaign, the Ad Council is underway.

Of course I'm describing the plan more explicitly than it may
appear to its designers and executors. And yet, the Ad Council
carefully plans its campaigns; each one must get approval not only
of the board, but of a Public Policy Committee, which "assures
that council campaigns are truly in the public interest, and are

not commercial or political." As the council rather quaintly puts the matter, it "has the largest client (in America)—the American people." With only one minor difference from other clients, I would add: the American people have no control over the advertising they get from "their" agency. The council decides just what words, ideas, attitudes, and actions are in the public interest. And the public can't take its account to another agency. But I am not just hinting at a prima facie likelihood that Ad Council campaigns add up to a general ideological effort, and that this effort reveals a somewhat peculiar conception of the public interest. Even a cursory look at present campaigns should leave no doubt that the pattern is there. It's as if the Ad Council had asked itself: what are the main political and social questions in America now, and how can we advance our views on each—without sounding controversial? For example— and in rapid summary:

—*Unemployment is over 10 percent.* The Ad Council's program: get businessmen to train and hire veterans, minorities, ex-cons, the disabled. But no action that might lead toward full employment. (I can't resist adding that the Ad Council boasts of having found (!) 250,000 jobs for vets, a million for the disadvantaged, and 850,000 summer jobs for young people. How it has done this while unemployment has steadily risen is an engaging puzzle.)

—*Energy shortages, now and in future?* The Ad Council prescribes carpooling, lower thermostats, slower driving, dimmer lights. But not development of solar or fusion power, or changes in the way industry makes energy choices, without our vote.

—*Malnutrition?* The Ad Council advises Americans on better diets. ("Food is More Than Just Something to Eat.") But no comment on expanding world food production or getting what the world now grows to the starving.

—*Population?* You guessed it—family planning for Americans, and nothing about raising the world's standard of living, the only humane and reliable way to curtail growth.

—*Pollution?* We've seen the answer to this one.

—*Health?* More people should choose health careers. (But who will pay for these workers or see that their services get distributed equitably, so long as health is largely bought and sold on the free market? The Ad Council, unsurprisingly, does not raise this question.)

—*Education?* "Give to the College of Your Choice," and to the United Negro College Fund ("A Mind is a Terrible Thing to Waste"). But nothing about the right of all to higher education.

—*Crime?* Employ ex-cons. And lock your cars.
—*Militarism?* Support the Reserve and the National Guard.
—*Race?* Build black capitalism.
—*A banking and credit system gone crazy?* Buy U.S. Savings Bonds, at interest rates far below the market—just as in 1942.

And so on, with uncanny completeness, through the whole array of issues that are, rightly, on everyone's mind.

It adds up to a rather consistent plan for America and the world. Keep power where it is now lodged, but conceal its presence. Avoid political change. Where the system is not working well, blame individual people, and recommend continence, thrift, neatness, hard work, good deeds, and—always—charity. Where the interests of the rich are threatened, let ordinary people trim their standard of living to bring about an end to growth. And these ads, recall, are said to be chastely nonpolitical.

This coherent program is advanced by a well-organized group of people drawn entirely from our dominant class. In effect, they are carrying on, through the public media, a struggle over ideas. But it is also a struggle over language, and often it is fought with the aid of what the National Council of Teachers of English has christened (after Orwell) "doublespeak." I've analyzed a few examples. Others from the Ad Council's campaign that deserve study include:

—"Community" and the related "Neighbor" (from the Red Cross campaign)—metaphors that suggest a simple, rural society, and deny the existence of impersonal relationships and large, powerful institutions that strongly limit our personal choices. This cluster of words and images is, of course, very commonly used to portray America as a nineteenth-century village. In the same spirit, a leader of the Ad Council itself says "we're the roof-raisers," as in Vermont or the old West—we're good neighbors who'll give a hand, get the house started. (From a public relations record put out by the Ad Council, as part of its "Report to the American People, 1973–74." From the report itself, and from radio, TV, and magazines, I have taken all my other quotations.)

—Another group of words and buried metaphors cluster around the idea of equality. The Red Cross helps people over the rough spots in life. These are clearly the exception, a smooth course the rule. Get people past the rough spots and there's nothing to block their pursuit of happiness. Similarly, in the Ad Council's world some people are "handicapped" and others "disadvantaged." The underlying idea is that of a race or competition in which we are all basically equal, except for special misfortunes—and charity can restore full equality by helping people over rough spots, hiring the handicapped, and so forth. The pattern of images does not allow for any permanent or *systemic* failure of equality.

—A third and last example—the phrase "public interest" itself, which accompanies every radio and TV spot of the Ad Council. The phrase asks us to think of a homogeneous public with a common interest—but how could this be so, as the public is now constituted? Brought down to earth, our interests conflict. But recurring phrases in Ad Council ideology—the "public good," "the needs of the country as a whole," "our problems"—tell us that conflict is a surface phenomenon, that politics is pretty much superfluous, and that no one really has power over any other person.

Needless to say, these ideas themselves are a political weapon of groups with illegitimate power that they conceal in order to preserve. And the rest of us had better expose the ideas in order to combat them.

14 On Teaching about Mass Culture

Mass *culture*. The term carries its own bad ideology. It hints that there is a mass out there different from "us." It more than hints that the masses are all alike. (Raymond Williams: "Masses are other people.") It suggests that they are responsible for Top-40 and "As the World Turns." And it rings as if spoken from a higher plane. For all that, I want mass rather than "popular" culture, the nearest brief alternative, because the latter has no critical edge at all, and falsely implies that The People made this culture as they made quilts and ballads. By *mass culture*, then, I mean culture produced by a few for many, through which the few try to turn the many *into* masses, the more easily to sell us to advertisers and sell commodities and the American way to us.

Why teach mass culture? I know you didn't ask that, but lots of academics do. It's a funny question; it could come only out of the humanities, where people congratulate themselves on teaching and preserving realms of experience remote from the daily experience of the majority. No one would think of condemning economists and biochemists because markets and metabolism have a place in our ordinary lives. Soap operas and shopping malls and superbowls dwell in and form consciousness, defining the real and the possible, and channeling the life energies of Americans, with a power matched only by that of family and job among all our institutions. Quite simply, to understand the world one must understand—and try to change!—mass culture. That goes double for teachers because our students, the young ones anyhow, spend and have spent more of their hours with mass culture than we. (More, for that matter, than *they* have spent on anything else but sleep.) If education is to demystify, liberate, and empower, it must deal with the culture of the marketplace.

That may suffice to exact a grudging tolerance from the culturally conservative professoriat. To leave the imperative at such a level of abstraction, however, is to be satisfied with a piety that opens the way to every conceivable academic use of mass culture. Teaching about mass media and mass entertainments is not in itself a radical act—no more than teaching Dante is intrinsically a conservative act. Beginning in the mid-sixties, mass culture seeped and then poured into the curricula of humanities departments. You remember the motives: to satisfy students' demands for relevance; to entice them into studying real culture; to provide them with topics for themes; to show the universality of our methods and theories; to prove ourselves hip; and most crucially, in the seventies, to bring the bodies back into our emptying classrooms and so preserve our jobs. Radicals whose motive was a ruthless critique of all things existing could have mixed feelings at best about some of our allies in challenging the monopoly of high culture, and about the educational and political results.

And of course this academic movement, like others grounded in opportunism or economic need, quickly sprouted a professional umbrella. The Popular Culture Association (PCA), founded in 1969 out of Bowling Green State University, has probably grown faster than any professional association or learned society in the history of American academe. The program for its convention in Pittsburgh ten years later included more than 150 sessions and well over 400 papers. It publishes the *Journal of Popular Culture* and a newsletter. The PCA defines itself as concerned with "productions . . . designed for mass consumption," but prints articles on the two-story log house in the Upland South and on western hay derricks along with articles on massage parlors in Washington, D.C., and on "Amos 'n' Andy." Yet lately it has spun off a new *Journal of American Culture*, because *JPC* was having to reject excellent articles simply for treating culture that was "not in the strict sense of the term *popular*." And out of that journal has sprung an American Culture Association, whose advisors include those well-known purveyors of the nonpopular, Steve Allen and Irving Wallace, and whose convention subjects include daytime TV, mass magazines, and rock.

What the hell, plunge first and define later when business is booming. And it is no doubt better for the PCA to be totally eclectic than dogmatically to pursue the conviction of its founders that mass culture "*reflects* the values, convictions, and patterns of thought and feeling generally dispersed through and approved by American society" (my italics; all quotations are from the program for the ninth annual convention). In fact, as the PCA gains respectability and establishment support, we should not worry much that its members get NEH funding for projects like a study of "elderly and/or retired detectives" in fiction. We should be more concerned that the PCA leadership may set the course of teaching in this area. NEH funded an interdisciplinary assault on that problem at Bowling Green two years ago. The goals PCA developed for its course on television:

1. Disabuse students of their false attitudes toward TV, including such notions as the *direct* influence of television on juvenile delinquency, alcoholism, consumerism in the American family.
2. Help students see that TV is interrelated with other media such as film, newspapers, literature, etc.
3. Help students consider what factors are used to judge the worth of television programs and lead them to a consideration of their own criteria.
4. Have students speculate about the future role of television in society including education, home entertainment, politics, community theatre, community, health and religious services.

(*Popular Culture Association Newsletter and
Popular Culture Methods*, March 1979)

I like the fact that these goals go beyond grooving with students and beyond a purely literary criticism, but nothing in the emphasis on society points beyond a sophisticated connoisseurship of things as they are.

Make no mistake: if you teach mass culture from a radical perspective you enter an arena of conflict, not so much with your Miltonic office mate who hates TV as with a popcult establishment that is by now comfortably academic and uncritical. You also enter into competition—though there are chances for collaboration too—with professional and vocational programs over on the other side of the campus, preparing students to join the consciousness industry. (Even at my liberal arts college, I've had many students headed for careers in broadcasting or advertising, who took my course in mass culture as part of their preparation, or to be exposed to the "other side.") And of course you are competing with the media themselves, promoting their version of reality all day and every day while you teach only three hours a week. So what else is new? Radical teaching of any subject in our present context fixes us in an adversary posture toward many of our colleagues, toward the institutions we work in, toward the institutions we teach about.

And yes, toward much that our students believe and feel. This is an especially delicate point for radical teachers of mass culture.

Though many students will come into our courses to examine critically their experience of mass entertainments, all of them carry
around that experience as an important part of themselves, and
many are enthusiasts eager to get academic credit for studying
what they already devour by choice. *Any* criticism can seem a put-
down of their own values. Most disastrously, our criticism can
seem indistinguishable from highbrow scorn, grounded in "taste,"
which usually amounts to either class hatred or the snobbishness
of the intellectual. A student in a course of mine, working class, an
athlete: "I think in 'Bread and Circuses' we're just bending over
backwards to find fault, and then being hypocritical about it. Intellectuals put themselves above everyone else and make it seem as
though you have the answers." I plead not guilty, but what use is
that? What I meant as criticism on behalf of his class came through
to him as criticism of his class, or at least of himself and things he
enjoys. So offended, I doubt that he learned much from the course.

More common, luckily, are students who feel a deepening of critical understandings they already half had, without a loss of pleasure or self-esteem. For they do bring contradictory feelings to
such courses. At the beginning of Bread and Circuses, when I ask
them to describe informally their experience of mass entertainments, the phrase "love-hate relationship" turns up over and over.
Mass culture is a feast as well as a swindle. We'd better savor the
feast while we analyze the swindle, teaching from "inside" this
contradiction, rather than as anthropologists.

And of course the students' addiction is also expertise. A happy
problem, that they "know" our subject more intimately than do
most of us. That's a tremendous resource. It opens the way easily to
a collaboration in learning that is more awkward when we teach
Chaucer or history of the novel. We should respect what students
bring to courses on mass culture, draw on that knowledge, help
sharpen and contextualize it, but *learn* from it. The educator must
be educated: when we teach mass culture, the only obstacle to
carrying out this injunction of Marx's is our own training in professional defensiveness.

But now I want to emphasize the other side of the equation.
What should *we* be contributing to our courses in mass culture, besides our politics, critical eyes and ears, respect, and anger? I have
three suggestions to offer.

1. In mass culture the personal and the political join more ex-
plosively than in almost anything else we teach. The media give us

heroes, image the good life, define personal attractiveness and worth, take hold of us by our needs, fears, felt inadequacies, loneliness—and on top of that, turn every social contradiction into a personal problem. I believe there are no more critical areas to penetrate, in teaching mass culture, than sexual politics and the family. In both areas a kind of war is going on between historical change in people's lives and the inventions of the hucksters and mythmakers. The women's movement, the "sexual revolution," the displacement of the traditional family, all have changed the terms on which we can be sold products, comforting stories, and the status quo. (And, to be dialectical about it, the selling of these things has also fueled the women's movement, the sexual revolution, and the breakup of the family.)

We should go well beyond identifying stereotypes, as we teach about such complex matters of sexual politics as the way advertisers (they've come a long way, too, baby) sometimes deny and sometimes obscenely appropriate women's struggles. Or the way TV shows work a hundred mutations on the image of the patriarchal family, while every ten minutes the commercials act as if each house contained a working father, a housewife, and two happy kids, with only the purchase of soap and cereal needed to avert any calamity. Political battles are being fought on such terrain, and we and our students are among the combatants.

2. This leads to my two cents worth of theoretical advice. Advertisers clearly try to manipulate us, in no region more viciously than that of our sexual and familial insecurities: to do so is their business. Put that together with the slightly less blatant political manipulation that runs from TV cop shows to *Reader's Digest;* add the fact, obvious to radicals, that almost all the news and commentary reinforces capitalist attitudes; top all this off with the equally obvious fact that the bourgeoisie owns the mass media—and it's easy to settle on a theory of manipulation. The dominant class, in such theories, consciously uses its ownership of the "means of mental production" to control them, and thereby to control our consciousness. Marx and Engels seem to encourage this view in the famous passage from *The German Ideology* from which I have just quoted (though not in the analysis that follows). Writers like Herbert Schiller (*The Mind Managers*), Paul Hoch (*Rip Off the Big Game*), and even Hans Magnus Enzensberger (*The Consciousness Industry*) develop it.

I don't think it adequate for most areas of mass culture. Take TV news.* It displaces class conflict, splinters politics into pragmatic "issues," buries even these under personalities, ignores ordinary people, lies about the rest of the world, and in general, well, you get the idea. But Rather and friends do not do these things by any political directive from corporate headquarters or the board of directors, though occasionally the higher-ups will step in to suppress a documentary or collaborate with the Pentagon. The roots of political mystification are tangled: they include (a) the fact that news must compete for profit and for our attention, and hence must be entertaining, dramatic, simple, punchy; (b) the class of those who produce the news—mostly technical, professional, lower managerial, and ambitious; (c) their self-definition as professionals, which in this case means "objective," uninvolved, and anti-ideological; (d) the need to produce news on short deadlines, which blocks serious investigation and leads to reliance on establishment sources and spokespeople; (e) the FCC and the Fairness Doctrine, which make newspeople leery of "extreme" views and thus draw safe limits to political discussions; (f) the historical origins of TV news in movie newsreels and radio, so that news tends to be visual first and analytic second if at all. (Read Edward Jay Epstein's *News from Nowhere* and Herbert Gans's *Deciding What's News* for an idea of these complexities.)

Gramsci's idea ("hegemony") of domination as a total way of understanding and living that spreads through all society is a better wedge into all this than theories implying conscious political control. We should be willing to learn in detail, and largely from establishment scholars, how the media become what they are, though we dispute the conclusions of those scholars. A lesser effort and a facile conviction that base determines superstructure may make our students properly cynical about what they see and hear on TV, but it won't equip them to deal with reality.

3. And that brings me to my third conviction: no reality without history. It's so fruitful and so easy, especially for humanities teachers, to stay with form and content analysis, that we may risk fetishizing the products the media turn out, almost as the New Critics did with literature. A good and essential corrective is to bring in the structure and economics of the mind industries. This is obvious, and I'll say no more. I put in a special word for history because I suspect that it's more often left out than is economics, and because I think that without it we can hardly hope to shake free of the

---

* This paragraph condenses a fuller analysis presented on pp. 171–86.

hypnotic now that we enter into when we consume mass culture. It's always *there*, inevitable, a kaleidoscopic spectacle of change that somehow remains always the same. Yet all the mass cultural forms and industries were vastly different just fifty years ago, and none of them but books and newspapers even existed as mass culture one hundred years ago. If our students—who of course know less of history experientially than we—learn that mass culture as they know it is a recent development, that it is largely a creation of monopoly capital, and that all its technologies could have developed quite differently within other social relations, they can more easily imagine a further transformation of mass culture, even perhaps a democratic one. That's why books like Eric Barnouw's *Tube of Plenty*, Stuart Ewen's *Captains of Consciousness*, Robert Sklar's *Movie Made America*, and Raymond Williams's *Television* are so valuable. And where such critical or radical histories don't exist, better make what use we can of mainstream and conservative histories like Foster Rhea Dulles's *America Learns to Play*, James Wood's *The Story of Advertising*, and Theodore Peterson's *Magazines in the Twentieth Century*.

I'd add a fourth point, equally crucial: in teaching mass culture we should always keep alternatives in view, and when possible tie learning to doing. The point, as someone said, is to *change* the world.

IV LITERACY
AND
POWER

15 Literacy, Technology, and Monopoly Capital

My late, lamented colleague Vernon Dibble once told me this rule of thumb: if a title comprises three words or phrases in a series, and their order makes no difference, then the lecture or article will be nonsense. (Vernon used a stronger word than *nonsense*, actually.) I hope to make some sense, although the three terms of my title could as well come in any sequence. In fact, the five sections of the chapter might themselves be rearranged. They represent five pieces of what I take to be a Big Picture, so big that to fill it all in would require a fat volume which I do not plan to write. So I ask the courteous reader to bear with my somewhat fragmentary method, here, and with an argument that cannot be decisive, only suggestive.

It may help if I indicate where I am heading. I claim that exhortations about the need for "computer literacy" have much in common with longer-standing debates about literacy itself; that both kinds of discussion usually rest on a serious misconception of technology and its roles in history; and that we can best understand the issues that trouble us by situating them within the evolution of our present economic and social system—a very recent historical process, going back little more than a hundred years. The whole discussion presumes that questions of literacy and technology are inextricable from political questions of domination and equality.

History

The earliest citations for the word *literacy* in the OED come from the 1880s. The word *illiteracy*, in the common modern sense, appears only a bit earlier. (Before that, it referred to lack of cultivation, or to ignorance.) The adjectives *literate* and *illiterate* have a much longer history; but again, before the late nineteenth century they had a global, qualitative meaning—well read and civilized, or the reverse—rather than indicating a line that divided those who could read and write from those who could not.

If this were 1850, we could not talk about literacy in the language we use now, nor with the same concepts. Of course people had been discussing for centuries the ability to read and write, and who should have it. But they did so without a mass noun that isolated that ability from other human practices and that referred to it as a measurable attribute of individuals, groups, or whole societies. That seems odd to me. Why did the concept and the term *literacy* come into play just when they did, toward the end of the last century?

We can get a hint by looking at the discourse within which writers (and doubtless speakers) began to use the words *literacy* and *illiteracy*. One of the *OED*'s earliest citations for *literacy* points us to the *New Princeton Review*, November 1888.[1] The word turns up in an article by George R. Stetson, called "The Renaissance of Barbarism," which laments and analyzes the rise in crime—statistically documented—since midcentury. He sees this quite specifically as a class phenomenon. There has been a widening "separation of those who have, from those who have not, a complete control of their appetites and passions"; the latter, he calls "the brutalized class," and to them he attributes almost all "the outrageous, inhuman, and barbarous crimes." That is why, although "Education is more general, our literacy greatly increased," moral degeneracy is also on the rise—with immigrants and Negroes contributing far more than their share.[2]

A companion article in the same issue, by James P. Munroe, ponders "The Education of the Masses." Munroe, like Stetson, worries about moral degeneration, idleness, and crime; like Stetson, he writes of these dangers in terms of class. There is a "dangerous class," composed mainly of immigrants, which may easily contaminate the class next to it, "the so-called working class." (His theory of class interaction: "Below a certain stratum of the social structure, all populations have a tendency toward degeneration,—a tendency enormously increased by contact with classes upon a still lower plane.") Munroe's concern is to provide the right education for these "slowly-plodding millions, without fame, almost without identity."

In this context he, too, uses one of the new words. He does *not* advocate repeal of compulsory education laws: "Not for one moment would I advocate illiteracy," he writes, even though at the moment, "the evils of mal-education" are "perhaps greater . . . than those of illiteracy." His solution: take the children of the masses—who are "unfitted or indisposed" to educate their children—from the parents at age two or three, put them in "kindergartens," and train them "to habits of cleanliness, order, neatness, and punctuality." To offset the cost of such education, Munroe advocates the abolition of free high schools, whose "higher education" is wasted upon most of the lower classes (pp. 348–52). I would note that Stetson also fixes upon education as a cause, and possible cure, for crime: a purely "intellectual" schooling has pushed out "religious and manual training," expanding literacy but not moral character (pp. 342–43).

I don't want to make these two articles bear too much weight, but I suggest we think about the soil in which our main concept took root. The argument over education for poor people had been joined long before the 1880s, of course. What catches my attention is how easily the new idea slid into that discourse. For it was a top-down discourse from the start, and its participants almost invariably took the underlying question to be: how can we keep the lower orders docile? Thus, for instance, Bernard de Mandeville: "Going to School . . . is Idleness, and the longer Boys continue in this easy sort of Life, the more unfit they'll be when grown up for downright Labour."[3] And, on the other side, Adam Smith: "An instructed and intelligent people . . . are always more decent and orderly than an ignorant and stupid one."[4] Once the lower orders came to be seen as masses and classes, the term *literacy* offered a handy way to conceptualize an attribute of theirs, which might be manipulated in one direction or the other for the stability of the social order and the prosperity and security of the people who counted.

From these origins, the concept evolved naturally to serve purposes of social diagnosis and reform. One could *measure* literacy scientifically. The first study of illiteracy in the United States was published in 1870,[5] but it was not until World War I, when 30 percent of recruits were unable to take the written intelligence test, that a movement toward systematic literacy testing got underway.[6] Literacy *tests* and census questions become evidence to fix the literacy *rate* of a society. After that, of course, we may thrill to periodic literacy *crises*, followed by back-to-basics movements. And international agencies may attack low literacy rates in third world countries with literacy *campaigns* designed to hasten modernization.

(Modernization theory held that a literacy rate of 40 percent was necessary for "takeoff" to occur.)

All of this—the analytic division of people into measurable quantities, the attempt to modify these quantities, the debate among professionals and political leaders over what's good for the poor— all this legacy still inheres in the discourse of literacy, even now, when almost everyone takes it for granted that literacy is a Good Thing, and when it would be hard to find a Mandeville to argue that the poor should be kept illiterate in order to keep them content.

Monopoly Capital

The term *literacy* came into use at about the time monopoly capitalism emerged. (See "Writing and Reading, Work and Leisure," essay 3, pp. 29–32, for an account of that transformation, which reshaped American society from the 1880s on.)

I do not think it a coincidence that the debate about reading admitted a new concept and took on a new emphasis in the midst of these epochal changes. Obviously the discourse of "dangerous classes" to which I have alluded gained impetus from the intense labor uprisings of the 1870s and 1880s, which challenged the industrial system and its hierarchies even as they were becoming ascendant. That system needed a mass of workers, and it needed them to be, precisely, "slowly plodding millions, . . . almost without identity." But its leaders and intellectual spokesmen could not reverse the management revolution that sought to deprive workers of human identity on the job. Nor was it possible yet to pay them decent wages. So the issue for those at and near the top of the hierarchy was how to channel and dampen the resentful energies of the new proletariat.

Sending in the Pinkertons, the militia, or federal troops was an option, and neither industrialists nor political leaders hesitated to use it. But they could not be at ease with the prospect of endless domestic warfare; also, the repeated necessity of using military force against the populace called into question the very legitimacy of the economic order and of the State. Those who thought and planned from the top down—including writers like Stetson and Munroe—cast about for ways to moderate tension and to discipline the subaltern classes under the sign of rationality rather than of sheer power. Universal public schooling was one strategy among many.[7] The idea of literacy harmonized nicely with that of the graded, uniform school system, through which each pupil would advance as far as ability permitted. Add the important fact that from 1880 on, the urban working class became increasingly *foreign*, and it is clearer still why a vigorous debate on social order called the concept of literacy into play.

More abstractly, monopoly capital added layers of complexity to our society, and also for the first time brought that complexity within the scope of national planning.[8] The successes of corporate design encouraged planning in other spheres, as well. A host of projectors and reformers emerged in the last quarter of the century, along with the institutions of social administration and social science. A habit took root of thinking analytically and from the outside about society. One could measure its dimensions, diagnose it with scientific authority, take its temperature, prescribe remedies. The concept of literacy fit naturally into this way of addressing the social world that is so characteristic of twentieth-century liberalism.

Technology

Against this background, I now marshal some reflections on technology—unsystematic, but I hope suggestive. First, as a kind of loosing-up exercise, I ask you to imagine some instances of the almost unimaginable.

1. Suppose that writing (a technology, as Walter Ong rightly insists) had been invented by slaves—say, in the Roman Empire—and for purposes of survival, resistance, and rebellion. How might they have devised a writing system to advance those purposes? Might it have been a shifting code, to preserve its secrets from masters? Might there have been a common form that could encode the different languages spoken by slaves? I don't know, but my guess is that writing would not have evolved as it did, had its inventors wanted it as an aid to solidarity and revolt.

2. What about printing? When Raphael Hythloday, Thomas More's traveler, showed European books to the Utopians, they quickly re-invented printing and papermaking: their sole purpose was to make available thousands of copies of the Greek classics, so that all who wished might pursue wisdom and the study of nature. Shortly after More wrote, the English adapted printing to a different use, in the *Great Boke of Statutes:* organizing the laws for their more rational administration and enforcement.[9] Would the Utopians, with their purely humanistic and relatively egalitarian aims, have developed the technology of printing in ways different from those that served state power? Certainly the printing technology

that served English radicals of the 1790s, with their plethora of small presses, pamphlets, and journals, was sharply different from the technology developed for mass circulation magazines, with gigantic rotary presses and photoengraving, to address people as a mass audience rather than as participants in a common discourse. (The 1790s term, *corresponding societies*, suggests a very different setting for technology from that indicated by our term, *mass communications*.)

3. Suppose that wireless communication had evolved, not under the guidance and for the needs of the British navy, the United Fruit Company, and commercial advertisers, but among women tinkering in their homes, sharing knowledge about domestic production, establishing networks of child care and concern. Every receiver is in principle a transmitter as well. Might we have had electronic systems that actually merited the name *communication*, rather than or in addition to *broadcasting?*

4. And what if the computer . . . ? I don't even know the right bizarre question to ask, but I do know that computers are an evolving technology like any other, shaped within particular social relations, and responsive to the needs of those with the power to direct that evolution. I will return to this subject shortly, for a mixture of anxiety and excitement about computers inevitably surrounds any discussion of literacy and technology today.

First, though, let me state the point of the in-some-ways absurd thought experiments I just asked you to conduct. Following Raymond Williams's helpful clarifications,[10] I have meant to call into question technological determinism (the idea that, e.g., TV somehow got invented, and from that accident many consequences have inexorably followed), and also what Williams calls "symptomatic technology" (the idea that TV was invented on the margins of the social process, and was simply deployed by other forces that dictate the direction of society—so that it is a *symptom* of consumerism, mass culture, passivity, or whatever). This second view is close to what I call "neutral techology"—the idea that every invention, still thought of as appearing independently, can be put to an infinite number of uses—humane and inhumane, tyrannical and democratic.

I agree with Williams that these views err in abstracting technology from society, sometimes in a way that makes it seem like a miraculous intervention in history. The history of radio and television, as told by Williams, or by Eric Barnouw in *Tube of Plenty*,[11] reveals quite a different process. The technology developed over a century and more, in ways far from accidental. Those with the vision, the needs, the money, and the power gradually made it what they wanted—a mass medium. (I exaggerate only a bit.) Technology, one might say, is itself a social process, saturated with the power relations around it, continually reshaped according to some people's *intentions*. The point is borne out with respect to electric lighting, the telephone, the chemical industry, and so forth, in David Noble's fine study, *America by Design*.[12] As a TV commercial aptly put it: "The future is being driven by technology, and Martin Marietta is masterminding it."

Perhaps I can make the point another way by entering a friendly objection to some characteristic formulations of Walter Ong, one of our most stimulating and learned writers on these matters. In *Interfaces of the Word*, for instance, he writes of "technological devices . . . which enable men to . . . shape, store, retrieve, and communicate knowledge in new ways."[13] Again, "writing and print and the computer enable the mind to constitute within itself . . . new ways of thinking" (p. 46). And, "the alphabet or print or the computer enters the mind, producing new states of awareness there. . . . the computer actually releases more energy for new kinds of exploratory operations by the human mind itself" (p. 47). My objections are, first, to phrases like "*the* computer," as if it were one, stable device; second, to these phrases used as grammatical agents ("the computer enables the mind . . ."), implying that the technology somehow came before *someone's* intention to enable *some* minds to do *some* things; and third, to phrases like "man," "the mind," and "the human mind," in these contexts, suggesting that technologies interact with people or with "culture" in global, undifferentiated ways, rather than serving as an arena of interaction among classes, races, and other groups of unequal power. Certainly Ong is no stranger to such ideas, and he may well agree with most of what I am saying. My point is just that technological determinism is a powerful ideology which tends to infiltrate our minds when we look the other way. I think we need to be on guard against it, when thinking about literacy or any other technology, including

Computers

About which I know remarkably little—so that I may now air my prejudices with only slight interference from the facts.

We are told (in the language of technological determinism) that computers are transforming the workplace and the home, not to mention the school, and that in response to this change, we need to provide "computer literacy" for everyone, or at least for the young. Paul A. Strassmann, vice president for "strategic planning" at Xerox's Information Products Group, holds that we are now at the end of the Gutenberg era and "the beginning of the 'electronic display' era." Adults ignorant of computers will soon be as restricted as those who today are unable to read. Software will become the language of the future, and "the dominant intellectual asset" of the human race, so that an "understanding of software . . . will be a primary component of literacy in the electronic age." [14] Many of those who worry about education see things the same way. The National Council of Teachers of Mathematics has committed itself to the proposition that "an essential outcome of contemporary education is computer literacy." The National Science Foundation funded a study to define computer literacy; its findings appeared in *Mathematics Teacher*.[15] The article listed sixty-four objectives for computer education (including forty "core" objectives), ranging from a grasp of how computers work to familiarity with computer crime. The authors acknowledged that achievement of these objectives would require more than a single course. Pressure increased on schools to provide such education.

Behind such pressure, of course, was the fear of parents and students that computer literacy will be required for many or most good jobs in the future. People like Strassmann encourage that view. He predicts that almost 30 million people—roughly one-quarter of the work force—will have "electronic workstations" by 1990, and use this means of communication about one-half the time they are at work (p. 117). I don't know just what Strassmann has in mind, but one may perhaps allay one's anxiety *or* euphoria, in anticipating this revolution, by looking around oneself right now.

For example: in my own department of twenty-three full-time workers, only one has an electronic workstation, and is required to possess a small degree of computer literacy. She is the junior secretary, and, at perhaps $12,000 a year, the worst paid of the twenty-three. (I don't believe the computer has improved her life or her temperament.) All the workers at my travel agency have electronic workstations, which have considerably routinized (and dehumanized) their work. So does the baggage agent at the airline. So does the teller at my bank. And I wonder if Strassmann's count included the check-out clerks at my supermarket, with their computerized scanners, which have reduced the skill required to an almost entirely manual one of the most repetitive kind. Or how about the young people behind the fast-food counter, whose computer keyboards no longer carry numbers and letters, but pictures of food items, so that the work could be done by someone who is both computer illiterate and just plain illiterate? Predictions that 50 to 75 percent of jobs will soon be "computer-related" sound intimidating, but how many of those jobs will call for even the slightest understanding of computers?[16]

I am suggesting that, seen from the side of production and work, the computer and its software are an intended and developing technology, carrying forward the deskilling and control of labor that goes back to F. W. Taylor and beyond, and that has been a main project of monopoly capital. As Taylor consciously sought to transfer all understanding of production to management and reduce the worker's role to that of a conduit for the transfer of commands into physical energy, engineers are shaping computers now so that those who work at them will be only keyboard operators. As Phil Kraft puts it, "all the skill is embodied in the machines"—in fact, that could be a definition of the term *user friendly*. ("Designing for idiots is the highest expression of the engineering art," in David Noble's words.)[17] In a special irony, engineers are programming some of their *own* skill into obsolescence, along with that of technicians, in the booming field of Computer-Assisted Design/Computer-Assisted Manufacture—CAD/CAM. And predictably, there are now programs for *programming*, aimed at reducing the need for intelligent programmers even as schools and colleges scramble to train them.

Of course there will be more jobs in the computer field itself. But that doesn't amount to much, as against the deskilling that is underway (or indeed, against the number of jobs *eliminated* through computerization). It seems that in 1995 there will be only half a million or so additional jobs in this field, compared to 800,000 new jobs for janitors.[18] Furthermore, the field is layered into specialties, which will be dead ends for most people in them. Operators seldom become programmers; programmers seldom become systems analysts; analysts seldom become designers or computer scientists.[19] Graduates of MIT will get the challenging jobs; community college grads will be technicians; those who do no more than acquire basic skills and computer literacy in high school will probably find their way to electronic workstations at McDonald's. I see every reason to expect that the computer revolution, like other revolutions from the top down, will indeed expand the minds and the freedom of an elite, meanwhile facilitating the degradation of labor and the stratification of the work force that have been hallmarks of monopoly capitalism from its onset.[20]

After this brief look at production, an even briefer glance now at consumption, before I skip back to literacy. Microcomputers *will* be in the homes of most people, without question (some forecasts see them penetrating the home market almost as universally as television has done). And to judge from some of my friends who are buffs, hobbyists, and addicts, some people *will* have their horizons widened and their minds challenged. (Though I also forecast even more broken marriages from this cause than have resulted from TV football coverage.) But I remain skeptical about the import of the change. Apparently, 80 percent of home computers in 1984 were used *exclusively* for games.[21] I bet many of them will fall into disuse, like other new toys. Yet the manufacturers are selling them hot and heavy, often appealing to the hopes and anxieties of parents in quite unscrupulous ways. Thus, one radio commercial featured a dad saying to a mom that if they bought a personal computer it could change their daughter's whole life. To Mom's incredulity, Dad explained that their daughter would get an edge on other kids at school that could get her into a prestigious college, and *that* could even affect whom she might *marry!* Mom was convinced. This appeal to hope and anxiety calls to mind strongly the pitch of door-to-door encyclopedia salespeople, thirty years ago.

Seen from *this* side of the market, computers are a commodity, for which a mass market is being created in quite conventional ways. And their other principal use in the home, besides recreation, most likely will be to facilitate the marketing of still *more* commodities, as computerized shopping becomes a reality. Thus our "age of technology" looks to me very much like the age of monopoly capital, with new channels of power through which the few try to control both the labor and the leisure of the many.

And the education? That is not my subject here; but a brief aside may be in order, to connect the instructional use of computers to my argument. In 1983, Stanley Pogrow lamented, in *Education in the Computer Age*, that schools were not responding well to the new "information economy." There were only 96,000 microcomputers in the schools, and they were not being used to improve learning for most students. He saw a high likelihood that in this decade, the dissatisfaction of parents and employers will go beyond "political activism" to *abandonment* of public schools, and to "environmental collapse" of a school system unable to adapt, with industry taking over this side of education.[22] Two other specialists in this area—Tim O'Shea and John Self—are confident that computers will become standard furniture in classrooms, but pose the danger and choices in this way:

Computers will cause great changes in education. Already there are examination halls in American universities where rows of nervous students type answers to multiple-choice questions at computer consoles and anxiously await their grade. There are also experimental classrooms where young children happily and confidently command a computer to draw pictures or play music, and articulately explain their latest computer program. Motivated by cost-effectiveness and efficiency, educators may try to use computers to turn classrooms into human battery farms. But there is a possibility that computers will be used to enhance the educational process and equip each learner with an exciting medium for problem-solving and individual tuition.[23]

Most people I've asked agree that O'Shea and Self's first alternative is ascendant at the moment, with computers being used as little more than electronic workbooks and data banks. That the liberatory possibilities explored by O'Shea and Self lag behind may have something to do with the way Pogrow's forecast is already proving to be wrong. There are now more than 500,000 computers in American schools, many of them gifts or nearly so from the manufacturers and from other companies. The motives for such generosity are not hard to imagine. Apparently, business will take care that its needs are met without the "environmental collapse" of public schools, and one cannot expect those needs to include many of the liberatory classrooms mentioned by O'Shea and Self. This is the first area of public education to be so stimulated and directed by business. Most likely, the technology of classroom computers—especially software—will serve purposes I have already described.

Now, none of these developments is foreordained. The technology is malleable; it does have liberatory potential. Especially in education, we have something to say about whether that potential is realized. But its fate is not a technological question: it is a political one.

Literacy

I have stated my outlook on these themes in enough ways, now, that you will know whether you find it congenial or not. I will not develop it in detail, with respect to the prospects for literacy in the United States today, but will just reflect on some of its implications.

Plainly, from this perspective it is not helpful to think of literacy as an invariant, individual skill, or as a skill whose numerically measurable distribution across a society (as in *literacy rate*) will tell us much of scholarly interest or human relevance. Literacy is an activity of social groups, and a necessary feature of some kinds of social organization. Like every other human activity or product, it embeds social relations within it. And these relations always include *conflict* as well as cooperation. Like language itself, literacy is an exchange between classes, races, the sexes, and so on. Simply recall the struggle over black English, or think on the continuing conflict over the CCCC statement, "Students' Right to Their Own Language," or the battle over generic male pronouns, for times when the political issues have spilled out into the open. But explicit or not, they are always there, in every classroom and in every conversation—just as broadcasting technology is an exchange that has up to now been resolved through control by the dominant classes, and participation by the subordinate classes in the form of Nielsen ratings and call-in shows.

That means we can usefully distinguish between literacy-from-above and literacy-from-below.[24] From the 1790s to roughly the 1830s, popular literacy in England was broad and vigorous (among men, at least), as artisans and the new industrial working class taught one another to read, formed corresponding societies, drafted petitions, put out pamphlets and books, held meetings. *The Rights of Man* sold 1.5 million copies by the time of Paine's death—equivalent to sales of 25 million in the United States today. This happened in a context where, as Donald puts it, "what we now specify as politics, education, literacy, journalism and recreation were still bound inextricably together. Their division into separate institutions was one effect of the ruling bloc's new techniques of power."[25] Those techniques won out, both in England and in the United States, as literacy was subsumed within state-run school systems. As we well know, the results here have provoked both patriotic self-congratulation and repeated literacy "crises" over the last seventy-five years— the latter meaning a periodic rediscovery by those at the top and their allies that after ten or twelve years of instruction in "English," very many citizens read and write badly.

But why should it be otherwise? Isn't the functional literacy rate just about what one would expect, given how schooling relates to the needs and life chances of the working class? (Shouldn't we expect similar results in computer literacy, once people understand the false promises behind that movement?) Likewise, top-down literacy campaigns in "developing" countries have been almost universally failures. In Cuba, on the other hand, during the single year of 1961, 750,000 illiterate adults learned to read and write, leaving only 250,000 illiterates there, or about 4 percent of the population. I've suggested that a literacy *rate* is in itself mystifying; but you can sense the *kind* of literacy and the context that supported it by reading some of the letters that "students" wrote to Castro, as their final "exam."

Dr. Fidel Castro Ruz
Dear Comrade:
I write this to let you know that now I know how to read and write thanks to our Socialist and democratic Revolution. That's why I'm writing to you, so that you can see with your own eyes. I take leave with a firm Revolutionary and democratic salute.
I used to be illiterate
Patria o Muerte
Teaching, we shall triumph.

Comrade Fidel Castro:
I am very thankful because I know how to write and read. I would like you to send me the Follow-Up books to improve my knowledge more in the reading and in the writing. To be an educated people is to be free.[26]

These peasants had learned to read and write in the context of a revolution, and with the aim of becoming full participants in it, not of passing from third grade into fourth or of meeting a college requirement. Their learning was saturated with politics, an activity of conscious liberation. Of course it did not happen spontaneously, and it *began* at the top in that Castro initiated the campaign. But he spoke for nearly all the people of Cuba when he articulated the goal of full literacy, and those people responded with energy because they saw the revolution as theirs, and literacy as contributing to it.

Cuba at that time had only 35,000 teachers, and they stayed in their classrooms teaching kids. The *brigadistas* who went out into the hills to live and work with peasant families were students, 90 percent of them between ten and nineteen years old, predominantly from the cities. More than 100,000 volunteered after Castro's call, in spite of the distances they would travel from home, the crude shacks they would live in, and the strangeness of their task (after just ten days of training). "I knew nothing about reading" (said a woman who was sixteen in 1961). My first motive . . . was not to teach. It was to be part of a great struggle. It was my first chance to take a stand."[27] They learned to use a primer and a book of readings, which began, not with "See Jane run," but with key political terms: "OEA," Spanish acronym for the Organization of American States; "INRA," the National Institute of Agrarian Reform. From the first day, the project of literacy was for these *campesinos* connected to their needs and their situation in the world. As David Harman (an adult literacy worker in Israel) said to Kozol, the pedagogical theories and classroom techniques don't matter a lot: "None of it works . . . unless it is allied with something else. That 'something else' is what they did in Cuba. It is the promise of a better life for every man and woman in the land."[28] The more recent literacy campaign in Nicaragua, which also offered "something else," used similar methods with similar results.[29]

Technique is less important than context and purpose in the teaching of literacy, and the *effects* of literacy cannot be isolated from the social relations and processes within which people become literate.

Enough. The age of computer technology will bring us some new tools and methods for teaching literacy. I hope we (or rather, those of us teachers who believe as I do!) will manage to shape that technology to democratic forms.

But this age of technology, this age of computers, will change very little in the social relations—the *class* relations—of which literacy is an inextricable part. Monopoly capital will continue to saturate most classrooms, textbooks, student essays, and texts of all sorts. It will continue to require a high degree of literacy among elites, especially the professional-managerial class. It will continue to require a meager literacy or none from subordinate classes. And yet its spokesmen—the Simons and Newmans and Safires and blue ribbon commissions on education—will continue to kvetch at teachers and students, and to demand that all kids act out the morality play of literacy instruction, from which the moral drawn by most will be that in this meritocracy they do not merit much.

But then monopoly capital will *also* continue to generate resistance and rebellion, more at some times than at others. I hope many of us will find ways to take part in that resistance, even in our daily work. Apparently we must learn to fight mindless computer literacy programs, as we have sometimes fought mindless drills in grammar and usage. We should remember that most programmed instruction, in addition to being mindless, builds in imperatives other than ours and other than those of our students. Computerized testing is likely to be undemocratic, not because the computer is, but because it will help realize the impulse toward inequality that is implicit in all standardized testing. We should be critically analyzing the politics of all these tendencies, trying to comprehend them historically, and engaging our students in a discussion of literacy and technology that is both historical and political. It's worth trying to reconstitute literacy as a process of liberation—but also to remember that work for literacy is not in itself intrinsically liberating. The only way to have a democracy is to make one.

16 The Strange Case of Our Vanishing Literacy

I spoke in the last essay about the peculiarly modern phenomenon of literary *crisis*. Every once in a while, people with cultural
authority scan the educational terrain, discover that it has turned
into a slough of despond, and gain access to the media for their
cries of alarm and their diagnoses. To my knowledge, the first such
crisis was in the 1890s. The second major one occurred in 1975–76,
when the nation was still reeling from the oil crisis of the two preceding years. I aired my own skeptical thoughts on the matter, in a
brief essay published by *The Chronicle of Higher Education*, in 1976.

On the rare occasions when American society takes notice, through
its more popular media, of English teachers, it does not usually
employ the customary academic language of self-scrutiny and self-
justification—"broad humanistic values," "personal growth," "the
best that has been thought and known in the world," and so forth.
It broods instead about why Johnny can't read and write.

The present is one of those times, and the current hullabaloo
makes a fascinating case study in the politics of education. The
Newsweek cover story in December 1975—"Why Johnny Can't
Write"—is the most elaborate expression of a new concern with
our doings, but readers of *Time*, the *New York Times*, the *Chicago
Tribune*, *Saturday Review*, *Change*, the *Yale Alumni Magazine*, *Reader's Digest*, and many other journals and newspapers, as well as
viewers of television, heard at length about this new crisis.

The talk they heard presents a consistent view. From quite varied
evidence it builds fat generalizations about a recent and frightening
historical change. Thus the editors of the *Yale Alumni Magazine* say
flatly that "students can't write." In *Newsweek* Merrill Sheils adds

that "students' reading ability is declining," and speaks of a "generation of semi-literates." The confidence behind these generalizations shows up in many an unhedged definite article: "the decline in writing ability" (*Time*); "the breakdown in writing" (*Newsweek*); "the decline in reading and writing ability" (Sidney P. Marland); "the inability of students to express themselves" (*Yale Alumni Magazine*); "the new illiteracy" (*Newsweek*).

Some analysts go further, leaping from the decline in certain kinds of performance to three possibilities that are graver still. First, the familiar one that our society is in the midst of a "literary breakdown" (Karl Shapiro). Second, the English language itself is in trouble (shades of George Orwell): A. Bartlett Giamatti discovers "something real and terrifying about the state of the English language"; Jean Stafford speaks of our "ailing language" and calls its condition "critical." Third, and most terrifying, the human mind may be passing through a dismal alteration. The very "ability to use language is withering" (A. Bartlett Giamatti); "we have ceased to think in words" (Jacques Barzun) and are spiraling down in a "regression toward the intellectually invertebrate" (Ronald Berman).

No wonder that, listening to such authorities, *Newsweek*'s correspondent worries that "we will soon find ourselves back in Babel."

I believe that the decline in literacy is a fiction, if not a hoax. So far as I can tell from a little reading on the subject, the available facts simply do not reveal whether young Americans are less literate than their counterparts in 1930 or 1960.

Here are some facts that support those who would like to use the definite article with *decline in literacy:*

—The verbal scores on American College Testing Program tests and the Scholastic Aptitude Test have gone down since 1964, with the biggest drop last year. Similar declines are recorded on other tests.

—The National Assessment of Educational Progress reports that in 1974, thirteen- and seventeen-year-olds wrote in a more "primer-like" style, with more run-on sentences, and with more incoherent paragraphs than did the same age groups in 1970.

—According to a large study run by the University of Texas and supported by the U.S. Office of Education, only 49 percent of people eighteen to twenty-nine years old have adequate command of the skills used in making a living and sustaining a household—compared to 60 percent of those thirty to thirty-nine years old.

But here are some facts that support the opposite view:

—*Preliminary* SAT scores were up between 1960 and 1966, and again between 1970 and 1972.
—The NAEP study showed that the percentage of good writers among seventeen-year-olds had gone up, that nine-year-olds were better writers than their counterparts four years ago, and that all three age groups adequately handled basics—spelling, punctuation, agreement, usage, and so forth.
—A study by the American Institutes for Research showed a slight improvement in reading-test scores for high-school seniors between 1960 and 1970.
—The National Assessment of Educational Progress found that the functional literacy rate for seventeen-year-olds increased from 88 percent to 90 percent between 1971 and 1974.

I apologize for this clutter of facts, but something like it is necessary in order to understand how little the pundits understand. The Educational Testing Service, the Office of Education, and two other organizations sponsored a wide survey of reading-test results in 1975. The researchers found no solid evidence of a decline in reading ability, and concluded this way: "We are now convinced that anyone who says he *knows* that literacy is decreasing . . . is at best unscholarly and at worse dishonest." Apparently we are, as so often, experiencing a media-created event.

When people set out to find the *causes* of an event that may or may not have happened, and whose nature is unknown, one can expect a certain amount of floundering. The most amusing side of the current debate is the cast of villains—plain and exotic, individual and collective—assembled by our writers to account for the decline in literacy. Here are some: the "creative school" among English teachers, structural linguistics, Webster's *Third*, less teaching of grammar, English teachers who themselves can't write, the fact that kids no longer read the Bible, educationists' jargon, the "new sentimentality," "the mono-syllabic speech habits of the young," open-admissions programs, the increase of mass education, the Free Speech Movement, Vietnam, Watergate, children's books, replacement of writing by telephone conversations, nonverbal parents, advertisements, popular songs, worship of the machine, the "complexity and illogic of the English language," students with tin ears, Kahlil Gibran, Kurt Vonnegut, Hermann Hesse, Abbie Hoffman, Zen Buddhism, the new primitivism, drugs, permissiveness, the federal government. And always poor television, with its "linguistic sludge" (*Yale Alumni Magazine*), its "paltry fare" (H. Mark Johnson), its "simplistic spoken style" (*Newsweek*), its "new plagues" of jargon (Jean Stafford).

If each of these things and people really does contribute to poor writing, it's astonishing that all of them taken together have not brought on terminal paralysis of the collective American forearm. Of course another possibility is that the decline in literacy has been accompanied by a decline in intelligence, especially pronounced among those who write about the decline in literacy.

Fortunately, studies are beginning to appear which, if noticed by the pundits, might help combat doublethink on this subject. Two of them were reported in *The Chronicle of Higher Education*. They bore not on the ontologically dubious decline in literacy, but on the quite real decline in some test scores over the past ten years. Here are three *other* facts that, taken together, suggest an interpretation rather different from what one can read in *Time* and *Newsweek:*

First, from 1971 to 1973 alone, enrollment of high school students in English courses dropped 11 percent nationally, while absences from school also increased. On the assumption that at least *some* of what English teachers teach shows up on tests, this could explain a lot.

Second, at the same time there were fewer dropouts from high school: that is, more students taking the standard tests from that part of the population that used to leave school before senior year.

And third, the decline in ACT scores has taken place almost entirely among women. Why? Between 1965 and 1975 the percentage of test takers who were women increased from 45 percent to 55 percent. The researcher inferred that this means young women are less excluded from education now: many who would not have had a go at college then are doing so now. Presumably this new group is less well prepared than the women who used to choose higher education. If so, the "decline in literacy" translates partly into an *increase* in equality and social justice. Is *that* what *Newsweek* is worried about?

Finally, it should at least be mentioned that an inverse correlation is well established between standardized test scores and number of siblings. People reaching their upper teens now come on the average from larger families than the same age cohort did fifteen years ago—or will fifteen years hence. So part of the decline in literacy is nothing more than the temporary reflex of a purely demographic fact.

When a cultural nonevent arouses wide concern, and when journalists, bureaucrats, and professors scramble to explain it, what most needs explaining is the journalistic phenomenon itself. Why the outcry? Why now?

Begin with the historical observation that each time the American educational system has rapidly expanded, admitting previously excluded groups to higher levels, there has been a similar chorus of voices lamenting the decline in standards and foreseeing the end of Western civilization.

Then consider that those who are quoted in the media belong almost without exception to our cultural and educational elite: A. Bartlett Giamatti, professor of English at Yale; H. Mark Johnson, teacher at a selective (though progressive) private school; Sidney P. Marland, president of the College Board; Ronald Berman, chairman of the National Endowment for the Humanities; Jean Stafford, a *New Yorker* writer; and Jacques Barzun, emeritus professor at Columbia.

Note further that most of the fuss is about the grammatical, stylistic, and conceptual abilities of the elite and near elite among our young people—those who are in college or hope to get there.

Finally, it should not be surprising that among those falling over each other to assign blame for "the" decline in literacy, conservative feelings are often in evidence. There's a tendency to indict the movements of the 1960s. Mass education and open admissions come under attack for lowering standards. Clearly the conflict over literacy in some ways parallels the conflict over race and IQ: underlying both is a continuing political argument about who shall be educated and what shall be the limits of equality in the U.S.

This controversy goes on always. But the forms it takes are important, and the present eruption of concern is a cloud of mystifications. The media, the pundits, and many spokesmen for my own profession have defined the problem as one of verbal manners, the performance of college students, and a deterioration of standards. Given this definition, the solutions are obvious: back to "basics," stricter grading, tougher standards for admission and advancement. There is pressure to make this branch of education more mechanical, less humanistic, more class bound, and less critical. To the extent that the pressure succeeds, my profession will have lost a skirmish in the battle over precisely those values it holds to be most important.

Meanwhile, there is a very different fight over literacy that deserves to be engaged. More worthy of concern than the supposed inarticulateness of Yale and Berkeley freshmen are the results emerging from the studies at the University of Texas of functional literacy, of the verbal abilities needed to get along minimally in our society. According to these studies, one American adult in five is functionally illiterate. And another large group is incapable of understanding such things as the concept of an equal-opportunity employer and the law against detaining an arrested person without bringing charges.

This is nothing new, and apparently nothing *Time* or *Newsweek* would care to do a cover story about. Why not? I think it's worth asking a different set of questions from those that the pundits and professors have so encrusted in nonsense. What would it take, by way of social change, to create full literacy? Why isn't this happening? Do those who control our economic and educational systems really want a totally literate work force, given that there are too few jobs to go around, and too few intelligent jobs for the literate and capable workers who now exist? And do they really want the most exploited people in the U.S. to command the skills of thought, speech, writing, and organization that are considered so essential for students at Yale and Berkeley?

17 On Speculacy

The liberal hope persists that by amending the system of education, and without changing the basic economic relations of our
society, we might make justice and democracy prevail throughout
the land. That hope infuses the thought and debate about literacy.
During the 1980s, literacy has attracted an increasing amount of
scholarly attention, partly in response to public airings of distress
like the one I analyzed in the last essay. One now begins to hear the
term *literacy theory* to refer to systematic thought on these matters.
Much of it is serious and clear-eyed, and I welcome it. But pious
hopes and a self-serving rhetoric of social improvement continue
to surround and confuse the good scholarship. I believe literacy
theory to be inseparable from broader social questions, and from a
history through which the spread of literacy has not in any simple
way been a triumph for ordinary people. In 1984 literacy theory
achieved the dignity of a large forum at the Modern Language Association convention. I tried to enter these concerns into the debate, in the following oblique way.

I'm going to ask you to listen to a parable—really an extended
analogy. Of course analogies prove nothing, and are always unfair.
But here goes, anyhow.

Imagine a society bearing no resemblance to our own, in which
over a period of centuries *gambling* has come to play a central role.
Even in the old days, gambling had some economic importance, as
in the outfitting of ships for long voyages to the spice islands, the
formation of joint-stock companies for colonization, the speculative search for gold, and the occasional wild scheme for investment
in the South Seas, which would enrich those who got in early and
impoverish those who came later. In addition, gambling was a favored leisure pastime among the rich, with a range of practices

from whist to horse racing. Also, a popular and autonomous culture of gambling flourished among the lower classes, with their cockfighting, bearbaiting, boxing matches, wagers on acts of speed or strength, and so on, posing a challenge to upper-class standards of decency and public order.

Through the nineteenth century, these leisure practices became more centralized and regulated: lotteries, sweepstakes, organized sports, and so forth. Gambling also assumed a far more significant place in economic life. Huge amounts of capital were staked on the building of railroads, with no guarantee that the lines would ever yield a profit. Banks flourished and failed. A stock exchange grew up and prospered, on the greed, hopes, and fears of the wealthy. People made and lost fortunes selling watered stock or trying to corner various markets. And the rapid triumph of production for exchange over production for use brought the basic activities of manufacture within the sphere of gambling. This new form of economic life expressed itself in a business cycle, alternating times of frenzied accumulation with times when many rich men lost their shirts. Many poor men and women did, too, and they responded often with strikes, bloody battles, and demands that they, rather than speculators, control the terms of productive activity.

Partly for this reason, a lively debate had gone forward through this period, among politicians, churchmen, businessmen, philanthropists, intellectuals, and social reformers, about whether the poor should be taught to gamble, or should be denied those skills. Some held that gambling among the poor would make them discontented with their station in life, would unfit them for the useful labor that was their destiny, and would encourage rebellion among them by admitting them to the secrets of the social order. Others argued that poor people *should* learn the elements of gambling, so that they might better carry out their roles in the market, and understand its rightness and inevitability; besides, if they spent their leisure hours in supervised gambling, that would keep them out of taverns and union halls, where crime and trouble were sure to arise. By the end of the century, the second group had decisively won the debate, and education in the basics of gambling was on its way toward becoming universal.

During the century and a half of this debate, two old words that figured in it gradually changed their meanings. The adjective *speculate* had meant "generally and deeply sophisticated in all practices, techniques, and understandings of risk taking"; it was close kin to such words as *cultivated, gentlemanly,* and *literate.* This meaning persisted, but by 1900 another one was crowding it out: "able, minimally, to carry out basic risk transactions like betting on a ball game or selling one's labor power." The adjective *unspeculate* passed through a parallel change; by 1900 it usually meant "completely unable to gamble." Right about that time, a brand new coinage entered the lexicon: the word *speculacy*. It too designated the basic ability to gamble, and it accompanied and facilitated a new conceptualization of these matters. In particular, it advanced two kinds of thinking. First, it could refer to an individual's attainment of specified elementary skills, like making a transaction at a pari-mutuel window or getting a job in a factory—rather than, as with the older words, evoking a whole way of life and a system of social relations that fostered it. From this way of thinking, to the *measurement* of speculacy, was a short distance. Standardized speculacy tests came into wide use, and each child moved toward adulthood trailing clouds of speculacy scores. Second, the new word could apply to the percentage of people in an entire society who had acquired the basic skills of gambling. Hence it became common to judge the progress of countries by their "speculacy rates." These in turn could be correlated with other social attributes like media participation, political participation, and urbanization, yielding theories of modernization, as well as speculacy campaigns in poorer countries, sponsored by international bodies.

As you can see, the word and the concept entered into and advanced a particular discourse among the powerful, one in which they sought to evaluate the condition, and shape the destinies, of the powerless, both at home and abroad. The word *speculacy* belonged from the start to a dialogue about social control. Yet it also helped *mask* the politics of domination. For one thing, most of the people behind speculacy movements genuinely wanted to help the lower classes get on well in the society. And, noticing that gambling was a main priority of the social system, many people in the lower classes *themselves* wanted their children to become speculate, and endorsed the educational measures that promised to make them so. Those measures did in fact help to make basic speculacy almost universal. Yet somehow they failed to inculcate more advanced speculacy (e.g., the ability to own and run a large commercial bank), and almost all bank owners continued to be the sons of bank owners, or of other successful gamblers. To some, this fact suggested an unfair system. But most well-to-do people took it to prove that the lower classes were incapable of rising above their natural station. And even many of the latter took their poor performance in speculacy classes and on speculacy tests as confirmation that their economic status was what they deserved. Both groups were strengthened in their acceptance of the status quo by observing that a few poor children *did* become highly speculate, and even rich and powerful.

Meanwhile, through the twentieth century, gambling grew both more exotic and more central to the society. It took such forms as third world loan rollovers, stock index futures, oil lease lotteries, investment in outer space, purchases of obscure paintings for millions of dollars, money market futures, declarations of bankruptcy in anticipation of lawsuits, investment tax credits, oil cartels, unfriendly takeovers, corporate bailouts, storage of nuclear waste, and mutual assured destruction. By late century, corporations and the state had also, between them, organized more of the leisure gambling of ordinary people, as they had earlier controlled the labor of the lower classes. Blackjack, roulette, craps, baccarat, slot machines, poker, lotteries, lotto, the numbers, sweepstakes, perfectas, trifectas, daily doubles, and other forms of betting on horses, dogs, and Basques, all came under such management, and helped transfer money from ordinary people to corporations and the state, in this way supporting still more gambling by those agencies. To be sure, pockets of traditional speculacy remained—church bingo games, office pools, the restricted gambling codes of the working class, black gambling, and so on. To some, these appeared to be forms of popular resistance, but most considered them inferior and archaic cultural activities that interfered with training in standard speculacy and held back those who practiced them.

These developments were punctuated at regular intervals by speculacy *crises*. College presidents, literary critics, and journalists would discover that young people couldn't gamble worth a damn any more, and would cite as evidence declining speculacy scores and howlers from students' papers, like writing "I bet" instead of "I bid," or thinking that "hopefully" referred to one's chances of winning, rather than to the arousal of one's emotions while scratching an instant lottery ticket. National commissions would be appointed to investigate the situation; they would prescribe more rigorous, old-fashioned training in speculacy, competency requirements for promotion and graduation, speculacy tests for teachers, and merit raises for those with the highest scores. These reforms, if instituted, would indeed raise basic speculacy scores. But strangely, they did not equip most students for ownership of large commercial banks, narrow the gap between rich and

poor, or produce certain other deep cultural changes held to accompany speculacy.

For, during this time, a body of speculacy theory had grown up,
grounded in the contrast between speculate and unspeculate—or
laboral—cultures. It varied widely from theorist to theorist, but
generally pointed to cognitive and attitudinal correlates of speculacy and laborality. Speculacy, for instance, grounds thinking that
is abstract, individualized, probabilistic, game-theoretic, monetarist, supply-sided, masculine, and quantum-mechanical; laborality
goes with thought that is concrete, collaborative, unidimensional,
pragmatic, feminine, and resentful. But although it was easy to
document such correlations, it was harder to find evidence that
speculate thinking derived from speculacy itself, rather than from
the contexts within which people learned and practiced speculacy.
For example, if a person had speculacy drilled into her in an inner-
city school, and practiced it on her job as a pari-mutuel clerk at the
dog track, she was unlikely to exhibit monetarist thinking—compared, say, to another person whose father owned a large commercial bank, who learned speculacy at Exeter and Harvard, and who
was vice president of a large commercial bank. Nor was there
much evidence that the higher forms of speculate culture *could* be
acquired in regimented schools, by young people who had little to
gamble with and only the faintest shot at a bank presidency. As a
speaker at the 1984 Modern Gambling Association convention put
it, "If you want a speculate people, you must want them to seize the
means of speculation."

Addressing a forum on speculacy theory, attended mainly by
friends of the destitute and working classes—advocates of what a
Brazilian theorist called "critical speculacy"—this speaker urged
all to remember how the concept of speculacy had emerged in a
discourse of domination, and how hard it is for those who oppose
domination to keep their bearings when they enter such a discourse. In concluding his remarks, he suggested an analogy between speculacy and literacy. He quoted, first, Antonio Gramsci:

Each time that, in one way or another, the question of language comes to
the fore, that signifies that a series of other problems is about to emerge [:]
the formation and enlarging of the ruling class, the necessity to establish
more "intimate" and sure relations between the ruling groups and the national popular masses, [and] the reorganization of cultural hegemony.

And second, he quoted James Sledd: "Friends of literacy should be
enemies of oppression."

18 Use Definite, Specific, Concrete Language

I now turn to particular issues in the teaching of literacy—or, to put it more humbly, English composition. The skills we teach and the ways we teach them have political implications. I favor what has come to be called "critical literacy."

My title is Rule 12 from Strunk and White's *The Elements of Style*, and it probably comes as close as any precept to claiming the unanimous endorsement of writing teachers. After E. D. Hirsch, Jr., in *The Philosophy of Composition*, develops his principle of "relative readability," grounding it in historical and psychological evidence, he turns for support to "the accumulated wisdom of the handbooks." (The ones he chooses are Strunk and White, Crews, McCrimmon, Lucas, Gowers.) He reduces their wisdom to ten or a dozen maxims each: there is much overlap from book to book, but only two maxims appear in nearly the same form in all five books, and my title is one of those two.[1]

Does anyone besides me feel uneasy when Strunk and White begin exemplifying this reasonable advice? For "A period of unfavorable weather set in," they substitute "It rained every day for a week." The rewrite is indeed more definite, specific, and concrete, and less pompous to boot. But it doesn't say the same thing, and in that difference there is a loss as well as a gain, especially if the writer means to relate the weather to some undertaking rather than just describing it. The original conveys—however inadequately—a more complex idea. The same is true when "He showed satisfaction as he took possession of his well-earned reward" becomes for Strunk and White "He grinned as he pocketed the coin."

In this chapter I look at the way some authors of textbooks show students how to be definite, specific, and concrete. The questions I have in mind as I do so are whether in teaching a skill like this we may inadvertently suggest to students that they be less inquiring and less intelligent than they are capable of being, and whether the teaching of basic skills is an ideological activity. To bring suspense down to a tolerable level, let me reveal now that my answer to both questions is Yes.

I examine just three textbooks, chosen not as bad examples—they seem to me lively, serious, and honest—but for these reasons: They are current (1978). They are second editions, an indication of acceptance in the market. Their authors have taught in a large city university, a community college in a large northern city, and two community colleges in a southern town and a southern city; such institutions are close to the center of the freshmen composition industry. All three textbooks give unusually ample attention to style, and in particular to the matters I am concerned with here.

I will look first at the second edition of David Skwire and Frances Chitwood's *Student's Book of College English* (Glencoe Press), and refer to a section in it titled "Specific Details." Skwire and Chitwood introduce the section by saying, "The use of specific details is the most direct way to avoid abstract writing." (And students *should* avoid it, since "abstract writing is the main cause of bored readers.") Detail is a plus. In fact, "within reason, the more specific the details, the better the writing." "Within reason" means that the detail must be relevant and neither obvious nor trivial. To illustrate, they offer three passages, labeled "Abstract (weak)," "More Specific (better)," and "Still More Specific (much better)." Here are the first and third.

1. Abstract (weak)

The telephone is a great scientific achievement, but it can also be a great inconvenience. Who could begin to count the number of times that phone calls have come from unwelcome people or on unwelcome occasions? Telephones make me nervous.

. . .

3. Still More Specific (much better)

The telephone is a great scientific achievement, but it can also be a great big headache. More often than not, that cheery ringing in my ear brings messages from the Ace Bill Collecting Agency, my mother (who is feeling snubbed for the fourth time that week), salesmen of encyclopedias and magazines, solicitors for the Policemen's Ball and Disease of the Month Foundation, and neighbors complaining about my dog. That's not to mention frequent wrong numbers—usually for someone named "Arnie." The calls always seem to come at the worst times, too. They've interrupted steak dinners, hot tubs, Friday night parties, and Saturday morning sleep-ins. There's no escape. Sometimes I wonder if there are any telephones in padded cells (pp. 348–49).

Consider now how revision has transformed the style of the first passage. Most obviously, one generalization—"unwelcome people"—disappears entirely, to be replaced by a list of eight people or types of people the writer doesn't want to hear from; another generalization—"unwelcome occasions"—is changed to "worst times," then amplified in another list. Seriation has become the main principle of structure. When items are placed in a series, the writer implies that they are alike in some respect. But in what respect? Here the angry neighbors and possessive mother are placed on par with salesmen and others connected to the writer only through the cash nexus. Are the callers unwelcome because the writer does not get along with his or her family and neighbors, or for a less personal reason: that businesses and other organizations in pursuit of money use the phone as a means of access to it? The answer may be both, of course, but in expanding the idea of "unwelcome people," Skwire and Chitwood add no insight to it. The specific details close off analysis.

The same holds for their treatment of "unwelcome occasions." An occasion is a time that is socially defined and structured: a party or a steak dinner, yes, but sleep and a bath are more private activities, hardly occasions. Of course a phone call is usually as unwelcome in the middle of a bath as during a party. My point is that in changing "occasions" to "times" and letting detail do the work, the germ of an idea has been lost: the idea that we like to control our own social time, and that the telephone allows other people to intervene and impose *their* structure. What the details communicate instead is a loose feeling of harassment—easier to visualize, more specific, but certainly not more precise in thought.

Other changes have a similar effect. "Headache" is more sensory than 'inconvenience," but less exact, and personal rather than social. The phrase "cheery ringing in my ears" is a distraction, from the perspective of developing an idea: the point is not the sound, but the fact, of the intrusions and their content, the social relations they put the writer into or take him or her out of. And where the final sentence of the original implicitly raised a fruitful question (why "nervous"?), the new conclusion—"Sometimes I wonder if there are any telephones in padded cells"—closes off inquiry with a joke and points up the writer's idiosyncrasy rather than the social matter under discussion.

On the level of speech acts, too, the rewrite personalizes, moves away from social analysis. In the first passage, emphasis falls on the general claims made about phones and the people who use them and are used by them. The rewrite buries those claims in a heap of reports of "my" experience, reports for which only the writer need vouch. The speaker of an assertion must be in a position to make it, or it isn't "felicitous," in Austin's terms. (I cannot felicitously assert that there is life in the next galaxy.) The writer of the second passage *risks* less by moving quickly from generalizations that require support from history and social analysis, to those that stand on private terrain. This reduction in scope accords well with the impression given by the rewrite of a person incapable of coping with events, victimized by others, fragmented, distracted—a kind of likable schlemiel. He or she may be a less "boring" writer, but also a less venturesome and more isolated person, the sort who chatters on in a harmless gossipy way without much purpose or consequence: a *character*.

If a student showed me the first passage (as the outline of a composition or the beginning of a draft), I would want to say that it expresses an interesting idea, inadequately handled to be sure, but begging for a kind of development that amplification by detail alone can never supply. The contradiction with which it begins is familiar but perplexing: How is it that so many of our scientists' "achievements," with all their promise of efficiency and ease, turn out to be inconvenient or worse in the long run? Why does an invention designed to give people control over their lives make many of us feel so often in the control of others? Why does a device for bringing people together (as its proprietors are constantly telling us in commercials) in fact so often serve as the carrier of frictions and antagonisms?

To make any headway with such questions it is necessary to stay with the abstractions awhile, penetrate them, get at the center of the contradictions they express, not throw them out in favor of lists of details. "Achievement": By whom? Who calls "science" into being, and engineers its discoveries into commodities? The telephone as we have it is a hundred-year-long achievement, of patent lawyers and corporate planners more than of Alexander Graham Bell. "Inconvenience": For whom? Not for the salesmen and bill collectors, presumably. And certainly not for executives barricaded behind secretaries making sure the boss talks only with people he wants to talk with, and at a time of his choosing. The telephone represents a network of social relations embedded in history. In order to gain any leverage on the badly expressed contradiction of the first passage, it is necessary to analyze some of those relations. Piling on the details, as in the rewrite, may create a kind of superficial interest, but no gain in insight. The strategy, as exemplified here, is a strategy for sacrificing thought to feckless merriment.

Skwire and Chitwood are concerned with adding detail. In the section I wish to consider from Winston Weathers and Otis Winchester's *The New Strategy of Style* (McGraw-Hill), the authors show how to make detail more specific. They do this under the heading "Texture," explaining that different subjects call for different textures: the simpler the subject, the more elaborate the texture. The maxim begs the question to an extent, since whether or not a given subject is simple or complex depends partly upon the diction used in exploring it. But apparently the first passage below is about a simple subject, since as the authors take it through four revisions their instructions all advise elaboration of texture. (*"Make your nouns more specific." "Make your adjectives more specific."*) Passage 2 is the second of the rewrites.

1. The country store was an interesting place to visit. In the very heart of the city, it had the air of a small-town grocery store combined with a feed and hardware supply house. There were flower seeds and milk churns, coal buckets and saddle blankets, all mixed together. Walking down the crowded aisles, you felt you had gone back to the past—to the time of pot-belly stoves and kerosene lamps and giant pickle jars. You could smell the grain, you could touch the harnesses, you could even sit down in the old wooden chair. When you finally left the store and were once more in the activity of the city, you felt as you sometimes do when you come out of an old movie into the bright light of reality.

2. Charlie's Country store was a spell-binding emporium. In the very heart of Minneapolis, Charlie's had the *dubious* charm of a smalltown grocery combined with a feed and hardware supply house. There were *zinnia* seeds and milk churns, *shiny* coal buckets and *garish* saddle blankets, all mixed together. Walking down its *quaint* passageways—*narrow, poorly lighted, but nevertheless immaculate*—you felt you had gone back to nineteenth-century America—to the lost years, the *faintly remembered* days of *squat* pot-belly stoves and *sturdy* kerosene lamps and *rotund, ceramic* crocks—meant for pickles or pastries. You could smell the cornmeal, you could touch the *leather* harnesses, you could even sit in the *stern* wooden rocker. And when you finally left this anachronism—and were once more

in the bustle of the city—you felt as you sometimes do when you come out
of an old cinema into the *blinding* glare of a *rocket-age* reality (pp. 135–38;
emphasis in original).

Passage 2 is the result of making nouns and adjectives more specific and also (though Weathers and Winchester don't say so) of
adding adjectives. Setting aside some words that might be criticized as elegant variations (e.g., "emporium," which suggests a
grander establishment than is implied by the rest of the passage),
consider the ways the description has become more specific.

1. The scene is particularized. The store is now Charlie's; the city,
Minneapolis; the past, nineteenth-century America. Note that this
change blurs the two main contrasts in which the description is
grounded, country versus city and present versus past. For the
sharpening of these contrasts, it does not matter whose store it is or
in what city, or whether the visitor travels back in imagination to
the U.S. or England. Some of the other specifics are equally irrelevant: zinnia seeds, pastries, cornmeal. The point, I take it, is not
the kind of flowers people used to grow, but that they had gardens;
not what kind of grain they used, but that they did more of the
work of preparing their own food, and that the arts of preserving,
packaging, and marketing were in a primitive state of development compared to our present attainments as represented by freez-
ers full of TV dinners and by the Golden Arches.

2. The writer's own impressions and values are placed in the foreground, most often adjectivally. The store is now *spell-binding*, its
passageways *quaint*, and so on through "dubious charm," "faintly
remembered," "stern," and "blinding." The writer has become much
more of a presence, reacting, exercising taste, judging. These responses seem to issue from no particular perspective; for instance,
what's "dubious" about the store's charm? They scarcely relate to
the content of the original passage, certainly not to the ideas latent
in it. They seem like the reflexes of a dilettantish tourist whose fugi-
tive sensations and values clutter the picture and block analysis.

3. Similarly, the adjectives highlight the thinginess of things,
their physical appearance, rather than what they are, what they
meant, how life might have been organized around them. "Shiny,"
"garish," "poorly lighted," "squat," "sturdy," "rotund," "ceramic."
The picture turns into a kind of still life, crowded with visual detail
apparently valuable in itself. Such emphasis on visible surfaces,
along with the aesthetic perspective, draws attention to a detached
present experience, dissipating the image of an earlier kind of civi-

lization in which most people lived on farms, the family was the main productive unit, few of people's needs were commercialized, and technology was manageable and local.

Like the telephone, the objects in the country store embody social relations. And even more clearly than the initial passage about telephones, Weathers and Winchester's original version supports a sense of history, of a society that has been utterly transformed so that most of the things in the store have lost their usefulness. The society these artifacts imply—in which local people grew the grain, harvested it, ground it into flour, and baked it into bread— has given way to one in which almost all of our labor is sold in the market and controlled by employers rather than expended at our own pace and to our own plans; and almost all of our consumption takes place through markets organized not by a village merchant but by distant corporations.

Of course the first passage doesn't say what I have just said, even by implication. But in the way it sets up contrasts and in the details it presents, it provides the ground and even the need for such analysis. The student who takes Weathers and Winchester's guidance in making the passage "richer," more "vivid," and more "intense" will lose the thread of *any* analysis in a barrage of sensory impressions, irrelevant details, and personalized or random responses. Once again, the rhetorical strategy scatters thought.

With my final example I turn to the injunction to use concrete language. The textbook is the second edition of *Composition: Skills and Models*, by Sidney T. Stovall, Virginia B. Mathis, Linda C. Elliot, G. Mitchell Hagler, Jr., and Mary A. Poole (Houghton Mifflin). Here are two of the passages they present for comparison in their chapter on forming a style, the first from Fielding's *Tom Jones*, and the second from Nevil Shute's *On the Beach*:

1. The charms of Sophia had not made the least impression on Blifil; not that his heart was pre-engaged, neither was he totally insensible of beauty, or had any aversion to women; but his appetites were by nature so moderate that he was easily able by philosophy, or by study, or by some other method to subdue them; and as to that passion which we have treated of in the first chapter of this book, he had not the least tincture of it in his whole composition.

But though he was so entirely free from that mixed passion of which we there treated, and of which the virtues and beauty of Sophia formed so notable an object, yet was he altogether as well furnished with some other passions that promised themselves very full gratification in the young lady's fortune. Such were avarice and ambition, which divided the domin-

ion of his mind between them. He had more than once considered the possession of this fortune as a very desirable thing, and had entertained some
distant views concerning it, but his own youth and that of the young lady,
and indeed, principally a reflection that Mr. Weston might marry again
and have more children, had restrained him from too hasty or too eager a
pursuit.

2. He went back to bed. Tomorrow would be an anxious, trying day; he
must get his sleep. In the privacy of his little curtained cabin he unlocked
the safe that held the confidential books and took out the bracelet; it
glowed in the synthetic light. She would love it. He put it carefully in the
breast pocket of his uniform suit. Then he went to bed again, his hand
upon the fishing rod, and slept.

They surfaced again at four in the morning, just before dawn, a little to
the north of Grays Harbor. No lights were visible on the shore, but as there
were no towns and few roads in the district that evidence was inconclu-
sive. They went down to periscope depth and carried on. When Dwight
came to the control room at six o'clock the day was bright through the
periscope and the crew off duty were taking turns to look at the desolate
shore. He went to breakfast and then stood smoking at the chart table,
studying the minefield chart that he already knew so well, and the well-
remembered entrance to the Juan de Fuca Strait (p. 390).

The authors have couched their discussion of style in historically
relative terms. Styles change, and students will want to choose
from among styles suited to contemporary life. Eighteenth-century
readers could "idle" over "long sentences"; "leisure is at a premium" now. Stovall and his colleagues do not absolutely value
Shute's style over Fielding's, but since they say that the earlier
style would strike the modern reader as awkward, stilted, colorless, complex, plodding, tedious and wordy, their counsel to the
student is reasonably plain.

They direct their judgment partly against Fielding's long and
complex sentences, partly against the quality of his diction. The latter is my concern. Stovall et al. object to phrases like "entertained
some distant view" and "had not the least tincture," and especially
to Fielding's dependence on the big abstractions, "passion," "virtues," "avarice," "ambition," words that "elicit no emotional response from the reader." They praise Shute for "concrete words"
that give life to the passage, citing "curtained cabin," "glowed in
the synthetic light," "surfaced," and "desolate shore." Later in the
chapter they urge the student to "strive for the concrete word."

Abstract nouns refer to the world in a way quite different from
concrete nouns. They do not point to a set of particulars—all curtained cabins—or to any one cabin. They are relational. For in-

stance, in speaking of Blifil's "avarice," Fielding calls up at least the relation of a series of acts to one another (a single act of acquiring or hoarding is not enough); of Blifil's feelings to these actions and to the wealth that is their goal; of those acts and feelings to a scale of values that is socially established (avarice is a sin, and so related to salvation and damnation); and of Blifil to other people who make such judgments, as well as to people whose wealth he might covet and who would become poorer were he to become richer. The term also evokes a temporal relationship: an avaricious person like Blifil seeks to become wealthy over time, and it is this future goal that informs his conduct. Abstract nouns that characterize people do so through bundles of relationships like these.

In short, one need not adopt an eighteenth-century faculty psychology, or expect Nevil Shute to adopt it, to see that Fielding's abstract nouns give a rich social setting to Blifil's sordid intentions. This setting is made more rich as, in context, Fielding humorously brings avarice into parity with love, under the higher-level abstraction of passion. (Herein another relationship, that of the narrator to his subject and his reader.) Abstractions are for Fielding a speculative and interpretive grid against which he can examine the events of the novel, and which themselves are constantly tested and modified by those events.

Shute's language in this passage, by contrast, sets his hero's actions against a background mainly of objects and of other people treated more or less as objects. The moral implications of the passage will have to be supplied by the reader. And there is no way for the narrator, given his style, to place that moral content in a dynamic relationship with social values, at least within the passage cited. This may be appropriate enough in a story from which society has literally disappeared; I do not mean to disparage Shute's diction, only to question the wisdom of commending it to students as plainly superior (for the twentieth-century reader) to Fielding's. Some important kinds of thinking can be done only with the help of abstractions.

In sum, as this textbook teaches the skill of using definite, specific, concrete language, it joins the other two in preferring realia to more abstract inquiry about realia, and to the effort to connect them. In doing so, it seems to me, the authors convey a fairly well-defined ideological picture to students. I would characterize this picture in these terms:

1. Ahistoricism. The preferred style focuses on a truncated pres-

ent moment. Things and events are frozen in an image, or they pass
on the wing, coming from nowhere.

2. Empiricism. The style favors sensory news, from the surfaces
of things.

3. Fragmentation. An object is just what it is, disconnected from
the rest of the world. The style obscures the social relations and the
relations of people to nature that are embedded in all things.

4. Solipsism. The style foregrounds the writer's own perceptions:
this is what I saw and felt.

5. Denial of conflict. The style typically pictures a world in which
the telephone has the same meaning for all classes of people, a
world whose "rocket-age reality" is just mysteriously *there*, outside
the country store, a world where avarice is a superfluous and tedious concept.

Furthermore—and I think this, too, a matter of the ideology of
style—the injunctions to use detail, be specific, be concrete, as applied in these books, push the student writer always toward the
language that most nearly reproduces the immediate experience
and away from the language that might be used to understand it,
transform it, and relate it to everything else. The authors privilege
a kind of revising and expanding that leaves the words themselves
unexamined and untransformed. Susan Wells has suggested that
Christensen's rhetoric does not open "to investigation the relations
among language, vision, and their objects,"[2] but takes those relations for granted. Her comment applies well to the use of detail
recommended in these textbooks.

In an epoch when so much of the language students hear or read
comes from distant sources, via the media, and when so much of it
is shaped by advertisers and other corporate experts to channel
their thoughts and feelings and needs, I think it a special pity if English teachers are turning students away from critical scrutiny of
the words in their heads, especially from those that are most heavily laden with ideology. When in the cause of clarity or liveliness we
urge them toward detail, surfaces, the sensory, as mere *expansion*
of ideas or even as a *substitute* for abstraction, we encourage them
to accept the empirical fragmentation of consciousness that passes
for common sense in our society, and hence to accept the society
itself as just what it most superficially seems to be.

Yet, it is good to keep readers interested, bad to bore them. Like
Hirsch's principle of readability, the injunction to be interesting is
on one level a bit of self-evident practical wisdom, not to mention

kindness. Whatever you are trying to accomplish through a piece of writing, you won't achieve it if the reader quits on you, or plods on in resentful tedium. But mechanically applied, the principles of interest and readability entail accepting the reader exactly as he or she is. The reader's most casual values, interests, and capacities become an inflexible measure of what to write and how to write it, a Nielsen rating for prose. What happens to the possibility of challenging or even changing the reader? If keeping readers' attention is elevated to the prime goal of our teaching, the strategies we teach may well lead toward triviality and evasion.

Yes, I also realize that most students don't handle abstractions and generalizations well. I know that they often write badly when they try, and how depressing an experience it can be to read a batch of compositions on free will or alienation or capital punishment. And I am aware of the pressure many English teachers now feel to teach basic skills, whatever they are, rather than critical inquiry.[3] But I can't believe that the best response to this pressure is valorizing the concrete, fragmented, and inconsistent worldviews that many of our students bring to college with them. Jeffrey Youdelman refers to colleagues he has heard say, "They can't handle abstraction . . . and therefore I always give them topics like 'describe your favorite room.'" Youdelman continues: "Already stuck in a world of daily detail, with limited horizons and stunted consciousness, students are forced deeper into their solipsistic prison."[4] Like him, I am concerned that in the cause of improving their skills we may end up increasing their powerlessness.

19 Writing and Empowerment

What are the roots of the powerlessness I invoked at the end of the last essay? Plainly, more forces conspire to create it than a teacher's injunction to use concrete language. The writer's situation is heavy with contradictions. She is eighteen years old, a newcomer to college, where she is invited both to assume responsibility for her education and to trust the college's plan for it; to build her competence and to follow a myriad of rules and instructions; to see herself as an autonomous individual and to be incessantly judged.

The writing class heightens these tensions. Writing. The word whispers of creativity and freedom; yet there is usage, there are assignments and deadlines, there is the model of The Theme, there are grades. We tell students to find their own voices, yet most feel subtly and not-so-subtly pressed to submerge their identities in academic styles and purposes that are not their own. They have little understanding of their world, and not all that much experience of it, but the academic paper calls for a knowing posture and for the routines of mastery.

Some of these contradictions inhere in the role of student, a transitional and mixed one. Some have their roots in the confusing ethos of college, which proclaims academic freedom in a community of scholars, even while making it clear that students aren't ready for full membership. And some blow into the classroom with the ideological winds of our social system: each one of us is the creator of his or her own destiny (yet the economy requires this many programmers, that many salespeople, and so on). Writing teachers would be paralyzed if they took upon themselves alone the task of disalienating English composition—as, in the 1960s, some of us naïvely hoped to make the individual classroom a liberated zone.

But even in circumstances not of our own choosing, we can contest the alienation of writing up to a point.

These are large issues. The writing practice I now want to discuss responds to them in a fairly small way. It does respond to them, though, and I would argue that ways of teaching composition that simply block out the social process around our teaching and our students' writing have little chance of fostering critical literacy. Also, having disparaged some standard ideas about "basic" literacy throughout this volume, and having attacked a common way of bringing student writing into relationship with the concrete world, I owe the reader at least some hints of an alternative way.

The one I single out for attention here makes use of interviewing; I have worked it into several composition courses, and sometimes made it the focus of an entire course (called Writing as Social Exploration). Reasons for that choice will appear along the way, and I will mention only one now, before becoming specific about this pedagogy. That reason: the interview write-up, as an essay form, has the signal advantage that most students are already familiar with its various conventions. Since before the turn of the century it has been a staple of newspaper and magazine journalism, and the live interview itself is everywhere to be seen on television: in news, in documentaries, in talk shows, even in commercials. Every student has "participated" in many interviews as reader or viewer; the genre belongs to a student's native idiom (as the academic essay does not), so an instructor needn't give elaborate instruction in methods of interviewing, or of transposing what happens in an interview onto the page.[1] This is not to imply that we should teach only what students already know, but only that mass culture can be a resource for teaching and learning, in ways other than something to write *about*. Of course, as students produce their own versions of a mass cultural form, they need to—and will—reflect critically upon its premises and limitations. That is a side benefit.

But I usually begin with a group interview, not with an interview in the standard, one-on-one format. This practice raises questions at the outset about capturing another's words and thoughts, questions that run from the technical to the ethical, and in fact tend to break down that distinction. I ask for someone to volunteer as subject; several do, and naturally students who step forward at this moment tend to be fairly extroverted and verbal. (Only once have I had a group interview fall flat because the subject became tongue-tied.) I ask each person in the class to prepare one or two questions, perhaps focusing on the passage from home to college or on what the interviewee expects of education, if the interview happens at the beginning of the school year.[2] Most students ask predictable questions; the interchange may tend toward the banal, but it will also be lively:

questions from the class . . . gathered a cautious momentum, finally tumbling into a natural rhythm.

"Do you enjoy classes at Wesleyan?" "Ever not want to go to class?" "Profs live up to your expectations?" "How is this music teacher eccentric?" . . . "How did you decide on Wesleyan?" "Apply to other schools?" "Did following your family's traditions hinder your individuality?" . . . "Think you've adjusted to college pretty well?" "How are you doing socially?" "Like frat parties?" "How do you handle the freedom of choosing classes?" . . . "Do you have a hard time disciplining yourself to study and yet find time to socialize?"

The flow of animated, conversational replies might have come from any of 607 freshmen.

There is such a variety of courses. I'm taking Chinese, a music class, an English. . . . Well, I like going to class because it gives me something to do. When I'm bogged down I don't like it so much. . . . Yes, I'd say all the profs are different, they're all very interested in what they're doing. . . . I'm studying different subjects than any I've ever studied before. I don't mean eccentric—that's too strong, but, well he flits around, he is a composer, talks real fast. He likes his work—all the professors do. He's so spontaneous, energetic . . . like he is dancing to music in his head.

We are close to the stock responses of orientation week here. In her write-up, Justine Cook[3] has marked that fact ("might have come from any of 607 freshmen"), and has shaped the material from her notes to emphasize the typicality of the event, with questions blended anonymously together, and answers grouped like fleeting scraps of talk, without a center.

Sarah Brown strikes that note, too, but her write-up is in the form of a monologue, deleting the questions, and presenting Jane as more individuated.

OK, I'm Jane Krenz. I'm from Baltimore. Go ahead, you guys; you can ask me anything. Classes: well, I'm taking beginning Chinese, Intro Psych—isn't everyone?—Music, and English 101, which I really like, because I like my teacher . . . [laughing]. I get a lot of pleasure out of my classes, because they really give me something to do. After the summer it's a new use of time. Except Chinese [twists her face into a grimace and then starts to laugh]. No, I'm just joking. But you might say that it's more than a challenge! . . .

All my professors here are really different; ha! You should see my music teacher. He's like, well, he's hard to describe. He flits around the room and he talks real fast—he's crazy! [laughing] I can't explain, but he's a composer, and he just runs around the room . . . sort of dancing. Eccentric's not the word; he just loves what he's doing. All my teachers are fascinated by their own work.

And Sarah concentrates and draws out one theme from the interview material that is less sunny, less superficial:

For a long time I didn't know how I felt about coming to Wesleyan. OK, do you want the truth? Wesleyan was not my first choice. I have a long family line here—I even have a cousin who's a freshman now. My dad went here, my uncle went here, and they've had a lot to do with the college since then; and I was afraid to follow in their footsteps. I didn't want to have to live up to their expectations—I knew they wanted me to come here. But even though deep down I *did* want to come here, I wouldn't admit it to anybody; I wouldn't give in to my dad and tell him I wanted to go to his school.

A rather different Jane emerges from this write-up. With photocopies of these and other versions in front of them, the class begins to argue out some vexing issues. Which version is more faithful? Faithful to *what?* Some students privilege the raw moment of the interview itself: only a verbatim transcript would honestly render it, they insist. But such an empirical—almost evidential—standard dissatisfies other students. A transcript would make the event appear inchoate, and would present Jane (or any but the most practiced interviewee) as out of focus, not the *person* we feel her to be. Wouldn't that be a worse kind of distortion? But any attempt to rearrange and highlight the material, to delete what seems trivial or irrelevant, to paraphrase and organize, to secure on paper the intuited meaning of Jane's words—any such attempt at a deeper fidelity brings the writer into the act as interpreter and judge, as surely as if he or she comments explicitly on the interview and its subject. The writer cannot dissolve into neutrality. And then there is the reader, to complicate the matter further. If the writer makes no inferences or choices, the reader certainly will: doesn't the writer's responsibility to event and interviewee include guiding those inferences toward fairness and insight? By this point the discussion has problematized any naïve standard of objectivity. Beyond that, it has begun to make clear that writing is itself a dense social relation that calls into play moral judgment and a kind of politics, not just a familiarity with conventions and rules. I think most instructors believe that, but we and our students often forget it. The interview paper keeps the perception alive.

Early on—still in the warm-up stage—I often have the class do a group interview of me. This underlines their ownership of the writing task in two ways. First, it demystifies my role in the class, opening up my goals and values as a subject for inquiry on the students' terms, taking them off the secret agenda. Second, it changes the relationship of their writing to what I have said in class, turning the latter into material for analysis and criticism rather than the graven words of authority. (I do not grade these write-ups; in fact, I hold off with grades altogether until well into the semester.)

There can be other kinds of preliminary interviewing tasks: for instance, pairing students to interview each other. Soon, though, I press them to formulate a common inquiry, which they can pursue by alternating interviews with analytic essays based on what they as a class have learned. Such themes include work, wealth and poverty (e.g., interviews with rich and poor students), conceptions of college and education. Here, banality often opens out into a sustainable interest; batches of interviews on the same question prompt inference and generalization, and invite new conceptions of the question itself. At this point, too, there can be a fruitful exchange between concrete and abstract writing, as the individual voice of one interviewee harmonizes or clashes with the voices of others, and as students find themselves driven beyond and behind details to find patterns of idea and culture that make sense of particulars.

Let me offer one example. I had organized a composition course around inquiries into mass culture, and the construction of the self. In the pair interviews it emerged that several students had an interest in fashion, and class discussion of chapters on clothes as both mass commodity and medium of social dialogue, in Stuart and Elizabeth Ewen's *Channels of Desire*,[4] had shown that many of the students were adept at reading "statements" encoded in dress. For their first interview with someone not in the class, I asked each student to find another who dressed in an unusual or striking way, and explore the implications of his or her style.

Unsurprisingly many of these interviewees were quite conscious of their wardrobes as extensions of social self, and assertive about their individuality:

Harold Twiss is an eighteen year old male from Manhattan. He has a slender build, a short afro, and is average height. . . . Having seen him on several occasions wearing clothes that could be labeled as unusual, such as bright pink socks, I chose him for the interview.

The first question that I confronted him with was, "How would you describe the way in which you dress, in one word?" His response was typical
of the entire interview; he said very confidently, "Harold." Hoping to pursue this thought, I asked him to describe the way he dresses, in two words;
his response was a clever, "My self." I then asked for a more traditional
three-word response, and he said, "I guess 'neat, conservative, yet new
wave."

(Tim Sullivan)

Although when pressed, Harold places himself at an unlikely inter-
section of social groups—conservative and new wave—he resists
definition of his outfits by social coordinates.

That opposition of individuality and the social turns up again
and again in these interviews (as does the word *unique*). Sometimes an interviewee makes it quite explicit, as happens at the end
of this excerpt from a write-up by Jack S.:

He calls his dress casual; his roommate and peers may call it unique.
Clad in blue sweats, a long-sleeve t-shirt, and a nice sweater lazily worn,
Derek sits cross-legged on his unmade bed and says, "I enjoy clashing
dressier clothes with rougher garments. It just gives you a rough-refined
feeling." . . .

He can be seen strolling about campus wearing a pair of sandals, sweat
pants, an untucked button-down shirt, and a tweed sportscoat. Inversely,
he can be seen in a pair of black shoes, nice pants, and a partially ripped
shirt. . . .

The manner in which he has acquired his rather large wardrobe is almost as interesting as the dress itself. Most of his articles that are not
hand-me-downs are purchased at tag sales or used clothing stores. He
owns six or seven dress jackets and an innumerable amount of button-
down shirts, yet the most he has ever spent on a garment is fifteen dollars.
One of his black shoes is missing a shoelace. When he is asked why, he half
jokingly replies, "The shoes cost 25 cents. If I put a shoelace in, it would
cost more than the shoes."

He will wear just about anything. When asked if there was one thing he
wouldn't wear, he paused for a little while and finally replied, "Women's
underwear." One thing he does protest is designer or status names, but he
also states, "I have some stuff from designers such as Pierre Cardin, but
the way I wear it, you could never tell."

While maintaining that his main purpose in his dress is comfort, he
does hint at some other motives. "I don't want to be classified into any
quote group, fashion, or mode. If how I dress is unique, then perhaps that
gives me a sense of individuality.

Apparently selfhood is hard to express, hard to attain, against the
threat of being "classified." This urgency unites people who dress

in sharply contrasting styles, as Maria G. found out by questioning a young man of much more *formal* appearance than is common at our college:

The person that I interviewed is a handsome, 6'2" male. I started off by asking him what he is trying to convey through his attire, and what attracted him to the clothes he wears. He answered with great confidence. "If a person my size was to dress in jeans and t-shirts, he would come across as a tough guy. I'm not a tough guy. I don't want to come across like that! That's why I wear ties and jackets, conservative clothing. I'm not the type of guy that likes to beat up people. I want to show that there's more to me than just size. When I walk down the street I don't want to intimidate old ladies or other people. At times I can see the fear. Also I don't want to look like a tough guy because I don't want other guys to try to force me to show how tough I really am. I dress to correct other people's misconception of myself."

Most students in the class picked up on this tension. In trying to understand or explain it, they moved naturally toward abstraction, trying out concepts like that of *ideology:*

Joan likes to dress "individualistically," and she calls her style of dress "a direct expression" of herself.

On an ordinary day, Joan can be seen wearing oversized sweaters and ample skirts—a look that *Mademoiselle* magazine recently featured. But, says Joan, she doesn't try to dress according to what she sees in advertising or magazines.

An aspect of Joan's clothing which is especially striking is her choice of accessories. She wears a wide copper bracelet along with other bangles on both arms. Added to this, she wears large hanging earrings which are also copper. "That's the part of me that's very natural," Joan says. "I bought the earrings from a man from Africa who dug the copper out of the earth himself. It's just my way to get away from the commercial."

In analyzing her fashion habits, Joan says the key for her is to be different. Why? "Because it's so easy to be like everyone else. I don't want to be that," she says. "I want to stand out in a crowd." That doesn't mean that she would sacrifice her good taste, though. "If it looks good, I'll wear it, but I would never buy something for the sake of being different."

This idea of non-conformity stretches far past fashion. Besides a fear of physically blending into the styles of the masses, people whose wardrobes are similar to Joan's reflect a desire to appear special or intellectually different. The ideology of conformity as evil or apathetic has played in their minds, forcing a desire for individuality.

(Dana Pollero)

Or *freedom* and *democracy:*

Julia is most often seen in loose-fitting, oversized, men's clothing, usually complemented with a pair of worn out old sneakers complete with holes. "I like to wear clothing that I don't have to constantly fix or adjust. Something which allows me to move and feel free in." . . .

"Your appearance is very personal and unique, and clothing should therefore create your appearance. It is the first thing someone notices about you, and should therefore be reflective of yourself." Julia insists that no one should try to be like anyone they are not, in any way. This even includes trying to dress like someone else. The most important thing is to be you, and to dress in your own style. . . . Julia's style of dressing implies a very broad sense of freedom and democracy. For she feels that people should be who they are, and that their clothing should be reflective of this. She views "fashion" as everyone's right to represent themselves as clearly as possible.

(Beth A.)

The abstractions retain a kind of solidity, because they rise from the specificity of the interview, from the spoken word and the worn-out sneakers.

Beth noted a political dimension in Julia's talk about clothing. A few students made that kind of connection quite specifically, as did Brad Fuller in his profile of a student with untucked shirts and untied shoes:

"Don't get me wrong, I don't have anything against conformity; in fact I like the idea of uniforms. Especially in China. I like their uniforms; however, it is a different kind of conformity there. They don't have a choice; it's law-enforced. In that area conformity works. Here I have a choice—I choose to be different in my clothing choice as well as my beliefs." . . .

The statement he is trying to make is clear: Eugene Finch is Eugene Finch. Eugene Finch is not the alligator on his shirt or a little red tag on his jeans. . . . I find congruence between his beliefs and his outfits. For an example, today's incident involving the marines in Lebanon: Eugene feels that the President should pull the troops out, but most of the other people that I spoke to thought that Reagan should send more troops, to exhibit the power of the United States. . . . When I told him that he was in the minority, he just said, "That's where I like to be."

And a few of the interviewees themselves turned out to have a conscious and fully articulated politics of fashion:

The young man sprawled on the lumpy dorm mattress, his head and back propped up by an overstuffed pillow. He is a good looking eighteen-year-old with a pleasant face. . . . Today he is wearing jeans, Nikes, and a fading t-shirt which has clearly been worn over a hundred times. Its scarlet lettering, "Holiday in Cambodia," will be a dingy pink after its next wash with his favorite detergent, Tide. . . . He is an inconspicuous and thoughtful clothes horse. He is as aware as any subscriber to *GQ* of the influential and message-laden nature of the fashion world in our society.

He began our interview with a discussion of American society and his personal punk outlook. "I will not accept blindly anything. Whenever possible, I try to find why something is done before I accept it. One of the aspects of our culture that punks question is appearance. American society and much of Western society in general puts great value on outward appearance. This seems a very poor criterion for judging people, as it tells little about them as a person beyond their wealth and background.

"As a response, punks dress and attempt to act differently from the rest of society. I, however, do not have a pink, six-inch, mohawk haircut. I, in fact, keep my hair relatively normally cut and do not wear dog collars or leather boots and jackets. I see such outward action as often mistakenly treated just as fashion is in the rest of society. That is not my view of the purpose: if punks merely created their own fashions and worshipped them in the same way that most people do regular fashions, then punk fashions would not be protest at all. I wear clothes that are comfortable and inexpensive. I complement these with t-shirts that make some sort of statement, either political or musical. I have chosen my own ways to protest society's overwhelming concern with appearances."

(Charlotte Oldham)

This student went on to characterize the outlook of "hardcore punk," the tendency to which he subscribed, and to tie its anger and hopelessness to unusable defense systems, starvation in the midst of plenty, and so on.

He accepted social classification, but only in a group whose credo he described thus: "Punk means thinking for yourself." The tension between a much-prized independence and the necessity of expressing it through signs associated with social groups was latent in all these interviews. Some interviewers reacted with suspicion:

Sitting across from Jessica, observing her—khaki pants, black Army boots, and her crew-cut hair style with streaks of pink through it, I can't help wondering if her clothing is expressing her individuality or if she is rejecting conservative values. Her gestures are feminine, but her appearance suggests a sense of masculinity. Her soft voice quickly contradicts the appearance. Her graduation picture on the wall shows an attractive girl with fairly long hair.

I asked Jessica if she thought her new haircut was more attractive than the style she wore when she took the picture. She said, "Yes, I feel I look better with the cut; I wanted something different and noticeable." I asked her, "But isn't your dress just a fad that happens to be in style?" She said, "My dress sets me apart from most people, and it expresses my individuality. It shows that I'm not afraid to be different; yes, it's a style, but it's my own style." But then I asked her if it wasn't the same style worn by punk rockers, and whether she listened to that form of music. She said, "I do enjoy punk rock music, and my dress is similar to that of most punk rockers and so-called new wavers." I asked her how this could be individuality when she is dressing the same as another group of people. She stated, "Although some other people dress the same as I do, it expresses my individuality because it's different from the accepted norm."

(John Rhea)

Other students who encountered this puzzle took it as the occasion for speculating on the limits and possibilities of dress as a social language. Bud H., for example, tried to grasp the historical dimension of the problem, as well as venturing a generalization about clothes as dialogue:

Bud: I'm very impressed by your wardrobe: how do you explain it?

Heather: Well, as a freshperson I was a definite hippie. I enjoyed the image but realized that it was just that—a fun image. It wasn't me, though, and near the end of the year I realized how ridiculous I had been. So I put most of my clothes in a box in Foss one and let people take what they wanted. What I have now was either given to me or is from the Salvation Army. I probably have a few things left over from my "hippie days." . . .

As Heather said, she used to be a "hippie," and I expect that she dressed like one. The hippies were protesting against an impersonal political and social system, and tried to embody their rejection of societal expectations in their dress. We can assume that in the early sixties this reaction could be considered as anti-fashion. Today the word "hippie" represents as much a stereotypical image as do the terms "preppy," "punk," or even "housewife." As such, it is no longer a personal reaction as much as a social stereotype. . . .

Heather's explanation of her "social development" led me to a general conclusion concerning dress as an individual expression. This is that as one's dress becomes more individual and subjective, one's implied values become less clear. As one's dress becomes more general or conformist, one's implied values become more obvious, while at the same time becoming more stereotypical (standard); and as such, chances are they are less genuine.

It was clear from this set of interviews that stand-out dressers were likely to proclaim their individuality in words as well. This was not a great surprise; after all, the class had sought out interviewees who were sending their sartorial messages in bold colors and shapes. But in the next stage of the inquiry we discovered something that precluded setting the assertive dressers entirely apart, as eccentrics and rebels. I asked the class to talk briefly, this time, with students who dressed in some quite recognizable convention.

A number of the responses did surprise the interviewers this time. For instance:

Lou: Why do you dress the way you do?

Bill: The clothes are comfortable and I find the preppy style appealing to me personally.

Lou: Don't you feel you're just "one of the preps"?

Bill: No, because people not only look at your clothes but at your physical characteristics. Preppy clothes fit me very well.

Lou: You said earlier that your use of preppy clothes conveys individuality and freedom. Explain.

Bill: I combine many colors, styles, and trends to formulate my own preppy look.

(Lou P.)

Normally, Steve Arkin dresses in classic clothes: cotton oxford shirts and crew neck sweaters purchased directly from the Brooks Brothers branch near his suburban Boston home. One might call him the king of convention, but ironically, he insists that he is a non-conformist. . . . "The word 'prep' means more than just a style of dress; it's an attitude that implies superiority and materialism," he says. Still, Steve doesn't reject the preppy style. "These clothes are timeless—they'll always be in style and you can turn them into a more mod type of thing. You can create a different look just by leaving the shirt tails out."

With these subtle changes, Steve feels he is making a statement. "I don't want to be like everyone else. That's boring. I'd rather be different." But difference can be measured in degrees. Steve would never dream of dressing in the truly non-conformist styles that are so unique to Wesleyan. "People who dress like that are dangerous," he thinks.

"I do associate myself with a group," he admits. "But it's a very small one. I'd describe the people in it as somewhat rebellious affluent adolescents who turn classical conservatism into neo-conservative mod."

(Dana Pollero)

Elliot Brown stands with his arms folded in the typical streetwise fashion. His expression as shown on his face is extremely serious, almost "deadly." More important is his manner of dress. On his head he wears a burgundy kangool hat tilted to the side of his head. Around his neck he wears a nameplate four times the usual size on which his nickname, "Skeets," is engraved. He is also wearing a dark blue, water-repellent Izod jacket with matching pants. And lastly, his outfit would not be complete without his meticulously clean white Nike sneakers; his laces are untied but carefully placed in their respective positions. If you were to stroll along the west side of Manhattan or Jamaica Avenue in Queens, you would find that Elliot is a carbon copy of every other guy who "hangs out" on the street corners of New York.

Oddly enough, Elliot doesn't feel that he is a conformist. He does feel that he must dress in this manner in order to be accepted. He considers his style to be a sign of status among his peers. Although he does wear a name-plate which is very common among his group, his is larger than most. Elliot explains that this is his way of standing above the crowd. In other words, he is an individual but at the same time conforming to his particular group.

(Emily C.)

Evidently, it was not just the bold dressers who subscribed to an ideology of the untrammeled individual. The discussion of these interviews led out from fashion, to reflection upon the kinds of students that came to Wesleyan, and on how they articulated their projects of selfhood. We talked about the college's buzzword, *diversity*. Why did that translate into the feeling that each person must have an identity that transcended membership in social groups? Was individuality the birthright of each person, or something that had to be achieved? If the latter, how did young people aspire to it? And which young people had the best chance to attain it, or—at least—to cherish it as a posible goal for themselves? It became clear that we were talking about social class, in manifestations quite a bit subtler than family income or attendance at a private school. Yet the generalizations about class and ideology and consciousness had their origins in boots, shawls, and t-shirts, and in what people said about why they wore these garments.

I like the possibility of building questions and insights in this way, through an exchange between interview and analysis. In addition, this kind of project fosters collaboration. A particular student's paper on selfhood and social groups, or on the paradox of promoting individuality through mass fashion, draws on interviews and commentary produced by the whole class, as well as on outside readings. Then a group of analytic papers generates further questions and hypotheses, which may lead to further interviews, and to readings unanticipated by students or instructor before the process began.

Meanwhile, students are learning how better to ask questions and how to listen; they are becoming more at ease, too, about talking with people different from themselves, sometimes on explosive subjects. In classes built largely around interviewing, students usually move "out" at this point, to inquiries less homely than the one into styles of dress. Sexuality is such a field. Twice I have had small groups of students develop projects around sexual issues; although it is no secret that people often misrepresent or misremember their sexual experience, I think much truth comes through in an interview like this one, to enlighten the interviewer and all who share her write-up:

Oh, OK, this is a long story. At the end of my second year, I had hit a sophomore slump of some kind, which is not unusual, but there were some unusual parts to it, I guess. I was uncomfortable, lonely, and unhappy for a lot of my sophomore year, and I really didn't understand why—basic unhappiness. My grades got me into some trouble, but in the second semester I pulled myself together again and finished the year in good academic standing. My parents, however, withdrew financial support from me because they decided, "We've paid enough for you to come to this place and you haven't *really* done that well."

Spring semester of my sophomore year was a very strange time. . . . Oh, one other thing that upset everybody, not just me, was that the lead tenor in Wesleyan's concert choir propositioned me. This had never happened to me before and I had never had to consciously consider the fact that I might be gay, and it—*wow, it scared the hell out of me!* I went through a lot of turbulence about that. It just kind of came out of the blue. I guess it wouldn't have upset me so much if I hadn't actually had tendencies in that direction to begin with, now that I think back on it. . . . So I had some work to do on the personal front, figure out myself. My parents, though very concerned, were not really able to help.

—How did they react?

Oh, I told them first of anybody, that I thought maybe my sexuality wasn't exactly typical, and I got what they had been trained with, or told. I got panic, some misinformation, and a little ridicule. They were concerned, though, and still loved me, but just didn't know what to make of it. . . .

—Do you still have an innate urge for sex?

Oh yeah!

—So how do you deal with that?

Well, I've found some nice men on campus who are interested in the same thing—oh, what do you mean?

—What I meant was: sex, as in "intercourse," that you can only have with a woman. In every man, isn't there a need for that type of sex?

No, there really isn't. It's kind of an exciting realization that, well, people are more versatile than that. I guess that's the nicest way I can put it. Sexual expression can take many forms. One of the most erotic experiences I ever had was with about nine other people in the back seat of a Ford Falcon. All we were doing was bumping around Maryland country roads in the middle of the night, and I was holding some girl's hand. I mean, that was beautiful. It was as nice a physical experience as anything else. There's a term that I love called "polymorphous perversity."

—What does that mean?

I'm not sure. Literally of course it would mean a sort of strangeness that takes many forms. As far as erotic things go, well, sexual expression can take many forms, and it *does*. People don't usually talk about most of them.

. . .

—Are gay men biologically different from straight men?

No. Really only transsexuals have an abnormal balance of hormones. Some gay men make great points of emphasizing their masculinity—me with this ridiculous haircut and me with my beard. Many men invest in other trappings such as a leather jacket and other similarly macho trappings to emphasize the fact that they *are* masculine. "There's nothing wrong with their hormones."

—Do you feel you have to prove your masculinity?

Oh, in some ways. It's a bit jokey to me. Sometimes I find it reassuring. Men are insecure and we're no different; we just have to assert our masculinity sometimes.

. . .

Let's talk more generally. Now that I'm gay—I know I am functionally for the most part gay—I always like to put those two phrases together. I know my orientation is not exclusively homosexual; it never was, probably never will be exclusively so. I know that and I am a student here, as opposed to being that way and not knowing it and being a student here. It gives people something more to deal with, for sure. It probably doesn't bother them all that much, but I think it's important for people whose sexuality is this way to show it. Not so as to be offensive, but just so as to be more consistent, internally, within themselves. I can see all kinds of reasons why a person would want to conceal his sexuality, if deviant, which mine is. It upsets colleagues and co-workers. It sort of makes an issue where it can be argued there's no need to make an issue.

. . .

I find it necessary, and I think it's honest, for me at some point in the context of friendship, with someone I'm getting interested in, to simply let them know that I *am* gay, and then they can figure out what to say back.

—Is that often an awkward situation?

Yes, it's a nerve-racking situation, and I think to avoid it, many times. I tend to avoid interacting on any personal matters with a man I do not know.

—So you're not likely to go up and introduce yourself to people that you'd like to get to know, or be outgoing?

Right, I've always tended towards introversion anyway.

—Do you feel your homosexuality has increased that?

No, it's just a part of the way I am. Pathos is not something I strive for; why bother? It's not pathetic to be gay. It *is* pathetic if you sit around feeling miserable about the fact, and you don't do anything about it, and you always think you have to hide it.

. . .

—How do you feel your homosexuality will affect your future goals and future career?

Well, Duke Ellington . . . talked about something called the Faggot Mafia in the world of music, and I've heard that in some ways it's just the old Hollywood story: if you plan to get to the top, one way to get there is to sleep your way. There's this group of gay musicians, entrepreneurs, and such, in the arts, that are sort of susceptible to that kind of persuasion, that type of manipulation. But I'm not into that. I'm not interested in using it to my advantage, and hope it's not used against me.

. . .

—How do you feel about being interviewed?

Pleased. It's an opportunity to communicate. I'm not out to recruit, by any means! It's just good to make people aware.

(Diana DeJoseph)

Students discover that this man's attitude is not unusual, though also far from universal. Many people want to talk, even about tricky matters, and even with a stranger, who will respect complexity or pain. Encouraged by that knowledge, some students venture further from the socially familiar. One small group undertook a series of interviews with rape victims. Jennifer Hilliard made her way into this subject through a city bureaucracy:

MRS. BETTY GREEN

When I stepped into the office I found Mrs. Betty Green with her head buried in a pile of papers. This dark haired, blue eyed, middle aged woman is the supervisor of the rape counselors for a metropolitan court system. As she stood to greet me I noticed a dark mark on the right side of her face. The mark travelled from her temple to the upper part of her jaw. I was later told by Mrs. Green that the mark was left after a guy raped her. She was eighteen when it happened. After the hand-shaking was done, she asked me to give her a couple of minutes to finish the papers on her desk. Then she handed me six photos. The pictures were of two young women. Two photos were of the girls before they were raped; two were of the girls, taken by the police photographer, after the rapes were reported; the last two were of the girls about a year after the rape. These were the two young women I would have the pleasure of talking to.

After I decided that my stomach had had enough of these horrible photos, I let my eyes roam about the office. The desk at which Mrs. Green sat was semi-circular in shape, and looked to be made of the finest oak. The chair in which she sat was a huge black recliner. The walls of the office were paneled in a deep, dark brown. One of the walls was covered with pictures of rape victims, before and after being attacked. When Mrs. Green finished with her task, our conversation began.

. . .

—First I'd like to know what motivated you to do this type of work.

Well, to make a long story short (she said), I myself was raped when I was eighteen. The counselor that handled my case was a big help. She would comfort me when I felt like crying. I guess it was because she knew exactly what I was feeling. You see, she had been raped herself when she was only sixteen. She helped me get my life together. I still want to cry sometimes when I look at myself in the mirror and this scar is staring back at me. I even have nightmares, but my husband is always there to hold me. I guess my experience as a victim was step one of my wanting to do this kind of work. Step two was definitely the counselor that handled my case. I knew I wanted to do something to help other victims.

. . .

KAREN HANSON

As a tall, slender woman with straight, blond hair which hung just past the nape of her neck, and green eyes so bright that they seemed to have captured the rays of the sun, stepped into the office, Mrs. Green rose from her chair and introduced the woman as Miss Karen Hanson. . . .

—Karen, when were you raped, and how did you feel afterwards?

After taking a deep breath, she replied, "I was raped when I was nineteen. I was living on campus, and on my way to visit my parents. I was just stepping into the elevator when these two guys rushed up behind me and pushed me to the back wall of the elevator. Before I could recover from the dizziness I felt because I hit my head on the back wall of the elevator when I was pushed in, we were already on the roof."

She takes another deep breath, as scenes of what had happened came into her mind, and tears began to swell in her eyes.

—You don't have to talk about it anymore if you don't want to.

"No, I have to talk about it. It keeps me from keeping it bottled up inside." She then continued, "They beat me up pretty bad. Then both of them raped me. After they decided that they had had enough fun, the two bastards beat me again. I came out of it with multiple bruises, two broken ribs, and a ruptured spleen. While I was lying there crying, my first thought was to jump right off that roof. But for some reason I didn't. I felt like a big piece of shit."

—You seem as though you've coped with the problem well. Is that true?

"I'd really love to believe I have," she laughed out. "I think I have. I'm not afraid of being touched by men anymore. I'm starting to relax now."

—Do you have nightmares about it?

"Yes," she responded with a sigh. "Some nights I wake up screaming. I don't have the nightmares as often as I used to. I guess I'll get over that. But damn, it's hard."

. . .

—What do you think made the guys want to rape you?

She looked me straight in the eyes and replied, "They were strung out. Those two guys were on Venus. I really don't think they knew what they were doing. I will say this, though, whatever the hell they were doing, they did it right on me."

—Do you hate them?

I hate what they did to me, sure. But I don't hate them. Sometimes I think I'm crazy for not hating them. I guess I don't because they were too strung out to even know whether or not they were standing.

. . .

As I walked outside into the afternoon sun, I could feel a huge lump in my throat. I gained pure respect for those two women I left behind in that office. I respected the strength and courage in each of them. And I hoped that I would be able to find within me that strength and courage to help me carry on in times of crisis.

The anguish of the discourse threatens the control conventionally exercised by an interviewer, and strains against the reassurance proffered by write-up formats. This is not a routine freshman comp exercise, and I would not expect many students to take the kind of risk Jennifer did. Still, a few go that far and farther. Jennifer herself followed these interviews by visiting a prison and talking with a convicted rapist. Two other students in the same class conducted a scary, two-hour interview with the leader of our state's Ku Klux Klan, in his well-fortified house. Such encounters are a limiting case, and often a high point. But the texture and achievement of a class's work do not depend upon such daring—and it would be unethical to ask it from young students who, after all, are enrolled in a writing course for one college credit.

Students find easier paths across social boundaries, listening to voices that come out of other experiences than their own. Class is one such line. Often, students have tried to hear what working-class people feel and think, and to catch the intonations of striving or defeat. (More than once, I have used Richard Sennett and Jonathan Cobb's *The Hidden Injuries of Class*, or books from Robert Coles's *Children of Crisis* series, as texts that humanize an inquiry like this.) Denise Paasche, tutoring a girl from a housing project, turned the "lesson" around, and made Gloria *her* teacher for a while:

The following is what Gloria, a fourteen year old high school student from Middletown told me about college education:

. . .

I think a college education is good. It gives you a better push. Say you're applyin' for a really good job, and someone else is also applyin' who hasn't been to college, but who's been workin' five years and seen more of the world. I think the person who's been to college will get the job. I don't really know why. When you don't go to college you can still be just as smart from being out in the world, but a college person has been exploring and meeting people from all over the place. Maybe they think you've been learnin' deeply, you know, what it's about, been testin' it, hitting the books. Person who's been workin' probably just been followin' orders. So the person with a college education gets picked. I guess that's the way society is now. I don't really know why, but college jus' gives you a kind of a push.

No, college doesn't really change you; well, you might be a little more knowledgy. You know, using big words, or things a little over somebody else's level.

Mos' kids go to college because they don't know what they want to do. You get to further your interests and see if that's what you really want. Also, society sort of says, 'If you go to college we'll have a better view of you.' Mos' people think they jus' should go, but lots of people are successful without college, my father for one. Most parents haven't been to college, you know, 'bout eighty percent. I think both my parents would've liked to go to college, but my mom got pregnant and then my dad had to work to support her. Too bad, because she was really smart, she got A's in her classes and everything. I bet she would've been a nurse by now.

Yeah, before parents didn't get college educations, they got pregnant, or somethin'. Now the kids are lookin' at the parents. They want to do better, want to do a bit more. They want to be able to support their parents, help them like they helped you. That's what I want to do.

I've been in Middletown all my life and I want to be out of here, to somewhere where they've never heard of Middletown. I'm keepin' up my grades, and I'm goin' to get into a nice college and be somethin'.

We upper-middle-class readers learn something from this of how a "nice college" looks to one not entitled by birth to attend one.

Gloria's aspirations pose little threat to the values of the more privileged students in my class, even though a few of her remarks might give pause to these "more knowledgy" ones. Some interviews with working-class people are more troubling. The middle-class listener reaches out with good will toward those who have a had a tougher time of it, but not everything he or she hears will please the liberal ear. Karin Hilding reports such words, but leaves them out of her final, sympathetic assessment:

At ten o'clock on a brisk Wednesday morning I entered the "Polish Dormitory." It is a large brick building that I speculated had one time been a refuge for new Polish members of the community, and had perhaps come to serve as a community center. The entrance led to a dim barroom with a few older men sitting around. After overcoming my surprise at the surroundings, I met the bartender. I slowly began to feel comfortable sitting down at the bar, asking these men questions, and listening to what was on their minds. They were mostly of Polish descent.

. . .

Harry, a large man about in his seventies, was sitting next to me, and spoke about black people in Middletown. "Are there conflicts between blacks and whites in Middletown?," I asked. "It all depends who's on top. We used to have feuds between different nationalities; now it's between blacks and whites. That's the big fight." Naively I asked, "What's the difference between whites and blacks?" At this he broke into laughter and let the others in on the joke. "You know the answer," he remarked. "You just have to look." In a more serious tone he continued, "It's not cause they're black or poor, but cause they don't want to work. Those who do work get punished by those who don't want to work." Later on there were other jokes around the bar about blacks.

. . .

When I brought up the topic of big business, all these men agreed that big business runs the country. The tax assessor pointed out that years ago Middletown was run by the Russell Company. "They owned the banks, the stores, everything. Ford Motors and Goodyear wanted to come in. Middletown was ideal with its river and the railroad, but the Russells wouldn't let them in." Harry brought up the view that today commercial industry has an advantage over the individual since they pay less per gallon of oil than home owners. I asked Harry about unions and he stated, "big business and unions are the same thing." At that remark someone brought up the workers' strikes in Poland. There was interest and sympathy expressed by them for the workers. They weren't, however, optimistic about the results of the strike. If the workers get anywhere, "It's only a matter of time before the Russians come."

. . .

As I got ready to leave, John [the bartender] pointed out that I had come on a good day, and he expressed his enjoyment of the variety of men that come to the bar. The friendliness and strong roots and opinions of these men gave me a good feeling. They expressed a sense of continuity. Perhaps it was a continuity of human problems and a togetherness in community.

Another student—like Karin, both open-minded and antiracist— cannot pass over the racism he hears voiced, though neither does it cancel the sympathy he feels for the young policemen with whom he drinks beer:

Rob Collins is a rookie cop in Middletown, and at 22 he is one of the youngest men on the force. He is a good example of what police administrators like to call the "new breed" of cop. His bachelor's degree and plans for graduate study in criminology are a facet of this, as is the extensive psychological and physical testing that he had to pass to be admitted to the group from which academy trainees are picked. Conscientious and happy with his work, Rob wanted to be a policeman, not just make a living. But if Rob is part of the new breed, there are many others on the force who differ from him. . . .

One auxiliary policeman I talked with, a Middletown native, had this to say: "These new kids are good cops, and I'd ride with them any day. But they want to talk everything out, reason with people too much. In a dangerous situation you need the brutal cop, the man who'll take some action. Here that seems to be the older guys, the guys who didn't get all this psychological training. On any police force you need a mix between the brutal cops and the 'nice guys.'"

. . .

That's the funny thing, and common, this split between old and new cops. Rob tells me that the thing about the job he didn't expect is the change in himself. He can see himself ten years from now, adopting the attitudes of the old cops. He says he can see how it happens. And while he thought that change wouldn't come to him, he feels it now. Here our conversation took a provoking turn.

"I didn't want to be a cop in my home town because of the huge ethnic element—there's always trouble. Here it's pretty quiet, mainly some nigger problems on the weekends. I won't hold it back, I'm prejudiced. Even black people make a distinction between themselves and niggers."

. . .

These are horrible, fascinating things, but I didn't feel comfortable enough with Rob to push him further, to ask him about the implications of his attitudes. I could sense him becoming wary of me.

What I was most interested in, and what I could least approach, were basic questions about the values of a man to whom the public trust has been given. How and why was there a double standard for blacks, for any people? Why the ambiguous attitude? What causes a young cop, especially a new breed cop, to adopt the attitudes of older, more provincial officers, attitudes he knows are unjust—attitudes he himself considers foreign to an ideal community? What in the job itself might account for this? Is it that basic nervousness caused by pumping adrenaline? Does the cop, who more than any other person is in danger from *other people*, seek some way to generalize about that danger, thus making it easier to recognize, by stereotyping its possible source (of course there are arguable dangers to this)? If this is true, are we, in demanding as we must that a policeman be fair, placing that officer in more danger? Can we ever expect, given the unfair society we have and given that policemen are human beings, an officer to be unprejudiced? Experience seems to prove that the answer is a depressing no.

(Paul Duke)

It is one thing to have correct opinions from the vantage point of the college on the hill, quite another to experience race from the police station or the "Polish Dormitory."

Interviews like these take us onto different terrain, raising questions like Paul's that cannot easily be resolved in the five-paragraph theme. They extend the field of vision from our elite college classroom; students' discoveries extend and test their book learning. Their writing enters into a process of re-knowing the world, a process that empowers as it perplexes.[5]

With that as a goal for the writing course, the individual paper as crafted performance matters less than it otherwise would. Still, no English teacher will deny that The Paper has its value to students; out of sheer self-interest, all would prefer reading sets of papers that teach us something, and perhaps even yield pleasure. I may have implied otherwise by reproducing only *excerpts* in this essay, and would like to conclude by printing one entire write-up that gave pleasure, of a sufficiently mixed sort. Let Jim Varney have the last words:[6]

"I want to help people on the streets . . . "

ARTHUR BRENT IS A RODNEY DANGERFIELD WHO SEEMS NOT TO WORRY ABOUT GETTING NO RESPECT. HE HAS BEEN AROUND—SEVEN YEARS IN THE AIR FORCE, UNEMPLOYED FOR A YEAR AND A HALF, A BARTENDER IN SEVERAL PLACES, AND, FOR THE LAST SEVEN YEARS, INVOLVED IN ONE OF AMERICA'S MOST ENIGMATIC SOCIAL INSTITUTIONS, PORNOGRAPHY. TODAY HE IS THE PROPRIETOR OF AN ADULT BOOKSTORE ("IN THE PHONE BOOK UNDER 'A,'" HE'LL TELL YOU, "'A' FOR ADULT.") IN BRANDON, CONN. HE SPEAKS IN AN EARNEST VOICE WITH AN EVEN MORE EARNEST FACE AS IF EVERYTHING HE TOLD YOU WAS NOT ONLY OF PROFOUND IMPORTANCE, BUT ENTIRELY JUSTIFIABLE AS WELL.

I've always had an interest in porn. Before I became employed here, I'd been into buying. You see I used to be a bartender and I became an alcoholic. I've been drying out for a while now and I'm better. Anyway, the guy who interviewed me for this job had been a bartender.

I'm really not your typical person behind the counter of an adult bookstore. I enjoy satisfying people's wants and needs, my job helps me solve their problems. A guy will come up to me and say, "I can't get it up," and I'll help him out. It's a peer counseling sort of thing.

I deal with fantasy. I provide pictures for masturbation fantasies. I allow people to vent their anger and frustration, soothe sexual repression that may have occurred in childhood. You see, porn is educational for many people. For example, marriage counselors send clients to buy dildoes. Even doctors refer to me. This job is part of a community service.

ARTHUR BRENT TALKS IN FRONT OF A TABLE WITH NEATLY STACKED DILDOES THAT HE CONSTANTLY REFERS TO AS "HEALTH AIDS." BEHIND HIM IS A KALEIDOSCOPE OF PICTURES BECKONING TO HIS CUSTOMERS WITH LEWD SMILES, MAGAZINES IN ROWS AND ROWS GLISTENING IN PLASTIC WRAPPERS. IN THE BACKGROUND IS THE FAINT,

INCESSANT HUM OF PEEP SHOW CAMERAS ("CHANGED WEEKLY," THE AD CRIES OUT-
SIDE THE STORE). A FLOCK OF SOMBER, ALMOST DETERMINED LOOKING MEN CLUS-
TER AROUND THE LIT FRAME TELLING THEM WHAT IS PLAYING IN WHAT BOOTH. NEW
SHIPMENT MAGS SPILL OUT OF THEIR BOXES DISPLAYING THE ENTICING TITLES, "TIT
FUCKERS" AND "EBONY HUMPER."

I want to get out of here. I'm bored. I don't get turned on unless I shoot
my own stuff. I can't find a challenge here, but I do like the paycheck (he
informs me that he is "very well paid"). It's just the same problems and
the same people.

You see, porn is really an upper middle class luxury. A good deal of my
clientele are white collar. (He nods at a man in a pinstripe suit furtively
glancing about trying not to use up his fifteen minute browsing limit too
quickly.)

Now, I want to get into social work, work that does not pay much. I'm
tired of drunks. This place is an underground meeting place for gays, men
that are looking for quick, no-strings sexual contact. Most of them are
married and have kids.

ARTHUR BRENT, FOR THE SIXTH TIME SINCE THE INTERVIEW BEGAN, GETS UP AND
TURNS A MAN'S ONE, OR TWO, DOLLARS INTO FOUR, OR EIGHT, ROUNDED, TWENTY-
FIVE CENT SATISFACTION PIECES. HE RETURNS TO DISCUSS HIS VIEWS ON PORN AS A
BENEFICIAL COG IN SOCIETY.

I don't have any bad feelings about what I do. I think porn should be
more available but controlled. Ten percent of the business is all the mob
does not own. You see, if the age of consent is sixteen, then the age for legal
exposure to porn should be sixteen (the law is eighteen in Conn.).

What I want to do is help people on the streets. Kiddie porn? All I can
say is it keeps kids off the street.

ARTHUR BRENT, WITH AN ALMOST DEFIANT EXPRESSION, LISTENS TO A DESCRIP-
TION OF "UNDER 21," A HOME DESIGNED FOR RUNAWAYS BY FATHER BRUCE RITTER
WHICH HAS BECOME A 24-HOUR HAVEN FOR KIDS RAVAGED BY NEW YORK STREET
LIFE. RITTER HAS SEEN TEENAGERS, BEREFT OF HEADS AND HANDS, LYING IN A
PUDDLE OF BLOOD IN THE DOORWAY OF "UNDER 21'S" MAIN OUTPOST ON THE BUTT-
SPRINKLED, BOOZE- AND URINE-STAINED STREETS OF TIMES SQUARE AND 42ND.
DAILY, HE DEALS WITH SEXUALLY VIOLATED FOURTEEN-YEAR-OLDS, AND SIXTEEN-
YEAR-OLDS WITH REARRANGED FACIAL DESIGNS. HE WATCHES EACH NIGHT WHEN
TEENAGERS HUSTLE THEMSELVES TO SURVIVE, ONLY TO BE BEATEN BY PIMP AND
JOHN ALIKE. HE SEES THIS. I'VE SEEN THIS. AND WHEN YOU THINK ABOUT IT, SO
HAVE WE ALL.

Look, first of all you've got to understand that it isn't as bad as the
people against it say it is. I know this business and kiddie porn is not
that bad.

I met a fourteen-year-old who was in the streets. I set him up with a guy
in New York who could get him hustling himself at a bar. I found that kid a

channel to get money. Believe me, I didn't do it until I called his parents and found out he was a total deadbeat. They wouldn't even take him back. I helped him out. I got him a job hustling. I found someone to take care of him.

ARTHUR BRENT, SOCIAL WORKER. I HOPE TO GOD HE'S LYING.

I know it's hard to morally justify my position. . . .

WITH A TAINTED NOTEBOOK, I LEFT HIS STORE. WALKING UP THE BUTT-SPRINKLED STREET IN BRANDON, I SAW THE SKY WAS MURKY. I WANTED TO GO HOME AND I WANTED TO STAY HOME. ARTHUR BRENT'S DISTORTED PHILOSOPHY RANG IN MY EARS.

Look, if the kids can understand sexuality then they can do it. You have to be sexually mature about this and if they like what they're doing, what's wrong with it?

This fourteen-year-old I told you about? He got raped at that "Under 21" place. It was the most traumatic thing that ever happened to him.

WELL, I GUESS THAT IS RIGHT. THINK HOW MUCH BETTER IT IS TO BE GIVEN A JOB HUSTLING YOURSELF. AT LEAST IT WILL KEEP YOU OFF THE STREETS.

20 Reflections on Class and Language

Two interviews are the starting point of this chapter. I got them from a video project called "The Unemployment Tapes,"[1] designed to explore through talks with local people the human costs, the sources, and the possible cures of unemployment in an old industrial area of Connecticut. The Connecticut Council for the Humanities funded the project, and I was a consultant to it. At the time (fall 1978) I was also reading and thinking about class and language, and it occurred to me that interviews like these might be helpful. No interview can ever be a "natural" context for the speech of the person interviewed, but at least these respondents had no reason to think that their language was being observed, except in the incidental ways that we all observe one another's language. The interviewers were not linguists, psychologists, or sociologists. They were friendly, casual, young, not personally intimidating. The interviews followed no fixed schedule; in this they were more like conversations than are many experiments and interviews in sociolinguistic research. Yet the subject and the goals of the questioning remained fairly constant throughout.

So here are the transcripts, with some names and places disguised.

A COUPLE AT A SHOPPING MALL

Interviewer: I'd like to ask you if you have jobs right now.
Respondents: Yes.
I: Have either of you ever been unemployed for any length of time?
R: No.
I: Well, would you say there was an unemployment problem in this area?
Man: Well, we're new in the area. We just moved in a couple of months ago. From what I've been reading there is unemployment in the area.
Woman: I would say so. There are an awful lot of people going to Oakfield and Hill County to get jobs. They're not staying in the valley.
I: Do you have any ideas about what causes that problem?

M: I have no idea.

W: Not enough industry up here. A lot of industry is just leaving the area.

I: How come?

W: Taxes are too high? There's no rebate or anything else for them.

I: So if we give a tax break and some other breaks to business, then—

W: I would say that there's no reason for businesses to stay in Connecticut. They're not getting any benefits from it. It's cheaper to go down to the South and get cheap labor now.

I: What happens when labor in the South matches labor up North?

W: They're going to have a problem.

I: Go overseas?

W: Possibly, yeah.

I: Then when labor overseas matches labor in the United States—

M: A vicious cycle.

I: What's the solution?

M: I don't know. If I knew I wouldn't be standing here.

I: Have you other thoughts on the subject?

W: I just wish they'd do something about it, that's all.

I: Who?

W: The government.

I: Could the government solve the problem?

M: I think they could make it a little easier. I don't think they could solve it. It's just going to—you're going to stop it here, it's going to start somewhere else. You're not going to be able to stop it. It's impossible. Like trying to stop war.

I: So it's part of the system?

M: I think so, yeah. I think it's part of life, but I think the government could make it easier.

I: Some people think a different system would solve the problem—

Both: I don't know.

I: A different economic system.

Both: I don't know.

THE MAYOR OF MILL TOWN

Interviewer: How do you think the high rate of unemployment has affected this community as a whole, in terms of its self image, in terms of its ability to deal with problems?

Respondent: Well, you know a very high percentage of unemployment is never a healthy condition, whether it's in Mill Town or anywhere else, and this lower Mill Valley region here has been pretty much plagued by high amounts of unemployment for at least fifteen to twenty years, and probably the greatest contributor to that would be the fact of how automation has taken over so much of the factory process that was once the main employer.

I: What are the other causes of unemployment, besides automation?

R: Well, I believe that automation is perhaps the chief cause of unemployment. Secondly, if we delve with other causes I would say it would be the lack of opportunity for the number of people that you have. We have a very densely populated area here, and like Mill Town with 6.2 square miles and you have over 21,000 people cramped into them, doesn't leave much space for industrial growth. In other words, we need to put our people to work. We need more facilities. We need more concerns here operating, businesses operating here, and we don't have the place to put them.

I: Whose responsibility is it to see that industry comes to, like, stop the high rate of unemployment? Do you see that as the responsibility of the government? Do you see it as the responsibility of business? Who puts pressure on business to do that? Whose responsibility is it?

R: Well, I don't think there is any one segment of society which, you're trying to point out, that is responsible. Like if it isn't there, that this is part of the responsibility of this particular segment. I think that it is very conducive to government to encourage industry in their area. I know I myself, as Mayor, am very anxious, and we have been working very hard, to fill up these remaining parcels we do have because it serves basically two purposes. It expands our tax base which makes life a little more comfortable for our citizens in terms of their tax bills, and secondly, it also in some effect provides more jobs which lowers that unemployment rate at least somewhat.

I: Do you think that the federal government should play a major role in bad economic times, as it is doing with CETA?

R: Well, certainly. I think that if you look at the entire history of our country, that it has always been the federal government that has come to the rescue. Take the great depression and all the federal programs that we used to bail it out. What you are really doing is, you stimulate the economy by priming up the pump and throwing money into the economy. That's—but by giving these people salaries and positions and all, they are going out and spending money, which gives business, the private sector, more of a stimulus, because they've got money coming in, they have the cash flow, and you hope for expansion.

I: Does that ever make you think about the economic system that we have, that it always has to be fed?

R: I think unfortunately it will always have to be fed. The government— the government—the federal government—the government in general are big partners in the private sector. I think they really prime a lot of money into them that, you know, makes things happen.

I: And you think that is the way it should be?

R: I don't think it's the way it should be. It would be wonderful to have private enterprise exist on their own, without any regulation or any help from government, but I don't feel that it is workable.

I: Why not?

R: Oh, for many, many reasons. I don't think first of all that private— well, you just take private enterprise as it is, and what if it wasn't regulated? I mean you take, again—going back historically, Standard Oil and all the great trusts that were brought together there in the early 1900s where a few people were making millions and millions of dollars—and which were like trillions today—and the majority of the people in the country, the standard of living was very, very low. It was when government came in and started to regulate the amount of profits that these people could make and to really decentralize the main business interest that people started to get a better standard of living. The unionism thing was all part of the entire movement, I believe, which created a better standard of living, and this was all done through government legislation.

Now I want to present in schematic form some rather sharp contrasts between the way the mayor talks and the way the man and woman talk, leaving aside all judgments about effectivenes, clarity, and intelligence.

A. Length and Complexity

1. The responses are much shorter in interview I. So are the sentences: there is no independent syntactic unit of more than sixteen words in I: six of the sentences in II are longer than thirty words.

2. There is little coordination and almost no subordination in I, except in sentences beginning "I think," "I would say," and so forth. There is much of both in II. For instance, in the sentence beginning "That's—but by giving . . . " the main clause is preceded by a gerund phrase and followed by a relative clause with an embedded appositive, then an adverbial clause that contains another appositive-like structure ("they have the cash flow"); there are several coordinate constructions along the way.

3. There are few explicit causal or logical connections in I, and many in II.

B. Modifiers

There are few adjectives and adverbs in I, and those mainly of degree. Modifiers are many and various in II, including derived adjectives ("industrial") and nouns used as modifiers ("*unemployment* rate").

C. Abstraction

There are few abstract nouns in I, many in II. Those in I appear mainly in simple constructions with the verb *be*, and are unrelated to one another: "There is *unemployment* in the area"; "*Taxes* are too high"; "There's no *rebate*." The abstract nouns in II appear in a variety of syntactic positions, and are often related syntactically and conceptually to one another. For example, in his fourth answer the mayor connects all the following nouns within a single sentence: "economy," "salaries," "positions," "business," "sector," "stimulus," "cash flow," and "expansion."

D. Reference to Context

The man and woman refer only a few times to the context of the discussion: "Oakfield," "Hill County," "down to the South," "Connecticut." The mayor not only anchors the discussion geographically to Mill Town with its 21,000 people in only six square miles, but also gives it a context in the social system (the economy, the government, etc.) and in history (the last fifteen to twenty years, the depression, the early 1900s). Note also that interview I includes one exophoric pronoun (a pronoun with no antecedent in the discourse): "I just wish *they*'d do something." There are none in II.

E. Reference to the Discourse Itself

There is virtually none in I, other than expressions of uncertainty, like "I think" and "I don't know." The mayor uses such constructions, and also refers to the discourse in at least four other ways:

1. He comments on the interviewer's question. For instance, when he begins his first answer, "Well, you know a very high percentage of unemployment is never a healthy condition," he in effect says, "That's a silly question," by stating a general principle that covers the situation and that should be obvious to anyone. Compare this to the beginning of his fourth answer.

2. He implicitly rejects the question: when asked who is responsible for reducing unemployment, he denies the presupposition that some *one* part of society is. When asked if the need for Keynesian measures makes him "think about the economic system," he simply reiterates the need for Keynesian measures, declining to answer the question (answer 5). When asked, next, if he thinks that is the way it should be, he does respond, but then goes on to show that the question is infelicitous—you cannot properly ask if X *should* be the case when X *must* be the case.

3. He comments reflexively on his own terms and statements: "In other words"; "I mean"; "Like if it isn't there"; "business, the private sector"; "money . . . the cash flow"; "the government—the federal government—the government in general."

4. He makes new starts in the middle of a sentence, indicating that he has reconsidered and thought of a better way to proceed: "That's—but by giving these people salaries"; "I don't think first of all that private—well you just take private enterprise"; "I mean you take again—going back historically." (The man in I does this once: "It's just going to—you're going to stop it here, it's going to start somewhere else.")

Contrasts like these run through all the unemployment tapes I have studied. People on the street, picked out as ordinary workers or perhaps unemployed people, were asked the same kinds of questions about unemployment as were officials, businessmen, and specialists. Speakers from the first group did not elaborate, rank, or expand their ideas much, did not make many distinctions, made few logical and causal connections, did not develop abstract ideas, did not relate their words very explicitly to context, and referred little to the discourse itself in a critical or metalinguistic way. Speakers from the second group rated high on all these measures.

In the last two decades, the sorts of contrast that emerge in these two interviews have drawn a lot of attention, especially in Britain. There a group of sociologists and linguists inspired and led by Basil Bernstein has done very extensive research on differences between working-class and middle-class speech. And Bernstein's concepts of "restricted" and "elaborated" codes[2] are now firmly planted in the center of this intellectual terrain—much respected and much criticized.

According to Bernstein and his colleagues, the elaborated code of the middle class runs more to subordination and modification than the restricted code of the working class. It includes more adjectives, adverbs, prepositions, complex verbs. It facilitates distinctions of all sorts, in particular logical ones. Elaborated code users distance themselves more from the immediate situation and from the content of their talk, through abstraction, through passives, through expressions of probability, through suppositions ("I think"), through questions and refusals to commit themselves quickly to definite interpretations of ambiguous experience. The elaborated code allows or encourages more individuation of response and more reflection on language itself. Restricted code users are more bound to the local, concrete situation. Much of their meaning is implicit—dependent on prior understandings of the context. (Hence they do not refer so explicitly *to* the context; exophoric pronouns are an extreme example.) In Bernstein's own words, the restricted code emphasizes "the communal rather than the individual, the concrete rather than the abstract, substance rather than the elaboration of processes, the here and now rather than exploration of motives and intentions, and positional rather than personalized forms of social control."[3] Again,

elaborated codes orient their users toward universalistic meanings, whereas restricted codes orient, sensitize, their users to particularistic meanings. . . . Restricted codes are more tied to a local social structure and have a reduced potential for change in principles. Where codes are elaborated, the socialized has more access to the grounds of his own socialization, and so can enter into a reflexive relationship to the social order he has taken over (p. 176).

By now it should be clear that the analysis assigns profound social values to the two codes and that it has wide political implications. Bernstein himself does not dwell on these, but does hint at the depressing circularity suggested by his findings. For instance, "One of the effects of the class system is to limit access to elaborated codes." In another article he argues that "the genes of social class may well be carried less through a genetic code but far more through a communication code that social class itself promotes" (p. 143). Putting these statements together, we can derive this principle of social continuity: the class system sorts people into elaborated and restricted code users; the codes perpetuate the class system.

The moral is drawn more fully in *The Politics of Communication* by Claus Mueller, who draws on Bernstein's research as well as many other studies of class, child rearing, language, and belief. Mueller argues that in advanced capitalist societies, a social order marked by severe inequality and the powerlessness of most people is sustained and legitimated, not so much by coercion (the police and the army) or even by manipulation (propaganda, censorship), as by

distortions of political communication which are related to the social structure insofar as it is expressed in class-specific language codes and socialization patterns, as well as to constraints on public communication. . . . Because of the restricted language code and rigid socialization patterns, the individual from the lower classes engages in arrested communication and tends to see the political universe as a static one and to abide by the prescriptions of external authorities (p. 84).

He thinks this impasse especially intractable because the codes are passed on in the home to very young children. He agrees with Bernstein that class differences in child rearing are decisive, and that working-class parents block the development of linguistic autonomy in their children through strategies of teaching and discipline that call on authority more than on reasoning and exploration. If this is so, neither school nor "Sesame Street" could easily undo the damage, even if school, for working-class kids, were an open and supportive institution. Mueller concludes that the only likely challenge to the legitimacy of the political system in countries like ours will come, not from the traditional working class, but from the intellectual and cultural "strata."[4]

Now I find myself in one of those strata and trying to challenge the legitimacy of power in the United States. For people in that position, marxism has long been the richest source of political practice. Few marxists would, even now, join with Mueller in giving up on the proletariat as the revolutionary class. A more common marxian position is that, indeed, some intellectuals defect from the capitalist social order, but they do not become thereby a revolutionary class or group in themselves; on the contrary, their task is to work politically and educationally (the two are really the same) within the proletariat, which is the leading force for revolutionary change. Marxism itself is, in this view, the system of ideas that derives from the experience of the working class—no proletariat, no *Capital*. But intellectuals must help give it voice, as Marx did, and so play at least a small role in the articulation of working-class consciousness.

If Bernstein and Mueller are right, however, there is a barrier to this task higher even than those raised by bourgeois control of police, schools, and media. Marxism as a system of ideas abstracts a great deal from local contexts and immediate experience; it cannot be given voice in a restricted code. If I may exaggerate, a bit, the implications of Bernstein's and Mueller's position: the revolutionary class in advanced capitalist societies, the class with the experience of exploitation and powerlessness and with the motive for socialism, has been excluded from the concepts and the very linguistic structures that must be used to express that experience and develop the institutions that will lead toward socialism. This would make the job of the revolutionary intellectual truly herculean. As I put it a while back, in the form of a question to myself and other radicals: "When we try to communicate to workers a socialist understanding of things, must we think of our task as, in part, making up a cognitive and linguistic deficit?"[5]

I couch this discussion in marxian terms to make clear my own commitment. But marxists are by no means the only ones who should be concerned about the social implications of Bernstein's research. Anyone who favors social equality, democracy, and a politically competent people, and does not see much of these in our society, should feel in these questions of class and language an urgency. For if Bernstein and Mueller are right, those who have available only a restricted code can do little more than passively observe the shaping of the future. Worse, there is probably as much potential for fascism as for democracy in the working class, since people raised by rule and nurtured in restricted codes tend "to abide by the prescriptions of external authorities."

I want now to turn a critical eye on the picture I have just drawn.[6] Bernstein and Mueller, whom I have allowed to stand for many others, advance an argument that has a hypnotic power. Once its underlying concepts and premises are allowed, the research leads inexorably to the conclusions I have sketched and to the political pessimism they sanction. But those concepts and premises are extremely problematic. It is my own belief that they are so defective as to invalidate the conclusions drawn from Bernstein's research, as well as the political interpretation of those conclusions that Mueller and others have offered. The trouble begins right at the beginning, with the concepts of class and code.

Take class. The idea of class that both Bernstein and Mueller deploy is drawn from mainstream social science. It is basically a heuristic concept, obtained by calibrating one or more such factors as income, education, and occupation, and selecting a cluster of them as convenient or experimentally handy. They may then be correlated with other variables: speech patterns, IQ, lifespan, child-rearing practices, beliefs, voting behavior, height, hair length, literally anything that can somehow be measured. Plainly there is no reason that any of these other factors might not be substituted for one of the original three, if doing so produced "better" correlations. Such a shift in definition would of course change the actual membership of each class, but that would not matter because the classes, within this framework, have no reality other than a heuristic one for the sociologist manipulating data. The unreality of this scheme is reflected in the fact that it can lead to three or six or any number (nine was the one in favor when I took sociology in college) of classes, which are no more than "strata situated along a continuum" (Mueller, p. 45), artificially segmented to the convenience—again—of the experimenter or theorist. Since this continuum of groups has no intrinsic relation to the structure of society or its historical evolution, correlations obtained within it do not much illuminate the way society works, but leave us within a closed explanatory circle where nothing has priority over anything else. There is no way to tell, for instance, whether occupational status explains speech patterns or vice versa—or both.[7]

A marxian idea of class is a much better foundation for discussion of these issues. Without going into the complexities of this subject, let me note that when we ground class in basic relations of production, the difficulties I've just listed disappear, and there is at least a *chance* of connecting class to something like language in a way that explains how society works, how it reproduces itself, and how it changes.

Note first that from this perspective Bernstein and Mueller are not talking of two classes, but mainly of two parts of the working class. Almost everyone included in both domains must sell his or her labor power in order to live, having no significant capital. (The exceptions: some independent professionals and small business people, apparently included in Bernstein's and Mueller's middle class.) The main distinction between the two is that most of the people they call working class sell their power to execute routine tasks at someone else's command—physical labor power,[8] in effect—while those they call middle class sell their power of conception—mental labor power—as well. Bernstein's working class (let me use the shorthand, "physical workers," for the moment) is limited mainly to executing someone else's plan, while his middle class (I'll say "mental workers") has at least a small role in the planning itself.

Once the discussion is so grounded, and for all the immense complexities that remain, Bernstein's results make a good deal of initial sense. For instance, his account of restricted and elaborated codes:

—Restricted, *context bound;* elaborated, *context free.* At work the context is almost entirely provided *for* physical workers by their bosses; mental workers can do more to shape the context of their work.

—Restricted, *concrete;* elaborated, *abstract.* At work, physical workers manipulate things, while mental workers manipulate ideas, numbers, and so forth.

—Restricted code, *predictable;* elaborated, more *individuated.* Physical workers are not paid to vary from set routines; employers value to some extent the individuality and creativity of mental workers.

—Restricted code, few *hesitations, expressions of uncertainty,* or *"metalinguistic" references to the discourse;* elaborated code, high on all these dimensions. Physical workers are limited to executing someone else's plan; mental workers have some responsibility for planning—precision and critical awareness in speech are important for them.

—Restricted code, *simple in syntax;* elaborated code, *complex,* with much *subordination, logical tissue, modification,* and so forth. Physical workers are not asked to make many connections, see broad relationships, understand the larger processes in which their work is embedded; the reverse is true for many mental workers.

Of course, young children—the subjects of much of Bernstein's research—do not work in factories or law firms. For the hypothesis I am sketching out to have any plausibility, it would have to derive "socialization" practices from the total experience of classes and subclasses in production. Bernstein's findings do point to such a connection, as a few examples will suggest:

—"Working-class" discipline of children stresses results, "middle-class" discipline, intentions. This corresponds to the distinction between execution and conception at work.

—"Working-class" parents teach skills; "middle-class" parents teach principles. This corresponds to what will be expected of the children later in their jobs.

—"Working-class" parents use "positional controls" (e.g., coercion: or, "Do it because your father says to do it"); "middle-class" parents favor "personal controls" (e.g., "If you don't clean up your room, your mother will have to do it, and she's very tired today"). Physical workers must learn to take orders without asking why. Mental workers need to know something of the rationale for what they do on the job.

From this pairing up of findings and causal hypotheses (overly schematic, to be sure),[9] a clear picture emerges. A class builds its life on its role in production. The social relations it experiences there may be embedded in its linguistic codes, and carried over into the kind of training it gives its children at home.[10] Now this is a very simple hypothesis, and may or may not turn out to be right. My point is that this approach to class at least permits us to work toward an explanation, in social structure and historical process, of the ways people talk, rather than leaving us enclosed in a limitless circle or measurable attributes, none with causal priority over the others. It roots language and consciousness in material life.

But within a marxian framework, this is still insufficient. I have been using a notion of class that is structural and static. In this way of thinking, a class is defined by its relationship to the means of production and to other classes. The concept is incomplete unless joined to one grounded in the continuous movement of history. In this second view, I do not simply and eternally *belong* to the professional and intellectual portion of the working class. Rather, in all my doings from day to day I and the people I mingle with and am affected by constantly *create* my class position. As, for instance, I confirm it by writing in this way to these readers, by continuing to work with my mind and my mouth more than with my hands, by failing to get rich enough so that I might if I liked stop working altogether, by sending my children to college so that *they* can work with their minds and probably also not get rich, and so on. From this perspective, class is not a permanent fact, but something that continually *happens*.[11]

As soon as we look at it in this way, a still different relationship of class and language comes into focus. My way of talking, whether "caused" by my class or not, is one of the important means by which I, in my relations with other people, re-create my class, confirm it, perhaps alter it. When I talk I mark myself, for others, as some kind of intellectual worker. Learning to talk that way was of course one prerequisite to securing myself a place in intellectual work. I might add that although my father did similar work, I don't believe I learned my code at home so much as in various acculturating institutions along the way to professordom.

Just as my father did not talk like an intellectual in the nursery, neither do I talk to my children as I talk to my colleagues. And I speak differently again when I'm lecturing in class, when I'm trying to explain at the electrical supplies store what kind of switch I need, and when I am a witness in court. To follow this line of thought is to call into question the second main term—"code"—in Bernstein's equation. He does allow that speakers of the elaborated code also can use the restricted code. I think it's more complicated than that. I don't "have" a code the way I have my Ford Escort out in the garage, to use whenever I go somewhere. If analogies are any use, a better one is probably to my wardrobe, from which I select in order to present myself in various ways on various occasions. Although there are clothes and ways of talking in which I feel most at home, sometimes I am *not* "at home," and I can confidently dress and talk to be comfortable in a variety of situations (though not all). But even that analogy won't do. Unlike a car or a ward-

robe, a code has no material existence in history, except as it is
ceaselessly re-created when people speak. The same is true of a
class, seen in the second marxian perspective. And of course when
we re-create a code by speaking, we almost always do so in collaboration with other people, and never in a setting that is socially
neutral. Whenever we talk we do so within a nexus of power, status,
intimacy or remoteness, family roles, institutional roles, designs
on one another, and so on. It is hardly an exaggeration to say that
the whole of society as I know it is present in or impinges on my
every verbal transaction.

Now this position, which I have laid out very generally and will
try to make more precise later, is a close neighbor to one of the cardinal principles of sociolinguistics. I mean the idea that for all of us
speech is variable. Sociolinguists speak of "variable rules," meaning, for instance, the frequency with which a New Yorker will use
or omit the postvocalic /r/, or with which a worker will say "he
don't" as against "he doesn't," in various situations. Along with
our grammatical abilities, we also tacitly know what counts as a
timely and appropriate utterance at different stages of a speech
situation, as well as how to relate through speaking to people of
various sorts (bosses, priests, kids), for various purposes (to buy a
hamburger or get a job), and in various genres (story telling, arguing, answering questions). It begins to seem very hard to disen-
tangle a single code from the dozens of ways that speech and
society impinge on each other.[12] The way one speaks at any time is
strongly influenced by the whole surrounding network of social circumstance, more than by relatively remote things like income, the
job status of one's parents, or the number of years one spent in
school.

This perspective applies not only to such constructs as "code"
and "vernacular," but even to the individual word itself. To quote
V. N. Volosinov:

Every sign . . . is a construct between socially organized persons in the
process of their interaction. Therefore, THE FORMS OF SIGNS ARE CONDITIONED
ABOVE ALL BY THE SOCIAL ORGANIZATION OF THE PARTICIPANTS INVOLVED AND ALSO
BY THE IMMEDIATE CONDITIONS OF THEIR INTERACTION.[13]

The sign, both in its form and in its meaning, is in Volosinov's view
"ideological": to simplify, it projects consciousness on reality, and
consciousness, in turn, derives from the organization of society.
Since different classes have different consciousness, and since for

the most part they use the same signs in communication, in each sign different ideologies intersect. The sign itself is, in Volosinov's words, "an arena of the class struggle" (p. 23).

That is a rather dramatic way to put it, but I think the point is right. Many words have alternative pronunciations that carry a marker of prestige or class. There is Labov's example of postvocalic /r/ in New York; there is *dese* versus *these;* in *My Fair Lady* there is "the /rayn/ in /spayn/" versus "the /reyn/ in /speyn/." When teachers "correct" kids on such matters, they comment on the kids' class. When a speaker who normally drops the *r* or says *dese* or /rayn/ talks with someone from a higher class or in a position of authority, he or she may shift to the more prestigious pronunciation or defiantly stand his or her linguistic and social ground. (I'm as good as you are, and I'll talk the way that's natural for me.) Such encounters may not be the heart of the class struggle, but they surely express conflict that is rooted in class.

As for meaning, consider the use of the word *industry* by the woman in interview I, and by the mayor of Mill Town. For her, industry is concrete (factories and machines), but also a remote and uncontrollable condition like the weather: "Not enough industry up here." Hence, not enough jobs—a fact of life. When the mayor says government should "encourage industry in their area," he speaks as a member of government who has some modest influence over the movements of industry. For him, industry is real people with interests that he can address, and with whom he is involved as other than just a seller of his labor power. *Industry* is the same sign in both sentences, but used in ideologically contrasting ways. For her, industry is an alien force, for him a set of valuable if evasive allies whom he wishes to help in their project of development. Both agree that it is good to have industry in the valley, but their political involvements in the matter are quite different. And they express their social situations in the ways they use the word.

It should be clear by this point, if you accept the argument, that Bernstein and Mueller ground their conclusions on a sociolinguistic method that in turn derives from damagingly static ideas of code and class, and of the links between code and class. In effect, Bernstein seeks to *correlate* two things, neither of which can be abstracted without distortion from the stream of social interaction, and both of which are incessantly re-created in every encounter.

In other words, we are dealing here with a phenomenon that is dialectical as well as dialectal. The power relations of a society permeate speech and shape it, while speech reproduces or challenges the power relations of the society. Please don't take me to be saying that class is only an artifact of the ways we talk to one another. But it would be equally wrong to say that the ways we talk are only an artifact of our class. The two are embedded in each other. Speech takes place in society and society also "takes place" in our verbal transactions with one another—which of course are inseparable from the economic and other transactions we enter. I have made this point a number of times now, insisting so much because it is important and, for social scientists at least, counter-intuitive.

But it is time to turn from theory back to the interviews and show how they may be seen afresh from this outlook. To begin with, both interviews explore the same subject, and the questions asked are quite similar in content. Nonetheless, the interview with the anonymous man and woman is in significant ways a quite different event from the interview with the mayor. One takes place in the street outside a shopping mall: it is impromptu. The other takes place in the mayor's office, by appointment. He has had time to prepare his thoughts. The mayor is interviewed because he is who he is; the specific identities and positions of the man and woman are of no consequence. They are selected precisely because they are representative, part of a mass. Again, the mayor is an expert on the economy of the valley. That is part of his job, while the man and woman suddenly find themselves on an intellectual terrain that is unfamiliar. Finally, the mayor is used to such encounters, and the man and woman are not. We may guess that the video equipment is at least a bit intimidating for them; it must make them feel that they are being observed, tested. Working with television is a more familiar challenge for the mayor. In a way, television is an extension of his office and his power, something he can use to his own ends if he is skillful. The television people are there by his sufferance and on his timetable: he begins the interview as in some ways their superior. So although the issues remain almost constant through the two interviews, social relations do not.

As you might expect, the participants also create their relationships differently in the two interviews, through the ways they talk to each other. For instance, the interviewer in I begins with four yes-no questions. This is a way of getting out some basic information, but it also establishes a particular social relationship. A yes-no question strictly limits the form of its answer. The questioner sets up a tight cognitive paradigm, asking only for some information to complete it. Of course the respondent may decline to play the game this way, but to do so requires a breach of decorum. By contrast, a *wh-* question frequently gives the respondent a kind of carte blanche as to how detailed and lengthy the answer may be. The three *wh-* questions with which interview II begins all accord the mayor that kind of freedom. On top of that, the first two questions to the man and woman request personal information. They do so in a respectful way; nonetheless, one condition for a felicitous question is that the questioner has the right to ask. If that right is not given by intimacy, it is usually given by virtue of some official purpose, as to bank officers considering loan applicants or to census workers. However gently, the sidewalk interviewer assumes such a prerogative. (Note that when he shifts to an impersonal question about unemployment, the man feels constrained to preface his answer with more personal information, by way of excuse.) The first question to the mayor, on the other hand, is not only general and impersonal but assumes much knowledge on his part. It positions him as an expert, someone whose opinion is worth knowing, in detail and on a highly complex subject. It is an invitation to expatiate.

These differences arise from no bias of the interviewers. On the contrary, since I know them I am confident in saying what I believe is also implicit in the interviews: that their sympathies lay more with the workers and unemployed people they met than with the managers, officials, industrialists, and bureaucrats. The differences stem from the speech situations themselves, and from moves the participants make that accept and confirm those situations. As a result of these moves the first interview proceeds somewhat like a quiz. When the interviewer shifts to *wh-* questions after a bit, it seems as if he is testing the man and woman. They respond like schoolchildren being drawn out against their will by an insistent teacher who is asking them to *have* opinions and ideas so that they may be judged. (Note especially the series of leading questions on cheap labor—a kind of catechism.) In interview II, by contrast, when the interviewer shifts to yes-no questions, their aim is to challenge and explore views that the mayor has already expressed. His position has itself become the subject of the discussion, and is in this way dignified. The interviewer is pressing him, as a serious antagonist.

Perhaps that is enough to establish my claim about the social dynamics of the interviews. One cannot know for sure how these people speak at other times, but the contrasts I have mentioned are certainly *sufficient* to have elicited a restricted code from the couple and an elaborated code from the mayor. Let me return, somewhat speculatively, to my initial analysis of the interviews, looking at Bernstein's categories from this new perspective:

A. Length and Complexity

The short responses and short, simple sentences of the man and woman are obedient answers of unprepared people who feel themselves tested and perhaps judged. Why not, with the camera looking on, and the questioner who clearly knows more than they about the subject? Their task, as I see it, is to avoid exposure or humiliation, to avoid the risk of saying something purely foolish. They take their leads from the interviewer, and try to sense from his reaction whether they have said the right thing. For them, "I don't know" is the ultimate defensive strategy, since it is at least not a wrong answer. The mayor is invited to dilate upon his subject; he does so, and in the complex (though often vapid) sentences appropriate to that task.

B. Modifiers

The man and woman are not being asked to individuate their opinions, to shade, specify, qualify. "Do you have any ideas about what causes that problem?" The interviewer is asking them to take a stab at it. A short, tentative answer is the natural response. But the mayor is invited to discourse on the "community as a whole," its "self-image," its ability to deal with problems." He could hardly take on this huge and complex subject without qualifying his answer along the way. Also, because of who he is, his words are important. They will go on record. They had better be measured and circumspect.

C. Abstraction

For the man and woman, terms like "industry," "taxes," "rebate," and "cheap labor" are hand-me-downs from TV, the newspapers, casual conversation about distant matters out of their control. They produce these terms as part of their role in the quiz, but the terms are alienated. The man and woman have nothing to back them up with, no way to relate them conceptually to one another and to reality. For the mayor, abstractions about the economy are rooted in his daily work: in technical reports bearing on decisions he must make, in talk with advisors, the Chamber of Commerce, state and federal bureaucrats. This is not to say that his account of unemployment is better than that of the man and woman. In my own view, automation is a shallow cause, and the lack of acreage in Mill Town an empty one, while the woman is right on target in pointing to the free flow of capital in pursuit of cheap labor. One may talk flaccid nonsense in elaborated codes, and hard truth in restricted ones; as the mayor's speech well illustrates, an elaborated code may serve as a bureaucratic smoke screen. At the same time, abstractions *are* a verbal medium the mayor is used to and works within. He manipulates them freely and voluntarily, rather than tentatively and with an air of talking someone else's language, under pressure. They are an instrument of power for him in this situation, and a token of powerlessness for the man and woman.

D. Reference to Context

The subject of the interviewer's questions belongs to the mayor's field of action. They already have a context in his work and thought. For the man and woman, government, the movements of corporations, unemployment, and history in the large sense are distant forces and events, not because of any cognitive or linguistic deficit, but just in that the couple are connected to such matters only through activities like drawing a wage, buying commodities, and voting, which relate them to the historical context only in fragmented and isolating ways—ways the mass media reinforce.

E. Reference to the Discourse Itself

The mayor's self-reflexive expressions, his comments on the interviewer's questions, his refusal to accept their premises, his new starts, all reflect the mayor's sense that he is in charge of the conversation. The questions are not, as he sees it, a form of power over him and a cage within which he must submissively remain. He can establish the terms and set the ground rules, up to a point. And what he says is important enough to warrant his taking pains, finding just the right formulation. (It may also be relevant to mention that the questioner in this interview is a woman.)

In all these ways the interviews embed power relations and speech conventions that existed prior to the encounters. But this is not to say that the speakers' codes reflect only the social relations that previously obtained. Choice is available at every point: note, for instance, how the mayor takes over leadership of the interview by volunteering the chief cause of unemployment without being asked, how he changes the terms of the questions, and so on. No law prevents the man and woman from doing likewise (though the power relations they walk into have nearly the force of law). The participants *create* the social relations of each encounter, in addition to inheriting them. In so doing they reproduce society. By such tiny increments is class made and remade.

If my argument is sound, then, a Bernsteinian explanation of these interviews badly misrepresents the social forces at work in them, assigning to static "class" differences in speech that express dynamic and changeable power relations.[14] More broadly, I have argued that this mistake follows from serious misconceptions of class and code. More the pity, because (1) Bernstein clearly meant it to serve the working class; (2) it has been highly influential, especially in Britain; and (3) the pedagogical inference drawn from it has generally been that we should teach elaborated codes to working-class kids, within the customary social relations of the school. Instead, I think the educational moral is roughly that of the 1960s reform movements, now much condemned: students should have as much responsibility as possible for their own educations. The habits of expressive power come with actual shared power, not with computerized instruction in sentence-combining or with a back-to-basics movement that would freeze students' language into someone else's rules, imposed from without. Respect the linguistic resources students have; make language a vehicle for achievement of real political and personal aims.

Finally, Mueller's political pessimism is justified only if we assume, as many leftists do (myself included at the time I first addressed these questions), that political consciousness is fixed, either at home in infancy and childhood or, even more deeply than that, by gross structural features of the society—if we assume that workers cannot become equal communicators and political participants step by step, and through action, but only by understanding, in a kind of conversion experience, the fundamental concepts of marxism. Movements toward worker self-management, co-ops, progressive credit unions, consumer movements, union organizing, populist movements of many kinds, are all fertile soil in which elaborated codes (better than that of the mayor, I hope) may grow along with the habit of democracy.

Notes

Preface

1. The nearness of my title to Williams's *Politics and Letters,* as well as my numerous citations of his work, rightly indicate the influence that work has had on my thinking about culture.

Chapter 1. The Function of English at the Present Time

1. Richard Ohmann, *English in America: A Radical View of the Profession* (New York, 1976): 303. One change I would make if I were writing the book now is in the title: not "America," but "North America" or "the United States."

2. Kurt Vonnegut's term, from *Wampeters, Foma, & Granfalloons: Opinions of Kurt Vonnegut, Jr.* (New York, 1974). "A *granfalloon* is a proud and meaningless association of human beings" (xv).

3. Some reviewers and critics considered that book marxist. I wish it had been: at many points its analysis would have had more coherence if firmly rooted in marxism. At the time, I knew too little of that tradition to make it my own, or write under its banner. Now, in case anyone is interested, I happily call myself a marxist (small *m*), and a feminist, radical, socialist. Not a Leninist.

4. What about the Soviet Union, someone asks. That is not the subject of this essay, but I am aware that the USSR is not a pacifist society.

5. I barely touch on post-structuralist theory in this book, and am not especially competent to do so. My understanding and assessment of its historical position owes most to Terry Eagleton, *Literary Theory: An introduction* (Oxford, 1983); idem, *The Function of Criticism: From "The Spectator" to Post-Structuralism* (London, 1984); and Perry Anderson, *In the Tracks of Historical Materialism* (Chicago, 1984).

6. I will not explain here why my views on this subject differ from many sunny forecasts about jobs in the high tech society to come. See "Literacy, Technology, and Monopoly Capital," in this volume.

7. The report of the NEH's Study Group on the State of Learning in the Humanities in Higher Education: reprinted in *The Chronicle of Higher Education,* 28 Nov. 1984.

8. E. D. Hirsch, "Cultural Literacy," *American Scholar* 52 (1983): 159–69; idem, "'English' and the Perils of Formalism," *American Scholar* 53 (1984): 369–79.

9. For instance, in 1986 Bennett was pressing the colleges to become cops in the fight against drugs. A university official commented, "I don't think we are here to tell students how to behave." Bennett replied, "Well, then, what *are* they there for?" (National Public Radio, 8 July 1986). Apparently the secretary saw no line between education and law enforcement.

Chapter 2. The Social Relations of Criticism

1. Jean-Paul Sartre, *What Is Literature?* trans. Bernard Frechtman (New York, 1966): 17–22.

2. Raymond Williams, *Keywords: A Vocabulary of Culture and Society* (New York, 1976): 76.

3. Antonio Gramsci, *Selections from the Prison Notebooks*, ed. and trans. Quinton Hoare and Geoffrey Nowell Smith (London, 1971): 8.

4. It may seem at first that the same could be said of the market for vaginal deodorants or power-driven leaf blowers. But those who stimulate or create the needs for *these* commodities are not the producers; they are marketers who do so through advertising.

5. I recall muttering with colleagues about a survey done by the Great Books people from Chicago in the early 1960s: What were the most important books of this century? Not a work of criticism appeared among the top hundred.

6. I developed this argument at length in chap. 9 of *English in America: A Radical View of the Profession* (New York, 1976).

7. Another vaguely remembered survey, this one just a few years ago, asked a variety of workers how they would spend the extra two hours of a hypothetical twenty-six-hour day. Professors led all other groups in answering that they would use those extra hours for work. I don't imagine they meant grading exams.

Chapter 3. Writing and Reading, Work and Leisure

1. William M. Payne, ed., *English in American Universities* (Boston, 1895): 20.

2. Ibid.: 12.

3. National Educational Association, *Report of the Committee of Ten on Secondary School Studies, with the Reports of the Conferences Arranged by the Committee* (New York, 1894): 86.

4. John B. Rae, "The Invention of Invention," in Melvin Kranzberg and Carroll W. Pursell, Jr., eds., *Technology in Western Civilization*, 2 vols., (New York, 1967), 1: 336.

5. Charles H. Hession and Hyman Sardy, *Ascent to Affluence: A History of American Economic Development* (Boston, 1969): 459.

6. Jeremy Brecher, *STRIKE!* (Greenwich, Conn., 1972): 101.

7. Theodore Peterson, *Magazines in the Twentieth Century* (Urbana, Ill., 1956): 6–11.

8. Alfred D. Chandler, Jr., *The Visible Hand: The Managerial Revolution in American Business* (Cambridge, Mass., 1977): 436–37.

9. I argue this in a work in progress, basing the claim on the research of Simon Kuznets, especially *Capital and the American Economy* (New York, 1961).

10. For a somewhat fuller account of these historical changes, see "Where Did Mass Culture Come From?," essay 9 in this volume.

11. Harry Braverman, *Labor and Monopoly Capital: The Degradation of Work in the Twentieth Century* (New York, 1974): 120–21.

12. Quoted by Wallace Douglas in "Rhetoric for the Meritocracy," in Richard Ohmann, *English in America: A Radical View of the Profession* (New York, 1976): 126.

13. Quoted in Ohmann, *English in America:* 292.

14. I take this term from Barbara and John Ehrenreich, "The Professional-Managerial Class," in Pat Walker, ed., *Between Labor and Capital* (Boston, 1979); I generally accept their account of the new class.

15. Arthur N. Applebee, *Tradition and Reform in the Teaching of English: A History* (Urbana, Ill., 1974): 31–32.

16. Payne, *English in American Universities:* 52, 93, 121.

17. George R. Carpenter, Franklin T. Baker, and Fred N. Scott, *The Teaching of English in the Elementary and the Secondary School* (New York, 1903): 329n.

18. I have labored, in revising this section of my argument, to respond to careful and helpful criticism by my colleague Gerald Burns, whose comments also saved me from a number of plain errors.

19. Theodore R. Sizer, *Secondary Schools at the Turn of the Century* (New Haven, 1964): 33–35.

20. Carpenter, Baker, and Scott, *Teaching of English:* 59, 61.

21. Percival Chubb, *The Teaching of English in the Elementary and the Secondary School* (New York, 1909): 240, 319.

22. J. F. Hosic, "Editorial," *English Journal* 5 (1916): 281–82.

23. John B. Opdycke, "New Wine in Old Bottles," *English Journal* 5 (1916): 392.

24. Quoted by Robert J. Connors, in "The Rhetoric of Explanation: Explanatory Rhetoric from 1850 to the Present," *Written Communication* 2 (1985): 64.

Chapter 4. A Case Study in Canon Formation

Carol Ohmann and I wrote this essay in 1976. Because it is collaboration, and also because its intent was partly to survey the life of Salinger's novel through its first quarter century, I have not updated it in any way except to add note 25, on *Partisan Review.* The essay explores the process of reading and commentary through which *The Catcher in the Rye* became what we called a "classic." It is thus a study in what everyone now calls "canon formation," and a kind of case history that exemplifies a process more broadly and speculatively viewed in essay 5.

1. Warren French, *J. D. Salinger* (New York, 1963): 102; James E. Miller, Jr., *J. D. Salinger* (Minneapolis, 1965): 5. Robert Gutwillig, "Everybody's Caught 'The Catcher in the Rye,'"*New York Times Book Review*, Paperback Book Section, 15 Jan. 1961: 38. Alice Payne Hackett, *70 Years of Best Sellers: 1895–1965* (New York: 1967): 13. The figure of 9 million is our estimate, based on this information: Bantam has sold just over 5 million copies since it became sole publisher of the novel in April 1964 (thanks to Peter McCue of Bantam for this figure). Assuming that about 1 million of

these were sold before the end of 1965, we conclude that over 4 million have been sold since Alice Payne Hackett's tally. *Catcher* was twelfth among all novels in American sales by 1965; our guess is that it is third or fourth now, and will soon be at the head of the list.

2. An exception is the review by William Poster, "Tomorrow's Child," *Commentary* 13 (Jan. 1952): 90–92. He places Holden in the upper-middle or lower-upper class, estimates Mr. Caulfield's income at between $30,000 and $100,000 a year, and calls Holden "typical not so much of this adolescent class as a whole, but of a specific and extensive part of it, namely, those individuals who think of themselves as exceptions to their class by virtue of their superior taste," those who "have nothing further to strive for within their class and cannot accept its usual goals." We do not entirely agree with this account, as will become evident later; but at least Poster sees the book as socially precise.

Other reviews appeared in *America*, 11 Aug. 1951; *Catholic World*, Nov. 1951; *Harper's*, Aug. 1951; *New Statesman and Nation*, 18 Aug. 1951; *Spectator*, 17 Aug. 1951; *TLS*, 7 Sept. 1951.

3. David L. Stevenson, "J. D. Salinger: The Mirror of Crisis," *The Nation*, 9 March 1957: 215.

4. George Steiner, "The Salinger Industry," *The Nation*, 14 November 1959: 360. Further quotations are from pp. 360–63, passim.

5. Donald P. Costello, "The Language of 'The Catcher in the Rye,'" *American Speech* 34 (Oct. 1959): 172–81.

6. Arthur Heiserman and James E. Miller, Jr., "J. D. Salinger: Some Crazy Cliff," *Western Humanities Review* 10 (Spring 1956): 129.

7. William Wiegand, "J. D. Salinger: Seventy-Eight Bananas," *Chicago Review* 9 (Winter 1958): 4.

8. Donald Barr, "Saints, Pilgrims and Artists," *Commonweal*, 25 Oct. 1957: 88–90.

9. Peter J. Seng, "The Fallen Idol: The Immature World of Holden Caulfield," *College English* 22 (Dec. 1961): 203–9. Frederic I. Carpenter, "The Adolescent in American Fiction," *English Journal* 46 (Sept. 1957): 314–15.

10. Unless of course Salinger himself was seen not only to have drawn an adolescent hero, but to have endorsed his attitudes, in which case critics addressed themselves to the writer's shortcomings, e.g., Maxwell Geismar in "The Wise Child and the *New Yorker* School of Fiction," *American Moderns: From Rebellion to Conformity* (New York, 1958): 195–209.

11. Jonathan Baumbach, "The Saint as a Young Man: A Reappraisal of *The Catcher in the Rye*," *Modern Language Quarterly* 25 (Dec. 1964): 467. Paul Levine, "J. D. Salinger: The Development of the Misfit Hero," *Twentieth-Century Literature* 4 (Oct. 1958): 97. Kermit Vanderbilt, "Symbolic Resolution in *The Catcher in the Rye*: The Cup, the Carrousel, and the American West," *Western Humanities Review* 17 (Summer 1963): 272.

12. George R. Creeger, *"Treacherous Desertion": Salinger's "The Catcher in the Rye"* (Middletown, Conn., 1961): 8. Dan Wakefield, "Salinger and the Search for Love," *New World Writing* 14 (1958): 70.

13. Authur Mizener, "The Love Song of J. D. Salinger, *Harper's*, Feb. 1959: 90.

14. David L. Stevenson, "J. D. Salinger: The Mirror of Crisis," *The Nation*, 9 Mar. 1957: 215.

15. Ihab Hassan, "The Rare Quixotic Gesture," in Henry Anatole Grunwald, ed., *Salinger* (New York, 1962): 148–49. Reprinted from Hassan's *Radical Innocence* (Princeton, 1961). First appeared in the *Western Humanities Review*, 1957. Heiserman and Miller, "Salinger": 132. Edgar M. Branch, "Mark Twain and J. D. Salinger: A Study in Literary Continuity," *American Quarterly* 9 (Summer 1957): 157.

16. Donald P. Costello, "Salinger and His Critics," *Commonweal*, 25 Oct. 1963: 133.

17. Geismar, "The Wise Child": 197–98.

18. Hassan, "Rare Quixotic Gesture": 139.

19. Carl F. Strauch, "Kings in the Back Row: Meaning Through Structure—A Reading of Salinger's *The Catcher in the Rye*," *Wisconsin Studies in Contemporary Literature* 2 (Winter 1961): 27.

20. Carpenter, "Adolescent in American Fiction": 316. Branch, "Twain and Salinger": 154.

21. Miller, *Salinger:* 12–17.

22. J. D. Salinger, *The Catcher in the Rye* (New York, 1964): 14–15.

23. Miller, *Salinger:* 13.

24. Notably these: (1) In "'Franny and Zooey' and J. D. Salinger" (*New Left Review* 15 [May–June 1962]: 72–82), Brian Way argued that *Catcher* is one of the few "contemporary American novels that have recreated in twentieth-century terms that simultaneous sense of character and society of the great nineteenth-century realists." School, he pointed out, "is the agency by which America more than most countries consciously socializes the immature for entry into the approved adult activities; and so a boy's relation to school becomes a microcosm of the individual's relation to his society. In this concentration upon a manageable network of representative relationships, we see at work the only method by which a novel can create with any living force the pressures of a society." Way went on to analyze both the successes and failures of the book in these terms, in an admirable essay. (2) Writing mainly about *Franny and Zooey*, but with reference to *Catcher* as well, Paul Phillips emphasized that "what Salinger's sensitive characters find so consistently repulsive is the vulgarity, the rampant selfishness, the fundamental hypocrisy and foulness of bourgeois conventions." We agree, though perhaps with milder epithets; we think Phillips was nearly right in holding that "Salinger's major limitation as a satirist is that he is generally unconcerned with world issues" ("Salinger's *Franny and Zooey*," *Mainstream* 15 [Jan. 1962]: 32–39). (3) Three years earlier, also in *Mainstream*, Barbara Giles said of Holden, "In a vague sort of way he senses that the mannerisms and general make-believe he hates would not be worth hatred if they didn't proceed from a system in which the 'dirty movies' and the Broadway productions that his father, the corporation lawyer, helps to finance, play a directly debasing role. In the helplessness of his hatreds he may even be said to sense, still more vaguely, the extent of a power and corruption he cannot name." She went on to say that Salinger's young people reject this system, "but with it they reject any further study of motive itself, demanding only certificates of purity from them-

selves" ("The Lonely War of J. D. Salinger," *Mainstream* 12 [Feb. 1959]: 2–13). We note that all three articles appeared in left-wing journals, well out of the *academic* mainstream. Establishment critics did not take up their lead. We had not heard of the three articles before we set out to write this piece.

Chapter 5. The Shaping of a Canon

1. See John Henrik Clarke, ed., *William Styron's Nat Turner: Ten Black Writers Respond* (Boston, 1968).

2. I make no large claims for my boundaries. They mark off, crudely, the time when publishing had become part of big business but before subsidiary rights had completely overshadowed hardbound novel publishing. My boundaries also mark the time when people born to one side or the other of 1930 attained cultural dominance and could most strongly advance their reading of the postwar experience. These years roughly enclose the rise and decline of 1960s movements as well as economic boom and the U.S. intervention in Southeast Asia. Anyhow, things have changed since 1975, both in the great world and in fiction publishing; accordingly I use the past tense when describing the process of canon-formation, even though many of my generalizations still hold true.

I speak of "precanonical" novels, meaning those that are active candidates for inclusion, not those that will in fact be canonical at some later time.

3. Jan Hajda, "An American Paradox: People and Books in a Metropolis" (Ph.D. diss., University of Chicago, 1963): 218, as cited in Elizabeth Warner McElroy, "Subject Variety in Adult Book Reading" (M.A. diss., University of Chicago, 1967).

4. See Simone Beserman, "Le Best-seller aux Etats-Unis de 1961 à 1970: Etude littéraire et sociologique" (Ph.D. diss., University of Paris [1975]): 280–92.

Surprisingly, neither this audience nor the ways it integrated novel reading into its social existence seem all that different from their counterparts in early eighteenth-century England, as described, for example, in chap. 2 of Ian Watt, *The Rise of the Novel: Studies in Defoe, Richardson, and Fielding* (Berkeley, 1957), or in "The Debate over Art and Popular Culture: English Eighteenth Century as a Case Study," by Leo Lowenthal (with Marjorie Fiske), in Lowenthal, *Literature, Popular Culture, and Society* (Palo Alto, Calif., 1968).

5. Saul Bellow, in Jason Epstein's interview, "Saul Bellow of Chicago," *New York Times Book Review*, 9 May 1971: 16.

6. Philip H. Ennis, *Adult Book Reading in the United States*, National Opinion Research Center (University of Chicago, 1965): 25. Other main needs were (1) "escape," which also implies a relationship between reading a book and the rest of one's social life (what one is escaping *from*), and (2) information, which I suspect is a need less often fulfilled by novels now than in the time of Defoe and Richardson. My appreciation is extended to Ennis, who is my colleague, for lots of help when I was first considering these issues.

7. Victor Navasky, "Studies in Animal Behavior," *New York Times Book Review*, 25 Feb. 1973: 2.

8. See Richard Kostelanetz, *The End of Intelligent Writing: Literary Politics in America* (New York, 1974): 207. Kostelanetz's estimate was confirmed by some of Beserman's interviews. Allan Green, who handled advertising for a number of publishers, including Viking, told her in 1971 that on the average, 50 to 60 percent of the budget went to the *New York Times Book Review* and another 10 to 20 percent to the daily *New York Times*. M. Stuart Harris, head of publicity at Harper, said he ordinarily channeled 90 percent into the *Times* at the outset, though once a book's success was assured, he distributed advertising more broadly (see Beserman, "Le Best-seller": 120).

9. See Beserman, "Le Best-seller": 168.

10. See Kostelanetz, *The End of Intelligent Writing:* 209, based on reports in Harry Smith, "Special Report: The *New York Times Book Review*," *Newsletter*, 30 July 1969, and "The *New York Times Book Review* (Part II)," *Newsletter*, 8 Dec. 1971.

11. For instance, the Sunday *New York Times* assigned only four of the novels that would become 1965's ten best-sellers to literary intellectuals: Julian Moynihan reviewed Bellow's *Herzog;* George P. Elliott, LeCarre's *The Looking Glass War;* Marcus Cunliffe, Stone's *Those Who Love;* and Peter Buitenhuis, Wouk's *Don't Stop the Carnival.* Only Moynihan wrote a thoroughly respectful and enthusiastic review; it was full of words and phrases like "masterpiece," "new and perennial," "great characters," "beautiful fluidity." Perhaps more important, he drew parallels both to contemporaries like Malamud, Salinger, Mailer, and Philip Roth, and to earlier writers like Joyce and Henry Roth, with the intention of putting Bellow in their company. The review all but says, "this one belongs in the canon." Elliott invoked Greene and Chandler, Cunliffe alluded to Graves and Wilder, but they used these comparisons in one way or another to demote LeCarre and Stone. Buitenhuis's review was dismissive; his *en passant* allusion was to the Marx Brothers. (I extend thanks to my student assistant, Pierce Tyler, for surveying reviews and digging up such information.)

12. See Julie Hoover and Charles Kadushin, "Influential Intellectual Journals: A Very Private Club," *Change* (Mar. 1972): 41.

13. See Charles Kadushin, Julie Hoover, and Monique Tichy, "How and Where to Find the Intellectual Elite in the United States," *Public Opinion Quarterly* (Spring 1971): 1–18. For the method used to identify an intellectual elite, see Kadushin, "Who Are the Elite Intellectuals?" *Public Interest* (Fall 1972): 109–25.

14. Like the Sunday *New York Times*, many of these journals singled out *Herzog* in the fall of 1964. The *New Yorker* gave it a lead review by Brendan Gill. V. S. Pritchett covered it for the *New York Review of Books*, in the only review of a 1965 best-seller devoted to just one book. The *New Republic* gave a lead review to Irving Howe, and the *Saturday Review*, to Granville Hicks. Only Pritchett was less than enthusiastic.

15. Kadushin, Hoover, and Tichy, "How and Where to Find the Intellectual Elite": 17.

16. See ibid.: 9.

17. See Kostelanetz, *The End of Intelligent Writing:* 107–8, based on Harry Smith, "The *New York Review* Gives Strong Preference," *Newsletter*, 5 Mar. 1969; and 110.

18. See, for instance, Leslie A. Fiedler, *The Inadvertent Epic: From "Uncle Tom's Cabin" to "Roots"* (New York, 1979). Fiedler's *What Was Literature? Class Culture and Mass Society* (New York, 1982) argues again for the primacy of people over professors.

19. As Jerome Klinkowitz states in his preface: "For even the well and intelligently read, 'contemporary American fiction' suggests Ken Kesey, Joseph Heller, John Barth, and Thomas Pynchon at best—and at worst Updike, Roth, Bellow, and Malamud." He contends that such a list misses "the direction which fiction will take, and is taking, as the future unfolds before us" (*Literary Disruptions: The Making of a Post-Contemporary American Fiction*, 2d ed. [Urbana, Ill., 1980]: ix).

20. Twenty-six of the forty-four responded. The survey accompanies an article by Melvin J. Friedman, "To 'Make It New': The American Novel since 1945," *Wilson Quarterly* (Winter 1978): 136–37. I don't know how the professors were selected or who they were, but almost every novel on this list was written by a white male with an elite educational background.

21. John Hawkes is the outstanding example of a novelist whose work has consistently impressed critics and professsors, without ever appealing to a wider audience. Should any of us be around to witness the outcome, it will be interesting to see if any of his books has a place in the canon forty or fifty years from now.

22. I omit novelists still alive in 1960, but whose possibly canonical work belongs to an earlier time—Steinbeck, Dos Passos, Hemingway, etc. I *include* those of an older generation (Porter, McCarthy) who did not publish a precanonical novel until the 1960s. I exclude novelists of foreign origin (Asimov, Kosinski, Nabokov) and writers mainly known for their poetry, plays, or criticism, unless (as with Dickey and Plath) they also produced a precanonical novel during this period.

23. I got this count by surveying the hardback and paperback best-seller lists in the *New York Times* from 1969 through 1975 and by checking the annual summaries in Alice Payne Hackett and James Henry Burke, *Eighty Years of Best Sellers, 1895–1975* (New York, 1977) for the rest of the 1960s. When I find time and patience to plow through the *Times* for that decade, my count will probably go up by a few.

24. For an account of this process that attributes it more to industrialism than to capitalism, see John Kenneth Galbraith, *The New Industrial State* (Boston, 1967). I prefer the analysis in Paul A. Baran and Paul M. Sweezy, *Monopoly Capital: An Essay on the American Economic and Social Order* (New York, 1966). In publishing, the ascendancy of media packaging over simple book publishing has continued apace in recent years. See Thomas Whiteside, *The Blockbuster Complex: Conglomerates, Show Business, and Book Publishing* (Middletown, Conn., 1981). The practices Whiteside describes, along with the growth of national bookstore chains, have further altered the dynamics of publishing, thereby providing another reason for terminating this study somewhere around 1975.

25. See my preliminary study of this process, "Where Did Mass Culture Come From? The Case of Magazines," essay 9 in this volume.

26. See, for instance, Raymond Williams, "Base and Superstructure in Marxist Cultural Theory," *New Left Review* 82 (Nov.–Dec. 1973): 3–16.

27. *The Marx-Engels Reader,* ed. Robert C. Tucker (New York, 1972): 136.

28. See Barbara and John Ehrenreich, "The Professional-Managerial Class," in Pat Walker, ed. *Between Labor and Capital* (Boston, 1979). The article originally appeared in *Radical America* (May–June 1977).

29. Every term of this characterization is a problem, and the whole subject vexed beyond apparent usefulness. (The debate over the Ehrenreichs' proposal in *Between Labor and Capital* should satisfy anyone on this point, as it applies to marxists.) There is not even agreement whether the people I refer to constitute a class, a subclass, a stratum, a contradictory location in the class structure, etc. For myself, I don't care which concept the reader prefers, so long as *in this context* we agree on what group we are talking about and agree that it has acted *as* a recognizable group. If the reader feels more at ease with the concept, from mainstream sociology and everyday talk, of the "upper middle class," that's all right too, though such a reader will, if he or she accepts my argument here, have to challenge the whole framework of theory from which that concept derives. Methodologically, I join the Ehrenreichs in holding that the point is not to "define" classes in some ahistorical way and that a notion of class is validated or invalidated by its power in theory, empirical explanation, and political practice. Hence I do not mean to be appropriating a preexisting definition of class in this essay and "applying" it to a particular situation and problem. Rather, I intend my argument and my evidence to help *develop* a more adequate picture of the way class has worked and works in the social process.

30. I am under no illusion that this study itself can stand apart from the canon-formation process; I am participating in that process, as I describe it. There is no help for that. I would insist, though, that my immediate purpose is not to tip the scales in favor of some novels and against others. My tally of precanonical novels includes some that I like very much indeed, some that I can't abide, and—in a fine gesture of impartiality—some that I haven't read. I do, of course, wish to influence the process in a broader way by calling attention to its narrow social base and to the parochial outlook it has produced.

31. Thus the precanonical novels display styles as various as those of Vonnegut, Malamud, and Brautigan; some novelists, like Updike, get high marks from the gatekeepers specifically for their styles; see essay 6.

32. Williams has used this concept since writing *Culture and Society, 1780–1950* (New York, 1958). Its most exact theoretical formulation is in his *Marxism and Literature* (New York, 1977).

33. It was fascinating, after twenty-five years, to reread the essay from which I remembered this phrase. Herbert Gold's "The Age of Happy Problems" (written 1956; rpt. in a book of the same title, New York, 1962). Gold offers a very precise early sampling of this consciousness.

34. For instance, the poorest 40 percent of families in the country received 16.8 percent of the income in 1947 and 16.9 percent in 1960, while the percentage going to the richest 5 percent went from 17.2 percent to 16.8 percent. The top 1 percent owned 23.3 percent of the nation's *wealth* in 1945 and 27.4 percent in 1962. These figures come from tables compiled by Frank Ackerman and Andrew Zimbalist, "Capitalism and Inequality in

the United States," in Richard C. Edwards, Michael Reich, and Thomas E. Weisskopf, eds., *The Capitalist System: A Radical Analysis of American Society*, 2d ed. (Englewood Cliffs, N.J., 1978): 298 and 301.

35. Godfrey Hodgson calls this outlook "liberal conservatism." See his excellent discussion in chap. 4, *America in Our Time* (New York, 1976). On p. 76 Hodgson enumerates six points of the ideological consensus which are very close to the analysis I give here.

36. That is, people relied on others, through the intermediary of the market, for more and more goods and services. In an ordinary day's "consuming," each of us depends on the past and present labor of hundreds of millions of workers worldwide. But of course this is easy to forget, since that loaf of bread magically appears on the store shelf and the only labor we *see* is that of the checker and the bagger.

37. Sylvia Plath, *The Bell Jar* (New York, 1971): 2.

38. Patricia Ann Meyer Spacks, *The Female Imagination* (New York, 1975): 145. She takes the concept from Therese Benedek.

39. J. D. Salinger, *Franny and Zooey* (Boston, 1961): 67. The two stories, which add up to a sort of novel, appeared earlier in the *New Yorker*. The Glass kids were already culture heroes for the reader of this fiction; people stood in line outside of bookstores on publication day to buy the book.

40. The other securely canonical work of the 1950s, *Invisible Man*, not only exhibits the characteristic inversion of sanity and insanity but comprehends racism itself within the illness story and the adolescent rite of passage.

41. Philip Roth, *Portnoy's Complaint* (New York, 1969): 111.

42. Bellow, *Herzog* (New York, 1964): 1, 2.

43. John Updike, *Rabbit Redux* (New York, 1972): 16.

44. These ideas derive from Antonio Gramsci, through the later work of Williams and people connected to the Center for Contemporary Cultural Studies at the University of Birmingham and to *Screen* magazine. E.g., Dick Hebdige, whose *Subculture: The Meaning of Style* (London and New York, 1979) is a fine study in this vein. Todd Gitlin has advanced the theory and analysis of hegemony farthest in the U.S. See esp. Gitlin's *The Whole World Is Watching: Mass Media in the Making and Unmaking of the New Left* (Berkeley, 1980).

Chapter 6. Style and Ideology

1. Fredric Jameson, *Marxism and Form: Twentieth-Century Dialectical Theories of Literature* (Princeton, 1971): 333–35.

2. Norman Podhoretz, *Doings and Undoings: The Fifties and After in American Writing* (New York, 1964): 252. Podhoretz wrote this essay long before publication of *Rabbit Redux*, but I see no reason for him to have changed his mind subsequently.

3. John Updike, *Rabbit Redux* (Greenwich, Conn., 1972): 351.

4. For an elaboration of this point, see the first chapter of Richard M. Ohmann, *Shaw: The Style and the Man* (Middletown, Conn., 1962).

5. I know that this point is in dispute among linguists. There is no space here to air the controversy; to those familiar with it, my position is plain. I do not believe the dispute bears on the interpretation I offer here.

6. Kurt Vonnegut, *Breakfast of Champions* (New York, 1975): 124–25.

7. Kurt Vonnegut, "Address to P.E.N. Conference in Stockholm, 1973," in *Wampeters, Foma, & Granfalloons* (New York, 1974): 229.

Chapter 7. Politics and Genre in Nonfiction Prose

1. Paul Hernadi develops a similar scheme in *Beyond Genre, New Directions in Literary Classification* (Ithaca, 1972), as do Robert Scholes and Carl H. Klaus in *Elements of Fiction* (New York, 1968) and its companion volumes on poetry and drama. But they add other dimensions to the relationship of author and audience, and since that relationship is my main concern, I shall use Northrop Frye's idea as my reference point.

2. Frye does touch on questions of power and social relations, especially in the first essay of *Anatomy;* but he does so in an idealized and ahistorical way that offers little help to this inquiry.

3. Raymond Williams, *Culture and Society, 1780–1950* (New York, 1958): 300.

4. Claudio Guillén, *Literature as System; Essays Toward the Theory of Literary History* (Princeton, 1971): 109.

Chapter 8. Teaching as Theoretical Practice

The following works are referred to in the nonlectures:

Elizabeth Ammons. *Edith Wharton's Argument with America.* Athens, Ga., 1980.

John Dos Passos. *The Big Money.* New York, 1969.

Terry Eagleton. *Marxism and Literary Criticism.* Berkeley, 1976.

R. W. B. Lewis. *Edith Wharton: A Biography.* New York: Harper and Row, 1975.

Barbara H. Solomon, ed. *Ain't We Got Fun? Essays, Lyrics, and Stories of the Twenties.* New York, 1980. The stories from this collection to which I refer are Katherine Brush, "Night Club," and James T. Farrell, "A Jazz-Age Clerk."

Edith Wharton. *The Age of Innocence.* New York, 1968.

1. In the very first class meeting I have posed some questions about the antagonistic relationship of many novelists to mainstream culture. Then I have explored uses of memory and of the remembered past as a response to history, in Cather's *My Ántonia.*

2. My second lecture on *The Age of Innocence* does attempt to place Wharton and her act of writing within the historical process.

3. Jim Merod, *The Political Responsibility of the Critic,* forthcoming (Ithaca, 1987).

4. I know from experience that a small number of them will also choose to become organic intellectuals, organizers, revolutionaries, but I don't think we should, or really can, direct our efforts toward that outcome, in standard literature courses.

Chapter 9. Where Did Mass Culture Come From?

1. Daniel Lerner, *The Passing of Traditional Society: Modernizing the Middle East* (New York, 1964): 56.

2. See, for instance, Herbert J. Gans, *Popular Culture and Mass Culture* (New York, 1974).

3. Herbert I. Schiller, *The Mind Managers* (Boston, 1973). Hans Magnus Enzensberger, *The Consciousness Industry* (New York, 1974).

4. Frank Presbrey, *The History and Development of Advertising* (Garden City, N.Y., 1929): 16.

5. C. Hugh Holman, "'Cheap Books' and the Public Interest: Paperbound Book Publishing in Two Centuries," in Ray B. Browne, Richard H. Crowder, Virgil L. Lokke, and William T. Stafford, eds., *Frontiers of American Culture* (Lafayette, Ind., 1968).

6. Theodore Peterson, *Magazines in the Twentieth Century* (Urbana, Ill., 1956), chap. 1.

7. Presbrey, *History and Development of Advertising:* 488.

8. Ibid.

9. S. S. McClure, *My Autobiography* (London, 1914): 131.

10. Salme Harju Steinberg, *Reformer in the Marketplace: Edward W. Bok and The Ladies' Home Journal* (Baton Rouge, La., 1979): 4.

11. Peterson, *Magazines in the Twentieth Century:* 5.

12. Alex Groner and the editors of *American Heritage* and *Business Week*, *The American Heritage History of American Business and Industry* (New York, 1972): 174.

13. Neil H. Borden, *The Economic Effects of Advertising* (Chicago, 1942): 48.

Other works to which I am indebted in less specific ways include:

On magazines: Edward Bok, *The Americanization of Edward Bok* (New York, 1921); George Britt, *Forty Years, Forty Millions* (New York, 1935); Frank Luther Mott, *A History of American Magazines*, 5 vols. (New York, and Cambridge, Mass., 1930–68).

On advertising: Stuart Ewen, *Captains of Consciousness* (New York, 1976); Ralph M. Hower, *The History of an Advertising Agency* (Cambridge, Mass., 1939); Julian L. Simon, *Issues in the Economics of Advertising* (Urbana, Ill., 1970); James Playsted Wood, *The Story of Advertising* (New York, 1958).

I have consulted various economic histories, but have been most influenced by the perspectives of Paul Baran and Paul Sweezy, and of Gabriel Kolko. In cultural theory I have taken my lead from Gramsci and, especially, Raymond Williams.

Chapter 10. Advertising and the New Discourse of Mass Culture

1. There, too, I gave an account of the emergence of monopoly capitalism; this essay alludes to or depends upon it at several points.

2. I originally presented part of this essay at the 1983 meeting of the Modern Language Association, in collaboration with Richard Terdiman, whose paper was on French newspapers, advertising, and department stores in the nineteenth century. I have adapted some of his ideas and terms—both from his MLA paper and from two chapters of his book in progress—to my own purposes.

3. Thanks for assistance to Cynthia G. Swank, archivist at J. Walter Thompson.

4. T. J. Jackson Lears noted this reading of Woolf's dictum in "From Salvation to Self-Realization: Advertising and the Therapeutic Roots of the Consumer Culture, 1880–1930," in Richard Wightman Fox and T. J. Jack-

son Lears, eds., *The Culture of Consumption: Critical Essays in American History, 1880–1980* (New York, 1983): 3.

5. Gustav A. Berghoff of the Rub-No-More Co., quoted by Glen Porter and Harold C. Livesay in *Merchants and Manufacturers: Studies in the Changing Structure of Nineteenth-Century Marketing* (Baltimore, 1971): 225.

6. Theodore P. Greene, *America's Heroes: The Changing Models of Success in American Magazines* (New York, 1970): 110–65.

7. Booth Tarkington, *The Gentleman from Indiana* (New York, 1900): 126. *McClure's* had printed a condensed version of the novel.

8. James Woodress, *Booth Tarkington: Gentleman from Indiana* (Philadelphia, 1955): 74–79; Keith J. Fennimore, *Booth Tarkington* (New York, 1974): 38–41. In addition to sources mentioned in this and the previous essay, I have also drawn upon Daniel Pope, *The Making of Modern Advertising* (New York, 1983), and Stephen Fox, *The Mirror Makers: A History of American Advertising and Its Creators* (New York, 1984).

Chapter 11. TV and the Sterilization of Politics

1. Horace Newcomb, *TV: The Most Popular Art* (New York, 1974).

2. Richard Sennett and Jonathan Cobb, *The Hidden Injuries of Class* (New York, 1973).

3. Stanley Aronowitz, *False Promises: The Shaping of American Working Class Consciousness* (New York, 1973): 7.

4. Edward Jay Epstein, *News from Nowhere* (New York, 1974): 90–91.

5. Hans Magnus Enzensberger, *The Consciousness Industry: On Literature, Politics and the Media* (New York, 1974): 11.

6. Karl Marx and Friedrich Engels, *The German Ideology*, in *Karl Marx: Selected Writings*, ed. David McLellan (Oxford, 1977): 176.

7. These figures have dropped somewhat since I wrote this article in the late 1970s; but in spite of cable's spread, the networks still dominate TV production.

8. Enzensberger, *Consciousness Industry:* 10.

9. Todd Gitlin, "Spotlights and Shadows," *College English* (April 1976): 790.

10. Ron Powers, *The Newscasters: The News as Show Business* (New York, 1977): 223–33.

11. Quoted in Epstein, *News from Nowhere:* 4–5.

12. Herbert Gans, *Deciding What's News* (New York, 1979): 162.

13. Antonio Gramsci, *Selections from the Prison Notebooks*, ed. and trans. Quinton Hoare and Geoffrey Nowell Smith (London, 1971). Todd Gitlin has helpfully developed these ideas and applied them to U.S. mass media, in *The Whole World Is Watching: Mass Media in the Making and Unmaking of the New Left* (Berkeley, 1980).

14. David Sallach, "Class Domination and Ideological Hegemony," in Gaye Tuchman, ed., *The TV Establishment; Programming for Power and Profit* (Englewood Cliffs, NJ, 1974): 162–3.

Chapter 12. Worldthink

This chapter stems from a talk I gave at the annual convention of the National Council of Teachers of English in November 1981. Thus a number of my examples are from that time, but anyone wanting to find a similar gathering in 1987 will have no trouble.

1. *In These Times*, 22 Dec. 1982–13 Jan. 1983.

2. Stephen Hilgartner, Richard C. Bell, and Rory O'Connor, *Nukespeak: Nuclear Language, Visions, and Mindset* (San Francisco, 1982).

3. Robert Scheer, *With Enough Shovels: Reagan, Bush, and Nuclear War* (New York, 1982).

4. Noting this anomaly, John Somerville proposed the alternate term "omnicide," in a letter to *Monthly Review* (June 1982): 61–62.

5. As this phrase stretches the meaning of "weapons," the implements that used to be called "weapons," and a lot more besides, have come to be designated "conventional" weapons, with a corresponding reduction of disgust at the idea of fragmentation bombs, napalm, agent orange, and other cruel innovations which would have been thought barbarous in the age of the rack and the wheel.

6. A much longer history lies behind this way of using the names of countries than behind the semantics of thermonuclear talk. But the two converge in our leaders' current picture of the world, which subordinates all peoples and all social process to the great battle of East and West.

7. *New York Times*, 6 Nov. 1981: A13.

8. It is interesting to note that Congress, in a pathetic attempt to impede our government's murderous El Salvador policy, has exacted a biannual certification (from that same government, of course) that the Salvadoran regime is making "progress" in human rights, as a condition of further military aid. This reassurance is apparently necessary in order to maintain the claim that our side is that of the angels. Naturally the certification dependably issues forth.

9. *CounterSpy*, Nov. 1981–Jan. 1982: 31.

10. This hideous nonsense goes on apace in 1986; "we" are not through with Libya yet.

11. *Newsweek*, 16 Nov. 1981: 59.

12. There may be a parallel usage among Soviet leaders. They at least make a distinction between a government and its subjects, but perhaps in their lexicon the phrase *the people* constitutes a similar subordination of social complexity to ideology.

13. I have lost the source of this quotation.

14. *In These Times*, 21–27 Oct. 1981: 11.

15. *New York Times*, 8 Nov. 1981: E2.

16. Patricia Derian, "Some of Our Best Friends Are Authoritarians," *The Nation*, 7 Nov. 1981: 469.

17. Ibid.

18. The editors of *Monthly Review* dug up this quotation and printed it on p. 9 of the Dec. 1982 issue. It is from *The Works of Theodore Roosevelt*, National Edition, ed. Hermann Hagedorn. (New York, 1926), 14: 368; and originally from a letter accepting the vice-presidential nomination, 15 Sept. 1900.

19. Of course there are excellent journalistic sources of fuller and more accurate information, such as *AMPO: Japan-Asia Quarterly Review, TCLSAC Reports* (on southern Africa), and *NACLA Report on the Americas*. But these reach only a tiny readership. And even such weak, if courageous, oppo-

sition may draw heavy artillery fire from the establishment, as in the "60 Minutes" attack (23 Jan. 1983) on the World Council of Churches and other religious social action groups, one of which has given NACLA financial support.

20. Raymond Williams has often pointed out that the word *communication* itself implies a false claim, in most usage, since it refers to messages that go in one direction only.

21. It is inseparable, too, from the more basic structure of capitalism, which casts ordinary people as material whose labor is a commodity, and as masses of consumers who must be mobilized to buy what they have produced—but that's another story.

Chapter 15. Literacy, Technology, and Monopoly Capital

1. Actually, the *OED* says December. It had never occurred to me that the *OED* could be wrong about something.

2. George R. Stetson, "The Renaissance of Barbarism," *New Princeton Review* (Nov. 1888): 336–37.

3. Bernard de Mandeville, "Essay on Charity and Charity Schools," in *The Fable of the Bees* (London, 1795): 180. First published in 1723.

4. Adam Smith, *The Wealth of Nations,* (London, 1910), 2: 269. First published in 1776. For an excellent account of these debates, see Richard D. Altick, *The English Common Reader: A Social History of the Mass Reading Public, 1800–1900* (Chicago, 1957).

5. Edwin Leigh, "Illiteracy in the United States," in *Annual Report of the Commissioner of Education* (1870): 467–502. Thanks to my colleague Gerald Burns for this reference. Burns also tells me that Horace Mann referred to the "stigma of illiteracy" as early as 1838, in his *Second Annual Report,* but I think this was the older usage of the term.

6. Daniel P. and Lauren B. Resnick, "The Nature of Literacy: An Historical Exploration," *Harvard Educational Review* 47 (1977): 381–82.

7. On this subject see, among many works, Michael B. Katz, *The Irony of Early School Reform; Educational Innovation in Mid-Nineteenth Century Massachusetts* (Cambridge, 1968); David B. Tyack, *The One Best System; A History of American Urban Education* (Cambridge, 1974); Samuel Bowles and Herbert Gintis, *Schooling in Capitalist America; Education and the Contradictions of Economic Life* (New York, 1976).

8. For the standard treatment of this theme, see Robert H. Wiebe, *The Search for Order, 1877–1920* (New York, 1967).

9. For some of the social consequences of this printing innovation, see Elizabeth L. Eisenstein, "Some Conjectures about the Impact of Printing on Western Society and Thought: A Preliminary Report," in Harvey J. Graff, ed., *Literacy and Social Development in the West: A Reader* (Cambridge, England, 1981): 58–59. I'm suggesting that social purposes like this had an impact on the technology as well.

10. Raymond Williams, *Television: Technology and Cultural Form* (New York, 1975): 10–14.

11. Eric Barnouw, *Tube of Plenty: The Evolution of American Television* (New York, 1982).

12. David Noble, *America by Design: Science, Technology, and the Rise of Corporate Capitalism* (New York, 1977).

13. Walter J. Ong, *Interfaces of the Word: Studies in the Evolution of Consciousness and Culture* (Ithaca, 1977): 44.

14. Paul A. Strassmann, "Information Systems and Literacy," in Richard W. Bailey and Robin Melanie Fosheim, eds., *Literacy for Life: The Demand for Reading and Writing* (New York, 1983): 116, 119.

15. David C. Johnson, Ronald E. Anderson, Thomas P. Hansen, and Daniel L. Klassen, "Computer Literacy—What Is It?" *Mathematics Teacher* 73 (1980). Thanks to Marilyn Frankenstein and Bob Rosen for pointing me to this and other articles on computers, and to Rosen for helpfully criticizing a draft of this article.

16. Ross Corson, "Computer Revolution," *The Progressive*, Sept. 1982, reports these predictions (by the U.S. Labor and Commerce departments and by corporations like IBM) and discusses this question.

17. Corson, "Computer Revolution," is my source for both of these quotations (p. 35).

18. Fred Pincus, "Students Being Groomed for Jobs That Won't Exist," *The Guardian*, 9 May 1984: 7.

19. Corson, "Computer Revolution": 35.

20. Pincus ("Students Being Groomed": 7) reports Bureau of Labor statistics suggesting that however much high tech *gear* may be around, high tech *employment* may be no more important in 1995 than it is today.

21. Douglas Noble, "The Underside of Computer Literacy," *Raritan* 3 (1984): 42. This article is another helpfully critical source.

22. Stanley Pogrow, *Education in the Computer Age: Issues of Policy, Practice, and Reform* (Beverly Hills, 1983): 92–94.

23. Tim O'Shea and John Self, *Learning and Teaching with Computers* (Englewood Cliffs, N.J., 1984): 1.

24. As does James Donald, in "Language, Literacy and Schooling," in *The State and Popular Culture* (Milton Keynes, 1982), a unit of the Open University course on popular culture. I found Donald's discussion particularly helpful, both for its historical account and for its theoretical position, and I have drawn upon it here. Myron Tuman also offers a good discussion of literacy as cause and effect, in "Words, Tools, and Technology," *College English* 45 (1983).

25. Donald, "Language, Literacy, and Schooling": 56.

26. Jonathan Kozol, "A New Look at the Literacy Campaign in Cuba," *Harvard Educational Review* 48 (1978): 358–59.

27. Jonathan Kozol, *Children of the Revolution: A Yankee Teacher in the Cuban Schools* (New York, 1978): 31.

28. Kozol, *Children of the Revolution:* 77.

29. See Robert F. Arnove, "The Nicaraguan National Literacy Crusade of 1980," *Comparative Education Review* 25 (1981).

Chapter 18. Use Definite, Specific, Concrete Language

1. The other is, avoid padding. E. D. Hirsch, Jr., *The Philosophy of Composition* (Chicago, 1977): 148–49.

2. Susan Wells, "Classroom Heuristics and Empiricism," *College English* 39 (1977): 471.

3. Obviously critical inquiry requires both abstractions and details, and a fluid exchange between them. I hope not to be taken as merely inverting

the values I have criticized and recommending the abstract and general over the concrete and particular.

4. Jeffrey Youdelman, "Limiting Students: Remedial Writing and the Death of Open Admissions," *College English* 39 (1978): 563–64. Anyone interested in the politics of rhetoric and composition should read this excellent article and that of Susan Wells, cited earlier.

Chapter 19. Writing and Empowerment

1. On occasion I have assigned the useful chapter on interviewing from William Zinsser, *On Writing Well; An Informal Guide to Writing Nonfiction* (New York, 1980).

2. Originally I adapted this exercise from Ira Shor, *Critical Teaching and Everyday Life* (Boston, 1980): 144–45. Shor's book, with the spirit of Paolo Freire behind it, is a rich source of pedagogies to empower.

3. Excerpts from student papers are reprinted with permission of the authors. Upon request, I have changed some of their names, and I have changed all names of those interviewed.

4. Stuart and Elizabeth Ewen, *Channels of Desire; Mass Images and the Shaping of American Consciousness* (New York, 1982). The class was also armed with Jeffrey Schrank's discussion of "pseudo-choice," in *Snap, Crackle, and Popular Taste: The Illusion of Free Choice in America* (New York, 1977); with Peggy Rosenthal's chapter on "The Power of a Positive Self," from *Words and Values: Some Leading Words and Where They Lead Us* (New York, 1984); and with a brief analysis of ideology in advertising, as that which assumes the reader *already* to have certain values and beliefs, from Judith Williamson, *Decoding Advertisements: Ideology and Meaning in Advertising* (London, 1978): 41–42.

5. Writing of this sort also brings students into the social dynamics of a literary genre, which I discussed in essay 7 in this volume (pp. 107–14). Those dynamics, too, become problematic for our class.

6. Varney's essay was published, with comments of mine, in *What Makes Writing Good; A Multiperspective*, ed. William E. Coles, Jr., and James Vopat (Lexington, Ma, 1985).

Chapter 20. Reflections on Class and Language

1. Thanks to Gerry Lombardi and Jan Stackhouse, who carried out the project and gave me copies of some of the tapes.

2. In this usage, a code is not a dialect or a language, but a way of mobilizing one's dialect in real situations. Bernstein also speaks of it as an "orientation."

3. Basil Bernstein, *Class, Codes and Control*, 3 vols. (London, 1971) 1: 143. In characterizing the two codes I have also drawn from research published in vol. 2 of this work, and in W. Brandis and D. Henderson, *Social Class, Language and Communication* (London, 1970), and P. R. Hawkins, *Social Class: The Nominal Group and Verbal Strategies* (London, 1977). Altogether, there are more than ten books in this series, edited by Bernstein and consisting mainly of research grounded in his ideas. Note: "positional" control is authoritarian: "personalized" control is more flexible and interactive. This may also be the place to note that Bernstein never, to my knowledge, defines *class*, but his references to the concept make it

seem that he identifies class with the parents' educational level and job status. Brandis spells this out technically in Appendix I of *Social Class, Language and Communication.*

4. Claus Mueller, *The Politics of Communication* (New York, 1975). Mueller notes that most of the studies he surveys define class "by education, occupation, and/or income" (p. 46). His own definition stresses education and occupation (p. 45).

5. Richard Ohmann, "Questions about Literacy and Political Education," *Radical Teacher* 8 (May 1978): 24–25.

6. In doing so, I have learned much from Raymond Williams, "Language," in *Marxism and Literature* (Oxford, 1977); Chris Sinha, "Class, Language and Education," *Ideology and Consciousness,* 1 (May 1977); William Labov, various articles, especially "The Study of Language in Its Social Context," in Joshua Fishman, ed., *Advances in the Sociology of Language* (The Hague, 1971); Dell Hymes, "Models of the Interaction of Language and Social Life," in John J. Gumperz and Dell Hymes, eds., *Directions in Sociolinguistics* (New York, 1972); Norbert Dittmar, *Sociolinguistics: A Critical Survey of Theory and Application,* trans. Peter Sand, Pieter A. M. Seuren, and Kevin Whiteley (London, 1976); Harold Rosen, *Language and Class: A Critical Look at the Theories of Basil Bernstein* (Bristol, 1972); and from other works cited later. Thanks also to Wendy Melechen and to the late Steve Ward, who explored these matters with me in a tutorial at Wesleyan University, to Johannes Fabian, who gave me helpful leads, and to Don Lazere, Wayne O'Neil, Barry Phillips, and Bob Rosen, who helpfully criticized a draft of this article (Lazere and Phillips disagree with me in major ways). It may be unnecessary to add that very little in this essay is "original."

7. In such an impasse, there is a tendency to look for causes in the *chronologically* prior years of childhood, hence in practices of "socialization." Aside from the theoretical arbitrariness of such a strategy, its political implications are obvious and rather nasty—e.g., the poor may be blamed for their own poverty; black parents may be held accountable for their children's failure in school; or, only a little more benignly, the liberals may set out to correct, in school, the cultural "damage" done at home.

8. This is so whether they are blue or white collar, assembly-line workers, keypunch operators, or McDonalds' robots doing it all for us. See Harry Braverman, *Labor and Monopoly Capital* (New York, 1974), chaps. 15 and 16, for an account of how clerical and service jobs have been reduced to smaller and smaller actions, requiring little thought on the worker's part. In this section of my argument I am relying on some basic distinctions that Braverman makes in his invaluable book, following Marx.

9. And of course I am omitting entirely some obvious differences in the kinds of schooling generally given to children of the two subclasses, not to mention different cultural environments at home (books, etc.), different relationships to television, and so on. Please excuse the drastic but necessary simplification.

10. Bernstein briefly mentions such an explanation in a memorable paragraph in *Class, Codes and Control,* 1: 143. But he does not develop it all, nor can it be derived from his conception of class.

11. The formulation is that of E. P. Thompson, in *The Making of the English Working Class* (New York, 1963), which renders a persuasive account of the way a group of people made themselves into a class through institutions like church, union, and party, and through struggles over work and life, as well as through cultural production—song, oratory, writing, etc.

12. Some sociolinguists—including Hymes and Labov—have even suggested that we drop the idea of grammatical competence and think instead of a flexible "communicative competence." This seems to me a damaging strategy, one that would forbid the abstraction from speech necessary for any systematic study of language. See Noam Chomsky's remarks on this subject in *Language and Responsibility* (New York, 1977): 53–58 and 189–92. But the work of these sociolinguists surely calls into question the abstraction, *code* (and probably that of *language*, too). Nor do I think it permits Labov's idea of the "vernacular," on which he settles in a kind of last-ditch attempt to get at the way people *really* speak when they are completely at ease. The vernacular he defines as "the style in which the minimum attention is given to the monitoring of speech" ("The Study of Language in its Social Context": 170; see fn. 6). For any person, the vernacular is the most systematic of his or her codes, hence the most worth studying. But studying it is nearly impossible, since people monitor and "correct" their speech when they think it's being observed, being noticed *as* speech. What surprises me is that Labov singles out the encounter of linguist-observer and "ordinary" speaker as so unusual in its ability to interfere with the vernacular. Speakers of one or another vernacular, unless completely isolated in rural valleys or perhaps prisons, are constantly in touch with bosses, officials, teachers, cops, and so on; and sociolinguists have documented well the "shift" of code that takes place in such encounters, mainly on the part of the subordinate person. Likewise, all speakers but the most lowly derelict or infant speak at times with people subordinate to them. Then there are also shifts from friend to stranger, from manipulation to just rapping, etc. The "vernacular" dissolves in real social contexts. Unlike grammatical competence, it is not the kind of idealization that helps get at what is systematic in language.

13. J. N. Volosinov, *Marxism and the Philosophy of Language*, trans. Ladislav Matejka and I. R. Titunik (New York, 1973): 21. It appears now that Bakhtin was actually the author of this work. See Katerina Clark and Michael Holquist, *Mikhail Bakhtin* (Cambridge, Mass., 1984): 147–48.

14. The mayor, it is worth noting, came from the industrial working class, and was a high-school baseball coach before entering politics.

Index

Page numbers in *italics* refer to illustrations.

About the Author

Richard Ohmann received a Guggenheim Fellowship in 1964; and a Rockefeller Foundation Fellowship in 1982, from which these essays on mass culture arose. He is the author of several books, including *English in America: A Radical View of the Profession* and *Shaw: The Style and the Man* (Wesleyan, 1962). Ohmann is a professor of English at Wesleyan University. He received his B.A. from Oberlin (1952) and Ph.D. (1960) from Harvard. He lives in Middletown, Connecticut.

About the Book

Politics of Letters was composed in Aster by G&S Typesetters, Inc. of Austin, Texas. It was printed on 60-pound Miami Book Vellum paper and bound by Arcata Graphics/Kingsport, Inc. of Kingsport, Tennessee. Design by Joyce Kachergis Book Design and Production, Inc. of Bynum, North Carolina.

Wesleyan University Press, 1987